Texas

WORLD BIBLIOGRAPHICAL SERIES

General Editors:
Robert G. Neville (Executive Editor)
John J. Horton

Robert A. Myers   Ian Wallace
Hans H. Wellisch   Ralph Lee Woodward, Jr.

John J. Horton is Deputy Librarian of the University of Bradford and currently Chairman of its Academic Board of Studies in Social Sciences. He has maintained a longstanding interest in the discipline of area studies and its associated bibliographical problems, with special reference to European Studies. In particular he has published in the field of Icelandic and of Yugoslav studies, including the two relevant volumes in the World Bibliographical Series.

Robert A. Myers is Associate Professor of Anthropology in the Division of Social Sciences and Director of Study Abroad Programs at Alfred University, Alfred, New York. He has studied post-colonial island nations of the Caribbean and has spent two years in Nigeria on a Fulbright Lectureship. His interests include international public health, historical anthropology and developing societies. In addition to *Amerindians of the Lesser Antilles: a bibliography* (1981), *A Resource Guide to Dominica, 1493-1986* (1987) and numerous articles, he has compiled the World Bibliographical Series volumes on *Dominica* (1987), *Nigeria* (1989) and *Ghana* (1991).

Ian Wallace is Professor of German at the University of Bath. A graduate of Oxford in French and German, he also studied in Tübingen, Heidelberg and Lausanne before taking teaching posts at universities in the USA, Scotland and England. He specializes in contemporary German affairs, especially literature and culture, on which he has published numerous articles and books. In 1979 he founded the journal *GDR Monitor*, which he continues to edit under its new title *German Monitor*.

Hans H. Wellisch is Professor emeritus at the College of Library and Information Services, University of Maryland. He was President of the American Society of Indexers and was a member of the International Federation for Documentation. He is the author of numerous articles and several books on indexing and abstracting, and has published *The Conversion of Scripts* and *Indexing and Abstracting: an International Bibliography*. He also contributes frequently to *Journal of the American Society for Information Science, The Indexer* and other professional journals.

Ralph Lee Woodward, Jr. is Director of Graduate Studies at Tulane University, New Orleans, where he has been Professor of History since 1970. He is the author of *Central America, a Nation Divided*, 2nd ed. (1985), as well as several monographs and more than sixty scholarly articles on modern Latin America. He has also compiled volumes in the World Bibliographical Series on *Belize* (1980), *Nicaragua* (1983), and *El Salvador* (1988). Dr. Woodward edited the Central American section of the *Research Guide to Central America and the Caribbean* (1985) and is currently editor of the Central American history section of the *Handbook of Latin American Studies*.

VOLUME 144

Texas

James Marten

Compiler

CLIO PRESS

OXFORD, ENGLAND · SANTA BARBARA, CALIFORNIA
DENVER, COLORADO

British Library Cataloguing in Publication Data

Texas. – (World bibliographical series; v.144)
Marten, James
I. Title   II. Series
016.9764

ISBN 1–85109–184–x

Clio Press Ltd.,
55 St. Thomas' Street,
Oxford OX1 1JG, England.

ABC-CLIO,
130 Cremona Drive,
Santa Barbara,
CA 93117, USA.

Designed by Bernard Crossland.
Typeset by Columns Design and Production Services Ltd, Reading, England.
Printed in Great Britain by
Bookcraft (Bath) Ltd, Midsomer Norton.

THE WORLD BIBLIOGRAPHICAL SERIES

This series, which is principally designed for the English speaker, will eventually cover every country (and many of the world's principal regions), each in a separate volume comprising annotated entries on works dealing with its history, geography, economy and politics; and with its people, their culture, customs, religion and social organization. Attention will also be paid to current living conditions – housing, education, newspapers, clothing, etc.– that are all too often ignored in standard bibliographies; and to those particular aspects relevant to individual countries. Each volume seeks to achieve, by use of careful selectivity and critical assessment of the literature, an expression of the country and an appreciation of its nature and national aspirations, to guide the reader towards an understanding of its importance. The keynote of the series is to provide, in a uniform format, an interpretation of each country that will express its culture, its place in the world, and the qualities and background that make it unique. The views expressed in individual volumes, however, are not necessarily those of the publisher.

VOLUMES IN THE SERIES

1 *Yugoslavia*, John J. Horton
2 *Lebanon*, C. H. Bleaney
3 *Lesotho*, Shelagh M. Willet and David Ambrose
4 *Rhodesia/Zimbabwe*, Oliver B. Pollack and Karen Pollack
5 *Saudi Arabia*, Frank A. Clements
6 *USSR*, Anthony Thompson
7 *South Africa*, Reuben Musiker
8 *Malawi*, Robert B. Boeder
9 *Guatemala*, Woodman B. Franklin
10 *Pakistan*, David Taylor
11 *Uganda*, Robert L. Collison
12 *Malaysia*, Ian Brown and Rajeswary Ampalavanar
13 *France*, Frances Chambers
14 *Panama*, Eleanor DeSelms Langstaff
15 *Hungary*, Thomas Kabdebo
16 *USA*, Sheila R. Herstein and Naomi Robbins
17 *Greece*, Richard Clogg and Mary Jo Clogg
18 *New Zealand*, R. F. Grover
19 *Algeria*, Richard I. Lawless
20 *Sri Lanka*, Vijaya Samaraweera
21 *Belize*, Ralph Lee Woodward, Jr.
23 *Luxembourg*, Carlo Hury and Jul Christophory
24 *Swaziland*, Balam Nyeko
25 *Kenya*, Robert L. Collison
26 *India*, Brijen K. Gupta and Datta S. Kharbas
27 *Turkey*, Merel Güçlü
28 *Cyprus*, P. M. Kítromilides and M. L. Evriviades
29 *Oman*, Frank A. Clements
31 *Finland*, J. E. O. Screen
32 *Poland*, Richard C. Lewański
33 *Tunisia*, Allan M. Findlay, Anne M. Findlay and Richard I. Lawless
34 *Scotland*, Eric G. Grant
35 *China*, Peter Cheng
36 *Qatar*, P. T. H. Unwin
37 *Iceland*, John J. Horton
38 *Nepal*, John Whelpton
39 *Haiti*, Frances Chambers
40 *Sudan*, M. W. Daly
41 *Vatican City State*, Michael J. Walsh
42 *Iraq*, A. J. Abdulrahman
43 *United Arab Emirates*, Frank A. Clements
44 *Nicaragua*, Ralph Lee Woodward, Jr.
45 *Jamaica*, K. E. Ingram
46 *Australia*, I. Kepars
47 *Morocco*, Anne M. Findlay, Allan M. Findlay and Richard I. Lawless

48 *Mexico*, Naomi Robbins
49 *Bahrain*, P. T. H. Unwin
50 *The Yemens*, G. Rex Smith
51 *Zambia*, Anne M. Bliss and J. A. Rigg
52 *Puerto Rico*, Elena E. Cevallos
53 *Namibia*, Stanley Schoeman and Elna Schoeman
54 *Tanzania*, Colin Darch
55 *Jordan*, Ian J. Seccombe
56 *Kuwait*, Frank A. Clements
57 *Brazil*, Solena V. Bryant
58 *Israel*, Esther M. Snyder (preliminary compilation E. Kreiner)
59 *Romania*, Andrea Deletant and Dennis Deletant
60 *Spain*, Graham J. Shields
61 *Atlantic Ocean*, H. G. R. King
62 *Canada*, Ernest Ingles
63 *Cameroon*, Mark W. DeLancey and Peter J. Schraeder
64 *Malta*, John Richard Thackrah
65 *Thailand*, Michael Watts
66 *Austria*, Denys Salt with the assistance of Arthur Farrand Radley
67 *Norway*, Leland B. Sather
68 *Czechoslovakia*, David Short
69 *Irish Republic*, Michael Owen Shannon
70 *Pacific Basin and Oceania*, Gerald W. Fry and Rufino Mauricio
71 *Portugal*, P. T. H. Unwin
72 *West Germany*, Donald S. Detwiler and Ilse E. Detwiler
73 *Syria*, Ian J. Seccombe
74 *Trinidad and Tobago*, Frances Chambers
76 *Barbados*, Robert B. Potter and Graham M. S. Dann
77 *East Germany*, Ian Wallace
78 *Mozambique*, Colin Darch
79 *Libya*, Richard I. Lawless
80 *Sweden*, Leland B. Sather and Alan Swanson
81 *Iran*, Reza Navabpour
82 *Dominica*, Robert A. Myers
83 *Denmark*, Kenneth E. Miller
84 *Paraguay*, R. Andrew Nickson
85 *Indian Ocean*, Julia J. Gotthold with the assistance of Donald W. Gotthold
86 *Egypt*, Ragai, N. Makar
87 *Gibraltar*, Graham J. Shields
88 *The Netherlands*, Peter King and Michael Wintle
89 *Bolivia*, Gertrude M. Yeager
90 *Papua New Guinea*, Fraiser McConnell
91 *The Gambia*, David P. Gamble
92 *Somalia*, Mark W. DeLancey, Sheila L. Elliott, December Green, Kenneth J. Menkhaus, Mohammad Haji Moqtar, Peter J. Schraeder
93 *Brunei*, Sylvia C. Engelen Krausse, Gerald H. Krausse
94 *Albania*, William B. Bland
95 *Singapore*, Stella R. Quah, Jon S. T. Quah
96 *Guyana*, Frances Chambers
97 *Chile*, Harold Blakemore
98 *El Salvador*, Ralph Lee Woodward, Jr.
99 *The Arctic*, H.G.R. King
100 *Nigeria*, Robert A. Myers
101 *Ecuador*, David Corkhill
102 *Uruguay*, Henry Finch with the assistance of Alicia Casas de Barrán
103 *Japan*, Frank Joseph Shulman
104 *Belgium*, R.C. Riley
105 *Macau*, Richard Louis Edmonds
106 *Philippines*, Jim Richardson
107 *Bulgaria*, Richard J. Crampton
108 *The Bahamas*, Paul G. Boultbee
109 *Peru*, John Robert Fisher
110 *Venezuela*, D. A. G. Waddell
111 *Dominican Republic*, Kai Schoenhals
112 *Colombia*, Robert H. Davis
113 *Taiwan*, Wei-chin Lee
114 *Switzerland*, Heinz K. Meier and Regula A. Meier
115 *Hong Kong*, Ian Scott
116 *Bhutan,* Ramesh C. Dogra
117 *Suriname*, Rosemarijn Hoefte
118 *Djibouti*, Peter J. Schraeder
119 *Grenada*, Kai Schoenhals
120 *Monaco*, Grace L. Hudson
121 *Guinea-Bissau*, Rosemary Galli
122 *Wales*, Gwilym Huws and D. Hywel E. Roberts
123 *Cape Verde*, Caroline S. Shaw
124 *Ghana*, Robert A. Myers
125 *Greenland*, Kenneth E. Miller

126 *Costa Rica*, Charles L. Stansifer
127 *Siberia*, David N. Collins
128 *Tibet*, John Pinfold
129 *Northern Ireland*, Michael Owen Shannon
130 *Argentina*, Alan Biggins
132 *Burma*, Patricia M. Herbert
133 *Laos*, Helen Cordell
134 *Montserrat*, Riva Berleant-Schiller
135 *Afghanistan*, Schuyler Jones
136 *Equatorial Guinea*, Randall Fegley
137 *Turks and Caicos Islands*, Paul G. Boultbee
138 *Virgin Islands*, Verna Penn Moll
139 *Honduras*, Pamela F. Howard-Reguindin
140 *Mauritius*, Pramila Ramgulam Bennett
141 *Mauritania*, Simonetta Calderini, Delia Cortese, James L. A. Webb, Jr.
142 *Timor*, Ian Rowland
143 *St. Vincent and the Grenadines*, Robert B. Potter
144 *Texas*, James Marten

Contents

A SHORT HISTORY OF TEXAS AND OF TEXANS xi

STATE OF TEXAS AND ITS PEOPLE 1

GEOGRAPHY AND NATURAL HISTORY 3
    General   3
    Maps and Atlases   5
    Exploration and Travel   6
    Flora and Fauna   10
    Environment   15

HISTORY 20
    Historiography   20
    General and Special Topics   22
    Spanish and Mexican Periods, 1540–1836   30
    Texas Revolution and Republic, 1836–1845   35
    Civil War and Reconstruction, 1845–1877   44
    The Gilded Age , 1877–1900   47
    Progressive Era, New Deal, and the Second World War,
       1900–1945   50
    Post-War Period, 1945–Present   54

MILITARY AFFAIRS 58

POLITICS AND GOVERNMENT 66
    Administration   66
    Parties and Elections   68
    Legal System   72

ETHNIC GROUPS 76
    Native Americans   76
    Mexican-Americans   84
    African-Americans   97
    Europeans   106
    Asians   110

Contents

WOMEN 112

RELIGION 118

SOCIAL CONDITIONS 124

URBAN AFFAIRS AND HISTORY 126

EDUCATION 136

ECONOMY AND BUSINESS 140
    Banking and Finance   140
    Agriculture and Ranching   143
    Industry   153
    Energy   156
    Trade, Transport and Technology   160
    Labour and Trade Unions   164

FOLKLORE AND LINGUISTICS 166

MEDIA 171

PERFORMING ARTS 173

FINE ARTS 177
    Literature   177
    Art   182
    Architecture   188

MEDICINE 193

SPORTS 195

REFERENCE WORKS AND BIBLIOGRAPHIES 199

JOURNALS AND PERIODICALS 203

INDEX OF AUTHORS, TITLES AND SUBJECTS 207

MAP OF TEXAS 231

A short history of Texas and of Texans

There is no single Texas. Texans relish the variety of terrain, climate, culture, economy, and lifestyles that flourish within the borders of this second largest of the United States. Her external borders are also shaped by widely divergent features. Oklahoma, across the Red River and wrapped over the Texas 'Panhandle' to the north, was, until the 20th century, 'Indian territory' and became home to many of the Native American groups driven out of Texas. To the east, Arkansas and Louisiana share the 'Old South' heritage proclaimed by many East Texans. The curving coastline of the Gulf of Mexico forms Texas's southeastern border and enables Texans to call their state the 'Third Coast' of the United States, while the long southwestern border with Mexico that extends up the Rio Grande River and the western boundary with New Mexico highlights the importance of Hispanic influences in Texas history and culture. Texans also proudly remind their fellow Americans that their state is the only one of the fifty states other than Hawai'i to have been an independent country, and they frequently feature the 'Six Flags' that have flown over Texas: Spain, France, Mexico, the Texas Republic, the Confederate States, and the United States. The literature on Texas history, natural resources, politics, society, and ethnic groups reflects this diversity and uniqueness.

Texas comprises 267,000 square miles – seven per cent of the area of the United States – that offer four different types of terrain. Coastal plains dominate the eastern third of the state, stretching from far northeastern Texas to a point east of the Big Bend of the Rio Grande River on Texas's southern border. These plains and the more northern interior lowlands rise gradually to the rocky Hill Country of the Edwards Plateau in south central Texas and to the Llano Estacado, the high plains of the Panhandle. The Edwards Plateau, in turn, rises to an extension of the Rocky Mountains in far West Texas, where a number of 8,000-foot peaks loom over the desert. Topography dictates that all of the major rivers in Texas naturally flow from the northwest toward the southeast. Rainfall ranges from plentiful – up to nearly sixty inches a year in the extreme east – to rare – under eight in the extreme west. Texans also enjoy a wide variety of weather patterns, from sultry summers and mild winters in the south and east to winter-time blizzards in the northern Panhandle and mountainous far west. Moreover, most of the state is subject to sudden 'Northers', fast moving cold fronts that blow out of the northwest and drop temperatures dramatically in a few moments or hours. Hundreds of 'twisters' spiral out of stormy skies every spring and summer and periodic hurricanes batter the coast of the Gulf of Mexico. A particularly severe tornado killed over 100 people in Waco in 1953, while in 1900 a hurricane virtually wiped out the island city of Galveston and killed 6,000 residents. The diversity of climate and terrain has, of course, nurtured an equal diversity of flora and fauna, from the forest of the Big Thicket of East Texas and high grasses of the plains to the cacti, mesquite, and brush of the western plains and desert. Important wildlife includes every species of poisonous snakes found in the United States; the ubiquitous armadillo; hundreds of species of birds; and longhorn cattle, the wild descendants of 16th century Spanish cattle which were domesticated for the cattle drives of the late-19th century. The bison, once common, is now gone from Texas.

The first humans entered the land that became Texas less than 10,000 years before the birth of Christ. Some early Native Americans, the Jumano, formed farming and hunting and gathering communities along the Rio Grande before dying out in the 16th century. Farther east, the Caddo, a confederation of perhaps two dozen tribes of Indians who also resided in parts of Louisiana, Arkansas, and Oklahoma, built villages and farms; 'Taychas', a word from the Hasinai division of the Caddo confederation that meant 'ally' or 'friend' eventually evolved into 'Texas'. The Caddo were also in a state of decline when the Spanish arrived in Texas. Two other primitive early tribes who depended on gathering food and had few allies among other Native Americans were the Tonkawa and Karankawa of the Gulf coast. Both tribes are remembered chiefly because they apparently practiced ritual cannabilism; they succumbed to extinction in the 19th century.

Other tribes pushed into Texas in the 17th and 18th centuries. The Wichita of central Texas established farms and extensive trade networks, while the Comanche roamed the Great Plains as nomadic hunters and warriors and, after centuries of resistance to Spanish and Anglo settlement, were finally driven out of the state in the 1870s. Other war-like plains tribes included the Kiowa and Kiowa Apaches, who in the 19th century allied themselves with the Comanche and shared their defeat, and the Lipan Apaches, who were forced into western Texas in the 18th century by the Spanish and by other Indian tribes, and who resisted the expansion of white settlement until the early 1880s. The history of the Native Americans of Texas was closely entwined with the history of the Spanish, through the development of the mission system, and with that of the Anglo-Americans, who saw them as obstacles to settlement. These cultures competed for the resources of Texas and fought dozens of distinct 'Indians wars'. Such conflicts, combined with the ravages of disease against which Native Americans had no immunities, eliminated many of them and forced virtually all the survivors out of Texas. Now, only tiny remnants of the Alabama-Coushatta and Tiguas remain on reservations in East Texas and El Paso, respectively.

Although their experiences obviously had a major impact on the course of Texas history and culture, the arrival of the first Europeans in Texas was hardly auspicious. The survivors of a failed Spanish expedition to Florida landed on Galveston Island in 1528; disease, malnutrition, and Karankawa Indians reduced their number from around ninety to only four. Six years later, led by Cabeza de Vaca, this small band stumbled into Spanish territory in northern Mexico. Their reports of rich natural resources and cities built of gold, together with those of later explorers, encouraged the Spanish to mount a major expedition in 1540 led by Francisco Vasquez de Coronado. Coronado searched through New Mexico, North Texas, and Kansas without finding any riches. He did, however, report that the land over which he had travelled seemed fertile. This failed to catch the Spaniards' imagination, and Texas remained relatively untouched by Europeans for well over a century.

This changed when a French expedition led by René Robert Cavalier, Sieur de La Salle, landed in Matagorda Bay in 1684. An attempt at permanent settlement failed, but the French threat, like their development of neighbouring Louisiana, sparked renewed Spanish interest in Texas. Franciscan missionaries, who had founded a settlement named Ysleta near present-day El Paso in 1681, formed the spearhead of the Spanish effort to establish footholds in Texas. By the 1720s, Nacogdoches and several other missions and towns had been built near the Red and Sabine Rivers in East Texas. A string of missions were perched along the San Antonio River at San Antonio de Béxar, the capital of the province, by the late 18th century, and other settlements appeared at La Bahía in southeastern Texas and along the Rio Grande.

Despite this activity, and their long-standing claims to the territory, the Spanish maintained only a tenuous hold on their rough frontier, which early in the 19th century was thinly settled by only 5,000 Spanish soldiers, missionaries, and ranchers who were challenged by the still powerful Comanche and Apache and by French and American explorers and adventurers. Much of the mission property had been secularized, and the Franciscan influence had dwindled after the turn of the 19th century. Short-lived rebellions against Spanish rule by Mexican revolutionaries and American 'filibusters' in 1812–13 and 1819–21 reflected the unrest throughout Spanish Mexico that resulted in the success of the Mexican independence movement in 1821.

The rise of Anglo-American influence in Texas coincided with the creation of the Mexican Republic. Desperate to make its potentially wealthy province profitable, the Mexican government granted vast tracts of land to foreign investors, or *empresarios*, to be settled by immigrants from the United States and several western Euopean countries. The most important *empresario* was Stephen F. Austin, whose father Moses had received a grant of 200,000 acres from the Spanish government which Stephen had to convince the new Mexican government to honour. The first group of families, the 'Old Three Hundred', began arriving in late 1821; by 1834, nearly 10,000 people lived on Austin's land.

This stage of Texas history lasted less than two decades. Anglos who moved to Texas chafed under the Catholicism to which they were required to convert. Disagreements broke out between the settlers, many of whom hoped to create an agricultural economy based on cotton and slaves, and the Mexican government, who had outlawed slavery in Mexico and hoped to do so in Texas. The erstwhile Mexican citizens complained that their sparsely settled region had little influence in the politics of Mexico or even in their own province, Coahuila y Texas. Additional conflicts over taxes and immigration policies, and the arrival from the United States of firebrands like William Barret Travis and Sam Houston, sparked meetings and overt resistance on the part of Texans, and arrests and occasional military crackdowns by the Mexican government. A campaign to centralize power by President Antonio Lopez de Santa Anna completed the Texans' alienation from the Mexican government, and open rebellion broke out in the autumn of 1835.

The Texas revolutionaries captured San Antonio late in that year, but suffered a devestating blow when Mexican forces massacred a group of 342 captured Texans at Goliad early in 1836. In March, less than 200 Texan defenders of the San Antonio de Valero Mission – a deserted mission called the Alamo near San Antonio – were overwhelmed by a Mexican Army led by Antonio López de Santa Anna. In the meantime, Texan revolutionaries, forgetting their initial goal of reform within the Mexican system, declared their independence from Mexico on March 2, wrote a constitution, selected an interim president, David G. Burnet, and appointed Sam Houston commander-in-chief of the hastily formed Texas Army. For six weeks Houston retreated into southeast Texas, followed by the Mexican Army and by fleeing refugees in what came to be known as the 'Runaway scrape'. On April 21, 1836, the Texans turned and attacked the larger Mexican force at San Jacinto and, crying 'Remember the Alamo' and 'Remember Goliad', inflicted over 800 casualties (out of 1,400 Mexican troops) and captured the survivors. Santa Anna agreed to Texas's independence – although the Mexican government did not – and the Texas Republic was born.

The next ten years were difficult ones for Texas. A huge majority elected Houston first president of the Republic, but personality and political conflicts between him and his rivals plagued the nation's short history. The growing presence of slaves in Texas prevented northern politicians in the United States (already deeply divided over the issue of slavery) from allowing the annexation of Texas to the United States, which Houston and most Texans supported. Expansionism during the presidency of Mirabeau B. Lamar caused Indian wars and renewed conflict with Mexico, whose armies invaded Texas three times in 1842 and occupied San Antonio twice. After bitter debate, the capital was moved from Houston to Austin. The Republic, without a proper financial system (banks were illegal under the Texas constitution) went deeply into debt. Houston returned as president in 1841 and continued working for annexation until, in February 1845, the United States Congress finally offered statehood, which the Texas Congress voted overwhelmingly to accept. On February 19, 1846, Texas officially entered the Union. James Pinckney Henderson became Texas's first governor and Sam Houston and Thomas J. Rusk its first United States Senators. The 1846–48 war between the United States and Mexico over the new state's western boundaries (Texans claimed territory that stretched nearly to Santa Fe, in modern New Mexico) resulted in a victory for the United States, which was aided materially by tough Texan soldiers. The war was, in effect, the final step in Texas's separation from Mexico; a congressional compromise in 1850 set the state's modern borders.

After two and a half centuries as a colony of Spain, fifteen years as a province of Mexico, and nine years as an independent nation, Texas had finally become a part of the United States. Her politics would be submerged in those of the nation and of the South; her economy would reflect tendencies typical of the developing West; her culture would represent a mixture of Hispanic, Western European, and African-American influences.

Politically, Texas shared the South's devotion to the Democratic Party and to slavery. By the 1860s, there were over 180,000 slaves in Texas (nearly 30 per cent of the total population) and the state was securely enmeshed in the cotton economy and in the rising wave of sectional politics that ultimately divided the nation. On March 2, 1861, the fifteenth anniversary of its entrance into the Union, Texas became the seventh state to secede from the Union. During the next four years of Civil War she contributed 60,000 trooops to the Confederate war effort. Aside from brief occupations of Galveston and South Texas by Union forces, the war barely scratched Texas. During the Reconstruction period that followed the war, Radical Republicans briefly controlled the state in the early 1870s, promoting equal rights for former slaves and a northern-style, active state government. After the Democrats regained power in 1874, they drew up a new state constitution, which limited the power and salaries of the governor and other state officials, established a number of elective positions (such as district and state supreme court judges and the state attorney general, comptroller, and treasurer), and reduced tax support for schools. As a reaction to Reconstruction and an affirmation of the limited government favoured by most Texans, the 1875 Constitution was extremely narrow and quite detailed. Over the course of the next century, 220 amendments were ratified by popular vote.

For the next eighty years the Democratic Party controlled the fortunes of Texas. Despite threats from inflationary 'Greenbackers' and agrarian protesters like the Populists, Texas generally remained a part of the 'Solid South', the conservative and evangelical political bloc centred in the states of the former Confederacy. At the state level, most politicians held to 19th century small-government, low taxes, and rural-minded policies until well into the 20th century. Important issues included prohibition, railroad construction, and the influence of the Ku Klux Klan in Texas politics. The limited power of the governor's office inhibited their influence on the course of Texas history, yet some chief executives stood out. James Stephen Hogg was a force for moderate reform in the early 1890s in his support for the regulation of railroad monopolies and for higher education. Jim 'Pa' and Miriam 'Ma' Ferguson were the most colourful governors during the first part of the 20th century. Something of a demagogue, 'Pa' won the gubernatorial election of 1914 but was impeached for corruption during his second term. Acting as a figurehead for her husband, 'Ma' Ferguson became the state's first woman governor, the first elected woman governor in the United States, in 1924 (she was also elected in 1932; Ann Richards became Texas's second female governor in 1990, nearly sixty years later). Texas Democrats who rose to national prominence included John 'Cactus Jack' Garner, a Speaker of the House of Representatives and vice president of the United States from 1933–41. Sam Rayburn served in Congress for forty-nine years and as Speaker for over two decades, while his protégé, Lyndon B. Johnson, served as Senate Majority Leader in the 1950s, vice president under John F. Kennedy, and as president from 1963–69.

Relegated to minority status, Texas Republicans argued internally over patronage and the role of African-Americans in the state organization. By 1960, however, conservative Texas Democrats, unable to agree with the social reform programmes of the national Democratic Party, began switching their allegiance to the moribund Republicans; in that year they elected John Tower to the United States Senate. Other signs of the resurrection of the Republican Party occurred during presidential election years. Although the Republican Herbert Hoover had narrowly won Texas in 1928, Dwight Eisenhower (in 1952 and 1956) and Richard Nixon (1968) carried the state more easily and Ronald Reagan campaigned successfully in both 1980 and 1984. William Clements became the state's first Republican governor in over a century in 1978, while Republicans became a force to be reckoned with in the state legislature in the 1980s. Texas finally had a bonafide two-party system.

Economically, between the Civil War and the early 20th century, Texas depended on the East Texas lumber industry, cottonseed oil processing, and flour milling, with vegetable and citrus fruit farming commencing in the Rio Grande Valley early in the 20th century. The most popular economic and cultural image of Texas for several decades before and after 1900, however, was of the ranching frontier. Texas longhorn cattle were the perfect animal for the long trail drives from South Texas to developing ranch country in Colorado and Wyoming, and to railheads in Kansas from which they were shipped to eastern packing plants. The rise of the cattle industry rescued Texas from the economic depression that plagued most southern states after the Civil War; 10,000,000 cattle were driven north from Texas in the 1870s and 1880s. Some Texas ranches occupied millions of acres. One of the most famous and most enduring, the King Ranch, grew from 75,000 acres of Nueces County to a total of 1,173,000 in 1925; in 1988, it still comprised over 800,000 acres. As railroads began spreading across Texas, the long drives became unnecessary. Fort Worth became an important railroad terminus and, by the early 20th century, a meat-packing centre in her own right. The extension of farming into ranch country, the development of tastier breeds of cattle, and over-production forced the Texas range cattle industry to shrink by 1890.

A short history of Texas and of Texans

The golden age of the cattlemen – which lasted only a generation – has been immortalized in American popular culture. Yet the most important economic event in Texas history was the discovery of oil. When the Spindeltop well 'came in' near Beaumont in East Texas in 1901, the Texas economy was changed almost literally overnight. Energy replaced cotton growing and processing as the major economic activity in the state. Over the next thirty years, vast oil reserves were located in other East Texas fields and in West Texas. Natural gas was also discovered and flowed through pipelines to markets in the northeastern United States. Houston's population skyrocketed, due to its role as a producer and seller of oil-drilling supplies and as a shipper of oil to the rest of the world. The oil boom created thousands of jobs, hundreds of fortunes, and proved to be a windfall to the University of Texas, which owned oil-rich land in the Permian Basin, and to Texas A & M University, which also recieved part of the profits. Texas became part of the international economy, enjoying the booms and enduring the busts that came with it.

For Texas, as for the rest of the United States, the lowest economic point of the 20th century came in the 1930s. A world-wide depression and faltering stock market ruined the prices of manufactured and agricultural products, and raised unemployment past 30 per cent. In West and North Texas, blizzard-like dust storms scraped off inches of topsoil and wrecked crops. United States government programmes under President Franklin D. Roosevelt's 'New Deal' funnelled nearly $1.5 billion into the state and created hundreds of thousands of jobs. The federal government's efforts helped Texans survive, but did not cure the basic economic ills besetting the country.

The coming of the Second World War finally ended the 'Great Depression'. Increased demand for petroleum products, jobs in war industries, and the creation of fifteen training camps and several prisoner-of-war camps in the state pulled Texas out of its economic doldrums. Huge war contracts encouraged the building of petro-chemical, synthetic rubber, and sulphur plants in southeastern Texas, and three quarters of a million Texans served in the armed forces.

Texas emerged from the war with a more diverse economy – although cotton, ranching, and the oil industry remained very important – and a more cosmopolitan population. In addition, the agricultural crisis of the 1930s and the opportunities for war industry jobs had sparked a rural-to-urban population shift that continues today. The garment and defence industries, the burgeoning financial and commercial sectors of the economy, and the development of computer and other 'high-tech' businesses combined with the still-growing oil industry and the rush to the 'Sunbelt' to draw Texans as well as 'Yankees' to Texas cities. Texas's population doubled in the period 1950–80 and reached seventeen million in 1987, making it the third most populous state in the United States: about one-third of the state's residents had been born outside of Texas and nearly a quarter had been born outside the South by this time. Three Texas cities – Houston, Dallas, and San Antonio – were among the top ten largest American cities, while only about one per cent of the state's population worked on farms or ranches. Economically and socially, the Texas of the 1990s was not the Texas of the 19th century.

Wide-ranging cultural changes also occurred during the 150 years after Texas won her independence. In 1980, sixty-six per cent of the Texas population was white, while twenty-one per cent was Hispanic, twelve per cent were black, and one per cent were 'other'. Texas society has always been characterized by ethnic diversity: black slaves accompanied the first settlers to Texas; Mexican-Americans, despite their small numbers during the 19th century, became a major element of the population by the 20th century; and European groups – with Germans probably the most conspicuous – have been a part of Texas since the earliest days of the Republic. The newest arrivals have come from Southeast Asia and continuing immigration from Mexico. All have, of course, brought their own languages, customs, and religions to the state. Yet, in the cases of African- and Mexican-Americans, conflict, rather than cultural sharing and integration, have characterized their relationships with the dominant white majority.

The first blacks in Texas suffered all the indignities, restrictions, and horrors of slavery. The Civil War and Reconstruction eliminated the institution; blacks in Texas still celebrate 19 June, 'Juneteenth', the day slaves in the state were officially freed and gained every legal right possessed by whites. However, during the last quarter of the 19th century and for more than half of the 20th, 'Jim Crow' laws segregated blacks and whites in public accomodations and conveyances, and several constitutional amendments effectively disfranchised blacks. Although a number of African-Americans (led by George Ruby and Matt Gaines) had served in the Texas legislature and scores of local offices during and just after Reconstruction, blacks were shut out of virtually all political offices from the late 19th century until the 1960s. In addition, dozens of blacks were lynched by mobs in the late 19th and early 20th centuries.

The long climb to legal racial equality for Texas blacks paralleled the civil rights movement in the rest of the United States. U.S. Supreme Court cases ended the 'white primary' in 1944 and segregation at the University of Texas in 1950. A number of public school districts began integration in the mid-1950s and restaurants, golf courses, and most other public places followed suit in the 1960s.

African-Americans began appearing in political and professional positions. One of the most admired and influential black Texans of the 1970s was Congresswoman Barbara Jordan of Houston who, after serving with distinction in the State Senate, became the first black southerner to win election to the United States House of Representatives since Reconstruction.

Although Mexican-Americans pre-dated blacks in Texas, they comprised only a small proportion of the population throughout the 19th century, with a low of 4 per cent in 1887. Economic depression and political turmoil in Mexico, and the opportunity for jobs – albeit low-paying ones – encouraged massive emigration to the USA after 1890. Despite restrictions placed on immigration to Texas from Mexico in 1917, illegal migration continued. Hispanics found extremely low-paid jobs as farm and ranch workers in South and West Texas and as pecan shellers and garment workers in cities such as San Antonio. They too endured discrimination, segregation, and violence. A 'Cart War' between Mexican and Anglo teamsters in 1857 and the 'Cortina War' of 1859 resulted in hundreds of deaths. Texas Rangers regularly preyed on *Tejanos* at election times or during labour disputes, while the tension caused by the Mexican Revolution and raids by Mexican border bandits sparked a backlash of Anglo violence during which Anglo vigilantes lynched between 3,000 and 5,000 Mexicans in the Rio Grande Valley between 1910 and 1920.

A number of political organizations struggled to represent Hispanics in Texas, notably *La Raza Unida*, founded in 1970. The same civil rights legislation and court cases that benefited blacks improved the quality of Hispanics' lives and they began entering politics in the 1960s. Henry Gonzales won election to the United States Congress in 1961 and Henry Cisneros was mayor of San Antonio for much of the 1980s, while hundreds of *Tejanos* served in local and state elective offices.

Just as Texas shared the rest of the United States' sometimes agonizing march toward civil rights, so did it acquire elements of the larger American culture and economy. Texas's primary distinctiveness among American states now lays in its history and its self-image. The 'Texas mystique' still exerts a strong pull on the minds of Texans and of other Americans, yet the contemporary problems of Texas match the problems of every urbanized, industrialized American state: pollution, crime, housing, racial tension, political inertia. Texas still depends too much on the oil industry, as the economic wreckage caused by the 1980s recession showed – but by the late 20th century, she has become, despite Texans' protestations, a little less 'Texan' and a little more 'American'.

The bibliography

A number of sometimes conflicting priorities determined the selection of books for this bibliography. All were written in English or are, in a few cases, English translations of works originally prepared in a foreign language. I sought coverage of both older works and more recent material with the latter predominating whenever possible. I worked toward a kind of symmetry in that topics of equal importance, or topics with roughly the same volume of available literature, should be represented, if at all possible, by approximately the same number of entries. Although some of the publishers of these books were, unfortunately, rather obscure, I tried to choose publications from fairly prominent university or commercial presses. I have also tried to avoid government publications, with only a few failures. Although I sought full-length monographs, I have made exceptions for two series of publications: the twenty- to thirty-page pamphlets on the ethnic groups of Texas published by the Institute of Texas Cultures, and an on-going series of thirty- to sixty-page booklets published on a wide variety of Texas topics by Texas Western Press. Many of these publications provide information on subjects unavailable in larger works. Virtually all of the entries are secondary sources, although a few published memoirs or autobiographies appear if secondary works on the same topic are unavailable, or if they have been published very recently, or if the introductions, notes and bibliographies, etc. provide useful information. A separate section provides short discussions of a number of periodicals and journals.

There are a few subjects for which the available books were so rare, arcane, or simply nonexistent as to make it impossible to offer a separate section. For instance, only two or three works on archaeology are included in the Native American section; most of the archaeological works to which I found references were highly technical reports which received such minimal distribution that they would be virtually inaccessible to users of this bibliography. Surprisingly, no book-length studies have yet been published on Asians living in Texas. In addition, although there is a plethora of easily available books on Texas history before 1900, the period since 1945 has not been thoroughly examined; the books in that section tend to be biographies of prominent politicians.

The works within each section are arranged alphabetically by author, except the journals and periodicals, which are organized by title. The placement and categorization of some entries is necessarily inconsistent. Biographies, for instance, are included in the sections devoted to works dealing with topics or periods in which the subject made his, or her, most important contribution. In other cases, however, the entry appears in the section that seems most appropriate. For example, books on women labourers appear in the women's section, not the labour section, while works on black soldiers have been placed in the African-American section rather than with Military Affairs. In these cases, I believe that the experiences of female workers were shaped more by their gender than by their rôles as labourers and that black soldiers have received attention, not because they were in the military, but because they were black. On the other hand, I have placed books on the folk culture and art of blacks, Mexican-Americans, and women alongside books dealing with those categories of experience for other Texas sub-groups and communities. Hopefully, the indexes will relieve any confusion my organizational choices may cause.

My approach to the works cited has been primarily descriptive. Although at times I have applied a critical eye to their content, my main objective has been to explain what the authors are trying to accomplish, their points of view, the information presented in the books (in the text, illustrations, appendixes, etc.), and how complete the authors' approaches seem to be. I have designed the bibliography to be an introduction to the literature of dozens of areas of inquiry on Texas, a jumping off point to further research. To this end, I have simply tried to determine how useful each book is and what audience would profit most from reading it.

Along with the authors included in this bibliography, I have used a number of terms to denote members of various racial groups. Although I have attempted to implement modern usages, many authors writing before the 1960s used terms that have fallen out of scholarly usage. The terms 'Indian' and 'Native American' are used interchangeably, as are 'black', 'African-American', and, in older works, 'negro'. Although some authors utilize the word 'Hispanics', I have tended to refer to the Spanish-speaking residents of the state with narrower terms like 'Mexican-American', 'Mexican-Texan', or *Tejano*. Finally, 'Anglo' is the term most commonly used by contemporaries, historians, and me to refer to a white Texan.

Acknowledgements

A number of people came to my aid in the preparation of *Texas*. Although they did not know it, David G. McComb and Joe B. Frantz were extremely helpful; their surveys on Texas history guided my preparation of the introduction. Research assistants provided by the Marquette University Department of History included Michelle

Sinka, Michael Haeft, Cathy Thom, and Pat Jung; they performed much of the leg work required of a project like this with competence and good humour. John Vogel kindly drew the map that accompanies this bibliography. I greatly appreciated the polite and unfailingly helpful aid provided by the staffs of the Memorial Library at Marquette University and the University of Texas Libraries. Special thanks go to Julie Gores and her excellent staff in the inter-library loan department at the Marquette library; without them, this project would never have been completed.

State of Texas and its People

1   **The super Americans: a picture of life in the United States, as brought into focus, bigger than life, in the land of the millionaires – Texas.**
    John Bainbridge.   Garden City, New York: Doubleday, 1961. 393p.

An affectionate, if unobjective look at the way that Texas has become 'the epitome of America'. Written as a series of articles in the *New Yorker* at a time when rich Texans were still something of a curiosity, Bainbridge's book examines the lifestyles of Texas's rich and famous. Although the 'larger-than-life' lifestyles of Texas millionaires have earned them condescension around the rest of the United States, the author argues that they are actually merely 'more' American than the rest of their countrymen. He focuses on their business practices, deal-making, dress, houses, conspicuous consumption, charities, and the ways that families pass their wealth down to the next generations.

2   **From Uncertain to Blue.**
    Keith Carter, introduction by Horton Foote.   Austin, Texas: Texas Monthly Press, 173p.

A collection of eighty of Carter's black-and-white photographs of people and sites in towns from all over East Texas; the unifying thread is the unusual names of the towns, such as Uncertain, Blue, Dime Box, Looneyville, and Ding Dong. There is no text, aside from the introduction and endnotes identifying the subjects of the pictures and explaining why Carter photographed them.

3   **Lost in west Texas.**
    Jim W. Corder.   College Station, Texas: Texas A & M University Press, 1988. 116p. (Wardlaw Book).

A pleasant and often eloquent memoir of West Texas by a Texas native and professor at Texas Christian University. His reminiscences and observations, frequently related through autobiographical vignettes, range over topics like the weather, family, the 1930s, and growing up in Texas. This slim volume provides a thoughtful 'feel' for West Texas and for Texas as a whole.

1

4 **Sam Houston's Texas.**
Sue Flanagan.   Austin, Texas: University of Texas Press, 1964. 213p.
maps.

The author, a photographer, traces Sam Houston's travels in the eastern half of Texas during his thirty-one years in the state through 113 black-and-white photographs of his homes, historical sites such as battlefields and campgrounds, important natural landmarks, and artifacts that belonged to Texas's greatest hero. Although the photographs are the most useful part of the book, the text is well-written and relies heavily on Houston's own speeches and writings. It also includes a yearly summary of his activities from 1832 (the date of his arrival in Texas) to 1863 (the year of his death).

5 **Landscapes of Texas: photographs from *Texas Highways Magazine*.**
Edited by John Graves.   College Station, Texas: Texas A & M
University Press, 1980. 158p. (Louise Lindsay Merrick Texas
Environment Series).

A coffee table book of dramatic vistas of Texas from the state's primary tourism magazine. The book includes hundreds of colour photographs of flora, fauna, weather, and natural and historic landmarks along with brief descriptions of each. The editor splits the book into sections based on the most commonly used geographical divisions of Texas: East Texas, the Texas Gulf Coast, West Texas, the Panhandle Plains, and Central Texas. Virtually all of the scenes presented are rural; urban life is basically ignored.

6 **Texas myths.**
Edited by Robert R. O'Connor.   College Station, Texas: Texas A & M
University Press, 1986. 248p.

O'Connor presents a wide-ranging compilation of essays on the creation and function of myths from all of the major ethnic groups of Texas – Native Americans, Mexican-Americans, Anglo-Americans and African-Americans. Also included are myths about frontiersmen, cattlemen, Texas wealth, and the notion of Texans' individualism. Other essays explore the influence of wealth and power on the clash of cultural myths, the ways myths create more cohesive family and ethnic groups, and the potential of myths to unify the often conflicting viewpoints of all elements of Texas society.

7 **Texans: oral histories from the lone star state.**
Ron Strickland.   New York: Paragon House, 1991. 335p.

A collection of about fifty of what the author calls 'minibiographies' of Texans from the main ethnic groups and from every part of Texas (although there are far more male respondents than female). The themes that emerge from these three-to-ten-page interviews deal with education (the lack of it and the desire for it); the natural environment; the reluctance with which Texans accept the homogenization of their state; local colour and pride; mentors and heroes; and the shared experiences of living in Texas. Strickland's subjects include oil men and cowboys, a high school dropout and an astronaut, the writers Elmer Kelton and Larry King, and a Texas Ranger.

Geography and Natural History

General

8 **At home in Texas: early views of the land.**
Robin W. Doughty. College Station, Texas: Texas A & M University
Press, 1987. 164p. maps. bibliog.

This is a gracefully written analysis of how American and European emigrants to pre-Civil War Texas applied their cultural backgrounds and preconceptions to the Texas wilderness. This process resulted in at least three perceptions of Texas: as a wild, but 'redeemable' region; as a nearly Mediterranean-style garden spot; and as a place that could be promoted as a fine land in which to make a home. The author contrasts the perceptions of Texas as a wilderness (a generally negative observation) and as 'nature' (a less judgemental attitude), and analyses the interplay of fact and fiction in the formulation of these ideas.

9 **Texas: a geography.**
Terry G. Jordan, John L. Bean, William M. Holmes. Boulder,
Colorado: Westview Press, 1984. 288p. maps. bibliog.

The authors attempt to dispel stereotypical portrayals of Texas landscapes and culture (treeless, anti-intellectual, violent) with a comprehensive view of Texas as it is. Although written as a 'geography', it contains a wealth of historical information. Organized topically, the book deals with issues such as the physical environment; demography, ethnicity, and linguistics; rural and urban settlement; industrial and agricultural geography; religion; and politics. A concluding chapter, 'Perceptual Regions,' describes how Texas stereotypes developed. Tables provide information on place names, manufacturing, voting patterns, religious affiliation, employment, and demography, while 150 maps and about 70 black-and-white photographs provide further data on various aspects of the geography – broadly defined – of the Lone Star State. The bibliography includes a wide selection of secondary works in history, geography, sociology, and anthropology, as well as published atlases.

10 **Imperial Texas: an interpretative essay in cultural geography.**
D. W. Meinig.   Austin, Texas: University of Texas Press, 1969. 145p.
maps. bibliog.

Meinig, a geographer, argues that Texas has evolved into a set of subcultures unified around a distinct set of symbols and a sense of destiny. He emphasizes early settlement patterns and later economic and political developments that have actually divided Texans along geographic, racial, linguistic, and religious lines. Nevertheless, these differences have been overcome by these groups' sense of allegiance to Texas as a place as well as a political entity, shared values and orientations, and participation in the unique development of Texas. The book is basically an exploratory essay that relies heavily on technical information and geographers' jargon, yet it remains a useful attempt to look at the myth of Texas nationalism from a scholarly standpoint. Also useful are the eighteen maps detailing the terrain, political and historical developments, racial and cultural regions, and the economies of Texas.

11 **The great plains.**
Walter Prescott Webb.   Boston: Ginn and Company, 1931. 525p. maps.
bibliog.

In this, his most famous work, Webb examines the experiences and adaptations of Americans as they left the wooded lands of the East and entered the Great Plains. He shows that the new lands required different weapons (the six-shooter) and new agricultural practices (barbed wire, windmills, dry farming), and that exposure to the plains affected the ways that the settlers interpreted the law, transported themselves and their products, and wrote about their lives. 'The history of the white man in the Great Plains', concludes Webb, 'is the history of adjustments and modifications'. The book includes separate chapters on Indian and Spanish responses to the plains, as well as nearly three dozen maps on such topics as weather patterns, vegetation, transportation, economic development, land use, and women's suffrage. Although frequently criticized in the decades since its publication for its geographic determinism (amongst other things), it has remained a useful jumping off place for two generations of western historians and geographers.

12 **La frontera: the United States' border with Mexico.**
Alan Weisman.   Tucson, Arizona: University of Arizona Press, 1986.
200p. maps. bibliog.

Although Weisman includes titbits of history and fifty-six photographs of landmarks and residents of both sides of the United States' border with Mexico (from the Gulf of Mexico to Baja California), this is actually a sympathetic and, at times, outraged, look at the problems such as drugs, illiteracy, racism, and poverty that currently plague border dwellers. The book highlights individuals who represent the problems as well as possible solutions to a region that, although it cuts through several states in two different countries, is united by economic dependence, unregulated urban development, government corruption, and severe social problems. The four chapters (out of a total of nine) dealing with the Texas border are 'Rio Grande City to Laredo', 'Laredo to Langtry', 'El Paso', and 'Big Bend'.

Maps and Atlases

13   Atlas of Texas.
Stanley A. Arbingast, Lorrin G. Kennamer, Michael E. Bonnie.
Austin, Texas: Bureau of Business Research, University of Texas at
Austin, 1967. 130p. maps.

This useful, although somewhat dated atlas presents 146 maps organized into five sections. Part one contains maps on various aspects of Texas's physical settings, such as political boundaries, precipitation, wind direction, and surface geology. Part two provides demographical information, such as county populations, rural-urban divisions, and ethnic makeup. Part three includes maps on transportation, recreation, and education, while part four furnishes agricultural data and part five covers manufacturing, mining, and the oil industry. The appendixes supply statistics on the growth of the state's largest cities from 1900-66 and on the population of the state's counties in 1940, 1950, and 1960.

14   Maps of Texas, 1527-1900: the map collection of the Texas State Archives.
James M. Day.   Austin, Texas: Pemberton Press, 1964. 178p. map.

Although Day includes a reproduction of an 1846 map of Texas, this is a catalogue of 2065 maps of the area now known as Texas drawn over a 400-year period. Organized chronologically, the collection includes maps of the region (including Mexico and the United States), of the Republic and State of Texas, and of individual counties and towns, as well as military maps, railroad maps, and maps of political districts. Each paragraph-long entry provides, when available, the name of the cartographer, the date and circumstances of its drawing, the map's dimensions, the materials used in making the map, brief comparisons with other maps, and the name of the original printer.

15   Mapping Texas and the Gulf coast: the contributions of Saint-Denis, Olivian, and Le Maire.
Jack Jackson, Robert Weddle, Winston DeVille.   College Station,
Texas: Texas A & M University Press, 1990. 112p. maps.

The authors trace the relationships between various French and Spanish cartographers and explorers who competed for this crucial new land in the 17th and 18th centuries. One useful aspect of the book is its publication of several previously unpublished maps of the Gulf Coast; another is its analysis of the politicization of cartography during the era of discovery and exploration.

16   Maps of Texas and the Southwest, 1513-1900.
James C. Martin, Robert S. Martin.   Albuquerque, New Mexico:
University of New Mexico Press, 1984. 174p. maps. bibliog.

After a thirty-page introduction on map making, printing, and marketing over the centuries, the authors present nearly sixty maps which show Texas as a vague territory north of Mexico, a rebellious province, an independent country, and a state. Most of the maps are accompanied by a one-page summary of their drawing, printing, and selling; analyses of their inaccuracies and of their strengths; and comparisons to earlier maps. The book clearly shows maps as diplomatic, political, and commercial tools.

17 **The mapping of the American Southwest.**
Edited by Dennis Reinhartz, Charles C. Colley. College Station,
Texas: Texas A & M University Press, 1987. 83p. maps.

The selections in this slim volume were chosen from papers presented at a symposium with the same name in 1983. David Buisseret writes on 'Spanish and French mapping of the Gulf of Mexico in the sixteenth and seventeenth centuries'; Dennis Reinhartz offers 'Herman Moll, geographer: an early eighteenth-century European view of the American Southwest'; Robert Sidney Martin describes 'United States army mapping in Texas, 1848-1850'; and Judith A. Tyner analyses 'Images of the Southwest in nineteenth-century American atlases'. In addition, the book contains twenty-four maps (including seven colour plates) of the Southwest dating from the 16th century through the end of the 19th century. The unifying threads of the essays are the ways in which maps became political and social artifacts rather than merely objective representations of terrain and geography.

Exploration and Travel

18 **William Bollaert's Texas.**
William Bollaert, Edited by W. Eugene Hollon, Ruth Lapham Butler.
Norman, Oklahoma: University of Oklahoma Press, 1956. 423p. map.
bibliog. (American Exploration and Travel Series).

Bollaert was an English-born chemist, explorer, soldier, and foreign agent for Portugal and Spain, who arrived in the Republic of Texas late in 1841 and stayed through the spring of 1844. He was apparently in the country to scout potential land purchases for a friend. The diaries, notebooks, and journals published here provide valuable details about life in Galveston, Houston, Austin, San Antonio, and points between during the years just before Texas was annexed by the United States.

19 **Diary of the Alarcón expedition into Texas, 1718-1719.**
Francisco Céliz, edited and translated by Fritz Leo Hoffman. Los
Angeles: Quivira Society, 1935. 124p. maps. (Quivira Society
Publications).

In 1718, Martin de Alarcón led a Spanish expedition deep into the wilderness of Texas as part of the on-going competition between France and Spain over East Texas. One result of his journey was the fouding of San Antonio. This is a transcript of the diary, lost for over two centuries, which was kept by the expedition's chaplain. The heavily annotated edition is preceded by a useful introduction that includes a brief history of Spanish interests in Texas from 1519 to 1718.

20 **Coronado's quest: the discovery of the southwestern states.**
A. Grove Day. Berkeley, California: University of California, 1940.
421p. maps. bibliog.

This is a very readable biography of Francisco Vásquez de Coronado and account of his explorations through present-day New Mexico, Arizona, Texas, Oklahoma, and Kansas.

21 **Bartlett's West: drawing the Mexican boundary.**
Robert V. Hine. New Haven, Connecticut: Yale University Press,
1968. 155p. map. bibliog. (Yale Western Americana Series).

John Russell Bartlett, an ethnologist, anthropologist, and artist, led the boundary
commission charged with establishing and mapping the official boundary between
Mexico and the United States in the early 1850s. Hine provides a cogent narrative of
the struggle to map the two thousand mile border. The book also includes fifty-seven
paintings, woodcuts, and drawings, most by Bartlett himself, of the landscapes, Indian
encampments, towns, and missions of Texas, New Mexico, Arizona, and California.

22 **Spanish explorers in the southern United States, 1528-1543.**
F. W. Hodge, T. H. Lewis. New York: Scribner's Sons, 1907. 411p.

Although it contains little in the way of historical explanation or scholarly apparatus,
this is a useful compilation in one volume of narratives of three of the most important
16th century Spanish explorers of the Southwest: Alvar Núñez de Cabeza Vaca,
Hernando De Soto, and Coronado.

23 **Beyond the cross timbers: the travels of Randolph B. Marcy, 1812-1887.**
W. Eugene Hollon. Norman, Oklahoma: University of Oklahoma
Press, 1955. 270p. bibliog.

Marcy (1812-87) was a map-maker, geographer, trail-blazer, authority on Indians, and
prolific writer. Although he served in the United States Army for fifty years, including
a stint as chief of staff for the Army of the Potomac during the Civil War, the author
emphasizes Marcy's five major expeditions into the Rocky Mountains and the
Southwest between 1849-58. Marcy's accomplishments included the selection of the
first reservation for southern plains Indian tribes and, in Texas, charting the Red,
Wichita, Colorado, and Brazos Rivers.

24 **Texas ranch life.**
Mary J. Jaques. College Station, Texas: Texas A & M University
Press, 1989. 363p.

Originally published in 1896, this reprint (there are no scholarly appendages in this
new edition) of an Englishwoman's memoirs of her visit to Texas in the 1890s describes
a period in Texas history not normally covered by travel accounts. Jaques' reactions to
Texas and Texans are often contradictory; she comments on their lawlessness,
independence, generosity, chivalry, brutality toward animals, and racism. She also
includes sections on women's work and on a side trip to Mexico.

25 **Texas auto trails: the northeast.**
Myra Hargrove McIlvain. Austin, Texas: University of Texas Press,
1984. 267p. maps. bibliog.

A useful, practical guide to automobile travel in northeastern Texas. Like the other
books in the series, this one describes the history, flora and fauna, architecture, natural
and man-made sites, museums, and restaurants along several routes. McIlvain provides
clear directions and, when possible, information on exhibits and hours of operation for
museums and other attractions. The author has included a number of maps for each
tour, as well as illustrations of many of the sites she mentions. The five routes, which
all begin in Dallas, are: the Pioneer Trail, sites of some of Texas's earliest Anglo

settlements; the Indian Trail, where Native Americans and whites fought over the fertile soils of east-central Texas; the Black Gold Trail through the East Texas oilfields; the Heritage Trail, where antebellum slaveowners created an 'Old South' culture; and the self-explanatory Red River Valley Trail.

26 **Texas auto trails: the south and the Rio Grande valley.**
    Myra Hargrove.   Austin, Texas: University of Texas Press, 1985. 248p.
    maps. bibliog.

This volume follows the same format as the previous title and offers four driving tours through South Texas, with several side-trips into Mexico. Starting in San Antonio, the trips include: the Immigrant Trail, which winds through the territory occupied by Spanish missions and Texas Revolution sites south and east of San Antonio; the Cattleman's Trail, leading south and west of the city to spots like the world-famous King Ranch; the Rio Grande Valley Trail, covering the coast from Corpus Christi to Padre Island and the western Gulf of Mexico (including Brownsville); and the Mustang Plains Trail, which takes travellers through the South Texas desert between the Nueces and Rio Grande Rivers (including Laredo).

27 **Texas auto trails: the southeast.**
    Myra Hargrove McIlvain.   Austin, Texas: University of Texas Press,
    1982. 285p. maps. bibliog.

This series of six tours radiates from Houston, and includes: the Ports Trail to San Jacinto and Galveston; the Industrial Trail through the 'Golden Triangle' of far southeastern Texas, with its refineries and chemical plants; the Big Thicket Trail, through the wooded preserves and lumber and oil resources of East Texas; the Heritage Trail in the Brazos River basin, trod during the 1820s by Stephen Austin's 'Old Three Hundred'; the Cattleman's Trail, where the Texas cattle industry first developed between Houston and Victoria; and the River Land Trail, which covers the delta regions of the Brazos, Colorado, and Lavaca Rivers.

28 **A journey through Texas; or a saddle trip on the southwestern frontier.**
    Frederick Law Olmsted.   New York: B. Franklin, 1860, 1969. 516p.
    (Burt Franklin Research and Source Works; American Classics in
    History and Social Science).

This is a famous and often-cited account of a journey through Texas in the mid-1850s by a confirmed Yankee and anti-slavery man. Olmsted, a native of New York who later designed Central Park in New York City and many other urban parks, published several books based on his travels through the South. He was particularly interested in studying the effects of slavery on the economy and culture of Texas, the interaction of Anglo-Texans with the Mexican-Americans and German-Americans living in the state, and the possibilities for the economic development of Texas. Olmsted's eclectic set of appendixes includes an historical chronology, population and economic statistics, meteorological data, a short bibliography, and assorted newspaper clippings on various topics. Overall, this is a serious, somewhat biased, yet astute reflection on ethnic and racial tensions and institutions in Texas on the eve of the Civil War.

29 **Travelers in Texas, 1761-1860.**

Marilyn McAdams Sibley.   Austin, Texas: University of Texas Press, 1967. 236p. maps., bibliog.

An extremely useful analysis of how travellers perceived Texas during the century before the Civil War. Gracefully written and reflecting a mastery of extensive sources, the book shows the many reasons travellers chose to record and publish their experiences. For some writing was a hobby, others wanted to make money, and still others had political or diplomatic objectives. The topics examined by the authors and by Sibley include the vagaries of travel on the Texas frontier, slavery, flora and fauna, towns, resources, Native Americans, government, law and order, and Texas culture in general. The sources that Sibley studies range from the reports of government officials, soldiers, diplomats, and priests, to the diaries, journals, and letters of private citizens. The author features published documents much more prominently than unpublished works. Sibley's thirty-page critical essay on sources is an extremely valuable guide to the accounts that she utilizes.

30 **On a Mexican mustang through Texas, from the gulf to the Rio Grande.**

Alexander E. Sweet, John A. Knox.   London: Chatto & Windus, 1884. 672p.

This book provides a generally light-hearted and eccentrically organized but informative description of Texas in the 1880s, with special attention paid to desperadoes, the cities of Texas, ethnic and cultural issues, legends, Native Americans, and noted personalities.

31 **Texas museums: a guidebook.**

Paula E. Tyler, Ron Tyler.   Austin, Texas: University of Texas Press, 1983. 327p. maps.

A practical guide to more than 500 Texas museums, including art, science, and historical museums as well as wildlife refuges and zoos. The Tylers provide the hours, fees, locations, and services of the museums and although some of the information is no longer accurate, this is still the most comprehensive guide to museums in Texas.

32 **Texas: a guide to the lone star state.**

Work Projects Administration.   New York: Hastings House, 1940. 718p. maps. bibliog.

The work of over 3,000 writers, volunteers, consultants, and editors under the auspices of the Texas Writers Project of the New Deal's Work Projects Administration, the guide is divided into three parts. Part one provides the history and status (in the 1930s) of Texas culture, government, resources, economy, religion, transportation, and institutions. Part two describes fifteen Texas cities and includes statistical profiles. Part three, which comprises three hundred pages, offers twenty-nine different auto tours of the state, with information on routes, facilities, and historical sites and other points of interest. The tone of the guide is matter-of-fact, with a certain amount of perhaps inevitable boosterism. All in all, this is a useful, compact history of Texas and an entertaining slice of Texas life just before the Second World War.

Flora and Fauna

33 **Plants of the Texas shore.**

Mary Michael Cannatella, Rita Emigh Arnold. College Station, Texas: Texas A & M University Press, 1985. 77p. map.

A straight-forward description and analysis in layman's terms, of the plants found on the gulf shore of Texas. After an introductory history of the coast and a description of its natural resources, the authors present chapters on the Barrier Islands, bays and marshes, and Chenier Plains. Their approach is more environmental than scientific, with non-technical descriptions of the plants and of the conditions that encourage their growth. Scores of black-and-white photos and drawings accompany the text. The appendixes include a list of all the plants on the Texas shore by habitat and short sections on area wildlife refuges (including their addresses and telephone numbers).

34 **Caprock canyonlands.**

Dan Flores. Austin, Texas: University of Texas Press, 1990. 200p. maps. bibliog.

A multi-disciplinary description of the natural and human history of the Texas Panhandle's Llano Estacado, or 'staked plains' – the author utilizes history, geography, geology, anthropology, poetry, art, ecology, folklore, mythology, and zoology. Throughout most of the book these themes are traced in chronological fashion. Flores offers, among other things, analyses of Comanche life, of the southern plains' flora and fauna, and of the ways that artists have represented this giant North Texas mesa. The conclusion promotes the preservation of this unique region of Texas. This is not a typical history or even environmentalist jeremiad; Flores' own deep feelings for and perceptions of this place inform every facet of his book, making it as much a description of his own relationship with the land as it is a simple natural history.

35 **Common Texas grasses.**

Frank W. Gould. College Station, Texas: Texas A & M University Press, 1978. 267p. (W. L. Moody, Jr. Natural History Series).

Less technical than its predecessor, Frank W. Gould's, *The Grasses of Texas* (College Station, Texas: Texas A & M University Press, 1975), *Common Texas Grasses* describes 150 of the most common of the state's grasses. Each species is accompanied by an illustration, a botanical description, and an analysis of its habitats and importance. A glossary is included.

36 **Fishes of the Gulf of Mexico: Texas, Louisiana, and adjacent waters.**

H. Dickson Hoese, R. H. Moore. College Station, Texas: Texas A & M University Press, 1977. 327p. map. bibliog.

A profusely illustrated (500 photos, 200 sketches) reference work on over 400 species of fish that live in the northwestern Gulf of Mexico above the Continental Shelf. One chapter explains how to identify fish while another provides keys to the families of Gulf fishes. Other chapters are devoted to sharks, skates, rays, and bony fishes. A glossary is also provided, as are eight appendixes on temperate and subtropical species, rare species, fresh water fish found in marine waters, salt water fish found in fresh water, spawning seasons, French, Cajun, Spanish, and Mexican names for gulf fish, and deep water fish.

37   **No woman tenderfoot: Florence Merriam Bailey, pioneer naturalist.**
Harriet Kofalk.   College Station, Texas: Texas A & M University
Press, 1989. 225p. bibliog.

Born in New York, Florence Merriam Bailey (1863-1948) spent over fifty years
traveling throughout the Southwest studying its wildlife, particularly birds. An unusual
blend of Victorian lady and adventure-loving pioneer, she was a self-taught
ornithologist who wintered in Washington, DC, but spent her summers conducting
field work. Bailey's life is presented chronologically; the bibliography includes a list of
the articles and books Bailey wrote between 1885-1939. Kofolk has included forty-
three black-and-white photographs of Bailey, her family, and scenes from her life.

38   **Texas wildflowers: a field guide.**
Campbell Loughmiller, Lynn Loughmiller.   Austin, Texas:
University of Texas Press, 1984. 287p. bibliog.

A guide to about 300 of the thousands of flowering plants that grow in Texas.
Although its title indicates that it can be used as a field guide, the book's organization
– species are organized alphabetically by scientific name, rather than by physical
characteristics or habitat – makes it difficult for a layperson to use easily. Yet the
authors' clear writing style presents important ecological, historical and botanical
information, and the pictures, many of them in colour, are spectacular.

39   **Connie Hagar: the life history of a Texas birdwatcher.**
Karen Harden McCracken.   College Station, Texas: Texas A & M
University Press, 1986. 296p.

Martha Conger Hagar (1886-1973) moved to Rockport, Texas, in the 1930s, and in
over thirty years of almost daily field observations, became Texas's most famous
birdspotter and a world famous writer about birds (as evidenced in the foreword by
famed bird watcher Roger Tory Peterson). A fairly basic biography, the book is
written in a conversational style that reflects the author's own obsession with bird
watching. This is, in fact, not only a biography, but a jargon-free account of bird life
along the Texas coast and of the growth and maturation of bird watching as a hobby
and as a scientific field. An index of bird names and an appendix of obsolete
designations and their modern equivalents are also included.

40   **The bird life of Texas.**
Harry C. Oberholser, edited by Edgar B. Kincaid.   Austin, Texas:
University of Texas Press, 1974. 2 vols. maps. bibliog.

Completed by Kincaid after Oberhauser's death and with nearly three dozen colour
paintings by Louis Agassiz Fuertes and hundreds of 'district' maps, this is a
comprehensive reference work. Each bird is mentioned twice, in a species description
and a subspecies description. The book provides a physical description of each bird, as
well as its habitat, range, abundance, habits, and calls.

41 **The nature of Texas: a feast of native beauty from Texas Highways Magazine.**
Frank Lively.   College Station, Texas: Texas A & M University Press, 1990. 124p. (Lonnie Lindsay Merrick Texas Environment Series).

Eighty colour photographs accompany twenty-two stories from the tourist magazine *Texas Highways*. In the first section, the pictures and text deal with every section of Texas, from the Big Thicket in the East to the Rio Grande, and from Palo Duro Canyon in the North to Port Aransas on the gulf coast. The second section is devoted to the state's flora and fauna, from mesquite to bluebonnets, and from insects to birds to range animals. This is a popular book highlighting the diversity of the wildlife of Texas.

42 **Birds of Texas and adjacent states.**
Roger Tory Peterson.   Norwalk, Connecticut: Easton Press, 1985. 304p. maps.

This is a field guide compiled by the United States' premier birdwatcher. The author arranges the birds with his 'Peterson System,' which uses patternistic drawings rather than anatomic descriptions to help bird enthusiasts identify birds. Texas is home to the greatest number of bird species of any of the United States; all 540 primary species can be found in this guide to Texas. The three appendixes include: 'accidentals' (birds seen five times or less in Texas); extinct and unsuccessful species; and silhouettes of Texas birds.

43 **Natural world of the Texas big thicket.**
Blair Pittman.   College Station, Texas: Texas A & M University Press, 1978. 99p. map.

Primarily devoted to nearly 100 one- and two-page full colour photographs of land and waterscapes, and plants, birds, reptiles, insects, and mammals of the Big Thicket in East Texas. This is intended for a popular audience. Although the photographs are the heart of the book, the text gives a brief overview of the Big Thicket's history, climate, geology, wildlife, and of developments such as railroads and the lumber industry which have affected the region.

44 **The birds of north central Texas.**
Warren M. Pulich, illustrations by Anne Marie Pulich.   College Station, Texas: Texas A & M University Press, 1988. 439p. maps. bibliog. (W. L. Moody, Jr. Natural History Series).

This guide to the birds of North Texas differs from Peterson's guides in that it is designed to help bird-watchers find birds rather than identify them. Along with dozens of distribution maps and a checklist of birds that have been spotted in each county of this region of Texas, the guide offers information on the habitats, habits, and abundance of every North Texas species.

45 **Birds of the Texas coastal bend: abundance and distribution.**
John Rappole, G. W. Blacklock.   College Station, Texas: Texas A & M University Press, 1985. 126p. maps. bibliog.

This is not a guide as such, but a reference work on the most common birds found along this stretch of the gulf coast. The authors categorize birds by species and provide information on habitat and migratory patterns. In some ways, the focus is more on the geographic area, and why and when birds come there than on the birds themselves. A wide selection of graphs, colour photographs, and black-and-white drawings and maps contribute to the book's usefulness.

46 Birds of Houston.
B. C. Robison. Houston, Texas: Rice University Press, 1990. 129p.

An amateur bird-watchers' guide to the fifty-four different species of birds that can be commonly seen around Houston, with hints on how to buy a good pair of binoculars and ways to attract birds. Robison divides the book into sections on doves, woodpeckers, blackbirds, summer birds, hawks, woodland birds, herons and egrets, and owls, and discusses their behaviour, appearance, habitat, and eating habits. Each species within these groups is described with reference to its habitat, the time of year it can be found in Houston, particular behaviour patterns and field markings that make them easily identifiable, and is presented in a colour photograph.

47 The bats of Texas.
David J. Schmidly, drawings by Christin Stetter. College Station, Texas: Texas A & M University Press, 1991. 224p. maps. bibliog. (W. L. Moody, Jr. Natural History Series).

With the most diverse bat fauna and the largest bat cave (Bracken Cave) in the United States, Texas is home to 4 families and 32 species of this flying mammal. Most of the book consists of accounts of each species, complete with more than 100 photographs and 28 maps. In addition, the authors provide a general discussion of bats (their appearance, distribution, classifications, evolution, biology, and life history), including sections on public health concerns and conservation efforts.

48 Mammals of trans-Pecos Texas.
David J. Schmidly. College Station, Texas: Texas A & M University Press, 1977. 225p. maps. bibliog. (W. L. Moody, Jr. Natural History Series).

This book contains an examination of 101 different species of West Texas mammals and discussion of how the region's climate, physical geography, soil, and vegetation impact on those species. The author lists each mammal by its Latin and its common name and provides information on eating habits, reproductive biology, habitat range, and behaviour. Domestic animals and game animals introduced to the region by man have been ignored, but non-native mammals that have come to live in the region naturally are included. Eighty maps, well over 100 illustrations, and a glossary make this an excellent reference for West Texas mammals.

49 Texas mammals east of the Balcones fault zone.
David J. Schmidly. College Station, Texas: Texas A & M University Press, 1983. 400p. maps. bibliog.

The definitive work on ninety different East Texas mammals. The author gives special attention to endangered species, economically important fur-bearing mammals, and game animals. The format is the same as for the author's work on mammals of the trans-Pecos (see entry no. 48).

50 **Wild flowers of the big thicket, east Texas, and western Louisiana.**
Geyata Sjilusgi. College Station, Texas: Texas A & M University
Press, 1979. 360p. map. bibliog.

The aim of this reference book is to help amateurs or even professional naturalists
identify the flowers of this region. Hundreds of colour photographs and a glossary of
the parts and structures of wildflowers accompany descriptions of the physical
characteristics, the conditions of growth, and the uses of each classification.

51 **The amazing armadillo.**
Larry L. Smith, Robin W. Doughty. Austin, Texas: University of
Texas Press, 1984. 134p. maps. bibliog.

This is a scholarly analysis of the state mammal of Texas. The authors call the
armadillo a 'generalist' mammal, with no specific feeding or habitat preferences, whose
adaptability has allowed it to flourish and expand its range since its introduction into
Texas 150 years ago. Twenty-one species of armadillo now live in South and Central
America and the southwestern United States. The book consists of four main sections:
the natural history of the armadillo; the animal's distribution and dispersal in the South
(including some areas east of the Mississippi River); human uses for the armadillo (as
food or for medical experiments); and an analysis of the armadillo in popular culture
(as pets, racers, and objects of art).

52 **Coastal Texas water, land, and wildlife.**
John L. Tveten. College Station, Texas: Texas A & M University
Press, 1982. 113p.

Intended for a popular audience, this book explains the interaction of plants, birds,
and animals on the beaches, dunes, and marshes of the Texas coast. Each habitat
receives its own chapter. The book features over 100 photographs of coastal
landscapes, shells, plants, and wildlife. Nature photographers will benefit from the
notes Tveten provides on some of his photographic techniques.

53 **Trees of east Texas.**
Robert A. Vines. Austin, Texas: University of Texas Press, 1977.
538p. maps.

Divided into fifty-nine sections – one for each family of tree found in East Texas, from
pines and cypress to persimmon and cactus – this is a listing and description of the trees
that grow in the most heavily forested region of Texas. Information provided for each
species within the families include common and Latin names, leaf and flower types,
size, range throughout the United States, the type of wood it produces, and in which of
the ten Texas 'tree zones' (categorized by soil type, region, and families of trees that
grow in them) the species flourishes. Vines provides a glossary of terms as well as 330
black-and-white drawings of branches and leaves and diagrams of the leaf parts and
forms of Texas trees.

54 **Birds of Big Bend National Park and vicinity.**
Roland H. Waner. Austin, Texas: University of Texas Press, 1973.
223p. map. bibliog.

This practical guide for birdwatchers in the spectacular desert and mountains of the Big Bend of the Rio Grande provides a history of birding in the National Park and its environs, and an annotated list of the 385 species of birds recorded in the area. Readers not only learn which birds frequent the park, but also when and where to spot them. A detailed, fold-out map is included, as are seventeen colour photographs of various landscapes and eight full-colour paintings of common birds by Howard Rollin and Anne Pulich.

55 **Naturalist's Big Bend: an introduction to the trees and shrubs,**
wildflowers, cacti, mammals, birds, reptiles and amphibians, fish and
insects.
Roland H. Waner. Santa Fe, New Mexico: Peregrine Productions,
1973. 160p. bibliog.

A biological 'smörgåsbord of facts' about the natural resources of Big Bend National Park and its vicinity. After several introductory chapters, the author devotes separate sections to the categories of plant and wildlife listed in the unwieldy title. The chapters are organized internally by geographical area (lowlands, highlands) and provide physical characteristics and habits of hundreds of species. Over 100 sketches and black-and-white photographs, as well as a brief section on walking and driving tours, enhance this useful volume.

56 **Cacti of the Southwest: Texas, New Mexico, Oklahoma, Arkansas, and**
Louisiana.
Del Weniger. Austin, Texas: University of Texas Press, 1970. 249p.
(Elma Dill Russell Spencer Foundation Series).

After an introduction, in which he provides a short history of cactus botany and prominent cactus botanists, Weniger provides separate chapters on eleven different genera of cacti, with each species in those genera discussed in detail. He describes each species' range, appearance, roots system, and flowers, offering information about the first botanists to describe and catalogue the species and the state of current research into its characteristics. A glossary, indexes of scientific and common names of cacti, and 332 colour photographs complement the text.

Environment

57 **Adventures with a Texas naturalist.**
Roy Bedichek. Austin, Texas: University of Texas Press, 1961. 2nd ed.
330p.

Originally published in 1947, this revised edition of the most famous book by Texas's best-known naturalist contains marginalia written in Bedichek's personal copy of the first edition. His purpose is to examine the impact of nature on mankind and on human culture, and the impact of man on nature. In twenty-two essays he discusses, among other things, the importance of highway fences (they can create miniature wildlife preserves), the ways that Mexican cliff swallows have utilized concrete bridges as dwellings, the dangers of indiscriminate hunting, commercial egg production, the cooperative relationships between various Texas ecosystems, the golden eagle, and nature in Texas folklore. Bedichek's observations are shrewd and moving, and this ranks with the finest personal ruminations on natural history.

58 **Karankaway country.**
Roy Bedichek. Austin, Texas: University of Texas Press, 1974. 2nd ed. 290p. maps.

In this series of essays, Bedichek focuses on the strip of the coast of the Gulf of Mexico between Corpus Christi and Galveston, the territory once occupied by the Karankawa Indians. The essays argue the necessity of a harmonious relationship between man and his environment, and cover such topics as whooping cranes, the Aransas wildlife refuge, wind and water erosion, prairie chickens, environmental damage caused by domesticated farm animals, and river pollution.

59 **Wildlife and man in Texas: enviromental change and conservation.**
Robin W. Doughty. College Station, Texas: Texas A & M University Press, 1983. 246p. bibliog.

After describing the different regions of Texas (coastal, mountainous, flat and rolling plains, brush, pine forest, and Rio Grande Valley), Doughty explains how Indians, the Spanish, Mexicans, Anglos, and German-Americans who lived in Texas adapted to and exploited the land and wildlife of Texas. Individual chapters detail these groups' initial perceptions, their use of wildlife for recreation (and the resulting decline in game and fish stocks), and 19th and 20th century efforts to conserve and manage Texas wildlife. The author argues that large-scale settlement and the developing oil industry took a heavy toll on wildlife in Texas, but that a number of environmental programmes – three tables provide information on funding provisions for the state wildlife programmes – are helping it to recover.

60 **Naturalists on the frontier.**
Samuel Wood Geiser. Dallas, Texas: Southern Methodist University Press, 1948. 296p. maps. bibliog.

This book contains short biographies of eleven prominent naturalists who worked in Texas from 1820-80. Geiser provides a synopsis of the men's lives, work, and discoveries; appendixes furnish a partial list of naturalists and collectors conducting research in Texas during the period, as well as a bibliography of their publications. The naturalists discussed individually are Jacob Boll, Jean Louis Berlander, Thomas Drummond, John J. Audubon, Louis Ervendberg, Ferdinand Lindheimer, Ferdinand Roemer, Charles Wright, Gideon Lincecum, Julien Reverchon, and Gustaf Wilhem Belfrage.

61 **Lady Bird Johnson and the environment.**
Lewis L. Gould.   Lawrence, Kansas: University Press of Kansas, 1988.
312p. bibliog.

A scholarly treatment of the environmentally minded wife of President Lyndon B. Johnson, Claudia 'Lady Bird' Johnson. Gould places Mrs Johnson's efforts in the contexts of the roles played by women in the conservation movement and the burgeoning roles of 20th century presidents' wives. He focuses on the beautification of America campaign for which Mrs Johnson is best-known, as well as her attempts to improve inner cities, control billboard construction along highways, and preserve California redwoods and the Grand Canyon in Arizona.

62 **The Big Thicket: a challenge for conservation.**
P. A. Y. Gunter.   Austin, Texas: Jenkins Publishing Co. 1972; College
Station, Texas: Texas A & M University Press, 1991. 172p. maps.
bibliog.

A profusely illustrated ecological history of East Texas's Big Thicket, with special emphasis on the destruction caused to it by lumbermen, rice farmers, and cattle raisers. The author, a philosophy professor and president of the Big Thicket Association, points out that reforestation after lumbering replaces trees but not forests. This is not a particularly technical or scientific description of the Big Thicket, but is, rather, a factual, historical and conservation-minded argument in favour of saving the last vestiges of wilderness in East Texas. Gunter also describes the long-term struggle to make the area into a National Park.

63 **Cannibals and condos: Texans and Texas along the Gulf Coast.**
Robert Lee Maril.   College Station, Texas: Texas A & M University
Press, 1986. 113p.

In this informally written book, the author focuses on two symbols of the Texas coast – Indians, among whom the Tonkawa and Karankawa were apparently cannibals, and condominiums – in order to illustrate the transformation of the coast since the 19th century. Maril chronicles how the population living along the gulf have adapted to this environment and to these changes, in terms of government, politics, economics, and family life. The author pays special attention to the ways that the ocean has been revered, neglected, and managed by the government. At the personal level, Maril speaks as a researcher, a traveller, and a father, who wants the environment to be used and developed wisely; he obviously hopes that this effort will contribute to that end.

64 **The climates of Texas counties.**
Natural Fibers Information Center.   Austin, Texas: Natural Fibers
Information Center, University of Texas at Austin, 1987. 569p. map.

An excellent source for basic weather information for Texas. After describing the ten climatic divisions of the state, with temperature, rainfall, and wind norms, it provides an alphabetical listing of each Texas county, with its annual climatic profile, seasonal descriptions, county statistics, and economic and physical characteristics. The second section consists of charts and graphs of temperature and precipitation statistics for each month of the year.

65 **Climate of Texas and the adjacent Gulf waters.**
Robert B. Orton. Washington, DC: United States Department of
Commerce Weather Bureau, 1964. 195p. maps.

A highly technical report compiled to furnish the National Aeronautics and Space
Administration in Houston with meteorological data necessary for the testing of space
vehicles and for the selection of landing sites. Each chapter is divided into three parts:
South Texas, the adjacent gulf waters, and North Texas. Information is provided on
sky cover, cloud ceiling height, visibility, wind, local physiography, and the synoptic
weather systems controlling these factors.

66 **Water and the future of the southwest.**
Edited by Zachary A. Smith. Albuquerque, New Mexico: University
of New Mexico Press, 1989. 278p. (Public Policy Series).

Fourteen interdisciplinary essays on water law, water policy, environmental issues, and
state, federal, and local government roles in all of these areas. The authors emphasize
the importance of water in this arid region's future prosperity, and aim to influence
policy in order to avert future crises. Part one, 'The Policy Environment', focuses on
the policy making process, water law, and estimates by state water resource managers
of future needs and problems. Part two, 'The Institutional Environment', studies
relations between the United States and Mexico, Indian water rights, federal-state
relations in each Texas county, military relationships, and the potential for the
development of national water policies. Part three, 'Allocation and Management
Issues', examines water transfers from one region to another, private water markets,
federal attempts to end barriers for transfers, and groundwater shortages.

67 **Land of the bears and honey: a natural history of east Texas.**
Joe C. Truett, Daniel W. Lay, foreword by Francis E. Abernethy.
Austin, Texas: University of Texas Press, 1984. 176p. maps. bibliog.

The authors detail the transformation of East Texas (primarily Angelina, Jasper, and
Tyler Counties) from a region with vast stretches of woods teeming with wildlife to a
developed and urbanized area devoid of much of its original natural wealth. Their
historical narrative of 150 years of change is entwined with partly autobiographical
stories of a family of hunters which show how their experiences and attitudes evolve
through the decades. Truett and Lay describe the disappearance of East Texas animal
and plant species and the ways that human uses for the land – agriculture, stockraising,
lumbering – have impacted on the environment. This is a very personal work reflecting
a deep commitment to conserving the nature of East Texas.

68 **'If you don't like the weather . . .': stories of Texas weather.**
John Edward Weems. Austin, Texas: Texas Monthly Press, 1989.
121p. bibliog.

An entertaining and anecdotal summary of the wide range of climatic conditions and
weather patterns enjoyed and endured by Texans. Weems devotes chapters to the ways
in which weather data are gathered, the conditions that govern Texas weather and
their sometimes extreme results, folk sayings regarding the weather, forecasting by the
National Weather Bureau and television meteorologists, and humans' psychological
responses to weather. Weems offers many amusing incidents and dozens of items of
trivia, but also a great deal of useful information.

69   **The tornado.**
John Edward Weems.   College Station, Texas: Texas A & M
University Press, 1977, 1991. 200p. map. bibliog.

An entertaining survey of tornadoes all over the world and of the kind of weather patterns that cause them. The focus is on the damage caused by tornadoes, on the bizarre incidents that occur during them, and on the experiences of their victims. It is also a personal narrative of the Waco tornado of May 11, 1953 which killed 114 people, injured hundreds more, and inflicted tens of millions of dollars worth of damage on that central Texas city.

70   **A weekend in September.**
John Edward Weems.   New York: Holt Publishing Co., 1957; College
Station, Texas: Texas A & M University Press, 1989. 180p. map. bibliog.

A fast-paced narrative of the 1900 hurricane that ravaged Galveston and killed 6,000 people. Based partly on interviews with survivors, Weems focuses on the meteorologists Isa and Joseph Cline, on the chronology of the storm, on heroic efforts to save lives by men like Police Chief Edward Ketchum, and on relief and rebuilding programmes in the hurricane's aftermath. Weems includes nearly thirty black-and-white photographs of Galveston before and after the disaster.

History

Historiography

71 **Texas through time: evolving interpretations.**
Edited by Walter L. Buenger, Robert A. Calvert.   College Station,
Texas: Texas A & M University Press, 1991. 304p.

Not merely a bibliography, *Texas Through Time* is a collection of twelve
historiographical essays that explore the work of historians of Texas in the context of
larger currents in American historiography. The guiding question is: why have Texas
myths survived in the face of more sophisticated and objective trends in the historical
profession? Written by the leading historians in Texas specialties like Texas-Mexican
culture, African-Americans in Texas, agrarianism, Progressivism, the New Deal,
women, urbanization and economics, the collective themes of the essays are; that
historians of Texas have generally ignored new perspectives and methods; that the
ideas of previous generations of historians have inhibited their successors; and that
Texans sense of their own identity prevented new interpretations that would threaten
comfortable stereotypes. Taken together, the essays challenge historians of Texas to
produce works less limited by provincialism and myth-making.

72 **A guide to the history of Texas.**
Edited by Light Townsend Cummins, Alvin R. Bailey, Jr.   Westport,
Connecticut: Greenwood Press, 1988. 307p. (Reference Guides to State
History and Research).

A very useful and up-to-date bibliography divided into two parts. The first consists of
eleven chapters detailing the monograph and periodical historical literature of Texas.
Several chronological chapters emphasize the political history of Texas, while
subsequent chapters explore the literature on Native Americans, African-Americans,
women, and Mexican-Americans. The appropriate books and articles are discussed in
essay form. One shortcoming is that the essay on the last seventy years of Texas history
has been allotted fewer pages than any other historical period since 1821. The second
part of the book consists of four- to ten-page essays on the fifteen most important

historical archives in the state. They include short histories of the collections and suggest fields of interest in which the collections might be helpful. Since many of the archives do not have published guides, it also is the best easily accessible source of information about those archives.

73 **The twentieth-century west: historical interpretations.**
Edited by Gerald D. Nash, Richard W. Etulain.   Albuquerque, New Mexico: University of New Mexico Press, 1989. 454p. maps. bibliog.

Thirteen essays on current scholarship in the modern West are divided into five categories: people, economy, environment, politics, and culture. Essays offer historiographical discussions of those fields and topics for further research. Among the topics included in the book are the shifts from an agricultural to an industrial economy and from rural spaces to urban spaces; the experiences of Chicanos, women, and Native Americans; environmental change and lumber and water resources; voting patterns and political reform; and western art and literature. Included are over two dozen tables and figures on population, metropolitan growth, voting, political affiliation, unemployment, and medical care. Although many of the essays deal with issues important to Texas, Texas is specifically mentioned in the essays on 'Mexican Americans in the New West', 'The changing face of Western literary regionalism', and 'The metropolitan region'.

74 **Essays on Walter Prescott Webb.**
Edited by Kenneth Philip, Elliott West.   Austin, Texas: University of Texas Press, 1976. 123p. bibliog. (Walter Prescott Webb Memorial Lectures).

Four of these five essays by students of Walter Prescott Webb (perhaps the best-known native-Texan historian) were originally delivered as a part of the Walter Prescott Webb Memorial lectures at the University of Texas at Arlington. They are not actually about Webb, but about the themes that Webb developed during his long career. After an introduction by the noted western historian Ray Allen Billington, Joe B. Frantz, in 'Walter Prescott Webb and the South', decribes the South's status as an economic colony of New England. W. Turrentine Jackson's 'Australians and the comparative frontier' shows how Australians have examined their frontier experience in an international context and offers a useful bibliography of works on various frontier periods. W. Eugene Hollon argues that the environment, resources, and geography of the West has shaped civilization throughout history in 'Walter Prescott Webb's Arid West: Four Decades Later'. The turmoil that has plagued international law in the 20th century, maintains George Wolfskill in 'The Webb "Great Frontier" Hypothesis and International Law', stems from the decline of European competition for western natural resources. Finally, 'Webb the Schoolteacher', by Walter Rundell, Jr. takes a look at Webb's educational career prior to his appointment to the faculty at the University of Texas; this essay was not delivered as a lecture, but won the annual Webb-Smith Essay Competition.

75 **Eugene C. Barker: historian.**
William C. Pool.   Austin, Texas: Texas State Historical Association, 1971. 228p. bibliog.

Perhaps the most important and certainly the most revered promoter of Texas history, Eugene C. Barker (1874-1956) was born in Texas, attended the University of Texas, and taught at the University for decades. In addition to writing several standard works on early Texas history, Barker served as director of the Texas State Historical Association as editor of the *Southwestern Historical Quarterly*, and as creator of the Eugene C. Barker Texas History Center archives. This straightforward narrative biography is simply organized; five long chapters deal with 'Youth and education', 'Years of growth', 'Barker and the forty aces' (the University of Texas), 'The historian at work', and 'The late years'.

76 **The making of a history: Walter Prescott Webb and the Great Plains.**
Gregory M. Tobin. Austin, Texas: University of Texas Press, 1976. 184p. bibliog.

Tobin focuses on the intellectual influence of Lindley M. Keasbey on the work of Walter Prescott Webb, especially in the latter's masterpiece, *The Great Plains*. Keasby was one of Webb's undergraduate professors; he believed that geography was a key determinant in the economic and social history of the United States. Although Keasby emphasized this geographical determinism at the global level, Webb applied it to a single region in North America. In effect, the author reconstructs the conception and composition of Webb's magnum opus. This is a useful and imaginative intellectual biography of Webb's career through the publication of *The Great Plains*.

77 **Clio's cowboys: studies in the historiography of the cattle trade.**
Don D. Walker. Lincoln, Nebraska: University of Nebraska Press, 1981. 210p.

A valuable analysis of the portrayal and the interpretation of the western cattle trade and the men who conducted it. Walker combines historiography with literary criticism beginning with the works of Joseph G. McCoy and Theodore Roosevelt and continuing through Marxist views of 'cowboy history'. Some of the chapter titles are very instructive: 'Freedom and Individualism on the Range: Ideological Images of the Cowboy and Cattleman'; 'The Fenceline between Cowboy History and Cowboy Fiction'; and 'Cowboy with a Sense of the Past'. Of particular interest are his analyses of the historian Walter Prescott Webb and the folklorist J. Frank Dobie. Scholarly yet entertaining, this is a welcome inter-disciplinary look at the historical and the imaginary images of cowmen.

General and Special Topics

78 **Texans, guns and history.**
Colonel Charles Askins. New York: Winchester Press, 1970. 246p. bibliog.

A colourful account of violence in Texas from the 1870s through the 1930s that tends to glorify the frontier stereotypes of Texas. Askins emphasizes Indian wars, famous lawmen (like Captain Lee McNelly of the Texas Rangers) and outlaws (like John Wesley Hardin and Bonnie and Clyde), border 'troubles', and trigger-happy ranch hands.

79 **Ghost towns of Texas.**
T. Lindsay Baker.   Norman, Oklahoma: University of Oklahoma Press,
1986. 208p. maps. bibliog.

After locating over 1,000 deserted Texas towns, Baker visited more than 300 and from those selected 89 to include in this book, which offered significant ruins, public access, and a fairly even geographical distribution through the state. Most were along railroads or near mines, military posts, or oil fields; the towns' residents disappeared when the soldiers moved on, the natural resources were used up, or the railroad traffic switched to distant highways. Brief narratives stressing the unique aspects of each town, as well as its similarities to others, complement 90 maps and nearly 200 black-and-white photographs in providing haunting slices of Texas's past.

80 **The history of Texas.**
Robert Calvert, Arnoldo De Leon.   Arlington Heights, Illinois:
Harlan Davidson, 1990. 479p. maps. bibliog.

The most recently published textbook for Texas history, it differs from its predecessors most obviously in its greater emphasis on social issues (ethnicity and urbanization) and on more recent Texas history. With well over 100 illustrations and maps (on topics like the Indians of Texas, prohibition, oil fields, railroads, ethnic settlements, and agricultural products), this is a useful introduction to Texas history for older high school students or first year college undergraduates.

81 **Galveston: a history of the island.**
Gary Cartwright.   New York: Atheneum, 1991. 338p. bibliog.

A popular history of Galveston Island. Cartwright examines the cannabilistic Karankawas who were the island's first inhabitants, the arrival of Spanish and French explorers like Cabeza de Vaca and Rene Robert La Salle, the occupation of the island by the pirate Jean Lafitte, the Civil War battle that took place in Galveston Bay, and the status of the Bay as a terminus of two railroad lines and major exporter of cotton and grain in the 1870s. The author also focuses on the Gilded Age rise of the Moody, Sealy, Kempner, and other prominent families, and the 1900 hurricane that killed one-sixth of the population. The island was the centre for rum-running during Prohibition, but by the 1950s reformers had cleaned up the city and begun restoring its historic buildings. This is an entertaining narrative of a prominent and colourful slice of Texan life.

82 **The Texas border and some borderliners: a chronicle and guide.**
Robert Joseph Casey.   Indianapolis, Indiana: Bobbs-Merrill, 1950.
440p. bilbiog.

A colourful, well-written popular history of the Rio Grande region from Brownsville to El Paso and from Spanish times through to the early 20th century. It includes short chapters on topics and people ranging from the Texas and Mexican Revolutions to West Texas oil to Lily Langtry (the English actress and inspiration for the name of Langtry, Texas). Casey emphasizes the violence and human interest stories of the Old West. The book is packed with photographs and other illustrations, as well as out-dated references to Texas landmarks and highways.

83 **Castle Gap and the Pecos frontier.**
Patrick Dearen. Fort Worth, Texas: Texas Christian University Press, 1988. 216p. maps.

Written by a novelist and unencumbered by scholarship, this colourful book studies six legends concerning Castle Gap, a break in a West Texas mesa often traversed by Indians and Anglos. Linked at least partly by quests for wealth, the tales include legends about a prospector who found a rich vein of gold but never revealed it to anyone else before his death, a lost wagon train allegedly buried in the desert, a dangerous ford across the Pecos River, a Fort Stockton ghost, and a mysterious salt lake. Dearen provides the history behind these legends, as well as the history of the telling of the legends.

84 **Lone star: a history of Texas and the Texans.**
T. R. Fehrenbach. New York: Collier Books, 1968. 719p. bibliog.

A popularly written account of Texas history that focuses almost entirely on the 19th century. Drawing on both secondary and primary published sources, Fehrenbach takes a fond but even-handed look at his state's often violent and always colourful history, especially the Texas Revolution, the Civil War era, and the Indian wars.

85 **Seven keys to Texas.**
T. R. Fehrenbach. El Paso, Texas: Texas Western Press, 1983. 140p.

Written by one of the best-known popularizers of Texas history, *Seven Keys* tries to determine what makes Texas and Texans different. At one point, the author compares Texas's role in the United States to Scotland's in Great Britain. Fehrenbach devotes chapters to the people, frontier, land, economy, society, politics, and transformations of Texas. The special history of this state helps explain the pride, loyalty, prejudices, conservatism, and territoriality that defines Texas. While a non-Texan may not agree that all of this amounts to 'a true ethnic identity', this is a very good example of the provincialism that characterizes the stereotypical self-image shared by many Texans.

86 **From the high plains.**
John Fischer. New York: Harper & Row, 1978. 181p. map.

The author, a journalist and former editor of *Harper's Magazine*, is the son of pioneers to the Texas Panhandle. This is an attempt to document the stories he heard growing up in this corner of the 'last' Old West. He considers work, religion, Indians, cowboys and cattle, Hispanics, and Texas 'sayings'. *From the High Plains* presents turn-of-the-century Texas colourfully without mythologizing Texas or Texans.

87 **Texas: a history.**
Joe B. Frantz. New York: W. W. Norton, 1976. 211p. maps. bibliog. (The States and the Nation Series).

A brief, breezy survey of Texas from pre-history through the 1970s by one of the state's best-known historians. Loosely documented and at times critical of Texan customs, policies, and attitudes, the book includes an annotated listing of historic sites in the state.

88 **A most singular country: a history of occupation in Big Bend.**
Arthur R. Gómez.   Sante Fe, New Mexico: National Park Service,
Department of the Interior; Provo, Utah: Brigham Young University
Press, 1990. 241p. maps. bibliog. (Charles Redd Monographs in Western
History).

This work traces, in a chronological manner, the history of the Big Bend region from
its centuries as an isolated, inhospitable frontier to its incorporation as a National Park
in the 1940s. The narrative includes the history of Indian fights, Mexican bandits, and
Anglo ranchers, as well as economic development (the mining and cattle industries)
and military activities (army operations between 1910-20 and air corps training).
Gomez also describes the debates over how best to exploit and preserve the natural
beauty of the Big Bend.

89 **Texas: from the frontier to Spindletop.**
James L. Haley.   New York: St. Martin's, 1991. 304p.

A chronological but episodic history of Texas from the arrival of Stephen F. Austin's
first colonists to the discovery of oil at Spindletop in 1901. The account does not
amount to a comprehensive coverage, but offers samples of Texas history. Although it
lacks detail, the plentiful illustrations and readable style make the book an adequate
introduction to 19th century Texan history.

90 **Social change in the southwest, 1350-1880.**
Thomas D. Hall.   Lawrence, Kansas: University Press of Kansas, 1989.
287p. maps. bibliog.

A monumental history of the Southwest from pre-history through the 19th century.
After establishing the prehistoric, ecological, linguistic, political, and social contexts,
Hall uses social theory to show how the indigenous peoples of the region interacted
with the Spanish invaders between 1540-1821. This is not a description of a static
colonial relationship, but an analysis of change over time, especially during the period
of Bourbon Reforms (1759-87). Of course, an important element of Spanish policy had
to do with the Native Americans who often resisted European encroachment; the
economic development and settlement of the area, with the help of American
merchants, and military conquest of the Spanish were ultimately unsuccessful. One
important aspect of this compelling book is that it does not compartmentalize
southwestern history into Spanish, Mexican, and American periods, but provides a
broad overview of change that cuts across artificial political and chronological
divisions.

91 **Great river: the Rio Grande in North American history.**
Paul Horgan.   New York: Holt, Rinehart and Winston, 1954. 2 vols.
maps. bibliog.

The first volume of this much-lauded work covers the period before and during the
Spanish occupation of the Rio Grande, while the second deals with the thirty years of
Mexican rule and subsequent occupation by the United States. Hogan has actually
written a history of the humans who inhabited the lands through which the Rio Grande
flows, emphasizing daily life as well as political and military events. This is, naturally, a
story of conflict, as successive cultures struggled for control of the vast area drained by
the 1900-mile long 'Great River'. Horgan tells the story with a novelist's eye for the
large sweep of history and the historian's eye for the telling detail.

92   **Texas graveyards: a cultural legacy.**
     Terry G. Jordan.   Austin, Texas: University of Texas Press, 1982. 147p.
     bibliog. (Elma Dill Russell Spencer Foundation Series).

A brief look by a cultural geographer at cemeteries as historical sources and as
reflections of cultural differences. Using an anthropological examination of artifacts
and a wide range of printed sources, Jordan explores ethnic and regional variations of
burial customs and the rituals created by the living to commemorate the dead. He
reveals important information about continuity and change in religious beliefs
(particularly ideas about death and nature) in social structures and in ethnic traditions.

93   **Texas crossings: the lone star state and the American far west, 1836-1986.**
     Howard R. Lamar.   Austin, Texas: University of Texas Press, 1991.
     82p. maps. bibliog.

Originially delivered as the first George W. Littlefield Lectures in American History at
the University of Texas at Austin, these three essays examine Texas as a route –
physical as well as figurative – elsewhere. 'Texas and the California gold rush' looks at
Texans and non-Texans traversing the state on their way to the West Coast gold fields
in the late 1840s and 1850s, while 'A breed apart' explores the impact of Texans and of
southerners in general after they arrived in California. 'Imperial strategies' analyses
forty years of attempts by Texans and the state government of Texas to connect their
state to California by rail; ironically, the Southern Pacific, which finally accomplished
that feat, was built by Californians. The five maps included provide very useful graphic
representations of the routes actually used to cross Texas.

94   **Between sun and sod: an informal history of the Texas panhandle.**
     Willie Newbury Lewis.   College Station, Texas: Texas A & M
     University Press, 1976. 178p. bibliog.

Lewis intends to illustrate the character of the land and people of the Panhandle
frontier, with an emphasis on the civilizing work of Clarendon, a Methodist utopian
community. The inhabitants featured in the book include hardy, determined buffalo
hunters, cowboys, and Methodists; the last group brought moral values and political,
economic, and educational institutions to the region. The author, who lived at
Clarendon early in the 20th century, uses a number of primary sources as well as her
own experiences yet she all but ignores the Native Americans who lived in the region.
According to the author, the text was completed years before its actual publication.

95   **Texas: a modern history.**
     David G. McComb.   Austin, Texas: University of Texas Press, 1989.
     198p. maps. bibliog.

A brief survey of Texas history from its Spanish origins to the present, popularly
written and without citations. After a chapter dealing with the terrain, climate, and
environment of Texas, McComb includes the usual stories of settlement, economic
growth, and politics. His final chapter examines 'The Texas Mystique' – the state's
culture and its image outside of its own boundaries. McComb provides a smooth
narrative and a sometimes critical look at Texas history and society. The book includes
many asides on personalities, sporting and historical events, and curiosities.

96 **Texas: all hail the mighty state.**
Archie P. McDonald.   Austin, Texas: Eakin Press, 1983. 266p. maps.

This is a general survey of Texas history from pre-colonial times through to the 1970s. The emphasis throughout, especially in the earlier parts, is on the land; how inhabitants fought over it, developed it, abused it, profited from it, and cherished it. The author also explains the special roles Texas has played in different eras of history, especially the Civil War, the Populist and Progressive periods, the World Wars, the civil rights movement, the space programme, and the energy crisis. The text is complemented by over sixty black-and-white photographs, sketches and paintings of people, places, and events.

97 **Texas after Spindletop.**
Seth S. McKay, Odie B. Faulk.   Austin, Texas: Steck-Vaughn, 1965.
247p. maps. bibliog. (The Saga of Texas Series).

A history of Texas from 1901, when oil was discovered at Spindletop near Beaumont, Texas, through the election of the Texan Lyndon B. Johnson to the presidency in 1964. The authors focus on political issues and politicians, from Prohibition and educational and prison reform from about 1910 to the resurrection of the Ku Klux Klan in the 1920s. They examine the lumber and oil industries, as well as agriculture during the 'boom' times of the decade after the First World War and the 'hard times' during the Depression of the 1930s. McKay and Faulk also emphasize gubernatorial politics and campaigns, and the economic growth that followed the Second World War.

98 **A nation within a nation: the rise of Texas nationalism.**
Mark E. Nackman.   Port Washington, New York: Kennikat Press,
1975. 183p. maps. bibliog.

This text examines the nationalistic exertions of white Texans from 1821-61. Nackman seems to believe in the legendary independent-mindedness of Texans and seeks to explain it in terms of the movement for Texas independence as well as the expansionism of the Texas Republic. The author believes that Texas was a haven for men unable or unwilling to live in the United States, and seems to attribute Texas nationalism not only to conventional economic and political motivations, but also to a less tangible restlessness and discontent with any sort of external limits.

99 **The Texas heritage.**
Edited by Ben Proctor, Archie McDonald.   St. Louis, Missouri: Forum
Press, 1980. 238p. bibliog.

A collection of essays by different historians on issues in Texas history. The first seven selections examine the state chronologically through Reconstruction; the next eight deal with special topics, including the cattle industry, the Texas Rangers, the struggle of *Tejanos* and African-Americans for equal rights, 'Texas Women versus the Texas Myth', the oil and gas industry, sports, and Texans in national leadership positions in the 20th century.

100 **The Texas Panhandle frontier.**
Frederick W. Rathjen. Austin, Texas: University of Texas Press,
1973. 286p. maps. bibliog.

Beginning with a physical history and description of the Texas Panhandle, the author
chronicles its history from aboriginal times to the 1890s. Much attention is given to
exploration of the region, the evolution of land use, and the gradual taking over of the
land by Anglo-Americans. Chapters are devoted to Native Americans, Spanish, and
Anglo-American explorers, buffalo hunters, military conquest, and occupation.
Statistical information on land management and agriculture is provided, and the seven
maps include information on topographic divisions and soil types, exploration and
railroad routes, battle sites, and locations of towns and forts.

101 **Texas: the lone star state.**
Rupert N. Richardson, Ernest Wallace, Adrian Anderson.
Englewood Cliffs, New Jersey: Prentice Hall, 1988. 5th ed. 464p. maps.
bibliog.

First published in 1943, this popular textbook on Texas history presents, in a matter-of-
fact way, the state's economic and political development. Although it is more objective
than many older histories of Texas, it pays only passing attention to ethnic and gender
issues. This is a very traditional look at Texas that, despite its recent revision, ends in
the 1960s.

102 **The cowboy hero: his image in American history and culture.**
William W. Savage, Jr. Norman, Oklahoma: University of Oklahoma
Press, 1979. 179p. bibliog.

This is not a history of cowboys, but a breezy history of the images of cowboys in
America that draws on literature, history, and popular culture. Savage examines
various aspects of cowboy myths and representations, including the cowboy as hero;
the ways any man can live vicariously as a 'cowboy' by dressing the part or by visiting a
'dude' ranch; cowboy music; the sexism inherent in the life style and the images of
cowboys; the marketing of cowboy goods and ideas; rodeo; and, finally, the eclipse of
the cowboy hero in the 1970s.

103 **Alamo images: changing perceptions of a Texas experience.**
Susan P. Schoelwer, Tom W. Geaser, Paul A. Hutton. Dallas, Texas:
DeGolyer Library and Southern Methodist University Press, 1985.
223p. bibliog.

A catalogue of an exhibition at the DeGolyer Library at Southern Methodist
University on the art, artifacts, literature, and movies about the central event in Texas
history and mythology. Profusely illustrated with black-and-white photographs, movie
stills, drawings, prints, woodcuts, and other kinds of Alamoiana, the book shows the
creation of Alamo myths and their ramifications (for instance, ignoring the
contributions of *Tejanos* to the cause of Texas independence and the expansion of
slavery brought about by the establishment of Texas as a republic and, later, a part of
the United States reflects a deep-seated racism). Throughout, historical truth
(regarding the battle as well as the previous lives of its participants) is placed in
counterpoint to the legends that have obscured the facts. The text and illustrations
provide a valuable study of the uses of legend in such diverse media as books, movies,
comic books, and advertisements.

104 **I'll die before I'll run: the story of the great feuds of Texas.**
C. L. Sonnichsen. New York: Devin-Adair, 1962. 371p. bibliog.
A colourful, readable, but thoughtful look at about a dozen 19th century Texas feuds.
Sonnichsen examines the conditions that spawned the feuds (particularly racial and
political tensions unleashed by the Civil War and Reconstruction), the families and
groups bound together by political or economic loyalties who fought them, and the
course of events of each feud. Two important threads run through most of the feuds:
the absence of effective mechanisms for enforcing the law and maintaining order, and
Texans' tendency to fight rather than retreat when challenged. Nearly half the book is
devoted to the three-decade-long Sutton-Taylor feud and to the Jaybird-Woodpecker
Feud of the 1880s.

105 **Big bend: a history of the last Texas frontier.**
Ronnie C. Tyler. Washington, DC: Department of the Interior,
United States Government Printing Office, 1975. 288p. maps. bibliog.
Prepared to accompany an exhibit on the Big Bend at the Amon Carter Museum of
Western Art, this is a chronological narrative of the Big Bend's history. The author
devotes chapters to the Bend's resources and environment, Spanish exploration and
settlement, early exploration and mapping by the United States army, American
settlement and economic development, the 'Mexican bandit' era, and the Big Bend's
more recent history as a national park. A major theme running throughout the book is
the important role that the United States and Mexican military and governments have
played throughout the region's history. Dozens of historic photographs, several colour
plates of important landmarks, and a sixteen-page description of historic sites make
this a very useful introduction to the Big Bend area.

106 **Red river in southwestern history.**
Carl Newton Tyson. Norman, Oklahoma: University of Oklahoma
Press, 1981. 222p. maps. bibliog.
Using an approach reminiscent of Horgan's work on the Rio Grande, Tyson's
traditional narrative portrays the Red River as a transportation route, as an avenue for
change, and as a locus for civilizations. He provides a history of this river that forms
part of Texas's northern boundary from the centuries of Indian occupation through the
20th century. It has served as a trade route from Louisiana into Indian territory and as
a source of conflict between the Spanish and French; it was a point of interest and a
highway for American settlement and a supply line for both the Union and the
Confederacy during the Civil War; more recently, it has provided electrical energy and
spawned economic development through the efforts of the United States government.

107 **Texas: an informal biography.**
Owen P. White. New York: G. P. Putnam's Sons, 1945. 268p. maps.
A popular general history that panders to the colourful side of Texas history and
accepts unhesitatingly the myth of Texas as a separate civilization. This biography is
notable for this sense of Texas nationalism – the state is ludicrously presented as an
'ally' of the United States during the Second World War – and as a good example of
pre-1960s historical writing which virtually ignores the experiences of Native
Americans and African-Americans and portrays Mexicans merely as opponents to
Anglo-American progress.

108 **They made their own law: stories of Bolivar Peninsula.**
Melanie Wiggins. Houston, Texas: Rice University Press, 1991. 220p.
bibliog.
Wiggins, a writer and resident of Galveston, uses local records, diaries, newspapers, and oral history to bring to life this isolated but colourful corner of Texas located on a peninsula jutting into the mouth of Galveston Bay. The peninsula was the home of Atakapa and Karankawa Indians and the site of one of the privateer Jean Lafitte's hideouts; Wiggins's tales of smuggling, hurricanes, and 'wildcat' oilmen emphasize local colour and the pre-modern history of the place.

109 **A history of Texas.**
L. J. Wortham. Fort Worth, Texas: Wortham Molyneaux, 1924. 5
vols. maps.
This multi-volume work provides a narrative of Texas history from 1820-1924. The first three volumes, however, only get as far as 1836; as a result, there is probably more here than anyone needs to know about the Anglo settlement of Texas and the Texas Revolution. It is useful as an example of a fairly early attempt to explain the sweep of Texas history and for the documents appended to each volume, such as early Indian treaties, lists of the 'Old Three Hundred' and of soldiers who fought at San Jacinto, early laws and Constitution of the Republic of Texas, and the Treaty of Guadalupe Hidalgo, which ended the Mexican War.

Spanish and Mexican Periods, 1540-1836

110 **The San Antonio missions and their system of land tenure.**
Felix D. Almaraz Jr. Austin, Texas: University of Texas Press, 1989.
100p. maps. bibliog.
The outgrowth of a National Park Service study of the four missions comprising the San Antonio Missions National Historical Park, this is a practical attempt to establish the original boundaries of mission land grants, to determine the configurations of its cultivation, and to find out what structures were built and when. Brief attention is also paid to the process of secularization of the missions in the early 19th century and the effects of urbanization as San Antonio developed. Useful appendixes include lists of grantees, descriptions of buildings, fees and payments, allotment of water resources, and some mission accounts of expenses and income.

111 **Tragic cavalier: Governor Manuel Salcedo of Texas, 1808-1813.**
Felix D. Almaraz Jr. Austin, Texas: University of Texas Press, 1971.
206p. bibliog.
A workmanlike biography of one of the last governors of Spanish Texas – he took office in 1808 and was assassinated five years later – whose life is in many ways a metaphor for Spain's crumbling Mexican and North American empire. A representative of the last generation of Spanish officials, Salcedo was no match for the

growing dissatisfaction of Mexican revolutionaries along the Rio Grande and American adventurers from Louisiana.

112 **The Spanish borderlands frontier, 1813-1821.**
John Francis Bannon. New York: Holt, Rinehart & Winston, 1970. 308p. maps. bibliog. (Histories of the American Frontier).

A synthesis based on secondary and published primary sources, this is an attempt to make Americans aware that the west of Daniel Boone and Kit Carson was complemented by a west explored and settled by the Spanish. Much of the book demonstrates the ways in which Spanish and Anglo settlement differed; for instance, the military and the church played important roles in the Spanish version of New World culture clashes with the Native Americans, unlike the English example on the Atlantic Coast. The expansion of Spanish settlement was directed, watched and controlled by the central government so that there was less room for self-reliance and self-expression for frontiersmen. There was much more cross-breeding with indigenous peoples on the Spanish frontier, as well as more mining and ranching and less farming. This is a useful corrective for Americans who claim the frontier experience as uniquely their own.

113 **The life of Stephen F. Austin, founder of Texas, 1793-1836: a chapter in the westward movement of the Anglo-American people.**
Eugene C. Barker. Austin, Texas: Texas State Historical Association, 1949. 2nd ed. 477p. maps. bibliog.

The classic biography of a hero of Texas history by a hero of Texas historiography. Gracefully written and very admiring of Austin (1793-1836), it places his life in the context of his family's westward movement after their arrival in America in 17th century New England, especially his father Moses' migration west to Missouri and Arkansas. The emphasis is on politics, and the author goes into great detail about general Texas history, especially, not surprisingly, the colonization of Texas and the events leading up to the revolution against Mexico. Very little information is provided about Austin's family life or personality.

114 **Stephen F. Austin, father of Texas.**
Carleton Beals. New York: McGraw-Hill, 1953. 277p. bibliog.

A breezy, information-packed narrative of the Texas founder written for readers at about the high school level; the author insists on referring to his subject as 'Steve' throughout the book.

115 **Coronado, knight of pueblos and plains.**
Herbert Eugene Bolton. Albuquerque, New Mexico: University of New Mexico Press, 1964. 491p. maps. bibliog.

A traditional but satisfying narrative of one of Spain's more spectacular efforts to explore its slice of the New World. Bolton places Coronado's 1540s trek through Arizona, Kansas, Oklahoma, and North Texas firmly into its political and economic contexts and the competition among conquistadors for riches and glory. Although obviously dated, the book's massive bibliography is an added attraction. Also dated is the book's Spanish point of view; Bolton all but ignores the ramifications of Spanish development on the indigenous peoples of the areas through which these explorers travelled.

116 **Texas in the middle eighteenth century: studies in Spanish colonial history and administration.**
Herbert Eugene Bolton. Berkeley, California: University of California Press, 1915; New York: Russell & Russell, 1962; Austin, Texas: University of Texas Press,1970. 501p. maps. bibliog.
Written by one of the deans of 'borderlands' history, this is a collection of essays based on vast research in Mexican and Spanish archives. Bolton stresses the political rather than the social and economic elements of Spanish settlement and of the diplomatic triangle between the Spanish, French, and Native Americans. Facts outweigh analysis; the twelve foldout maps (some from the 18th century) are quite useful.

117 **Six missions of Texas.**
James Day. Waco, Texas: Texian Press, 1965. 194p.
Organized around six colour paintings of Texas missions by Granville Bruce (prints of the paintings are included in the book) and with an introduction by the then-Governor John Connally, this is not a particularly scholarly work. However, the essays that accompany the paintings do provide serviceable narratives by well-known Texas historians of the La Bahía mission in Goliad and of the five missions in the San Antonio area: Concepción, San José, San Francisco de Espada, San Juan de Capistrano, and, of course, San Antonio de Valera, the mission that came to be called the Alamo.

118 **Spanish and French rivalry in the Gulf region of the United States, 1678-1702.**
William E. Dunn. Austin, Texas: University of Texas Press, 1917. 238p. maps. bibliog.
This little-revised Columbia University dissertation presents a factual, chronological look at the exploration and colonization of the Gulf of Mexico from Florida to Texas, including French Louisiana and Spanish Texas. Dunn's research in Spanish sources is prodigious; his political and diplomatic narrative, therefore, tends to stress the Spanish point of view.

119 **The last years of Spanish Texas, 1778-1821.**
Odie B. Faulk. The Hague, Netherlands: Mouton, 1964. 156p. bibliog. (Studies in American History).
This is basically a narrative of the political, economic, and administrative history of the last four decades of Spanish Texas, with separate chapters on religion, culture, and Indian policy. Faulk stresses Spanish successes (such as the initial exploration and mapping of the region and the Spanish imprint on its laws, place names, and architecture) as well as its failures (the Indians were not permanently converted to Christianity or made vassals to the Spanish King, Spanish soldiers never secured the land, and Spanish migrants could not settle all of the vast territory). Although the author seems to admire the local administrators who tried to do their jobs despite receiving little help from Madrid, he suggests that latter-day administrators were hardly the hardy adventurers of the age of conquest. The system of initiative and reward which fueled the conquest of America, was replaced by law, relative security, and purely administrative concerns, which smothered individual initiative and contributed to the fall of the empire.

120   **A successful failure.**
Odie B. Faulk.   Austin, Texas: Steck-Vaughn, 1965. 218p. maps.
bibliog. (Saga of Texas Series).

A brief and mostly descriptive narrative of the exploration and settlement of Texas from 1519-1810. Faulk describes the earliest exploration of Texas by Alvar Núñez Cabeza de Vaca in 1528, Francisco Vásquez de Coronado's search for the fabled Seven Cities of Cíbola in 1540, missionary efforts by the Franciscans beginning with Friar Augustin Rodríguez in 1581, and the founding of the first permanent mission in Texas in 1681 near present-day Juárez. The author also describes Spanish and French tension over rival claims on the Texas coast between the 1690s and 1730s, the beginnings of Spanish colonization, and conflicts between and among missionaries, military leaders, and Apache and Comanche Indians. Economic development consisted of farming and raising livestock near the *presidios* and missions. Faulk's last chapter discusses Anglo incursions and intrigues in Texas, which set the stage for the Texas Revolution in the 1830s.

121   **Moses Austin: his life.**
David B. Gracy II.   San Antonio, Texas: Trinity University Press, 1987. 303p. maps. bibliog.

A straightforward biography of New England-born Moses Austin (1761-1821), the father of Stephen F. Austin. A merchant and operator of several lead mines, Austin migrated from Connecticut to Virginia and on to Missouri; he received the original Spanish land grant for 200,000 acres in Texas and permission to settle three hundred families on it. Unfortunately, he died before he could implement the plan, and his son went on to establish the first Anglo settlement in Texas.

122   **The Alamo chain of missions: a history of San Antonio's five old missions.**
Marion H. Habig.   Chicago: Franciscan Herald Press, 1968. 304p. bibliog.

A general reference work that includes the history of the five missions in the 'Alamo chain' of Franciscan missions and sketches of ninety-three of the missionaries who worked in them. The two dozen additional illustrations include diagrams depicting the layouts of several of the missions; appendixes include statistical information, the names of the principal Indian tribes associated with the missions, and the names of the presidents of the missions.

123   **Storms brewed in other men's worlds: the confrontation of Indians, Spanish, and French in the southwest, 1540-1795.**
Elizabeth A. H. John.   College Station, Texas: Texas A & M University Press, 1975. 805p. maps. bibliog.

A chronological study of the interaction between the indigenous peoples of the Southwest (from Louisiana to New Mexico) with the invading Spanish and French, from first contact in the 1540s to the dissolution of Spanish power in the 1790s. Among the featured tribes are the Apache, Navajo, Comanche, Ute, Wichita, Tonkawa, Hopi, Pueblo, and Caddo groups. Well over half the book's twenty-one chapters are devoted at least in part to Native American groups living at least partly in Texas. John emphasizes the ways that tribal heritages and traditions influenced their struggles to cope with European encroachment.

124 **The Spanish missions of Texas.**
Walter F. McCaleb. San Antonio, Texas: Naylor Company, 1954.
121p. bibliog.
McCaleb takes a very pro-Franciscan point of view in chronicling the struggle of the
order to cross from New Mexico over into Texas to Christianize the natives there. He
describes both the successful and the failed missions and explains their intricate
relationships with Spanish civil and military authorities, especially the conflict between
religious fervour and mundane administrative concerns. Widely researched in Spanish
records and accompanied by about a dozen black-and-white photographs of the
mission structures as they appeared in the 1950s, the book is organized in a
chronological fashion.

125 **Borderland in retreat: from Spanish Louisiana to the far southwest.**
Abraham P. Nasatir. Albuquerque, New Mexico: University of New
Mexico Press, 1976. 175p. maps. bibliog.
A useful introduction to the larger colonial developments in which Texas was originally
settled. In describing the expansion and contraction of New Spain in North America,
this narrative pays close attention to the interaction of Spain with both Native
Americans and with the other European powers fighting to establish colonies in the
New World. Told from the Spanish point of view, the book highlights political forces
and military leaders.

126 **The revolutionary decades, 1810-1836.**
David M. Vigness. Austin, Texas: Steck-Vaughn, 1965. 215p. maps.
bibliog. (Saga of Texas Series).
A general history, based on secondary sources and without citations, of the settlement
of Anglo-Americans in Texas and their later rebellion against the government of
Mexico. Vigness tries to place the political and military events in Texas during this
period in the contexts of United States and Mexican history. He presents the heroes of
Texas in a favorable light; Stephen F. Austin, for instance, is portrayed as the ideal
man for the role of colonizer of Texas, willing to compromise when necessary in his
dealings with Indians and the Mexican government. Despite the Mexican belief that
Austin's colonists had betrayed the Mexican government, the author argues that most
Texans fulfilled their agreements with Mexico and resorted to arms only when
attacked.

127 **The Mexican frontier, 1821-1846: the American southwest under
Mexico.**
David J. Weber. Albuquerque, New Mexico: University of New
Mexico Press, 1982. 416p. maps. bibliog. (Histories of the American
Frontier).
A widely honoured and extremely useful synthesis of the history of the expansion of
the United States and retreat of Mexico in the Southwest. Weber links the separate
experiences of Texas, New Mexico, California, and Arizona, within the larger trends
and issues of internal politics, the economy, the society, the military, and the Church.
These colonies are viewed from south of the Rio Grande, especially in terms of the
effects the Mexican Revolution against Spanish rule had on the Southwest (it generally
forced the colonies to form closer economic ties with the United States). Weber
concludes that these far-flung provinces shared a common set of problems and

responses that culminated in their rejecting their colonial status within the Mexican Republic. Nearly 30 illustrations of major figures and places and 9 maps showing mission sites, Indian trails, land grants, and other geographic details amplify the text.

128 **San Juan Bautista: a gateway to Spanish Texas.**
Robert S. Weddle.   Austin, Texas: University of Texas Press, 1968.
469p. map. bibliog.

Located in present-day Guerrero, Coahuila, San Juan Bautista was the northern-most Spanish mission in the early 18th century and the starting point for the development of Texas missions until the 1770s. This exhaustive book examines the mission's role both as a facilitator for other settlements and as a mission and town in its own right, taking the story up to the early 19th century.

129 **The San Saba mission: Spanish pivot in Texas.**
Robert S. Weddle.   Austin, Texas: University of Texas Press, 1964.
238p. maps. bibliog.

An in-depth narrative of a central Texas mission to the Lipan Apaches in the 1730s. Although quite Eurocentric – Indians are frequently referred to as 'savages' or with other derogatory terms – it provides a useful look at the political, diplomatic, and religious motivations for establishing the mission; daily life at the mission; and tensions between the Spanish settlers and the Indians they intended to convert, including the 1758 massacre of many of the priests and the subsequent abandonment of the military outpost established with the mission.

Texas Revolution and Republic, 1836-1845

130 **British interests and activities in Texas, 1838-1846.**
Ephraim Douglass Adams.   Baltimore, Maryland: The Johns Hopkins University Press, 1910; Gloucester, Massachusetts: P. Smith, 1963.
264p. (Albert Shaw Lectures on Diplomatic History).

American and Texan contemporaries believed that Great Britain had a very deep interest in the future of the Texas Republic, including preventing its annexation by the United States and encouraging the abolition of slavery in Texas. Adams argues that ending slavery was very much a secondary interest for the British, whose primary goal was to use their friendship with Texas to provide a check on United States expansion; of course, neither of these scenarios were realised. This is a very old but still reliable look at this nearly forgotten element of the diplomatic history of the Texas Republic.

131 **The expansionist movement in Texas, 1836-1850.**
William C. Binkley.   Berkeley, California: University of California
Press, 1925; New York: Da Capo Press, 1970. 253p. maps. bibliog.
(The American Scene).

The Texas Republic was well-known for its expansionist policies, and border controversies frequently arose between Texas and the Republic of Mexico, and the American Territory of New Mexico. Binkley's still-respected book provides the diplomatic and (to a lesser extent) political contexts for this territorial aggressiveness on the part of the Texans. Texas expansionism is also seen in the light of earlier Spanish and Mexican policies and in the larger 19th century westward movement of the United States.

132 **The Texas revolution.**
William C. Binkley.   Baton Rouge, Louisiana: Louisiana State
University Press, 1952. 132p. (Walter Lynwood Fleming Lectures in
Southern History).

A vast amount of learning and study is condensed into these four brief, interpretative essays originally delivered as part of the Fleming Lectures in 1950. The essays examine the transition of Texas from a sparsely settled frontier province of Mexico to an independent country and seeks to explain the economic and institutional factors for the Revolution and the birth pains with which Texans had to deal. The separate pieces – on conditions in Texas just before the outbreak of revolution, the events leading up to the beginning of the conflict, the internal struggle over a constitution, and the onset of relative stability after the revolution – together present a number of insights regarding the origins of Texas. The transition from a subsistence to a commercial agricultural economy and the desire on the part of Anglo settlers for institutions like schools and self-government conflicted with the Mexicans' rather static notions about the colonial future of Texas. Texas's problems differed markedly from those of other Mexican provinces and caused Texans to seek relief from a central Mexican government that had to weigh Texan grievances against the greater good. Binkley also shows that the Revolution was a continuation of the old Mexican struggle against European interests and methods.

133 **The Texan Santa Fe trail.**
H. Bailey Carroll.   Canyon, Texas: Panhandle-Plains Historical
Society, 1951. 201p. maps. bibliog.

In 1841, the Republic of Texas sent an expedition of about 320 soldiers and civilians to establish a secure trade route from Austin to Santa Fe, which was at that time still a part of northern Mexico. Led by Hugh McLeod, the effort failed and its members ended up in Mexican prisons. Carroll spent a generation painstakingly establishing the expedition's exact route and day-by-day experiences. The text includes a brief journal kept by a member of the expedition.

134 **David G. Burnet.**
Mary Whatley Clarke.   Austin, Texas: Pemberton Press, 1969. 303p.
map. bibliog. (Presidents and Governors of Texas).

A laudatory narrative that emphasizes Burnet's experiences during and contributions to the Texas Revolution. Burnet (1788-1870) was a New Jersey native who came to Texas for his health in 1817 and served as president of the Republic during the dark days of

36

the Revolution and briefly in the early 1840s. He was best-known for his bitter opposition to Sam Houston, which originated with Burnet's attacks on Houston's handling of the Texas Army during the Revolution.

135 Thomas J. Rusk: soldier, statesman, jurist.
Mary Whatley Clarke. Austin, Texas: Jenkins, 1971. 274p.

Rusk (1803-57) came to Texas on the trail of men who had stolen a horse from him in South Carolina; he stayed and soon became a revolutionary. He signed the Texas Declaration of Independence and served as inspector general and secretary of war in the early days of the Republic. He went on to fight Indians, serve as senator and Chief Justice, and to promote Texas's annexation by the United States. He was one of Texas's first two United States senators. Clarke provides a serviceable, although non-critical, biography of one of Texas's early heroes.

136 Adventure in glory, 1836-1849.
Seymour V. Connor. Austin, Texas: Steck-Vaughan Co., 1965. 270p. maps. bibliog. (Saga of Texas Series).

A year by year chronicle of Texas during the exciting period of Revolution and independence. Connor emphasizes the creation of governmental institutions, threats from Indians and Mexicans, diplomacy, immigration and colonization, annexation by the United States, the Mexican War, and Texas's part in the debate over the Compromise of 1850. This is primarily a very useful political history; social and economic issues are not prominently featured.

137 Sam Houston: colossus in buckskin.
George Creel. New York: Cosmopolitan Book Corporation, 1928. 340p.

A biography of Houston (1793-1863) that is notable because it is frequently cited and because its author led the United States' propaganda campaign during the First World War. This defensive and heroic chronology of the life of Texas's most famous citizen has no references and no bibliography.

138 Jose Antonio Navarro: co-creator of Texas.
Joseph M. Dawson. Waco, Texas: Baylor University Press, 1969. 127p.

The San Antonio-born son of Corsican-Spanish immigrants, Navarro (1795-1871) was a rancher, merchant, revolutionary, and politician. This biography deals in a straightforward way with Navarro's life and contributions and stresses his importance in early Texas history. This is a deeply felt if not deeply researched or sophisticatedly written book; it is one of the few full-length biographies of a prominent *Tejano*.

139 Sam Houston: the great designer.
Llerena Friend. Austin, Texas: University of Texas Press, 1954. 394p. bibliog.

Perhaps the most famous and most scholarly of the biographies of Sam Houston, it was originally written as a dissertation at the University of Texas at Austin. Firmly rooting her story in Texas and national politics, Friend avoids previous historians' obsession with Houston's larger-than-life qualities and looks at him as a practical politician and statesman who served as president of the Republic of Texas and as governor and senator of the state of Texas. Friend focuses not only on Houston's activities in Texas, but also on his role in the national Democratic Party after 1846, his opposition to southern sectionalism and secession, and his frequent (if brief) presidential campaigns. This is an admiring, but very professional study.

140 **Anson Jones: the last president of Texas.**
Herbert Gambrell.   Austin, Texas: University of Texas Press, 1964.
2nd edition. 530p. map. bibliog.

This well-received 1948 book, re-issued with an extensive, expanded bibliography, is a lively account of the life and times of the last chief executive of the Republic of Texas. Jones (1798-1858), a failed physician, drifted into Texas in 1833 and soon became involved in the events that resulted in Texas' independence. Gambrell thoroughly recounts the colonization of Texas by Anglo-Americans, the development of the Texas Revolution, the climactic San Jacinto campaign, and especially the diplomatic and political history of the Texas Republic. Jones leaped to prominence as a soldier and politician, including stints as Minister to the United States, secretary of state, and president. The author attempts to demonstrate that Jones's influence in developing foreign policy and in seeking annexation was at least equal to that of the much better-known Sam Houston.

141 **Mirabeau Bonaparte Lamar: troubador and crusader.**
Herbert Gambrell.   Dallas, Texas: Southwest Press, 1934. 317p. map.
bibliog.

A journalist and politican in his native Georgia, Lamar (1798-1859) arrived in Texas in 1835 and almost immediately became embroiled in revolutionary activity. He rose from the rank of private to major general in the Texas army and served as vice president in 1836. His term as president from 1838-41 was noted for its aggressive expansionism, anti-Indian policy, and spiraling budget. Gambrell tries to improve Lamar's generally poor political reputation, at least in comparison to his frequent opponent, Sam Houston. Based on primary and secondary sources but without citations, this sixty year-old book is still the standard biography on Lamar.

142 **Sam Houston with the Cherokees, 1829-1833.**
Jack Gregory, Reunard Strickland.   Austin, Texas: University of
Texas Press, 1967. 206p. maps. bibliog.

A chronicle of the most mysterious period of Houston's life: his three-year stay with Cherokee Indians after his resignation as governor of Tennessee and prior to his arrival in Texas. The authors rather successfully attempt to establish his activities and his true relationship with his hosts during this time and argue that this was no wilderness idyl, but a formative period in Houston's career and character. His activities on behalf of Cherokee interests would later shape his Indian policies; his friendship with this group of Indians helped secure the northern border of Texas during his presidency of the Texas Republic.

143 Samuel May Williams, early Texas entrepreneur.
Margaret Swett Henson.   College Station, Texas: Texas A & M
University Press, 1976. 190p. maps. bibliog.

A scholarly biography of Williams (1795-1858), a merchant and financier who also served as one of Stephen Austin's top assistants after reaching Texas in 1822. Henson stresses Williams' financial and arms-procurement contributions to the Texas war effort and the fledgling economy of the Republic of Texas. Although he damaged his reputation with unwise land speculations, he is notable as one of the region's first settlers and as the founder of Texas's first independent bank.

144 The Texas Republic: a social and economic history.
William R. Hogan.   Norman, Oklahoma: University of Oklahoma
Press, 1946. 338p. maps. bibliog.

A matter-of-fact, thoroughly researched account of what the author calls the 'everyday existence of a frontier democracy'. Individual chapters are devoted to immigration, housing and food, travel and roads, economic problems, leisure activities, education, Texas-style tall tales and literature, religion, health, the legal system, and the individualistic nature of early Texans. Despite the fact that it all but ignores Native Americans, Hispanics, and even immigrant Germans, this is a quite useful, if unsophisticated, social history of the Texas Republic.

145 Rebellious ranger: Rip Ford and the old southwest.
W. J. Hughes.   Norman, Oklahoma: University of Oklahoma Press,
1964. 300p. map. bibliog.

A nearly worshipful biography of John 'Rest In Peace' Ford (1815-97), one of a handful of 19th-century Texan heroes who played no role in the Texas Revolution but was nonetheless active throughout this period. Ford was a physician, journalist, surveyor, and fairly minor politican, but his most famous contributions came as a Texas Ranger in countless operations against Indians, Mexicans, and, during the Civil War, Yankees. Not surprisingly, Hughes highlights Ford's career as a Ranger.

146 Deaf Smith, incredible Texas spy.
Cleburne Huston.   Waco, Texas: Texian Press, 1973. 141p. bibliog.

A pedestrian narrative of the life of Erastus 'Deaf' Smith (1787-1837) who was, as the dramatic title suggests, a legendary scout, spy, and leader during the Texas Revolution. Smith arrived in Texas in the early 1820s. Although the book emphasizes his escapades during the Texans' fight for independence, it also includes descriptions of Smith's frontier business ventures, none of which were particularly successful.

147 The raven: a biography of Sam Houston.
Marquis James.   Indianapolis, Indiana: The Bobbs-Merrill Co., 1929.
489p. maps. bibliog.

The best-known biography of Houston, this is a very entertaining and durable narrative. James worked closely with Houston's grandchildren and relies heavily on family traditions and anecdotes. Very admiring and straight-forward, its usefulness has declined in the more than sixty years since its publication, as more complex views of Houston and of Texas have appeared.

148　**The Texas revolutionary experience: a political and social history, 1835-1836.**

Paul D. Lack.　College Station, Texas: Texas A & M University Press, 1992. 376p. maps. bibliog.

A useful corrective to older versions of the revolutionary period in Texas history. This newest scholarly look at the Texas Revolution studies revolutionary era politics and society. Lack's most unique contribution is his contention that Texans were not united in fighting their revolution. The majority refused to serve in the Texas military, and racial tension – between Anglos and Mexican-Texans, and because of whites' fears of the potential for a slave uprising – also plagued Texans.

149　**Duel of eagles: the Mexican and United States fight for the Alamo.**

Jeffery Long.　New York: Morrow, 1990. 431p. maps. bibliog.

A detailed narrative of the battle for the Alamo and the events that preceded and succeded it. The rather odd sub-title, which seems to ignore the fact that the United States was not officially involved in the Texas Revolution, indicates the major conceptual problem with the book. Texas heroes are provided with vivid – if rather stereotypical – characterizations.

150　**The Texas-Santa Fe pioneers.**

Noel M. Loomis.　Norman, Oklahoma: University of Oklahoma Press, 1958. 329p. maps. bibliog.

A scholarly examination of the 1841 journey by Anglo-Texans into New Mexico, which ended in their capture and imprisonment by the Mexican army. Loomis places the expedition in the context of Texas President Mirabeau Lamar's aggressive foreign policy and his desire to bolster the Texas economy by opening trade routes and extending Anglo influence into Mexico's territory. The author concludes that while the expedition was not strictly a military operation, it was hostile (toward Mexico) in intent. Ten maps show the Texans' routes into Mexico, while a number of appendixes provide rosters and information about Mexican commanders, prisons, and other details.

151　**A time to stand.**

Walter Lord.　New York: Bonanza Books, 1961. 255p.

A popular history of the Alamo that emphasizes the lives and fates of both the Texans trapped inside the crumbling mission and the Mexicans besieging them. Exciting battle descriptions and moving excerpts from letters and diaries complement one another.

152　**De Witt colony of Texas.**

Edward A. Lukes.　Austin, Texas: Jenkins Publishing, Pemberton Press, 1976. 269p. maps. bibliog.

A useful look at Spanish and Mexican emigration policies and at Anglo-American settlers in Texas. Most of the book deals with the colony founded by Green De Witt in 1825 near Gonzales, including the social and economic patterns that emerged as the colony's population increased, the transition from a subsistence to a market economy, urban growth, Indian relations, and problems with the Mexican government. Operations by the Mexican Army during the War for Independence virtually destroyed the colony. Included are eleven maps showing the boundaries and population distribution of the colony from 1825-31.

153   **Turn your eyes toward Texas: pioneers Sam and Mary Maverick.**
Paula Mitchell Marks.   College Station, Texas: Texas A & M
University Press, 1989. 323p. maps. bibliog.

A scholarly yet readable dual biography of Samuel (1802-70) and Mary (1818-98) Maverick, the first generation of one of most prominent families in Texas. Marks emphasizes the public life of Sam – he participated in virtually every important event in Texas between 1835 and the Civil War – and the private life of Mary, who was frequently left at home alone in San Antonio to manage the Maverick household and family. This is a useful look at Sam's involvement with politics, but an even more useful analysis of marriage, family life, slavery, and Indian-white and Anglo-Hispanic relations in frontier Texas.

154   **Slavery and the annexation of Texas.**
Frederick Merk.   New York: Knopf, 1972. 290p.

As the title of his book indicates, Merk considers the political controversies surrounding the 1845 annexation of Texas by the United States in light of the growing controversy over the expansion of the institution of slavery. Texas's joining the Union was one of the occasional crises that demonstrated the fragility of the ties that bound North and South together. The most entertaining and useful element of the volume is its analysis of the pro- and anti-annexation propaganda that flowed from both sides of the slavery issue; many Congressional speeches, newspaper editorials, and personal letters are reprinted in the book's second half.

155   **After San Jacinto: the Texas-Mexican frontier, 1836-1841.**
Joseph Nance.   Austin, Texas: University of Texas Press, 1963. 642p.
maps. bibliog.

For more than a decade after the Battle of San Jacinto, the Republic of Texas and Mexico fought a kind of cold war: the issues included the debate over the exact border between Mexico and its former colony, the role of Texans in various Federalist schemes against the Mexican government, and Texans' attempts to secure their country's frontiers. Nance focuses on Texas-Mexican relations along the thinly populated southern and southwestern frontier between the two countries and with the role the Indians played in the contest between the two competing cultures. He also discusses trade relations and the extension of settlement during those fleeting times of peace between Mexico and Texas and delves into the alliances, battles, and expeditions that occurred in less peaceful times. This is the best book available on the issues that eventually contributed to the outbreak of war between Mexico and the United States in 1846.

156   **Rise of the lone star: the making of Texas.**
Andreas Reichstein, translation by Jeanne F. Wilson.   College
Station, Texas: Texas A & M University Press, 1989. 303p. map.
bibliog.

The English translation of this 1984 book by a German historian is at times rather clumsy, but Texas historians have generally received this award-winning revisionist interpretation of the Texas Revolution with enthusiasm. Reichstein rejects the

Barkeresque 'clash of cultures' interpretation of the revolution and its implicit racism. He chooses instead to place the conflict in the context of United States and Mexican expansionism and land speculation, the spirit and policy of Manifest Destiny, and the acquisitiveness of the groups attempting to settle this frontier between nations. In fact, he refuses to call the conflict a revolution at all; it was not an attempt by the 'Revolutionaries' to alter Mexico or to create social change, but to position themselves for annexation to the United States. This is not a romantic presentation of old legends, but a tough, thoroughly researched, and fresh look at a favourite topic of Texans.

157 **Sam Houston's wife: a biography of Margaret Lea Houston.**
William Seale. Norman, Oklahoma: University of Oklahoma Press, 1970. 287p. bibliog.

Taking advantage of manuscripts previously unused by historians – and used here with permission of the Houston family – this biography not only provides a narrative of the life of Margaret Lea Houston (1819-67), but also attempts to determine her effect on her famous husband's career. The author barely mentions Margaret's life before her marriage to Houston; his rather heroic emphasis is on the moral support she provided throughout Houston's stormy career and the inner strength that helped Margaret endure frontier conditions and long separations from her husband.

158 **A political history of the Texas Republic, 1836-1845.**
Stanley Siegel. Austin, Texas: University of Texas Press, 1956. 281p. map. bibliog.

A traditional and scholarly political history of the Republic of Texas. Among the topics considered are the colonization of Texas; Stephen Austin's role in the Texas Revolution; Sam Houston's tenure as president; Mirabeau Lamar's conflict-ridden term in office and his failure to resolve his country's dispute with Mexico; and the debates in the United States Senate over Texas that were finally ended with annexation in 1845. This is a good, no-nonsense source on the political careers of Houston and Lamar, as well as Texas luminaries like James Pickney Henderson, James Hamilton, and William Wharton.

159 **Ashbel Smith of Texas: pioneer, patriot, statesman, 1805-1886.**
Elizabeth Silverthorne. College Station, Texas: Texas A & M University Press, 1982. 259p. bibliog. (The Centennial Series of the Association of Former Students, Texas A & M University).

An uncritical but scholarly biography of this multi-talented doctor, agricultural reformer, diplomat, and politician. Smith (1805-86) was the Texas Republic's Minister to France and England and Secretary of State, won three terms to the Texas state legislature, helped found the state's Democratic Party, fought in the Mexican and Civil Wars, served as a regent of the University of Texas, and founded Prairie View Normal School and the University of Texas Medical School. This straight-forward biography emphasizes politics, but does not ignore Smith's medical career – he produced a long list of publications on yellow fever and cholera – or his contributions to education.

160   **The annexation of Texas.**
Justin Harvey Smith.   New York: Brooklyn Public Library, 1911; New
York: AMS Press, 1971. 496p. bibliog.

A still serviceable survey of the issues surrounding the annexation of Texas by the
United States. After discussing the settlement of Texas by Americans in the 1820s and
the eventual separation of the colony from Mexico, Smith examines the new Republic's
diplomatic relations with European powers and the United States and the impact of
public opinion on the formation of those countries' foreign policies. It also looks at
British attitudes towards slavery, political conditions in northern Mexico, the
possibilities that Texans saw in remaining independent, and the debate over
annexation in the United States (including the initial failure of an annexation treaty
and the role of annexation in presidential politics, especially in 1844).

161   **Six who came to El Paso: pioneers of the 1840's.**
Rex W. Strickland.   El Paso, Texas: Texas Western College Press,
1963. 48p. bibliog.

A brief but well-researched look at the early settlement of El Paso, which is basically a
collective biography of six of El Paso's first settlers: Ben F. Coons, Parker H. French,
J. W. Magoffin, Hugh Stephenson, Simeon Hart, and Frank White. The emphasis is
on their pioneer experiences rather than the development of the El Paso area.

162   **William Barrett Travis: his sword and his pen.**
Martha Anne Turner.   Waco, Texas: Texian Press, 1972. 318p.

A utilitarian narrative of Travis's role in the Texas Revolution (as a propagandist and
leader) and especially of his command of the 'last stand' at the Alamo. Turner includes
very little about Travis's life previous to his arrival in Texas, and obviously greatly
admires this hero of the Revolution. Although she is concerned with the facts, she is
unwilling to avoid the legend of Travis's life. She also allows her sources to lead her to
express rather racist attitudes in her treatment of Mexicans. The highlight is the
profusion of illustrations of key people, places, and artifacts of the Revolution.

163   **Dream of empire: a human history of the Republic of Texas, 1836-1846.**
John Edward Weems.   New York: Simon & Schuster, 1971. 377p.
maps. bibliog.

A popular history with a rather unique format of the Republic era in Texas based on
secondary sources and on the memoirs, journals, and letters of a dozen diverse people.
Weems's informants include two women, a preacher, two physicians, a Texas Ranger,
a soldier, a businessman, and a would-be politician. The standard events of the period
– the Revolution itself, continued conflict with Mexico, Indian troubles, annexation –
are recounted through the differing perspectives of these ordinary people.

164   **James Pickney Henderson: Texas' first governor.**
Robert Glenn Winchester.   San Antonio, Texas: Naylor, 1971. 116p.
bibliog.

Another biography of a hero of the Texas Revolution. This is a brief account of
Henderson's life based entirely on secondary sources. Henderson (1808-58), a native of
North Carolina, came to Texas in 1836 with a contingent of volunteers to fight in the
Texas Revolution. He quickly rose to the rank of brigadier general, and served as a
diplomat, secretary of state, and attorney general during the Republic period. In 1846

he was chosen as Texas's first governor, an office he left in order to serve as a major general in the Mexican War. His last service to his adopted home came in 1857, when he was elected to the United States Senate. This is a short, straight-forward, and uncriticial biography.

165 **Sam Houston: American giant.**
M. K. Wisehart. Washington, DC: Robert B. Luce, 1962. 712p. bibliog.

A detailed, but less than objective biography of Houston based on extensive research in secondary sources and on published primary sources (including eight volumes of Houston papers which had just been published as the book was being researched). Wisehart concentrates on Houston's character and follows him through the prominent phases of his life: his journey to Texas; his role in the Revolution (especially as commander in chief of the Texas army, his decision to sacrifice the Alamo, and his long retreat in the weeks leading up to San Jacinto); as president, United States Senator, and governor; and as an opponent of secession before the Civil War. The theme of the book is Houston's taming of his natural impetuosity and rebelliousness; he appears as a calculating, careful, and resolute fighter and as a prescient intellect.

Civil War and Reconstruction, 1845-1877

166 **Secession and the union in Texas.**
Walter L. Buenger. Austin, Texas: University of Texas Press, 1984. 255p. maps. bibliog.

A well-written and persuasive analysis of the attitudes of Texans about the Union and about secession in the two years leading up to the Civil War. Using qualitative as well as quantitative evidence, Buenger examines the growing importance of the plantation economy and of the pressure to conform to southern extremists' demands; that pressure proved too strong, and most members of the fragmented Unionist 'Opposition' succumbed to secession. Buenger's greatest innovation is his emphasis on the cultural and geographic origins of Unionists and secessionists.

167 **A southern community in crisis: Harrison County, Texas, 1850-1880.**
Randolph B. Campbell. Austin, Texas: Texas State Historical Association, 1984. 443p. map. bibliog.

A unique and valuable account of Harrison County, Texas (on the Louisiana border in far northeastern Texas) from the antebellum period through Reconstruction. Campbell bases his account on manuscript sources and on close readings of manuscript censuses and tax rolls between 1850-80. Harrison County was one of the most populous counties in antebellum Texas and the most 'southern'; it was heavily involved in the cotton plantation economy and the slave system. The author seeks to determine the effects of economic growth, war, and Reconstruction on wealth-holding, political power, and social relationships within the county. He finds that, despite the ravages of war and the humiliation of Reconstruction, the groups who owned the wealth, controlled the politics, and dominated society in the county remained on top at the end of the era.

168   **Wealth and power in antebellum Texas.**
       Randolph B. Campbell, Richard G. Lowe.   College Station, Texas:
       Texas A & M University Press, 1977. 183p. map. bibliog.

A heavily quantitative analysis of personal, real, and slave property holding in Texas on the eve of the Civil War. The authors divide the state into four regions (based on climate, economy, soil, and population) and discover that wealthholding of all kinds was extremely centralized throughout the state. Extensive reading in the secondary literature allows Campbell and Lowe to place Texas in a national context. *Wealth and Power in Antebellum Texas* is especially useful as a source of economic information; its fifty tables include a wide variety of statistical approaches to wealth distribution, slave ownership, and agricultural property, among other things.

169   **The Matamoros trade: Confederate commerce, diplomacy, and intrigue.**
       James W. Daddysman.   Newark, Delaware: University of Delaware
       Press, 1984. 215p. maps. bibliog.

Texas and Mexico shared the only border between a neutral country and the Confederacy. With the growing effectiveness of the Federal blockade, Confederate cotton was traded for guns and supplies in Matamoros, which grew from a sleepy border town across the Rio Grande from Brownsville into a major port. This is a very useful narrative that presents the evolution of this trade system in chronological fashion. Especially instructive is Daddysman's analysis of the corruption that flourished in Matamoros even to the extent that northern merchants became involved in trading with Confederate agents.

170   **Kirby Smith's Confederacy: the trans-Mississippi south, 1863-1865.**
       Robert L. Kerby.   New York: Columbia University Press, 1972. 529p.
       maps. bibliog.

A detailed account of events during the last two years of the war in the region west of the Mississippi River which was something of a backwater theatre for both sides after the Union won control of the Mississippi in the summer of 1863. The Trans-Mississippi (Texas, Arkansas, Louisiana, and Missouri) was, for Confederate commander Gen. E. Kirby Smith, a vast region that he had to defend with too few troops and resources. Kerby concentrates on the military, economic (especially the illicit cotton trade), and political (at the state and the Confederate levels) aspects of the war in the far western Confederacy. Although he is often critical of Confederate decisions, this is basically a thoroughly researched narrative of events in this often over-looked area. This is by far the best and certainly the most substantial history of the Trans-Mississippi Confederacy.

171   **Texas divided: loyalty & dissent in the lone star state, 1856-1874.**
       James Marten.   Lexington, Kentucky: University Press of Kentucky,
       1990. 180p. map. bibliog.

The author investigates the growth of dissent against southern and Texan values and institutions during the antebellum period, the rise of Unionism and disaffection during the war itself, and the continuing importance of the issue of loyalty during the Reconstruction years. He also examines the ways that Texans attempted to eliminate dissent before, during, and after the war. An important factor in dissent and vigilance against dissent was the presence in Texas of large numbers of blacks, German immigrants, and Mexican-Americans.

172 **Reconstruction in Texas.**
Charles William Ramsdell.   New York: Columbia University Press, 1910; Austin, Texas: University of Texas Press, 1970. 318p. bibliog.

The classic study of Texas during the years following the Civil War. The book reflects Ramsdell's tutelage under William A. Dunning, the scholar who helped establish the interpretation of Reconstruction as a time of corruption and misrule under Radical Republican 'carpetbaggers' from the North and 'scalawags' and blacks in the south. Although dated in its interpretation, *Reconstruction in Texas* still remains a good source for factual information. Some of this traditional view of Reconstruction appears as late as 1962 in W. C. Nunn, *Texas Under the Carpetbaggers* (Austin, Texas: University of Texas Press, 1962).

173 **White terror: the Ku Klux Klan conspiracy and southern reconstruction.**
Allan W. Trelease.   New York: Harper and Row, 1971. 557p. bibliog.

A detailed account of the rise and decline of the first K K K from 1868 to the early 1870s. Trelease describes the Klan as a 'conspiracy' to subvert normal legal processes and as a political tool designed to defeat Radical Reconstruction. Although the book has been criticized for exaggerating the extent of the conspiracy and of the Klan's organization, it is nevertheless useful for the wealth of information it presents and for its strong point of view. Despite the fact that Texas actually had less formal Klan activity within its borders than southern states farther east, the author covers the state's own racist hate groups like the Knights of the Rising Sun and features the violent 1868 election in Texas.

174 **Texas in turmoil, 1849-1875.**
Ernest Wallace.   Austin, Texas: Steck-Vaughn, 1965. 293p. maps. bibliog. (Saga of Texas Series).

A dramatic account of Texas from the end of the Mexican War to the end of Reconstruction. Wallace emphasizes political and military events and personalities related to the sectional conflict and to the frontier experience, and tends to sympathize with conservative Texans (due to their tradition of leadership, their 'gallantry', and their determination) over 'Radicals' like A. J. Hamilton and Carl Degener. Aside from its rather old-fashioned attitudes about issues such as black suffrage, this is a generally reliable account and is the only survey of this period in Texas history.

175 **Colossal Hamilton of Texas: a biography of Andrew Jackson Hamilton, militant unionist and reconstruction governor.**
John L. Waller.   El Paso, Texas: Texas Western Press, 1968. 152p.

A biography of the ardent Unionist Andrew Jackson 'Colossal Jack' Hamilton (1815-75). Hamilton, a native of Alabama, was a pre-war attorney general and congressman who helped lead those Texans who opposed the state's secession from the Union in 1861. Driven from the state during the war, he became a brigadier general in the Union Army and served in the largely symbolic post of military governor of Texas. After the war, he served as provisional governor for a year and led the conservative wing of the fledgling Republican Party. Although not particularly objective, this is a reliable account of the career of one of Texas's leading Civil War-era dissenters.

The Gilded Age, 1877-1900

176 The cattle kings.

Lewis E. Atherton. Bloomington, Indiana: Indiana University Press, 1961. 308p. bibliog.

Although Atherton self-consciously attempts to overcome the antiquarian and popular historical images of the West and of cowboys, this is actually a very admiring portrait with a multitude of illustrations of the role of ranchers in the economy, society, and politics of the West. According to the author, these men contributed to the development of the West and of the United States in a number of ways: they created an often ambivalent, romantic image of the western past; they helped the 'rugged individualism' exemplified in their own lives to become more ingrained in American culture; they promoted stability through their business practices and concern for law and order; they often led their region in the implementation of scientific agriculture. This is an intriguing, although one-sided look at the aspirations, accomplishments, and heritage of the men who dominated the Gilded Age West. No single chapter deals solely with Texan ranchers, but references to Texans and to Texas are sprinkled throughout the text.

177 Farmers in rebellion: the rise and fall of the Southern Farmers Alliance and People's Party in Texas.

Donna A. Barnes. Austin, Texas: University of Texas Press, 1984. 226p. bibliog.

The Southern Farmers Alliance – a late 19th century agrarian movement that grew to three million members by 1891 – originated in Texas and drew much of its leadership and strategies from Texas. Barnes' analysis utilizes and evaluates structural strain and mobilization theories of protest movements in the light of Southern Alliance techniques and experiences. The farmers of the South and West were protesting, among other things, the exploitative crop lien system that with low cotton prices in the late-19th century had reduced southern farmers, blacks and whites alike, to near peonage conditions. The alliance tried to improve the lot of farmers by promoting cooperative marketing and purchasing. During the 1890s, the Alliance's political arm, the People's Party, began to dominate the movement; electoral failure killed the Alliance by 1900. Barnes has provided a useful analysis of agrarian protest in its sociological context.

178 Reconstruction to reform: Texas politics, 1876-1906.

Alwyn Barr. Austin, Texas: University of Texas Press, 1971. 315p. maps. bibliog.

A scholarly account of Gilded Age politics in Texas, when the Democratic Party struggled to develop and maintain its dominance of the Texas political system. Barr has organized his analysis in a basically chronological fashion, with chapters devoted to movements and issues like Greenbackers (those who favoured an inflationary paper currency), land policy, prohibition, agrarian discontent, labour, railroad regulation, the silver issue, Populism, and Progressivism. The author pays closest attention, of course, to the Democratic Party and all of its factions and challengers, but also covers the Republican Party, which was increasingly controlled by whites primarily concerned with patronage from the federal government. Barr maintains that Gilded Age politics in Texas revolved around the developing state and national economies (he stresses lumber, agriculture, oil, and stock-raising interests); religious identity and ethnic groups (Germans, Mexicans, African-Americans); and personalities. He sees the Democrats as a coalition of a number of interests controlled by the Anglo, evangelical majority. This is an excellent work by one of the deans of Texas historians.

179 Sul Ross: soldier, statesman, educator.

Judith Ann Benner.   College Station, Texas: Texas A & M University Press, 1983. 259p. bibliog.

A straight-forward narrative of the life of Lawrence Sullivan Ross (1838-98), an Indian fighter and Texas Ranger, Confederate brigadier general and post-Civil War sheriff, state senator and governor (1887-91), president of Texas A & M University and namesake of Sul Ross State University. Benner provides a useful chronicle of these phases of Ross's life, but also stresses the complexities and changes in his character; he was fearless of physical danger but sensitive to criticism; hot-headed in his youth but a model of self-control in maturity; adored by Texans but personally modest; roughly educated but a major contributor to the state's educational system. This is a scholarly biography of a prominent member of the second generation of Texan heroes.

180 The great buffalo hunt.

Wayne Gard.   New York: Alfred A. Knopf, 1959; Lincoln, Nebraska: University of Nebraska Press, 1972. 324p. bibliog.

A journalistic look at the buffalo hide industry of the 1870s and 1880s in Texas and other parts of the Great Plains. Gard describes the hunting process, the Indians' bloody reaction, and the legends sparked by the activities of a very few men during a very short period of time. The emphasis is on colour; the author includes only very brief accounts of the importance of buffalo to scores of Indian tribes and of the long-term effects of the virtual extinction of the animals. The tone of the book is best summarized by a passage in which Gard refers to the buffalo hunters as 'mighty men' outwitting the 'redskins who wanted their scalps'. Another popularly written account of buffalo hunting on the plains and its ramifications is Mari Sandoz' *The buffalo hunters: the story of the hidemen* (New York: Hastings House, 1954; Lincoln, Nebraska: University of Nebraska Press, 1978).

181 Democratic promise: the Populist movement in America.

Lawrence C. Goodwyn.   New York: Oxford University Press, 1976. 718p. maps.

This is probably the best, and one of the most controversial analyses of the Populist Movement in the 1880s and 1890s. In addition to providing an exhaustive narrative of the history of the Farmers' Alliance and of the People's Party, Goodwyn explores the economic programmes sought by the Populists, the party's relationship with black farmers, the social origins and benefits of the agrarian movement, methods of spreading the agrarian gospel, regional differences within the movement, and especially the movement's ideological background and evolution. This is an excellent work; Texas is featured as one of the movement's centres.

182   **Populist vanguard: a history of the Southern Farmers' Alliance.**
Robert C. McMath, Jr.   Chapel Hill, North Carolina: University of
North Carolina Press, 1975. 221p. map. bibliog.

McMath's book is a scholarly chronicle of the National Farmers' Alliance and
Industrial Union, or the 'Southern Farmers' Alliance', as it was commonly known.
This was the largest of the three main farmers' alliances in the United States in the
1880s and 1890s. The Southern Alliance was started in 1877 in Lampasas County,
Texas, as a small farm club called the Knights of Reliance; at its height in the 1880s it
had 1.5 million members in thirty-two states. This straightforward narrative focuses on
the organization and expansion of the Alliance, its community based interests, and its
ill-fated shift to politics via the People's Party. Two useful appendixes profile Alliance
leaders and provide membership statistics in seventeen states from 1875 to 1892.

183   **Not without honor: the life of John H. Reagan.**
Ben H. Proctor.   Austin, Texas: University of Texas Press, 1962.
361p. bibliog.

A deeply researched biography of one of Texas's best-known 19th-century politicians.
Reagan (1818-1905) came to Texas from Tennessee in 1839 and served as a state
legislator, district judge, and Congressman. In 1861 he became Confederate
Postmaster-General, a post he filled throughout the Civil War. During Reconstruction
he was a rather moderate Conservative; he returned to Congress in 1875 and served in
the United States Senate from 1887-91. Although he was an advocate of limited
government, he favoured the creation of the Interstate Commerce Commission and
served on the Texas Railroad Commission from 1891-1903. This is a very useful look at
one of Texas's least flamboyant but most respected public men.

184   **The southwestern frontier, 1865-1881.**
Carl C. Rister.   New York: Russell & Russell, 1928. 336p. maps.
bibliog.

A dated, but still useful analysis of the 'opening' of the Southwest after the Civil War,
with West Texas as one of the primary foci. Rister emphasizes the gradual
'disappearance' of the frontier due to economic development, with separate sections on
the destruction of the great buffalo herds, the cattle industry, and the railroads.
Perhaps two-thirds of the book deals with Indian policy (which the author often
criticizes as short-sighted from a military point of view) and army operations against
Comanches and Apaches. The author's tone is very pro-development; approving of the
elimination of obstacles to white civilization.

185   **Temple Houston: lawyer with a gun.**
Glenn Shirley.   Norman, Oklahoma: University of Oklahoma Press,
1980. 339p. bibliog.

A pleasant, often dramatic, and extremely admiring biography of Sam Houston's
youngest son. Temple Houston (1860-1905) became a renowned orator and attorney
on the Texas Panhandle and Oklahoma frontiers and served the Lone Star State as a
district attorney and state senator. This profusely illustrated volume focuses on
Houston's eccentric dress, his gun-slinging, and his political and legal careers within
the contexts of frontier life and justice.

186 **George W. Brackenridge: maverick philanthropist.**
Marilyn McAdams Sibley.   Austin, Texas: University of Texas Press, 1973. 280p. bibliog.

A straightforward, thorough, sympathetic, but balanced account of the life of an extraordinary Texan. Brackenridge (1832-1920) migrated to Texas from the midwest in the 1850s as a member of an entire family who made their mark in Texas business and philanthropy. As a Unionist, Brackenridge fled the state during the Civil War; he returned afterwards to found the First National Bank in San Antonio and to work tirelessly for the University of Texas as a regent, contributor, and promotor. Despite his stature, he continued the dissenting ways he had begun during the Civil War; he belonged to the Republican Party and was generally sympathetic to African-American causes. Sibley's clear, scholarly work smoothly combines biography, business history, political history, and family history.

Progressive Era, New Deal, and the Second World War, 1900-1945

187 **Damning the Colorado: the rise of the Lower Colorado River Authority, 1933-1939.**
John A. Adams.   College Station, Texas: Texas A & M University Press, 1990. 176p. maps. bibliog. (Centennial Series of the Association of Former Students, Texas A & M University).

An analysis of the struggle between public institutions and public interests to control the unpredictable and often dangerous Colorado River of Central Texas. The New Deal finally allowed the Lower Colorado River Authority to be established with millions of federal dollars, which, with the Tennessee Valley Authority as a model, resulted in the building of a system of dams, reservoirs, and hydroelectric power stations along the lower reaches of the Colorado. Among the topics examined in this handsomely illustrated book are water resource development and the sometimes uneasy relationships between private utility interests, conservationists, and politicians. The success of the LCRA set a precedent for additional federally funded water and reclamation projects in the West.

188 **Crusade for conformity: the Ku Klux Klan in Texas, 1920-1930.**
Charles C. Alexander.   Houston, Texas: Texas Gulf Coast Historical Association, 1962. 88p. bibliog.

A description of the purpose, organization, membership, influence, methods, and decline of the K K K in Texas between 1920-30. Alexander claims that the motivations of the Texas Klan stemmed less from nativism and racism than from a yearning to correct the ills of urbanization and a quest for moral and social conformity. Its political orientation made it one of the most powerful interest groups in Texas during the 1920s.

189 **Boss rule in south Texas: the progressive era.**
Evan Anders.   Austin, Texas: University of Texas Press, 1982. 319p.
maps. bibliog.

A look at South Texas politics in the 1890s and early 20th century in the context of the
rise of 'boss rule' in American politics after the Civil War. Anders applies social
science models of urban 'bossism' to the rural areas of South Texas to explore the
mechanics of county 'rings'; the relationships between the bosses and government
agencies like the Texas Rangers and between violence and racial tension. The author
demonstrates that bosses used the votes of lower-class Mexican-American and Anglo
residents (which they won through bribery and opposition to prohibition) to stay in
power and to protect their various corrupt enterprises. Racial violence obviously grew
out of this system, but the bosses also intimidated and killed their Anglo competitors,
when necessary. In fact, at least one of the bosses, Manuel Guerra, was Hispanic; he
acted no differently from his colleagues. Progressive reformers, using Populist rhetoric
and hoping to take advantage of the region's modernizing economy, tried to eliminate
the bosses' power by disfranchising *Tejano* voters.

190 **Hood, bonnet, and little brown jug: Texas politics, 1921-1928.**
Norman Brown.   College Station, Texas: Texas A & M University
Press, 1984. 568p. bibliog. (Texas A & M Southwestern Series).

The first of a proposed two volume study of politics in Texas during the 1920s and
1930s. Brown's prodigious research in manuscript collections (at the state and national
level) and in Texas newspapers helps him explore three main issues in Texas politics:
the activities and influence of the Ku Klux Klan, prohibition, and the careers of
Miriam 'Ma' Ferguson and James 'Pa' Ferguson. The author shows that James
Ferguson dominated politics in the Lone Star State between 1914-34. He explains the
evolution of Progressivism into conservative efforts to protect moral standards and
cultural values; analyses the role of pro-business interests in the state's politics;
examines the role of women after the passage of the 19th Amendment to the
Constitution granted them suffrage; and details Texas's role in national politics
(including the state's rejection of the 1928 Democratic candidate for president, Al
Smith, an anti-prohibition urban Catholic). This is a close analysis of the major
currents in 20th century Texas, expertly placed in the context of national issues and
events.

191 **Texas and the Mexican revolution: a study in state and national border
policy, 1910-1920.**
Don M. Coerver, Linda B. Hall.   San Antonio, Texas: Trinity
University Press, 1984. 167p. bibliog.

An analysis of the interplay between the United States, Mexican, and Texas
governments during the revolutionary decade after 1910. This Mexican revolution, like
its predecessors, often spilled over into Texas because of the long shared border and
the string of 'twin cities' perched on opposite banks of the Rio Grande. Juarez, across
from El Paso was the most dangerous and important source of tension, but there were
also problems at Matamoros (Brownsville) and Nuevo Laredo (Laredo). Many of the
leading Mexican revolutionaries actually operated out of Texas. Differences frequently
arose over conflicts between the state's border policy and the federal government's
foreign policy. Even at the national level, the war and state departments were often at
odds; while it sometimes made sense to do nothing in response to a border incident in
the larger scheme of foreign policy, it rarely seemed that way to Texas officials. Part of

the problem was that the United States president for most of this period was Woodrow Wilson, who cared little about foreign affairs and when he did get involved tended to worry more about Europe. His idealism frequently clashed with Texans' realism, and the issues raised by intra- and inter-government conflicts were not resolved until peace returned to Mexico.

192　**James Stephen Hogg: a biography.**
　　Robert C. Cotner.　Austin, Texas: University of Texas Press, 1959.
　　617p. maps. bibliog.

An extremely thorough and scholarly account of the life of the first native-born governor of Texas. Hogg (1851-1906), a lawyer, was a member of a famous political family. He worked as a district attorney and as attorney general before serving as a Democratic governor between 1891-95. A Texas-style Progressive, he worked for rational practices and government regulation in business (especially railroads) and for education reform. In a time of often impassioned extremism, Hogg was basically a moderate, even in matters of race. Although he served as governor during the 1890s, his role as one of Texas' leading Progressives actually places his career and this biography into the history and historiography of the post-1900 period.

193　**Progressives and prohibitionists: Texas Democrats in the Wilson era.**
　　Lewis L. Gould.　Austin, Texas: University of Texas Press, 1973.
　　339p. map. bibliog.

A case study of the interaction between the national Democratic Party and the southern branches of the party upon which Woodrow Wilson relied so heavily for electoral support. Although the national party was moving toward an urban, multi-cultural polyglot of interest groups, Texas Democrats remained evangelical in their religious outlook and 'dry' in their moral temperament. Yet Texans supported Wilson heavily at the polls and three Texans served in Wilson's cabinet. Wilson led his Texas followers toward a more positive view of government power, and reformers in Texas also began pushing for Progressive reforms like women's suffrage and business regulation. This is a scholarly but accessible book on an important period in the formation of the modern Democratic Party at the national level and in Texas.

194　**Littlefield land: colonization on the Texas plains, 1912-1920.**
　　David B. Gracy II.　Austin, Texas: University of Texas Press, 1968.
　　161p. maps. bibliog.

Written by a great-great-nephew of Major George W. Littlefield, the founder of the Littlefield Land Co, this is the story of his efforts to encourage settlement in Lamb County, Texas. Major Littlefield turned his Yellow House Ranch into a real estate company in 1912. He built his planned community on a grid and subdivided it for settlement. He attracted the usual small-town businesses (a post office, a bank, a store), as well as people employed in farming, the lumber industry, and ranching. In addition, a large contingent of Mennonites also settled on Littlefield land. Several maps, an extensive bibliography, twenty black-and-white photographs, and an appendix of the original land buyers provide important information for this little-known episode.

195 1941: Texas goes to war.

Edited by James Ward Lee. Denton, Texas: University of North Texas Press, 1991. 300p.

An entertaining and often nostalgic compilation of nearly 300 black-and-white photographs, contemporary letters, and reminiscences from Texas scholars and writers like Elmer Kelton, F. E. Abernethy, and Don Graham, of their experiences during the Second World War. The emphasis is on the home front: rationing, industry, urbanization, volunteerism, technological change, and the state's shifting economy.

196 Galveston, Ellis Island of the west.

Bernard Marinbach. Albany, New York: State University of New York Press, 1983. 240p. bibliog. (SUNY Series in Modern Jewish History).

Marinbach recounts the history of a little-known phase of American, immigrant, and Jewish history. Between 1907-14, about 9,000 Jews disembarked at Galveston, Texas, and continued on to nearly every state in the union. The author places the so-called 'Galveston Movement' – the migration of mainly Russian Jews – in the context of other proposed solutions for the plight of Eastern European Jews. Among the problems encountered by the new immigrants were competition for jobs with resentful Anglo-Americans and the opposition by the United States government to the programme, which led to some deportations. Marinbach details the work of the Jewish Territorial Organization, the Jewish Emigration Society (in Kiev), and the Jewish Immigrants' Information Bureau and also describes the experiences of these immigrants during their journey and after their arrival. This book is less about Galveston than it is about one small part of the Jewish diaspora, but it nevertheless fills an interesting niche in Texas historiography.

197 The year America discovered Texas: centennial '36.

Kenneth Baxter Ragsdale. College Station, Texas: Texas A & M University Press, 1987. 325p. bibliog.

A look at how the 1936 Texas Centennial (as celebrated primarily in the Dallas/Fort Worth area, where over seven million people attended a myriad of exhibitions) was seen by its promoters as a means of alerting the rest of the United States to the past accomplishments and future potential of Texas in order to create national interest in the Texas economy. The idea for the commemoration originated with local advertising executives and was adopted by commercial leaders and politicians. Ragsdale provides a narrative of the planning stage as well as the events themselves, and argues that the activity and tourism spawned by the Centennial helped stimulate the development of modern Dallas/Fort Worth. In addition, it caused Americans to recognize Texas as more than just a vestige of the old Wild West, which, in turn, helped integrate Texas into the rest of the country.

198 Mr. House of Texas.

Arthur D. Howden Smith. New York: Funk & Wagnalls, 1940. 381p.

Written by a journalist who knew him well, this is a familiar, but stuffy and old-fashioned, anecdote-filled biography of Edward M. House (1858-1938). The son of a wealthy Galveston merchant, House was a Democratic Party operative who served as campaign manager for Governor James S. Hogg and other Texas Democratic gubernatorial candidates; as an aide, advisor, and trouble-shooter for Pres. Woodrow

Wilson; and as one of five American Peace Commissioners at Versailles following the First World War. This is a very positive look at House's life, stressing his involvement with United States foreign policy and with the League of Nations.

199 **The depression in Texas: the Hoover years.**
Donald W. Whisenhunt. New York: Garland Publishing, 1983. 249p. bibliog.

This is less a political and more a cultural history of Texans' response to the Great Depression of the late 1920s and early 1930s. Texans at first denied the reality of the depression; they failed to understand how fluctuations in the stock market could affect their agriculturally oriented economy. As the depression deepened, however, they began looking for reasons. The Populist tradition caused many to blame businessmen and the Republican Party; religious fundamentalism led others to blame a sinful society. As hard times dragged on, Whisenhunt argues, Texans had to shed some of their rugged individualism and to accept an expanded federal government presence in their lives through relief programs of various kinds. The author argues that the highly touted individualism of Texas was transformed during the depression into a willingness to try anything – including agricultural reform and federal aid – that would alleviate the crisis. This is a rare and scholarly look at 1930s Texas.

Post-War Period, 1945-Present

200 **Red scare! right-wing hysteria, fifties fanaticism, and their legacy.**
Don Carleton. Austin, Texas: Texas Monthly Press, 1985. 390p. bibliog.

An analysis of the anti-Communist 'Red Scare' in Houston in the 1950s. The rapid economic and social changes and the development of left-wing political groups in Texas's largest city during the 1930s and 1940s sparked a back-lash among the city's elite against labour unions and other liberal organizations. Two of the most important anti-communist groups were the Committee for the Preservation of Methodism and the local chapter of the Minute Women of the United States; they opposed any real or perceived 'communist' or socialist activity, especially among Houston's educators. The anti-communists conducted their campaigns virtually unopposed from 1951-54, and although their movement (like the national anti-communist movement better-known as 'McCarthyism') died out by the mid- to late-1950s, their legacy remained. This is a decidedly unsympathetic account of a significant conservative movement.

201 **The Years of Lyndon Johnson.**
Robert Caro. New York: Alfred A. Knopf, 1982, 1990. 2 vols. maps.
bibiog.

The first two volumes of this massive biography of Lyndon Baines Johnson (1908-73)
the only United States president from Texas, cover the period up to his 1948 election
to the United States Senate. Caro has produced nearly 1400 pages of exhaustively
researched but extraordinarily biased biography. Volume one, subtitled *The Path to
Power*, takes Johnson's life up to his years in Congress; volume two, *Means of Ascent*,
covers only seven years in his life. The author stresses mostly Johnson's negative
characteristics: his love of power and compulsion to dominate other people. his use of
money as a lever to get what he wanted, and his secretive nature, especially concerning
his personal finances. Critics have applauded the vast amount of information
accumulated by Caro, but have decried the shrill, one-sided attacks on Johnson's
character and the author's refusal to acknowledge any sort of sincere beliefs on
Johnson's part on the 1960s issues of civil rights and the war on poverty.

202 **Congressman Sam Rayburn.**
Anthony Champagne. New Brunswick, New Jersey: Rutgers
University Press, 1984. 188p. maps. bibliog.

An analysis of the political style and methods of Rayburn (1882-1961), who served as a
Democratic congressman from Texas for forty-nine years and as Speaker of the House
for seventeen. Rayburn began representing the 4th Congressional District northeast of
Dallas during the Woodrow Wilson administration; he remained a self-professed old-
fashioned politician throughout his career. His was a very personal style; he exuded
small-town friendliness, excelled at developing networks of allies in Texas and in
Washington, DC, worked hard to serve his constituents, tried not to alienate his
opponents, and earned a reputation as a compromiser. Basing his work on Rayburn's
speeches, some correspondence, and interviews with colleagues, associates, and
observors, Champagne pays much more attention to the sources of Rayburn's political
effectiveness than to the issues with which he was involved. Appendixes include a
number of tables on the demography and voting patterns of Rayburn's 4th District. For
another insider's biography of Rayburn, see D. B. Hardeman and Donald C. Bacon's
Rayburn: A Biography (Austin, Texas: Texas Monthly Press, 1987).

203 **Lyndon B. Johnson: the exercise of power.**
Rowland Evans, Robert Novack. New York: New American Library,
1966. 597p.

Based on the authors' observations as long-time Washington reporters, and on two
hundred interviews, this is not a standard biography, but a study of the ways in which
Johnson 'sought, achieved, and dispensed power', especially after he became Senate
Democratic Leader in 1953. They argue that Johnson's political personality was a
mixture of ruthlessness and compassion, modesty and self-promotion, and posit that
power was Johnson's primary goal throughout his career. They provide useful case
studies of how Johnson dealt with certain situations in his career: foreign policy crises,
elections, and potentially damaging rumours. Although the authors seem to admire
Johnson's political skill, they are sometimes critical of the ways in which he applied it.

204 **Maury Maverick.**
Richard Henderson. Austin, Texas: University of Texas Press, 1970.
386p. bibliog.

A solid, well-researched and balanced narrative of Maury Maverick's (1895-1954) political career. Anderson portrays Maverick as a political radical, committed to free speech, racial justice, civil liberties, and an active government. As mayor of San Antonio, United States Congressman during the 1930s, and federal bureaucrat in the 1940s and 1950s, Maverick was that rare specimen in pre-1960s Texan politics: a successful liberal. This is a scholarly, detailed, and positive – although not white-washed – biography of a major 20th century Texan.

205 **Allan Shivers: the pied piper of Texas politics.**
Sam Kinch, Stuart Long. Austin, Texas: Shoal Creek Publishers, 1974. 247p.

Allan Shivers (1907-) was a long-time Democratic politican who served in the state senate, as lieutenant governor, and three-times as a governor in the early 1950s. A conservative, he convinced many Texas Democrats to vote for the Republican Dwight D. Eisenhower in the 1952 presidential election. In the 1960s he served as president of the United States Chamber of Commerce. This is a chronological narrative that presents the facts, with very little criticism of this often controversial figure.

206 **The death of a president, November 20–November 25, 1963.**
William R. Manchester. New York: Harper and Row, 1967. 710p.
maps. bibliog.

Written at the personal request of the president's widow, this is a detailed and fast-moving narrative of the assassination of Pres. John F. Kennedy in Dallas. Manchester recreates the days leading up to and after the assassination and the murder of Lee Harvey Oswald, the man commonly assumed to have killed Kennedy. The author provides information on the movements and reactions of family members, the president's staff, his vice president, the Texan Lyndon B. Johnson, and Texas law enforcement officials, and places the incident in the contexts of national political issues and pressures facing the president, who was not popular in Texas. Manchester seems to favour the 'lone gunman' theory – that Oswald was acting alone – but he presents other scenarios as well. More controversial than Manchester's work are two books by authors who suspect cover-ups and conspiracies: David W. Belin's *Final disclosure: the full truth about the assassination of President Kennedy* (New York: Scribner's, 1988), and David S. Lifton's *Best evidence: disguise and deception in the assassination of John F. Kennedy* (New York: Macmillan, 1980).

207 **Texas and the Fair Deal, 1945-1952.**
Seth Shepard McKay. San Antonio, Texas: Naylor, 1954. 437p.
bibliog.

An analysis of Texas's growing involvement in and dissatisfaction with national and international political issues in the immediate post-Second World War period. Overwhelmingly conservative Texans had never willingly accepted President Franklin Roosevelt's New Deal programmes in the 1930s, nor did they accept President Harry S Truman's Fair Deal programmes of the 1940s. McKay pays close attention to Texan issues such as educational and legal reform and to important Texas elections such as the Rainey – Jester gubernatorial contest in 1948 and the Lyndon B. Johnson – Coke

Stevenson United States Senate race in 1948. A straightforward and useful political history.

208 **Postwar readjustment in El Paso, 1945-1950.**
Patricia Rescheuthaler. El Paso, Texas: Texas Western Press, 1968.
43p. bibliog.

A useful, brief case study of one Texas city's economic and social adjustment to conditions immediately following the Second World War. El Paso grew markedly in the 1940s, and became heavily dependent from an economic standpoint on nearby military installations. Housing was a problem in this early example of a 'Sun Belt' boom-town; racial tension and labour conflict also plagued the city. Yet another element of this little book is its analysis of the impact of the rapidly growing business sector in post-war El Paso.

209 **The lone star: life of John Connally.**
James Reston. New York: Harper & Row, 1989. 691p. bibliog.

An appreciative, breezy, and detailed biography of John Connally (1917-), protégé and best friend of Lyndon Johnson, a Democrat who converted to the Republican Party, Texas governor, Secretary of the Navy and of the Treasury under President Richard Nixon, and in the 1970s and 1980s perennial candidate for higher office. Connally was one of the movers and shakers of Texas and national politics from the 1950s through the 1970s. He was also a stereotypical 'high roller' who was frequently suspected of corruption and, after a series of unwise business deals, declared bankruptcy in the 1980s. Reston, a well-known political columnist, uses his knowledge of national politics to place Connally in that context. An intriguing appendix examines the John F. Kennedy assassination investigation; Connally was severely wounded in the attack that killed President Kennedy.

Military Affairs

210 **Between the Enemy and Texas: Parsons's Texas Cavalry in the Civil War.**
Anne J. Bailey. Fort Worth, Texas: Texas Christian University Press, 1989. 208p. maps. bibliog.

A straightforward account of a single cavalry brigade operating in Texas and Louisiana between 1862-65. The emphasis is on their campaigns and skirmishes, on the leadership of its commander, Colonel William H. Parsons, and on the difficulty of keeping a unit in the field in the chaotic and resource-poor Trans-Mississippi region of the Confederacy.

211 **Texans in Revolt: The Battle for San Antonio, 1835.**
Alwyn Barr. Austin, Texas: University of Texas Press, 1990. 72p. maps. bibliog.

In a tightly conceived analysis of the first major campaign of the Texas Revolution, the author describes the Texans' capture of this important Mexican outpost. He examines the events of late 1835 and early 1836 from their military and political viewpoints and explodes the widely held myth that the victors overcame a three to one numerical disadvantage.

212 **The second Texas infantry: from Shiloh to Vicksburg.**
Joseph E. Chance. Austin, Texas: Eakin Press, 1984. 216p. bibliog.

A thorough and useful history of a single Texas Civil War regiment. With notable members like Colonel Ashbel Smith and Private Sam Houston Jr, the Second Texas was raised early in the war and all but destroyed in the Vicksburg campaign in 1863, where it surrendered to Federal forces. Most of the men were paroled and returned to Texas, where they served for the remainder of the war. The narrative is complemented by a complete roster of the men who served in the unit and selections of songs and poetry relating to the regiment.

213 **Frontier forts of Texas.**

Roger N. Conger, (et al). Waco, Texas: Texian Press, 1966. 190p. map.

Narratives by eight authors of the history of eight forts built in Texas between the antebellum and Reconstruction periods. Each historian examines daily life, frontier settlements that developed nearby, and military operations that originated from the installations. Comparative information is provided on twenty-two other military establishments. The forts, their locations, and the years in which they were built are: Brown (Brownsville, 1846), Bliss (El Paso, 1848), Belknap (North Texas, 1851), Mason (Central Texas, 1851), Clark (on the Rio Grande, 1852), Davis (near the Davis Mountains in West Texas, 1854), Concho (San Angelo, 1867), and Sam Houston (San Antonio, 1876).

214 **Wolves for the blue soldiers: Indian scouts and auxiliaries with the United States Army, 1860–90.**

Thomas W. Dunlay. Lincoln, Nebraska: University of Nebraska Press, 1982. 304p. bibliog.

The standard analysis of the United States Army's use of Indian scouts during the height of the 19th century Indian wars. Dunlay explores the motivations and experiences of both sides in this study of a very unique example of the relationship between whites and Native Americans in the West. Although the author casts his net over the entire West, Texas is discussed in the book; Texas Rangers utilized Cherokee, Tankawa, Lipan, and even Comanche tribesmen as scouts in their pre-Civil war operations against the Comanche.

215 **Crimson desert. Indian wars of the American southwest.**

Odie B. Faulk. New York: Oxford University Press, 1974. 237p. maps. bibliog.

Organized more or less chronologically and focusing on atrocities (committed by both sides), military campaigns, battles, and Indian-white negotiations between the years 1846–86, this is a useful introduction to the military perspective of the Indian wars in Texas and the rest of the Southwest. In Texas, Faulk emphasizes the Apache campaign on the edge of North Texas and the long-standing wars against the Comanche in the Panhandle region of the state.

216 **Battles of Texas.**

Joe B. Frantz, (et al). Waco, Texas: Texian Press, 1967. 190p.

A book written in a popular style in which eight historians describe eight battles which had a major impact on Texan history. Three are from the Texas Revolution: the famous last stand at the Alamo (March 6, 1836), the massacre of Texas revolutionaries by the Mexican Army at Goliad (March 27, 1836), and the Texans' stunning victory over the Mexicans at San Jacinto (April 21, 1836). Two chapters are devoted to battles between Texans and Indians during the years of the Republic of Texas: the Battle of the Neches River (July 16, 1839), the decisive battle of the Cherokee War, and the Battle of Plum Creek (August 11, 1840), which pitted Texans against Comanche and Kiowa Indians. Also considered are the Battle of Palo Alto (May 8, 1846), one of the first battles of the Mexican-American War; the Battle of Sabine Pass (September 8, 1863), in which Dick Dowling's handful of Confederate artillerymen routed an invasion of East Texas by a much larger Union force; and the Battle of Adobe Walls (June 27,

1874), the fight between Kiowa-Comanches and buffalo hunters that sparked the 1874–75 Red River War.

217 **The ragged rebel: a common soldier in W. H. Parsons's Texas cavalry, 1861-1865.**
B. P. Gallaway.   Austin, Texas: University of Texas Press, 1988. 186p. maps. bibliog.

Although Civil War literature is filled with first person accounts from every military rank and biographies of most of the prominent and not-so-prominent commanders, few 'common soldiers' have earned their own biographies. This book is notable chiefly for bringing seriousness and scholarly method to the life of David Carey Nance, a private who eventually rose to the rank of sergeant. Although Gallaway uses sketchy sources imaginatively, he provides little new information. Nevertheless, this rare account of the Civil War in the Trans-Mississippi region is an important source for the common soldiers' point of view.

218 **The buffalo war.**
James L. Haley.   Garden City, New York: Doubleday, 1976. 290p. maps. bibliog.

An examination of the Red River War of 1874-75, which was sparked at least in part by the slaughter, by white hunters, of the massive buffalo herds on the southern plains. It became the largest military campaign against Native Americans – specifically the Comanche, Kiowa, Cheyenne, and Arapaho – up to that time, and resulted in the final subjugation of three of these very powerful Indian tribes and the securing of the region from central Kansas to central Texas for white settlement. Haley's well-written narrative highlights combat and atrocities, but also provides useful accounts of the complex relationships between hostile Indians and whites, 'Peace' Indians and 'War' Indians, the Army and the United States Indian Bureau, and among ambitious army officers. The war included the famous battle of Adobe Wells, in which hundreds of Indians unsuccessfully attacked a handful of buffalo hunters. Haley provides nearly sixty illustrations, most of which are portraits of noted chiefs and officers.

219 **Sentinel of the southern plains: Fort Richardson and the northwest Texas frontier, 1866-1878.**
Allen Lee Hamilton.   Fort Worth, Texas: Texas Christian University Press, 1988. 251p. maps. bibliog. (Chisholm Trail Series).

An exciting narrative of an important outpost in United States Army campaigns against Kiowas, Commanches, and Kiowa-Apaches during the decade or so just after the Civil War. The fort was built in 1866 in Jack County (northwest of Fort Worth) and abandoned only twelve years later as the frontier moved westward. Five thousand troopers passed through the installation; three major campaigns and hundreds of patrols originated there. Hamilton emphasizes combat episodes in the fort's history, but also sketches the daily life of the men assigned there and the fort's physical surroundings. With extensive notes and dozens of illustrations, this is a work for serious historians of the frontier but also for general readers.

220 **The Texas navy: in forgotten battles and shirtsleeve diplomacy.**
Jim Dan Hill. Chicago: University of Chicago Press, 1937; Austin,
Texas: State House Press, 1987. 224p. maps. bibliog.

A narrative of the development and battles of the Texas Navy under the command of
Commodore Charles Hawkins and Secretary of the Navy Robert Potter. Despite
chronic problems with wretched equipment and ill-trained crews – both of which are
thoroughly documented – the Navy played a crucial role in denying reinforcements to
the Mexican Army during the San Jacinto campaign of 1836. The author highlights in a
chronological fashion the political battles over the Navy and its role in the often
complicated diplomatic relations between the Republic and the Mexican, French, and
English governments.

221 **Wings over the border: the Army Air Service armed patrol of the United
States-Mexico border, 1919-1921.**
Stacy Hinkle. El Paso, Texas: Texas Western Press, 1970. 67p.
bibliog.

A brief but unique personal account by a former United States Army pilot who flew
into Mexico during the 1919 campaign against Mexican revolutionary bandits. Hinkle
provides information about air patrols, the bandits themselves, and the kidnapping and
ransoming of flyers by the 'bandits'. Sources include a pilot's log, official records, and a
wide range of newspaper reports.

222 **Rangers and regulars.**
George E. Hyde. Columbus, Ohio: Long's College Books, 1952.
143p.

A rare and unscholarly but useful summary of Spanish, Mexican, and American
military campaigns against and policies toward the Indians of the southern plains,
especially the Apaches and Comanches.

223 **The military conquest of the southern plains.**
William H. Leckie. Norman, Oklahoma: University of Oklahoma
Press, 1963. 269p. maps. bibliog.

A scholarly and useful narrative of military operations by the United States Army
against the Comanche, Kiowa, Kiowa-Apache, southern Cheyenne, and Arapaho from
the 1860s to 1875. Events in Texas are adequately covered, although there is little
mention of the Texas Rangers and other state efforts to deal with Indian problems.
Although there is some limited discussion of the political context and of Indian policy,
and of the Indians' motivations in fleeing their reservations, this is basically a military
narrative from the whites' point of view.

224 **Fort Belknap frontier saga: Indians, Negroes, and Anglo-Americans on
the Texas frontier.**
Barbara A. Neal Ledbetter. Burnet, Texas: Eakin Press, 1982. 300p.
maps. bibliog.

Ledbetter highlights individuals and events from the history of Young County's long-
term military establishment. Although it focuses on an 1864 massacre and kidnapping
of a number of white settlers by Kiowa Indians, and the legends that arose about the
incident, the book provides vignettes of incidents ranging from the turn of the 19th

century to the late 1880s. Not surprisingly, the military is an important element in these stories, but the author also pays close attention to the experiences of civilian settlers, black as well as white. The book is marred by an anti-Indian bias, but does provide useful evidence about the intersection of cultures on the West Texas frontier.

225 Plains Indian raiders.

Wilbur S. Nye.   Norman, Oklahoma: University of Oklahoma Press, 1968. 418p. maps. bibliog.

A basic history of United States Army campaigns against the southern tribes from 1864-75 in Kansas, Indian Territory, and Northern Texas. Although the text is scholarly and well-written, it is overshadowed by 112 black-and-white photographs of the chiefs, warriors, and daily life of the Kiowa, Apache, Comanche, Cheyenne, and Arapaho taken by the photographer William S. Soule. This is a useful introduction to the warfare on the southern Plains and an important collection of images from that period.

226 Confederate cavalry west of the river.

Stephen B. Oates.   Austin, Texas: University of Texas Press, 1961. 234p. maps. bibliog.

An examination of the cavalry units serving the Confederacy west of the Mississippi River. Lacking the 'spit and polish' of their counterparts in the eastern theatre, the cowboys and farmers who enlisted in the 114 western cavalry regiments and 47 battalians were natural riders and shooters who often were able to overcome their poor equipment and limited supplies to perform daring raids and operations that often played important roles in the overall strategy of the western theatre. Oates provides much information about tactical and strategic topics, but also devotes chapters to organization, food and clothing, and arms and mounts. Appendixes provide a list and an estimate of the strength of every Confederate cavalry unit west of the Mississippi River.

227 Wings over the Mexican border: pioneer military aviation in the Big Bend.

Kenneth B. Ragsdale.   Austin, Texas: University of Texas Press, 1984. 266p. map. bibliog.

An enjoyable, affectionate, but thorough narrative of military aviation in the rough wilderness of the Big Bend between 1929–44. Originally established to patrol the Mexican border, the air corps base created on Elmo Johnson's ranch later became an important training site. Ragsdale's themes include the growth of the Army Air Corps as a military force, the gradual replacement of young adventurers by professional flyers, the changes in aviation technology, and the informal nature of life on the post. Short on analysis, but packed with information, *Wings over the Mexican Border* is a solid work on a little-known aspect of Texas history.

228 Along Texas old forts trail.

Rupert Richardson, B. W. Aston, Ira Donathon Taylor.   Denton, Texas: University of North Texas Press, 1990. 114p. maps. bibliog.

A tourist guide to the 19th century military installations of the Texas Panhandle and West Texas: Forts Richardson, Phantom Hill, McKavett, Belknap, Chadbourne, Mason, Griffin, and Concho. Along with easy to follow directions and maps, the authors provide short histories of the forts and information on lodging, restaurants, and annual events at the forts and in the nearby towns.

229   **Fort Griffin on the Texas frontier.**
Carl Coke Rister.   Norman, Oklahoma: University of Oklahoma
Press, 1956. 216p. map.

Fort Griffin, located in Shackelford County in northwest Texas, was established in 1867 and abandoned in 1881. Rister stresses the 'Wild West' aspects of the history of this frontier crossroads: the soldiers who served at the fort, of course, but also buffalo hunters and gamblers, Kiowas and Comanches, ranchers and cowboys. The author also includes in his narrative the town that grew up around the military post and the factors that made it an important institution in late 19th century Texas. Topically arranged and based on secondary and primary sources, the book is clearly and colourfully written.

230   **Albert Sidney Johnston: soldier of three republics.**
Charles P. Roland.   Austin, Texas: University of Texas Press, 1964.
384p. maps. bibliog.

Johnston (1803-62), a Texan, was one of the most distinguished officers in the pre-Civil War United States Army and one of the first Confederate heroes during the war. From the Blackhawk War in the 1830s to the Mexican War in the 1840s and the Mormon 'War' of the 1850s, Johnston served in most of the antebellum period's hot spots. This admiring but scholarly biography stresses Johnston's high moral character, tremendous sense of duty, and outstanding leadership skills. As one of the highest-ranking Confederate generals during the first year of the Civil War, Johnston commanded the western theatre's main southern army; in April 1862, he was killed at the Battle of Shiloh. Seventeen maps of battlefields and regions and 14 black-and-white illustrations add to the text.

231   **War scare on the Rio Grande: Robert Runyon's photographs of the border conflict, 1913–1916.**
Frank N. Samponaro, Paul J. Vanderwood.   Austin, Texas: Texas
State Historical Association, 1991. 160p.

An edition of 88 duotone and 20 half-tone photographs taken by a Brownsville, Texas, photographer during the volatile period from 1910 to 1920. Runyon made some thirteen thousand prints and negatives of the region during this time, featuring incidents from the Mexican Revolution, 'bandit' raids across the border, and the resultant United States military build-up. The text is drawn from traditional historical sources and examines United States-Mexican relations and the events chronicled by the photographs. See also the authors' *Border fury: a picture postcard record of Mexico's revolution and U.S. war preparedness, 1910–1917* (Albuquerque, New Mexico: University of New Mexico Press, 1988).

232   **Hood's Texas brigade: Lee's grenadier guard.**
Harold B. Simpson.   Waco, Texas: Texian Press, 1970. 512p. maps.
bibliog.

Three Texas regiments and a number of units from other southern states served in Texas's most famous Civil War unit, which was commanded early in the war by General John B. Hood. Perhaps 4,700 out of the 5,300 original recruits were killed, wounded, or captured and others deserted. This is definitely a 'drums and bugles'-style military history. Simpson relies on a wide variety of primary and secondary sources in chronicling the brigade's history from its enlistment in 1861 to its long walk home at the end of the war. His primary emphasis is, naturally, on the brigade's battles and marches. Along with a number of photographs of officers and sites associated with the unit, the author has included a dozen maps of the major battles in which it fought.

233 **Sabers on the Rio Grande.**
Jerry Thompson. Austin, Texas: Presidial Press, 1974. 235p. bibliog.
Begining with a discussion of the Coahuiltecans Indians and passing quickly to the Spanish conquest, the book chronicles the history of the Laredo area throughout the Civil War. The emphasis is on military history, as this border town often became a battleground between Spanish and Mexicans, Indians, Texans and Mexicans, Confederates and Yankees, settlers and Indians, and even factions of Mexican revolutionaries. Thompson also discusses the blending and clashes of cultures and the development of political systems as they were affected by frequent warfare and conflict. Woven throughout the book are descriptions of military post life, Indian 'management', and life in Laredo.

234 **If these walls could speak: historic forts of Texas.**
Robert M. Utley. Austin, Texas: University of Texas Press, 1985.
64p. map. bibliog.
A brief look at ten Texas forts in use before, during, and after the Civil War, featuring eighteen colour paintings by J. U. Salvant of buildings from the posts. The text, by noted western historian Robert Utley, provides a short history of each fort, including their missions – which ranged from fighting Indians to fighting Union troops during the Civil War – and the lives of the people who lived in them. The paintings are based on architectural plans and old photographs; parts of a few of the forts are still standing as abandoned ruins. Included in the volume are Forts Brown, McIntosh, McKavett, Lancaster, Richardson, Griffin, Concho, Davis, Bliss, and Ringgold Barracks.

235 **The Indian frontier of the American west, 1846-1890.**
Robert M. Utley. Albuquerque, New Mexico: University of New Mexico Press, 1984. 325p. maps. bibliog. (Histories of the American Frontier).
A very useful account of all of the major Indian-white conflicts in the last half-century of westward movement. Utley includes not only an instructive narrative of familiar campaigns, battles, and other military episodes, but also an explanation of the culture clash that led to conflict between these groups and of the politics and economics of government policies toward Native Americans. Using his own extensive research in many phases of western history, as well as the work of scores of other historians, the author focuses not only on well-known plains tribes, but also on the 'Five Civilized Tribes' in Indian Territory. He argues convincingly that the plains tribes were reacting not so much against whites as against the reservation system. Utley's book is useful for those interested in Indian policy in Texas mainly because it provides the broad picture of government policy, although he does examine such Texas incidents as the Kiowa raids and white retaliation of the 1870s.

236   **Ranald S. Mackenzie on the Texas frontier.**
Ernest Wallace.   Lubbock, Texas: West Texas Museum Association,
1964. 214p. maps.

A standard biography of the commander of the 4th United States Cavalry from 1871-78, who led the campaigns in Texas against the Kiowa and Comanche in the early 1870s. He also explored previously uncharted areas of the southern plains. Although his research is solid, the author glosses over the dispossession of the Indians represented in Mackenzie's career; the colonel was a bonafide Indian hater who firmly believed in his mission.

237   **Commodore Moore and the Texas navy.**
Tom H. Wells.   Austin, Texas: University of Texas Press, 1960. 218p.
map. bibliog.

Commodore Edwin Ward Moore (1810–65) left the United States Navy in 1839 as a lieutenant and immediately became commander of the fledgling Texas Navy, which had only six ships at the time. For the next seven years, he fought for resources and authority with Sam Houston and others, and eventually built a respectable force that was instrumental in Texas's struggles with Mexico in the early 1840s. Appendixes list commanding officers of Texas Navy vessels, their vessels, and Navy regulations.

238   **Texas' last frontier: Fort Stockton and the trans-Pecos, 1861-1895.**
Clayton Williams.   College Station, Texas: Texas A & M University
Press, 1982. 457p. maps. bibliog.

A relentlessly chronological look at the campaigns and personalities associated with Fort Stockton, in Pecos County in far West Texas, from the Civil War through to the turn of the century. The author, a son of one of the area's original pioneers, has drawn on a wealth of primary and secondary sources and oral tradition to illustrate the Indian fights, outlaws, feuds, ranchers, and the daily lives of soldiers and civilians in this vast, wild corner of Texas. Although it is idiosyncratic and, at times, quite informal, the book provides much information and three dozen illustrations within its useful and colourful narrative.

239   **Soldiers, sutlers, and settlers: garrison life on the Texas frontier.**
Robert Wooster.   College Station, Texas: Texas A & M University
Press, 1987. 240p. maps. bibliog. (Clayton Wheat Williams Texas Life
Series).

A heavily illustrated and straightforward description of the lives of military and civilian inhabitants in dozens of Texas military installations between 1848–90. Seventy black-and-white sketches of daily life and several diagrams of typical physical layouts augment chapters on the construction of forts, the lives of dependents, economic concerns, uniforms and weapons, routine duty and combat, the role of sutlers (civilian storekeepers), and society and culture on the posts. Wooster takes care to place those experiences in the context of military policies toward the Indians, and also examines relationships between soldiers and civilians, males and females, and blacks and whites.

Politics and Government

Administration

240 **They sat in high place: the presidents and governors of Texas.**
James T. De Shields.   San Antonio, Texas: Naylor, 1940. 484p.

This is a fairly useful but decidedly unscholarly collection of short biographies of every president (1836-46) and governor of Texas through to 1939. The author is unabashedly proud of these Texas politicians; the flattering biographies are accompanied by portraits of each subject. This is a useable source for basic biographical information on the first forty of Texas's chief executives, if not for honest criticism.

241 **The chief executive in Texas: a study in gubernatorial leadership.**
Fred Gantt.   Austin, Texas: University of Texas Press, 1964. 396p.
map. bibliog.

Gantt divides this basic analysis of Texas governors into four parts; the development of the governorship, the governor as executive and administrator, the governor and the legislature, and the political role of the governor. Although he provides background from earlier periods, his emphasis is on those governors who served under the 1876 Constitution, and especially those who occupied the office since 1920. The author covers the formal powers and informal influence wielded by the governors; the leadership styles and personalities of individual governors; and their executive, administrative, and political roles. This study is packed with information, including many photos of people and political memoribilia and thirteen tables detailing election statistics, appropriations, constitutional amendments concerning the governors' office, and campaigning. Despite its exhaustive coverage, it lacks deep analysis; in addition, it is out of date in that Texas now has a viable two-party political system.

242 **Texas government.**
Stuart MacCorkle, Dick Smith. New York: McGraw Hill, 1974. 7th
ed. 578p. maps. bibliog.

An often-revised and nearly ubiquitous primer on Texas state government as shaped
by the precise, massive state constitution (which comprises nearly one hundred pages
of the text). The book's twenty-two chapters focus on such issues and departments as
the legislative process, the financial organization of the state, the governor's office,
public education, welfare, the judiciary, regulation of the oil and gas industry, highway
administration, county and local governments, and intergovernmental relations.
Thirteen maps provide information on the resources, roads, counties, educational
system, and political districts in Texas, and a sixteen page appendix lists all the state
agencies. Although it reads like a textbook (which, of course, it is) this is a thorough
and exceedingly useful introduction to the constitution and the government of Texas.

243 **The public lands of Texas, 1519-1970.**
Thomas Lloyd Miller. Norman, Oklahoma: University of Oklahoma
Press, 1971. 341p. 12 maps. bibliog.

A straightforward, chronological approach to the administration and disposition of the
public lands of the region that became Texas. Part one briefly details the land policy of
the Spanish and Mexican governments, while part two devotes separate chapters to the
relationships between the public lands of the Republic and State of Texas to such
issues as colonization, soldiers' benefits, internal improvements, schools, and court
claims. Part three looks at the administration of Texas's 'appropriated' lands, including
land with mineral and timber resources and land devoted to education and asylums, as
well as the operations of the state's general land office. A supplement to this volume is
the highly statistical, analytical, but rare *Financial history of the public lands in Texas*
by Aldon S. Lang (Waco, Texas: Baylor University, 1932), which argues that Texas's
huge supply of public land available for sale retarded the development of an equitable
tax system but also led to wide-spread land ownership, and, because the income of
certain lands was set aside for specific purposes, good transportation facilities and a
good public school system.

244 **State and local government in Texas.**
Caleb Perry Patterson, Sam B. McAlister. New York: Macmillan,
1961. 3rd edition. 500p. bibliog.

Designed as a textbook for Texas undergraduates, this methodical volume is filled with
statistics, flow charts, and the nuts and bolts of Texas government. Chapters are
devoted to the party system, the executive and legislative branches, finance, education,
health care, labour, public safety, business regulations, the legal system, prisons, and
natural resources. The authors also include sections on nominating candidates,
lobbying, and the relationship between state and federal laws. Despite its title,
however, the book barely mentions local government; only the last two chapters deal
with county and municipal administration.

245 **The Texas Senate: volume one: Republic to Civil War, 1836-1861.**
Edited by Patsy McDonald Shaw.   College Station, Texas: Texas A &
M University Press, 1991. 408p. bibliog.

The first of five planned volumes, this is a useful reference tool that provides brief
biographies of the men who served in the Senate of the Texas Republic and the Texas
State Senate through 1861. Written by a number of authors who utilized a wide variety
of primary sources, these mini-biographies provide basic biographical data as well as
information on the senators' personalities and the issues with which they dealt. Also
included are discussions of Senate proceedings throughout the period and fifty-nine
black-and-white photographs.

246 **Early economic policies of the government of Texas.**
Lee Van Zant.   El Paso, Texas: Texas Western Press, 1966. 48p.
bibliog.

A short, useful analysis of government policies on, and the economic effects of,
railroad construction and immigration during the 19th century, particularly in terms of
land grants and government regulation.

Parties and Elections

247 **Money, Marbles, and Chalk.**
Jimmy Banks.   Austin, Texas: Texas Publishing, 1971. 277p. bibliog.

An uncriticial look at Texas politics from the 1940s through 1970, which highlights the
rise to national prominence of such men as John Connally, Lyndon B. Johnson,
George Bush, Preston Smith, and Lloyd Bentsen. The author presents flattering
portraits, especially of the Texas Republicans of the 1960s; adjectives like 'masterful',
'fascinating', and 'amazing' frequently appear in his descriptions. Banks presents an
insider's view of the big-money, high stakes Texas political atmosphere and suggests
that this tough political arena produces superior politicans worthy of national attention
and office.

248 **The ambition and the power.**
John M. Barry.   New York: Viking, 1989. 768p.

A popularly written account of Jim Wright's years as Speaker of the House of
Representatives. The author claims that he had nearly total access to Wright and
cooperation on both sides of the House aisle, which means his book is loaded with
often irrelevant details and is not particularly objective in its portrayal of Wright.
Barry does provide insights into Wright's driven personality, such as his impatience, his
quest for wealth, and his despair when his personal ethics were challenged. The book is
especially useful in detailing the fall of Wright, but loses its balance when it attacks the
House Ethics Committee investigation. *The Ambition and the Power* is far too long, far
too detailed, and far too biased, but it does contain some important insights and a
wealth of useful information.

249 **Dr. Lawrence A. Nixon and the white primary.**
Conrey Bryson. El Paso, Texas: Texas Western Press, 1974. 96p.
bibliog.

A concise but useful introduction to Lawrence A. Nixon's efforts to end the political
disfranchisement of Texas blacks, particularly the whites-only nominating primaries.
He emphasizes victorious cases taken before the United States Supreme Court that set
legal precedents for black participation in the Texas political system. Bryson also
examines black leaders in both the Republican and, much later, the Democratic
Parties.

250 **A history of the Republican Party in Texas, 1865-1965.**
Paul Casdorph. Austin, Texas: Pemberton Press, 1965. 315p. bibliog.

A scholarly account of the incidents, issues, and personalities associated with the
steady growth of the Republican Party in Texas during the century after the Civil War.
Casdorph places Texas Republicans in the context of national Republicanism,
particularly during Reconstruction and the eras of Theodore Roosevelt and Dwight D.
Eisenhower. He also pays close attention to the party's internal struggles, especially
concerning the issue of race and the battle over whether the black majority or white
minority would control the party during the late 19th and early 20th centuries. An
extensive bibliography, thirty black-and-white illustrations, and an appendix listing
every Texas Republican delegate to national party conventions from 1868-1964 makes
this a useful source for Texas Republican history.

251 **Texas at the crossroads: people, politics, and policy.**
Edited by Anthony Champagne. College Station, Texas: Texas A &
M University Press, 1987. 309p. maps.

The author offers a series of essays that provide a status report on the vital political
issues facing Texas in the late 20th century. Utilizing nearly fifty graphs and tables
providing statistics on demographics, crime, welfare, immigration, ethnicity, voting
patterns, urbanization, natural resources, transportation, prisons, and energy consumption, the essayists provide an overview of the dynamics of the state's population,
industrial development, and political interests, followed by articles on water resources,
energy policy, educational reform, funding higher education, highway policy, crime
and the correctional system, and welfare reform.

252 **Race and class in Texas politics.**
Chandler Davidson. Princeton, New Jersey: Princeton University
Press, 1990. 344p.

Davidson draws on the predictions of political scientist V. O. Key, Jr. a native Texan,
who believed before it was fashionable that Texas would lead the South in establishing
a competitive two-party system as a replacement for the old politics of race and
discrimination. Davidson's analysis of this process shows that the belief that Texas was
controlled by an 'Overwhelming Conservatism' was actually a myth and reveals the
basis for a future liberal coalition in 1940s Texas. He then examines blue-collar and
upper class interests in the state, as well as the issues that eventually led to a liberal
'breakthrough', the rise of right wing Republicanism, and the consummation of Key's
model. A number of tables provide quantitative evidence on voting patterns,
Congressional voting records, and voters' income and occupation.

253 **The life and death of the solid south: a political history.**
Dewey W. Grantham.   Lexington, Kentucky: University Press of
Kentucky, 1988. 257p. maps. bibliog. (New Perspectives on the South).
Describes and analyses the causes of the rise during the late 19th century, the success
during the first half of the 20th century, and the decline during the last three decades of
Democratic Party hegemony and white exclusivity in the American South. Grantham
focuses on the post-Second World War growth of a viable two-party, bi-racial (at least
in the political sense) South. This shrewd examination by a noted historian provides a
useful national context for the factionalization of Texas Democrats along 'liberal' and
'conservative' lines and the corresponding growth of the Republican Party among
Texans.

254 **The establishment in Texas politics.**
George N. Green.   Westport, Connecticut: Greenwood Press, 1979.
306p. bibliog. (Contributions in Political Science).
Green believes that Texas drifted away from traditional southern politics during the
1930s, 1940s, and 1950s, entering a demagogic period characterized by harsh anti-
labour laws, the suppression of academic freedom, segregation, corrupt elections, an
impotent daily press, and the absence of public-service oriented politicians. Obviously
fascinated as well as disapproving, the author highlights scandals, influence peddling,
and the importance of big-money interests in Texas. He argues that the emergence of
the Texas Republican Party as a viable force in the 1950s coincided with the
stabilization and increased effectiveness of Texas politics. Based on wide research in
primary sources, this is an original look at a pivotal time in Texas political history.

255 **Black victory: the rise and fall of the white primary in Texas.**
Darlene Clark Hine.   Millwood, New York: KTO Press, 1979. 266p.
bibliog. (KTO Studies in American History).
This is the story of two decades of legal battles against Texas's whites-only Democratic
primaries. In 1923, Dr. Lawrence Nixon of El Paso was denied the opportunity to vote
because of his race. Four United States Supreme Court cases resulted from his struggle
and the efforts by the NAACP, culminating in 1944, in *Smith v. Allwright* which
overturned the white primary in Texas. Hine details all of the major cases before the
Supreme Court and the questions they raised, and places the efforts to overturn voting
discrimination in the Lone Star State within the contexts of the court's very restricted
interpretation of the 14th and 15th Amendments; the rise of disfranchisement and
white primaries elsewhere in the South; and the evolving nature of NAACP challenges
to discrimination. *Smith v. Allwright* marked a shift in the Supreme Court's role and its
success was an important landmark along the road to *Brown v. Topeka Board of
Education* and other revolutionary Civil Rights decisions of the 1950s and 1960s.

256 **Republicanism in reconstruction Texas.**
Carl H. Moneyhon.   Austin, Texas: University of Texas Press, 1980.
319p. maps. bibliog.
An extremely useful account of the formation and policies of the Texas Republican
Party during the decade after the Civil War. Moneyhon focuses on the personalities
and elections that built the party, and on issues such as black suffrage, support for the
national Republican Party, internal struggles between blacks and whites and between
'Radicals' and moderates for party leadership that ultimately led to the Party's

dwindling power, despite its control of the state government in the late 1860s and early 1870s. This is a thorough, revisionist interpretation of Reconstruction; 'carpetbaggers' did not overrun Texas and Republicans were no more corrupt than Democrats. Seven maps break down the ethnic groups of Texas and reveal voting patterns (against secession, for Republican Governor Edmund J. Davis in 1869 and 1873, and in legislative elections), while appendixes provide names of delegates to the state constitutional conventions of 1866 and 1868-69, and other quantitative information.

257 **The Texas political system.**
Dan Nimmo, William Oden.   Englewood Cliffs, New Jersey: Prentice-Hall, 1971. 166p. maps.

A 'systems analysis' of Texas politics, in which the authors analyse election results, political parties, pressure groups, governor-legislative relations, and geography in order to create a working model of the state political system. They also show how Texas fits into the entire United States political system, arguing that Texas's political impact on the rest of the country is considerable because of its great wealth, resources, and special needs and attitudes. Their findings are fleshed out by three maps that reveal minority distribution in Texas counties, social class rankings of Texas counties, and the distribution of political cultures within the United States (all as of 1960). A number of statistical tables provide information on poverty, ethnicity, interest groups, the number of legislative measures introduced and made into law between 1961-69, and white attitudes on racial integration.

258 **From token to triumph: the Texas Republicans since 1920.**
Roger M. Olien.   Dallas, Texas: Southern Methodist University Press, 1982. 309p. bibliog.

Another history of 20th century Texas Republicans that emphasizes their steady shift from a small party concerned mostly with distributing patronage from the national party and from the Republican administrations of the 1920s to a vibrant and competitive party in the 1980s. Olien downplays the corrupt 'bossism' of the early years and highlights the hard work, shrewd strategy, and grassroots support – including that of women – that lifted the party out of its doldrums in the Eisehower 1950s.

259 **Texas government today: structures, functions, political processes.**
Beryl E. Pettus, Randall Walton Bland.   Homewood, Illinois: Dorsey Press, 1984. 3rd ed. 538p. maps. bibliog.

A survey of Texas government that methodically examines a variety of topics: the Texas State Constitution of 1876; the impact of political parties and ethnic and interest groups on the political system; the operations of the legislature and the governor's office; the criminal justice system; civil liberties; metropolitan and rural problems in an inter-governmental context; local government; public finance; education; transportation; public assistance; state regulations; and the politics of the budgetary process. Eight maps, fifty-seven tables, and nearly thirty charts and graphs provide demographic, revenue, tax, and public policy data.

260 **Party and factional division in Texas.**

James R. Soukup, Clifton McCleskey, Harry Holloway. Austin,
Texas: University of Texas Press, 1964. 221p. maps. bibliog.

A comprehensive examination of fourteen elections (four presidential, seven
gubernatorial, and three US Senate races) between 1946-62. The authors seek the
effects of geography, location, historical tradition, the economy, race and ethnicity,
and urbanization on Texas politics and voting patterns. The maps and statistical tables
showing voting patterns in a number of elections by party, income, geographic
location, ideology, ethnicity, employment, and differences between candidates are
extremely useful. The authors argue that in the 1930s and 1940s a liberal-conservative
rivalry developed in Texas; they conclude that Texas politics was guided during the
next two decades more by that ideological dichotomy than by any other single factor.

261 **Texas in the 1960 presidential election.**

Oliver Weeks. Austin, Texas: University of Texas Press, 1961. 80p.
maps. (Public Affairs Series).

This is a case study of how local and state issues and trends impact on national
elections. The liberal Democratic candidate John F. Kennedy narrowly won Texas (by
less than 25,000 votes) in 1960, although the Republican Dwight D. Eisenhower had
won easily in Texas in 1952 and 1956. In this book, Weeks tells part of the story of
Texas's transition from a one- to a two-party state beginning in the late 1950s. By the
1960s, Texans had begun to reject sectionalism as the primary factor in determining
party loyalty and were moving toward class and interest group politics. In Weeks' view,
sectional issues like race and states' rights were being replaced by industrialization and
urbanization – and their attendant problems – as the primary factors in determining
how Texans voted.

Legal System

262 **The Spanish element in Texas water law.**

Betty Eakle Dobkins. Austin, Texas: University of Texas Press, 1959.
190p. maps. bibliog.

Laws regulating access to and preservation of water resources are vital in a rapidly
developing but semi-arid state like Texas. Dobkins argues for the continuing
importance of Spanish precedents in Texas water law two centuries after the opening
of Texas to white settlement. Spanish law was based on experiences in the arid
portions of Africa and Spain, shaped by an irrigation-centered agriculture, and
organized around a community based society. It played down property rights and
relied on a central administration, and depended on an attitude that did not take
plentiful water resources for granted or make water policy a by-product of land law. As
a historian hoping to shape future policy, the author urges Texans to realize that water
is not abundant and must be wisely used; individualism and ownership must become
less important than a just resolution of conflicts and wise administration of limited
resources.

263 **Death row.**
   Bruce Jackson, Diane Christian.   Boston, Massachusetts: Beacon
   Press, 1980. 292p.

This emotional and depressing book includes lengthy extracts from sixty hours of taped interviews with and a few letters from twenty-six of the 105 men waiting to be executed at Huntsville Prison, Texas, in April 1979. Jackson and Christian virtually ignore the legal issues involved in specific cases or in the death penalty in general, choosing instead to focus on the 'community' of prisoners on death row: how they endure the waiting, occupy their time, get along with one another, and their view of the world. Chapters discuss the prisoners' transition to the limbo of death row, religion, and their relationships with their families. Stark photographs of the inmates and the cell complex in which they live complement the text.

264 **The power vested: the use of martial law and the National Guard in
   Texas domestic crises, 1919-1932.**
   Harry Krenek.   Austin, Texas: Presidial Press, 1980. 181p.

Between 1919-32, the Texas National Guard was invested with powers normally reserved for the famous (and infamous) Texas Rangers, who had earned a reputation for abusing their power during the early 20th century. As a result, when local labour or racial disputes escalated beyond what was in the power of local officials to control, National Guard units were sent in to re-establish order. During the thirteen years after the First World War, the guard intervened in Galveston, Denison, Mexia, Borger, and in the East Texas oil fields; Krenek provides detailed accounts of these incidents. In 1932, the Rangers were once again made responsible for such affairs and the Guard continued its traditional work of providing relief during natural disasters and as a means of last resort in controlling crowds.

265 **Houston police: 1878-1948.**
   Louis Marchiafava.   Houston, Texas: Rice University, 1977. 119p.
   bibliog.

Published in volume 63 of Rice University Studies, this is a study of the professionalization of the Houston police force after it replaced the city marshall system of law enforcement. By 1895 Houston had twenty-four policemen. Houston's growth obviously impacted seriously on its police force, and Marchiafava examines the expansion of the duties of policemen to include social and community services, the addition of women (as matrons in the city jail) to the force in 1900, and the establishment of professional organizations and labour unions among policemen. This is a useful narrative of the formative years of an important law enforcement institution in Texas.

266 **Texas prisons: the walls came tumbling down.**
   Steve J. Martin, Sheldon Ekland-Olson.   Austin, Texas: Texas
   Monthly Press, 1987. 289p. map.

The state of Texas operates twenty-seven prisons and processes over thirty-thousand new inmates annually. This is an examination of the Texas Department of Corrections's largely autonomous status prior to the 1980s, when reformers began chipping away at the problems of overcrowding, mentally retarded inmates, and secret and often corrupt business practices. The authors place the reforms in the context of the prisoners' rights movement, which was itself an outgrowth of the 1960s civil rights movement, as well as the growing activism and policy-making of courts in regard to the administration of the system. *Ruiz v. Estelle* was the central court case in Texas prison reform; it made its slow way through the courts from 1972-85. Martin and Ekland-Olson provide a history of that case, examine the conditions it attacked, and discuss the reforms that it mandated.

267 **Gunpowder justice: a reassessment of the Texas Rangers.**
Julian Samora, Joe Bermal, Albert Pena. Notre Dame, Indiana: University of Notre Dame Press, 1979. 179p. bibliog.

A revisionist work highly critical of one of the state's best-known institutions – the Texas Rangers, the only state-operated law enforcement agency of its kind. The authors focus on the 20th century in detailing a litany of Ranger mistreatment of Mexican-Americans, which has ranged from harassment to brutality to false arrests and imprisonment, often during political campaigns or labour disputes. A useful, if not necessarily balanced corrective to popular myths about this unique institution. The authors base their conclusions on traditional historical sources such as government reports and newspapers, but also on interviews (although only two informants were actually Rangers).

268 **Texas high sheriffs.**
Thad Sitton. Austin, Texas: Texas Monthly Press, 1988. 279p. bibliog.

A collection of interviews with eleven rural Texas sheriffs. Sitton has not altered these reminiscences and his introduction highlights their benevolence, hard-work, and community stature. The result is a rather unbalanced and entirely favourable view of local law enforcers. The sheriffs' accounts emphasize their adventures and the crimes they have solved; they also complain that modern regulations, legal restrictions, and court oversights of the criminal justice system limit their effectiveness to enforce the law.

269 **Roy Bean: law west of the Pecos.**
C. L. Sonnichsen. New York: Macmillan, 1943. 207p. bibliog.

A colourful account of Sam 'Roy' Bean (ca. 1830-1903), a Kentuckian who, after adventures during the California Gold Rush and as a Confederate partisan in New Mexico during the Civil War, landed in San Antonio in 1866. After gaining and losing several fortunes and getting into legal troubles, he relocated to the country beyond the Pecos River in West Texas, where he opened a saloon and became justice of the peace at the tiny town of Vinegaroon (Bean later renamed the town Langtry, after the English actress Lily Langtry). Much of this biography describes his unusual career on the bench; he held court in a room adjoining the saloon and, with no formal legal training, dispensed pragmatic and eccentric justice.

270 **Penalogy for profit: a history of the Texas prison system, 1867-1912.**
Donald R. Walker. College Station, Texas: Texas A & M University Press, 1988. 216p. bibliog. (Texas A & M Southwestern Studies).

The author shows that as the Texas prison population swelled between the end of the Civil War and the beginning of the First World War, state policy-makers insisted that the prison system make a profit. As a result, in the late 1860s they began leasing convict labourers to railroads, a practice commonly used throughout the South.

Despite evidence that they were treated harshly by their supervisors, the government continued leasing prisoners simply because it was profitable. Sugar cane growers, mining companies, levee construction contractors, and lumber companies all benefited from the policy. By the 1890s, Populists began demanding an end to the convict labour system, and after the turn of the century, Progressives continued the campaign. Led by George W. Briggs, a San Antonio journalist, the campaign to stop convict labour succeeded in 1912. Walker provides a dozen rare photographs of convict labourers, and a number of tables detailing the age, crimes, and race of Texas prisoners throughout the period.

271　**The Texas Rangers: a century of frontier defense.**
Walter Prescott Webb.　Boston, Massachusetts: Houghton Mifflin, 1935. 583p. bibliog.

A popular but out-dated study of the Texas Rangers, from their years as rather irregular units fighting Mexicans and Indians in the 1830s and 1840s to their incorporation as a formal part of the Texas law enforcement system. They enforced prohibition, fought Mexican bandits, and searched for German spies during the First World War. Webb clearly admires the Rangers, and emphasizes their heroism and hard-fighting determination; he ignores their use as storm troopers against Mexicans and their frequent abuse of the wide-ranging powers granted to them. Nevertheless, this provides a comprehensive history of the first century of the Ranger organization, with entertaining anecdotes and useful biographies of leading Rangers.

Ethnic Groups

Native Americans

272 **Indians of the upper Texas coast.**
Lawrence Aten. New York: Academic Press, 1983. 370p. maps.
bibliog. (New World Archaeological Record).

A highly technical archaeological study of the indigenous peoples along portions of the Texas coast. Aten has attempted to reconstruct the demographic and social characteristics and the material culture of ancient tribes like the Akokisa, Bidai, and Atakapa, with emphasis on the effects of the region's topography, climate, and geology on the Indians. He has fashioned chronologies of these groups long before white contact and has dated artifacts found at a number of places. Most of his research took place at four modern-day sites: the Wallisville Reservoir, the Trinity River Delta, the Harris County Boys School, and near Galveston Bay. Dozens of maps, a number of black-and-white photographs of artifacts, and a variety of charts and graphs add to the analysis of the author's field work.

273 **The Indians of Texas in 1830.**
Jean Louis Berlandier, edited by John C. Evers, translated by Patricia Reading Leclerq. Washington, DC: Smithsonian Institution Press, 1969. 209p. maps. bibliog.

Jean Louis Berlandier was a French biologist commissioned by the Mexican government to accompany a military expedition into Texas from 1827-29. He collected data on the geography, soil, minerals, plant life, and animals of Texas, as well as on the customs and dispositions of the Indians of southern, central, and eastern Texas. Many of the specimens and artifacts that Berlandier collected are now in the Smithsonian Institution in Washington. The informative text is objective, thorough, and scientific, at least by early 19th century standards, and is accompanied by over 50 illustrations of Indian life and artifacts and various sites in Texas, and by 2 maps showing the Frenchman's travels and the locations of Indian tribes in Texas.

274 **The Hasinais: southern Caddoans as seen by the earliest Europeans.**
Herbert Bolton, edited by Russell M. Magnaghi. Norman,
Oklahoma: University of Oklahoma Press, 1987. 194p. map. bibliog.
(Civilization of the American Indian).

This is the edited text of a work that Bolton, one of the ground-breaking 'borderlands' historians, never published. Magnaghi up-dated the bibliography and clarified the footnotes and the conclusions are Bolton's. Bolton provides an historical narrative of this east Texas tribe, members of the Caddaon linguistic group who built an advanced society in what are now Cherokee and Houston Counties. Chapters are devoted to social life, tribal politics and economy, material culture, religion, and ways of waging war. Bolton demonstrates the importance of Spanish documents in researching the ethnology of borderlands Indians.

275 **Kiowa voices.**
Maurice Boyd. Fort Worth, Texas: Texas Christian University Press,
1981. 2 vols. maps. bibliog.

In 1975 Kiowa leaders formed the Kiowa Historical and Research Society to record and preserve the tribe's cultural traditions. Volume one, 'Ceremonial Dance, Ritual, and Song', provides the history and text (and some of the music) for songs and dances such as the Sun, Buffalo, Scalp, Black Legs, Feather, and Rabbit Dances as well as songs dealing with Christianity, peyote, and the wind. Volume two, 'Myths, Legends, and Folktales', provides tribal oral traditions regarding topics such as life and death, time, horse-buffalo culture, courtship and marriage, migration to the southern plains, and warfare. Sources include written documents, oral interviews, and tapes of Kiowa ceremonies and songs. Nearly 450 illustrations (paintings, diagrams, photographs) help to make this massive work a valuable reference tool.

276 **Comanche texts.**
Elliott Canonge. Norman, Oklahoma: Summer Institute of Linguistics
of the University of Oklahoma, 1958. 156p.

A sampling of some of the most important genres of Comanche stories and fables, taken from recordings of elderly Comanche women living in Oklahoma in the early 1950s. The categories are coyote stories, in which the coyote is presented as sly, shiftless, and untrustworthy; fables and fairy tales, morality tales that show relationships between Comanches and animals; adventure stories, in which brave Comanches defeat enemies such as the Osage; and tales about hunting and preparing food. The texts are printed in Comanche as well as English, and are accompanied by a twenty-five page vocabulary of Comanche words and more than forty illustrations.

277 **Chief Bowles and the Texas Cherokees.**
Mary Whatley Clarke. Norman, Oklahoma: University of Oklahoma
Press, 1971. 143p. maps. bibliog. (The Civilization of the American
Indian).

An even-handed narrative with many illustrations of the life of 'The Bowl', Di wa'li, or Chief Bowles (ca. 1756-1839), the leader of a band of Cherokees who migrated to East Texas from the southeastern United States in 1819. After Bowles and his group cooperated with the Mexican government in putting down an Anglo rebellion in the 1820s, they were never trusted by their white neighbours. In 1839, the Texas Senate rejected a proposed treaty and President Mirabeau Lamar demanded the Cherokees' expulsion. A brief war broke out and Bowles was killed at the Battle of the Neches; his followers were driven by the Texans into Indian Territory (Oklahoma).

278 **Mythology of the Wichita.**
George A. Dorsey. Washington, DC: Carnegie Institution, 1904. 351p.

Still an important source, this collection of sixty Wichita stories were gathered in 1903. A brief introduction to the history and culture of the Wichita (another Caddoan group) precedes the stories, which are divided into three categories: the creation story, transformation stories (60 per cent of the book), and stories from the late 19th century. The stories are clearly re-told, with no linguistic or folklore theory attached to them.

279 **Traditions of the Caddo.**
George A. Dorsey. Washington, DC: Carnegie Institution, 1905; New York: AMS Press, 1976. 136p.

This is a re-telling of seventy stories collected by the author between 1903 and 1905 dealing with the Caddoan religious system, folk culture, and ceremonial organization. The Caddos were originally an agricultural tribe living on the lower Red River in Louisiana who were pushed into Texas by white settlers and adopted the plains Indians' buffalo hunting lifestyle. These tales include creation myths; the origins of night and day, and of various animals, stars, lightning, and the moon; and the mischievous coyote, who had been banished from the Caddo shortly after creation and frequently caused trouble. Abstracts of the tales appear at the end of the book.

280 **The Texas Cherokees: a people between two fires, 1819-1840.**
Dianna Everett. Norman, Oklahoma: University of Oklahoma Press, 1990. 173p. bibliog. (The Civilization of the American Indian).

The 'fires' in the title refer to a series of tensions within the Texas Cherokees: between their ideals of tribal harmony and the reality of factionalism; between following ancient traditions and accomodation to whites; and between white pressure on the Cherokees to move west from the southeastern United States and the resistance they met from western tribes. The Cherokees are portrayed as a people trying to protect their political and moral self-determination, in spite of larger processes and developments beyond their control. Everett devotes separate chapters to their removal to Texas and their acquiescence to white demands (1828-35), their neutrality during the Texas revolution (1836-38), and the last Cherokee war in Texas and the tribe's final removal to Indian Territory (1839-40).

281 **Comanches: the destruction of a people.**
T. R. Fehrenbach. New York: Alfred A. Knopf, 1974. 557p. maps. bibliog.

Fehrenbach provides a broad survey of the Comanches, or Nermernuh – 'True People' – from pre-Columbian times through the 19th century. He describes Spanish-Comanche contact, which marked the introduction of the horse to the plains Indians (and gained the Comanches their reputation as the plains' greatest horsemen). The second half of the book concentrates on their relationship with Anglo-Texans, emphasizing military conflict and the gradually tightening circle of negotiations that resulted in the Comanches' exile to reservations by 1875. Sympathetic to the

Comanches, Fehrenbach casts a rather negative light on the Texas Rangers. Nearly forty photographs and lithographs enhance the narrative.

282　The Kickapoos: lords of the middle border.
Arrell M. Gibson.　Norman, Oklahoma: University of Oklahoma Press, 1963. 391p. map. bibliog. (Civilization of the American Indian).

First encountered by whites in the Great Lakes region, the Kickapoo (who belong to the Algonquian linguistic group) eventually migrated to such diverse places as Wisconsin, Illinois, Indiana, Ohio, Michigan, New York, Pennsylvania, Iowa, Missouri, Kansas, Oklahoma, New Mexico, and Texas. Gibson portrays them as independent, ruthless, opportunistic, and not a popular tribe among other Indians. They also stubbornly resisted encroachments by French, British, and Americans and refused to accept reservation life or to assimilate into white culture until the 20th century. The Kickapoo began arriving in Texas around 1804; the emergence of an independent Texas ended a generation of peace and conflict between them and white Texans lasted until 1880. They often raided Texan ranches from refuges in Mexico and in 1865 they actually defeated Texas forces at the battle of Dove Creek. This is not an ethnology of the Kickapoo, but a history of their movements and warfare from the 17th century into the 20th.

283　United States-Comanche relations: the reservation years.
William T. Hagan.　New Haven, Connecticut: Yale University Press, 1976. 336p. maps. bibliog. (Yale Western Americana Series).

A straightforward historical narrative of Comanche-white relations from the initial treaties between the plains tribes and the Federal government in the 1860s to the Comanches' reservation experiences and the land allotment programme after the turn of the century. Hagan focuses on the formation of policy in Washington, the execution of that policy, and its impact on Comanche culture and existence. Two important elements of the book are its analyses of the contradictory goals and motivations of policy makers and lobbyists – sympathetic reformers, pragmatic Congressmen, expansionist cattlemen, and railroad developers – and of the relationships among government officials, Indian agents, and the Comanche themselves.

284　The Comanches: lords of the south plains.
E. Adamson Hoebel, Ernest Wallace.　Norman, Oklahoma: University of Oklahoma Press, 1952. 381p. map. bibliog.

Drawing on both anthropological and historical sources, this is an ethnohistory of the Comanche from Spanish times to the 20th century. The authors examine Comanche culture, political and tribal structures, warfare, the importance of horses and buffalo to their culture and economy, the gender-based division of labour, material culture, and the impact of the tribe's relationship with whites including treaties, warfare, and reservation life at the turn of the 20th century.

285　Tonkawa texts.
Harry Hoijer.　Berkeley, California: University of California, 1972. 106p. (University of California Publications in Linguistics).

A collection of twenty-seven Tonkawa stories is presented here in Tonkawa and in English, as told by John Rush Buffalo to the author between 1928 and 1931. There are two categories of stories. 'Night Stories', which describe the time before humans existed, when birds and animals roamed the earth and spoke like men, feature the coyote, a divinity who owns all the animals on which the Tonkawas depend for food. Most of these stories are about the coyote's relationship with other animals. The other category comprises 'Old Stories', adventures that took place in the distant past. They are often tales of Tonkawas interacting with animals or meeting natural and man-made challenges.

286   **Kickapoo tales.**
William Jones.   Leyden, Netherlands: E. J. Brill, 1915; New York: AMS Press, 1974. 143p. bibliog. (Publication of the American Ethnological Society).

A collection of eleven Kickapoo tales, presented in both English and Kickapoo and divided into three categories: culture hero tales, animal tales, and miscellaneous tales (which deal with supernatural, moral, and family issues). The author collected the tales in 1903. This volume also includes linguistic material; Jones concludes that both woodland and plains Indian elements, and even a few European elements can be found in Kickapoo mythology.

287   **Culture complexes and chronology in northern Texas: with extension of Puebloan datings to the Mississippi Valley.**
Alex D. Krieger.   Austin, Texas: University of Texas Press, 1946. 366p. map. bibliog.

A report linking southeastern and southwestern archaeological discoveries, dating the cultural factors and artifacts found at a number of excavations, and seeking to place Puebloan cultures farther east than they have previously been thought to have existed. Krieger divides the book into sections on the Panhandle and western plains, north central Texas, and northeast Texas, and includes a section on similarities and relationships between Puebloan and Caddoan cultures. This is a highly technical and extremely scholarly look at Puebloan agricultural and trade economies during the prehistoric and early historical periods. Fifty illustrations of artifacts and an eighty-page bibliography make this an important source for early Indian life in Texas.

288   **The Mexican Kickapoo Indians.**
Felipe A. Latorre, Dolores L. Latorre.   Austin, Texas: University of Texas Press, 1976. 401p. map. bibliog.

Although the Kickapoo no longer live in Texas (this anthropological study examines the Coahuila Kickapoos living in the Mexican village of El Nacimiento) the Kickapoo played an important role in 19th century Texas. While their history and migrations from Wisconsin to Mexico have been well-chronicled, this is the first ethnographic survey of these Indians. The Kickapoo have retained a strong tribal identity; the Latorres devote most of their book to the Kickapoos' contemporary culture and lifestyle, with chapters devoted to habitations, language, food, dress and personal care, political and legal organizations, life cycles, the passing of knowledge from generation to generation, rituals, religion, and magic. Two dozen photographs of Kickapoo life, tables showing land holdings, membership in tribal clans and alcohol consumption, and a glossary of Kickapoo terms further enhance this book.

289   Kiowa years: a study in culture impact.
      Alice Marriott.   New York: Macmillan, 1968. 173p. map. bibliog.

This is a slightly eccentric look at some aspects of Kiowa culture. Part one is based on
a tale told to the author by an aged Kiowa in 1935. It is the true story of the leader of a
Kiowa band who in the late 1860s and early 1870s led raids against white Texans, who
was eventually captured and killed by soldiers. The story demonstrates aspects of
Kiowa culture such as preparations for war and buffalo hunting, and the importance of
rituals like the Sun and Gourd Dances. Part two examines modern gourd dancers,
while part three discusses other aspects of traditional Kiowa life, such as work,
building shelter, the importance of the buffalo, and religious beliefs. The author
discusses the important impact on Kiowa culture of reservation life and contact with
whites.

290   The Kiowas.
      Mildred P. Mayhall.   Norman, Oklahoma: University of Oklahoma
      Press, 1962. 364p. map. bibliog. (Civilization of the American Indian).

An ethnohistory of the Kiowa from pre-Columbian times to the present. Mayhall
focuses on Kiowa relationships with other southern plains tribes like the Apache,
Osage and Comanche; with the Spanish; and with Anglo-Americans, including battles
as well as treaties. In addition to examining Kiowa culture before the invasion of
Europeans, the author also discusses changes to Kiowa ways after they came into
contact with the dominant Anglo-American culture. Along the way, she describes the
hide calendars on which the Kiowas noted significant events. The book ends with a
discussion of Kiowa acculturation, beginning at the end of the 19th century, and of
current efforts by the Kiowa to keep their culture alive.

291   Calendar history of the Kiowa Indians.
      James Mooney.   Washington, DC: Smithsonian Institution Press,
      1979. 331p. map. bibliog.

This book is a facsimile edition of the 1898 publication. The book contains 186
pictographs taken from Kiowa calendars that denote battles, deaths of prominent men,
treaties, and other significant events in Kiowa history. The author examines the
calendars from ethnological, sociological, and historical points of view, and discusses
Kiowa relations with white men and with other tribes of Native Americans.

292   The Indians of Texas: from prehistoric to modern times.
      W. W. Newcomb, Jr.   Austin, Texas: University of Texas Press, 1961.
      404p. maps. bibliog.

Newcomb, an anthropologist, offers a useful starting point for the study of Texas
Indians. Indian scholars in Texas have to face the problem that virtually all of the
Native American groups associated with Texas disappeared many years ago – some
even before Anglo-Americans entered the area. Newcomb attempts a comprehensive
look at the Indians of Texas; his synthesis embraces history, linguistics, and
archaeology. He successfully resists the temptation to concentrate on the Comanche,
who are perhaps the best-known Indian tribe of Texas. The author admits that value
judgements enter into his analysis; each chapter is devoted to a different tribe, ranked
in ascending order of technological productivity.

293 The rock art of Texas Indians.
W. W. Newcomb, Jr.   Austin, Texas: University of Texas Press, 1967.
239p. maps. bibliog.

An ethnological survey of the traditions, locations, and subject matter of Texas Indian rock artists from prehistoric as well as historic times. Newcomb, who organizes his analysis by geographic areas, explains that most Texas tribes did not have well-established rock art traditions; the exceptions lived in the Hueca Tanks and Pecos River areas. His analysis is based on 161 paintings of rock art executed by the artist Forrest Kirkland in the 1930s. The author has also included over forty black-and-white photographs of the sites, seven maps of the different regions covered in the book (with the sites designated), and comparisons to rock art in western Europe, Africa, South America, and Australia.

294 Hasinai: a traditional history of the Caddo confederacy.
Vynola Beaver Newkumet.   College Station, Texas: Texas A & M
University Press, 1988. 144p. bibliog.

Newkumet examines the history of three sub-confederacies which made up the Caddo nation, based chiefly on oral history and on analyses of the most important ritual dances of the Caddo (Hasinai is the Indian term for Caddo). Newkumet focuses on the functions of each dance: for instance, the drum dance helps to explain the origins of the Hasinai, the bear dance ensured good hunting, and the corn dance helped produce a plentiful corn crop. Other examples include the women's dance (which dealt with family relationships), the Cherokee dance (health), and the turkey dance (history). The book also provides information on Hasinai clothing, housing, relationships with other southwestern tribes, dialects, and their efforts under the Indian New Deal during the 1930s to revitalize their tribal government. Thirty-five black-and-white photographs from the 19th and 20th centuries illustrate scenes from Caddo ceremonies and daily life.

295 Bad medicine and good: tales of the Kiowas.
Wilbur S. Nye.   Norman, Oklahoma: University of Oklahoma Press,
1969. 291p. maps. bibliog.

A collection of over forty 18th and 19th century Kiowa tales collected by the author during the 1930s. Some deal with famous warriors, warrior societies, and battles and raids against Comanche, Mexicans, and other enemies, while others deal with Kiowa religious beliefs (hence the title), and still others describe customs involving eagles, the ceremonial use of eagle feathers, and the importance of the buffalo to the Kiowa. Unencumbered with scholarly apparatus, this is a very straightforward presentation of some of the Kiowa's most important oral and cultural traditions.

296 Indians of the Rio Grande delta: their role in the history of southern
Texas and northeastern Mexico.
Martin Salinas.   Austin, Texas: University of Texas Press, 1990. 193p.
maps. bibliog. (Texas Archeology and Ethnohistory Series).

The author attempts to relieve the prevailing confusion over the ethnicity and names of the various Indians who lived in the Rio Grande Delta and to create a chronological history of the groups native to this area, as well as those displaced groups who relocated to the Delta. Salinas examines variations in environment, population density, and language as ways of determining cultural differences, and tries to connect specific tribal groups to specific Spanish missions. He finds that at least forty-nine Indian groups lived in the area before 1800, and concludes that the documentary and archaeological evidence is still too scattered to conclusively identify linguistic groups and many cultural characteristics. Although it provides much useful information – however tentative – this is a very technical and often dry piece of work.

297 **Indian life in Texas.**
Charles Shaw, foreword by James A. Michener.   Austin, Texas: State House Press, 1987. 203p. bibliog.

A wide-ranging book intended for the general audience. Although the text is derivative and sometimes misleading, the strength of this book comes from Shaw's pen-and-ink drawings of Indian customs, material culture, and lifestyles. The book is divided into four sections: prehistory, 1600-1836, 1837-1900, and the 20th century. The final section is illustrated with a photographic essay by Reagan Bradshaw of contemporary Texas Indians.

298 **Source material on the history and ethnology of the Caddo Indians.**
John Reed Swanton.   Washington, DC: Government Printing Office, 1942. 332p. maps. bibliog.

A description of all aspects of Caddo culture in Louisiana, Arkansas, and East Texas since the beginning of contact with whites. The author depends primarily on the diaries and journals of Spanish explorers and missionaries, Anglo settlers and military officers, and letters and reports from the Bureau of Indian Affairs of the United States government. The topics include population; origin legends; history; physical, mental and moral characteristics; material culture (food, clothing and personal adornment, dwellings, and crafts); social rituals and functions (birth, child-rearing, marriage, division of labour based on gender, clan and government structure, ceremonies, punishments, war, trade, burial); and religious and medical beliefs and ceremonies. Twenty-nine black-and-white photographs from the late 19th century show Caddos and some of their artifacts, while the appendix contains three documents relating to the Caddos written by Spanish officials in the 18th century.

299 **Columbian consequences: archeological and historical perspectives on the Spanish borderlands west.**
Edited by David Hurst Thomas.   Washington, DC: Smithsonian Institution Press, 1989. 503p. maps. bibliog.

The editor of this volume of thirty essays declares that the book will look at the cultures of the Southwest from a 'cubist' perspective through interdisciplinary and multi-dimensional analyses that attempt to show how Europeans and Indians interacted with and affected each other. The issues covered in the essays include health, economy, art, and material culture. The authors are geologists, historians, archaeologists, and, mostly, anthropologists whose writing is often quite technical and of varying accessibility. Papers that deal specifically with Texas examine the material culture of mission Indians and other elements of the relationships between Native Americans and the Spanish at the missions; another essay studies the rock art of the central Rio Grande region. Twenty-two maps and a number of charts on health and economic matters help flesh out the articles.

300 **Indian tribes of Texas.**
   Dorman H. Winfrey, (et al). Waco, Texas: Texian Press, 1971. 178p.

An attempt to remedy the slighting of Texas Native American groups, who have not received the attention they deserved because some are extinct, others were pushed out of Texas, and still others have combined or been incorporated into Mexican or Anglo-American culture and languages. As a result, little is known about the diverse tribes of Texas. The eight chapters, each by a different historian, examine the Alabama-Coushatta, Caddo, Comanche, Karankawa, Kiowa, Lipan Apache, Tonkawa, and the Wichita. The authors describe the culture and history of each tribe and the ways each reacted to contact with other tribes and with Europeans. They also compare them to more well-known tribes with similar customs and stress their unique characteristics. Among the topics covered for each group are daily life, government, crops, warfare, and how each has been depicted in and been affected by Texan and American history.

Mexican-Americans

301 **Race and class in the southwest: a theory of racial inequality.**
   Mario Barrera. Notre Dame, Indiana: University of Notre Dame
   Press, 1978. 261p. bibliog.

Blending history with social science theory and methods, the author describes the development of the unequal position of Chicanos in the Southwest. Current conditions are placed in their historical contexts: in the 19th century, economic motives sparked American expansion into Mexican territory and displacement from the land shaped subsequent Chicano employment patterns and immigration. Urbanization created Mexican-American communities in Anglo cities and helped to create a small Chicano middle-class. Fluctuations in the United States and Mexican economies have seriously affected Chicano employment. The author favours a Marxist structuralist model to illustrate the role of the state in class conflict and he uses one American corporation, International Harvester, as an example of the employment practices and economic decision-making that continue to exacerbate the problem. Forty statistical tables and graphs provide information on population, employment, and the class structures of minorities in the Southwest.

302 **Cuanderismo: Mexican-American Folk Healing.**
   Juan Antonio Chavira, Robert T. Trotter II. Athens, Georgia:
   University of Georgia Press, 1981. 204p. bibliog.

The authors call this an 'ethnography of healing theories and practices' among Mexican-Americans. Approaching their subject as anthropologists doing field work, Chavira and Trotter observed folk-healers who actually practiced their craft full time (seeing at least five patients a day); most of their research was done in the Rio Grande Valley counties of Hidalgo, Cameron, and Willacy. After examining the history, cultural context, theories, rituals, and spiritual and mental elements of the healing process, they argue that cultural and community factors and norms are at least as important to these people as scientific factors, despite increased access to modern medical facilities. A glossary of medical and Spanish terms is also included.

303 **Equality of opportunity for Latin-Americans in Texas.**
Everett R. Clinchy. New York: Arno Press, 1974. 221p. bibliog.
(Mexican-American Series).

In this 1954 political science dissertation from Columbia University, Clinchy studies the social, economic, and educational discrimination against Latin-Americans in Texas and places it in the context of similar situations in other states. Although the book is obviously dated (it was written before the Civil Rights movement of the 1950s and 1960s) it does provide a useful analysis of post-Second World War efforts to ease discrimination against Hispanics. The impetus came with the agricultural labour shortage of the early 1940s, when the Mexican government refused to allow workers to migrate to Texas because of widespread discrimination. The 'Good Neighbor Commission' established a state agency to eliminate the problem and created an educational programme as well. Although these were pioneering attempts to deal with racial discrimination in Texas, their effects were limited, especially in terms of economic issues.

304 **Chicano workers and the politics of fairness: the FEPC in the southwest, 1941-1945.**
Clete Daniel. Austin, Texas: University of Texas Press, 1991. 237p. bibliog.

Daniel examines efforts by President Franklin D. Roosevelt's Fair Employment Practices Commission to break down racial and ethnic barriers in southwestern workplaces, especially in defence industries, during the Second World War. The Chicano community in the Southwest was divided into at least four groups: labourers, intellectuals, the middle class, and businessmen. Since they were unable to form a political solidarity based on their common ethnic identity, they were less successful than blacks in overcoming workplace discrimination. More importantly, the Hispanic community was dominated by the 'Immigrant Generation', who looked at life in the United States as a transitory experience; they refused to enter mainstream American life, retained their Mexican citizenship, and were not motivated to participate in labour or civil rights movements. Although they gained only minor victories, the efforts of Chicano workers during the Second World War set the stage for later civil rights activities, encouraged the eventual assimilation of many Mexican-Americans, began the training process for American-born Hispanic leaders in the post-war Chicano movement, and led the way toward a stronger sense of ethnic solidarity in coming years.

305 **Ethnicity in the sunbelt: a history of Mexican Americans in Houston.**
Arnoldo De León. Houston, Texas: Mexican American Studies/ University of Houston, 1989. 255p. maps. bibliog.

A study of the evolution of the Houston *barrio* by the leading historian of Mexican-Texans. De León divides his work into three parts. Part one describes the political and cultural elements of the Mexican community in Houston before large numbers of immigrants began arriving in the 1920s. Part two, which covers the 1930s through to the 1960s, examines assimilation and growth, accommodation and protest among the Mexican-Americans in Houston. Finally, part three details the continuing immigration from Mexico and other parts of Latin America, the increasing pluralism within the Hispanic community, and the Chicano movement of the 1960s and 1970s.

306 *San Angeleños*: **Mexican-Americans in San Angelo, Texas.**
Arnoldo De León.   San Angelo, Texas: Fort Concho Museum Press,
1985. 173p. bibliog.

In this history of Mexican-Americans in a moderate-sized West Texas city, De León applies the larger themes of his other books to a town with the same ethnic ratio as the state of Texas. Although this is not a deeply researched book, it is rooted in the local primary sources of San Angelo, a city of 73,000 people, 25 per cent of whom are Hispanic. De León stresses ethnic identity and culture, and political and community activism, and argues that there has been much assimilation into Anglo-American society, but that there has also been significant continuity. In addition, he argues that, as in the region as a whole, there has been a great deal of cultural amalgamation between the races.

307 *Tejanos* **and the numbers game: a socio-historical interpretation from the federal censuses, 1850-1900.**
Arnoldo De León, Kenneth L. Stewart.   Albuquerque, New Mexico:
University of New Mexico Press, 1984. 119p. maps. bibliog.

A very useful source of basic information on Mexican-Texans gleaned from a close analysis of the United States manuscript census schedules for the last half of the 19th century. Individual chapters deal with the historiography of Mexican-American culture, Hispanic immigration to Texas, economic issues, family life, and rural-urban contrasts. The text – complemented by twenty-five tables and two maps – examines such issues as segregation, education, employment, household composition, marital patterns, wealth, and residence patterns.

308 **The *Tejano* community, 1836-1900.**
Arnoldo De León.   Alburquerque, New Mexico: University of New
Mexico Press, 1982. 277p. map. bibliog.

An excellent study of the ways that *Tejanos* 'took environmental, social, economic, and political circumstances . . . and developed a bicultural identity that equipped them to resist oppression'. De León takes a topical look at this dual identity of Mexican-Americans living in Texas during the 19th century, with chapters devoted to politics, rural and urban contexts, daily life, religion, folklore, and entertainment. The story is one of interaction as well as conflict between Anglos and *Tejanos*; the theme is how the latter formed a distinctive culture amid poverty and oppression. Amplifying his arguments are twenty tables on education, wealthholding, employment, and political participation.

309 **They called them greasers: Anglo attitudes toward Mexican-Americans in Texas, 1821-1900.**
Arnoldo De León.   Austin, Texas: University of Texas Press, 1983.
153p. map. bibliog.

A brief but important study of the institutionalization of attitudes that came to dominate the cultural, religious, and political perceptions of *Tejanos* by Anglos and the interactions between races. De León takes a chronological approach within topical chapters; he argues that racism, not merely cultural chauvinism, was the source of discrimination that ranged from racist jokes to overt violence throughout the 19th century. This is a detailed, objective, but powerful examination of one side of the unhappy and ancient conflict between these two races and cultures in Texas.

310 **The future is *mestizo*: life where cultures meet.**
Virgilio P. Elizondo. Bloomington, Indiana: Meyer-Stone Books, 1988. 111p.

This is a Hispanic theologian's plea to create a new culture based on religious concerns and biblical examples out of the different and often conflicting cultures of the Southwest. Much of the book is autobiographical; both of the authors' parents were Mexican immigrants to San Antonio's west side who eventually owned their own grocery store. His odyssey from San Antonio's *barrio* to his role as a priest at the cathedral in which his parents married, and as a professor of theology, is the story of encountering new cultures (San Antonio's German-Catholic schools, a Catholic seminary, and France, where he received his doctorate). His own life has convinced him that Anglos and Hispanics are forming a new culture in the Southwest, one that stresses diversity and possibilities, rather than differences and stereotypes.

311 **The Mexican-American border region: issues and trends.**
Raul A. Fernandez. Notre Dame, Indiana: University of Notre Dame Press, 1989. 147p. maps.

This synthesis of published sources is a good introduction to United States-Mexican border history. The author methodically sets up contrasts within the border region in his first chapter, then devotes separate chapters to the history of water use, the long history of frequently illegal migration (mainly from south to north), the Rio Grande, and the more recent industrialization of the border region. Fernandez's final chapter is more suggestive than historical in its attempt to predict the future of economic policies and growth in the area.

312 **The United States-Mexico Border: a politico-economic profile.**
Raul A. Fernandez. Notre Dame, Indiana: University of Notre Dame Press, 1977. 174p. map.

A predecessor to Fernandez's previously mentioned work, this provides an historical context for what the author sees as a great deal of cultural and geographic unity on both sides of the Rio Grande. Yet economic progress has not proceeded in a rational manner because the United States has developed into a rich country whilst Mexico has remained underdeveloped and relatively poor. The result, maintains Fernandez, is that profits – due in large measure to the pool of cheap labour crossing into the United States from Mexico – keep the United States from seeking to initiate change, while poverty and political corruption prevents Mexico from initiating change.

313 **From *peones* to *politicos*: class and ethnicity in a south Texas town, 1900-1987.**
Douglas E. Foley. Austin, Texas: University of Texas Press, 1988. 2nd ed. 318p. (Mexican-American Monograph Series).

An anthropological and historical study of the ways that the 6,000 Anglo and Mexican-American residents of one town in the South Texas vegetable-producing region have dealt with racism and economic inequality since 1900. Topics such as labour organizations, management, race relations, and cultural and political institutions are traced through three historical eras: the Anglo-dominated period of 1900-30, the rapidly changing period from the 1930s to 1970, and the politically vibrant 1970s and 1980s. The author (with research help from Clarice Mota, Donald E. Post, and Ignacio Lozano) relies on traditional historical sources and months of field work which included conducting hundreds of interviews, taking fifty detailed 'life histories' of residents, and observing scores of meetings and classrooms. The appendix contains tables on population, the economy, ethnicity, and occupations. This, the second edition of the book originally published in 1977, brings the analysis up to 1987.

314 **Latinos and the political system.**
      Edited by F. Chris García.   Notre Dame, Indiana: University of Notre
      Dame Press, 1988. 501p.

A series of essays by sociologists and political scientists that examine the involvement of Mexican-Americans, Cuban-Americans, and Puerto Ricans in United States politics. The topics of these wide-ranging papers include the political activism and participation of Latinos; Latin American representation at the local, state, and federal levels of government; educational policy; and public employment. Four essays deal directly with Texas: Joseph D. Sekul's 'Communities Organized for Public Service: Citizen Power and Public Policy in San Antonio'; Susan A. MacManus and Carol A. Cassel's 'Mexican-Americans in City Politics: Participation, Representation, and Policy Preferences' (Houston); Karen O'Connor and Lee Epstein's 'A Legal Voice for the Chicano Community: The Activities of the Mexican-American Legal Defense and Educational Fund, 1968-1982' (the Fund's headquarters are in San Antonio); and Rudolfo O. de la Garza, Robert D. Wrinkle, and Jeffrey L. Polinard's 'Ethnicity and Policy: The Mexican-American Perspective' (on Travis and Hidalgo Counties).

315 **United we win: the rise and fall of *La Raza Unida Party*.**
      Ignacio García.   Tucson, Arizona: Mexican-American Studies and
      Research Center at the University of Arizona, 1989. 284p. bibliog.

At the centre of the Chicano movement of the 1960s and 1970s was the *Raza Unida Party*. The author of this well-received analysis of the organization was a participant in the activities he describes, but he also did extensive research in contemporary newspapers, personal paper collections, and oral histories. García focuses on the leading personalities of the movement and their activities from 1969 to the party's collapse in the late 1970s. He describes its Texas origins in the Mexican-American Youth Organization in the mid-1960s, its electoral success in the early 1970s – again, mainly in Texas – and its fight against racial discrimination. The book also details *La Raza Unida*'s internal debates between rural and urban, national and regional, and ideological and practical interests. Although García is hardly a disinterested observer, he is fair, and his work provides a cogent analysis and many details about an often ignored movement.

316 **Desert immigrants: the Mexicans of El Paso, 1880-1920.**
      Mario J. García.   New Haven, Connecticut: Yale University Press,
      1981. 316p. maps. bibliog. (Yale Western American Series).

An analysis of early Mexican settlers in El Paso, who worked largely in agriculture or in industries such as smelting in the late 19th and early 20th centuries. Their appearance in El Paso created a dual community; they were separated by culture, language, and race from the Anglo-American community. Their status as menial labourers also separated them from white Texans, who tended to be white collar professionals who exploited the unskilled Mexican labourers. García describes the development of the *barrio* in El Paso, including its schools, politics, and social life, the Mexican influence on the larger El Paso and southwestern culture, as well as the importance of Mexican labourers to the Texas economy. A number of tables present statistics on immigrants from Mexico, wages, occupations, and household composition.

317 **Mexican Americans: leadership, ideology, and identity, 1920-1960.**
Mario J. García. New Haven, Connecticut: Yale University Press, 1989. 364p. bibliog. (Yale Western Americana Series).

García challenges the contempt of 1960s Chicano activists for earlier Mexican-American leaders and intellectuals as accommodationists who neglected their own culture and failed to fight enthusiastically against discrimination. García argues that these middle- and working-class leaders were reformers rather than radicals who strove to end discrimination on the job and in the classroom. Their ultimate goal was integration, not separation; yet their activities prepared the way for the more volatile and nationalistic Chicano movement of the 1960s. The book is organized into three parts that examine the middle class, labour and the left, and Mexican-American intellectuals. Although García emphasizes Texas and California, he considers the entire region and places the experiences of Mexican-Americans in the context of other ethnic groups in the United States, especially African-Americans.

318 **Rise of the Mexican American middle class: San Antonio, 1929-1941.**
Richard A. Garcia. College Station, Texas: Texas A & M University Press, 1991. 256p. bibliog. (Centennial Series of the Association of Former Students, Texas A & M University).

An examination of the tension between traditionalist Mexican immigrants in the San Antonio *barrio* and the rising Mexican-American generation who were far more willing to seek assimilation through education, political activity, and economic advancement. The young *Tejanos* wanted to become Americans politically while remaining Mexicans culturally. Garcia effectively studies the ramifications of these disagreements on the issues and institutions of class, church, family, education, politics, and urban problems.

319 **Chicanos and Native Americans: the territorial minorities.**
Edited by Rudolph O. de la Garza, Z. Anthony Kruszewski, Tomas A. Arciniega. Englewood Cliffs, New Jersey: Prentice Hall, 1973. 203p.

A collection of papers delivered at the 1972 Workshop on Southwestern Ethnic Groups: Sociopolitical Environment and Education. The sociologists and political scientists involved in the workshop sought to improve understanding of the values and political behaviour of Native Americans and Chicanos and to determine how the political system has responded to their needs. The essays attempt to find unifying threads for the experiences and interests of the three major non-Anglo ethnic groups in the United States – although blacks are not included in the title, their experiences are occasionally considered. Especially interesting to those seeking information about Texas are Tomas A. Arciniega, 'The Myth of the Compensatory Education Model in the Education of Chicanos'; Susan Navarro Uranga, 'The Study of Mexican-American Education in the Southwest: Implications of Research by the Civil Rights Commission'; and David E. Wright, Esteban Salinas, and William P. Kuvlesky, 'Opportunities for Social Mobility for Mexican-American Youth'.

320 *Los Chicanos*: an awakening people.
John Haddox. El Paso, Texas: Texas Western Press, 1970. 44p. bibliog.

This is a very brief, but useful, survey of Chicano ideology as it stood in 1970. Haddox, a philosopher, explains the values and culture of Chicanos, decries the discrimination in public education (the barrier of language, the problems caused by enforced acculturation), examines Mexican-American stereotypes, and shows the Chicanos' need to retain their identities.

321 **Learning to be militant.**
Herbert Hirsch, Armando Gutiérrez. San Francisco, California: R & E Research Associates, 1977. 146p.

A heavily statistical case study by a pair of political scientists of Chicano activism in Crystal City, Zavala County, Texas. The town has long been dominated by Anglo-Americans, although most of its residents are Mexican-Americans, many of whom work in the surrounding spinach fields. The authors examine a number of issues – economic, educational, racial, familial, religious, and political – in trying to explain the conditions within an ethnic community that contribute to the rise of militancy. In this case, ethnic identity sparked a rise of consciousness among Hispanics that encouraged the development of a local chapter of *La Raza Unida* Party.

322 **A history of Hispanic theatre in the United States: origins to 1940.**
Nicolas Kanellos. Austin, Texas: University of Texas Press, 1990. 240p. bibliog.

Kanellos seeks to show how Hispanics created art in the face of adversity, promoted racial pride, and demonstrated 'cultural continuity and adaptability in a foreign land' through their theatre. His thoroughly researched monograph is packed with names and dates and other facts on the Hispanic theatre from the 18th century to the eve of the Second World War. Separate chapters focus on Los Angeles, San Antonio, New York, and Tampa, and are organized around the most important theatres in those cities. San Antonio's greatest contribution to the Hispanic theatre was in the development of 'tent theatres' – a cross between a circus and vaudeville – and on the theatre's role in developing a vibrant Mexican-American culture in San Antonio. In Los Angeles, on the other hand, the key development was the rise of professional theatres, while in New York City the theatre brought together all of the different Hispanic national groups. There is also a short section on Mexican-American theatres in other Texas cities such as Laredo (a leading centre of Texan theatre before the surge in Mexican immigrants to San Antonio in the 1910s), El Paso, and towns in the Rio Grande Valley. Kanellos includes nearly three dozen illustrations of prominent actors, theatres, and memorabilia, as well as a glossary of Hispanic words.

323 **Latin Americans in Texas.**
Pauline R. Kibbe. Albuquerque, New Mexico: University of New Mexico Press, 1946; New York: Arno Press, 1974. 302p. bibliog.

A report by a Texas journalist on conditions and issues facing Latin Americans in Texas just after the end of the Second World War. Kibbe provides brief historical backgrounds of Texas and of Hispanics in Texas, and chapters (full of statistics) on education, housing, sanitation, health, employment, the cotton industry, migrant labour, and social and civil inequality. She also offers a long section of suggestions on

how to solve the problems of racism and discrimination through economic
development, better education, and the development of effective leadership among
Mexican-Americans.

324 *Del Pueblo*: a pictorial history of Houston's Hispanic community.
   Thomas H. Kreneck.   Houston, Texas: Houston International
   University, 1989. 246p. bibliog.

A self-styled 'public history' aimed at revealing and explaining the Hispanic heritage of
this decidedly non-Hispanic city. The emphasis is on individual contributions and the
development of a sense of community among Houston's Hispanics in the 20th century.
Hundreds of photographs, many from the Houston Metropolitan Research Center at
the Houston Public Library, reveal scenes of Hispanics as students, musicians,
businessmen, celebrities and public figures (from politicians to television anchor-
persons), and as failures (in flop houses, for instance). The substantial text is
workmanlike, chronological, and very sympathetic to the problems and culture of
Houston's Hispanics.

325 **The Mexican-American workers of San Antonio.**
   Robert Garland Landolt.   New York: Arno Press, 1976. 379p. maps.
   bibliog. (The Chicano Heritage Series).

A study of the problems of San Antonio's Mexican-American working population,
such as poor education and housing, inadequate labour skills, and poverty. Landolt
seeks to find the roots of the problems which prevent full utilization of Mexican-
Americans in San Antonio's economy. He looks at political, educational, health, and
social and cultural obstacles that inhibit Mexican-Americans' entrance into skilled
professions. The author provides the historical roots of these circumstances and the
inter-racial relationships with blacks and whites that evolved over time, along with the
impact of events like the World Wars and the Great Depression. He concludes that a
disparity in the quality of life between Chicanos and Anglos in San Antonio stemmed
from all of the above factors, as well as the stagnant production economy of a city
dependent on military bases for much of its economic activity. Fifty tables show
sociological and demographic data such as employment rates, occupations, and
educational attainment among Mexican-Americans in the city.

326 **Culture conflict in Texas, 1821-1835.**
   Samuel Harman Lowrie.   New York: Columbia University Press,
   1932; New York: AMS Press, 1967. 188p. map. bibliog. (Studies in
   History, Economics, and Public Law).

A dated but interesting approach to race relations in Texas prior to the Texas
Revolution. The author presents, one by one, the various elements which served as a
foundation for 'culture conflict' in Texas, such as environment, composition of
population, conditions of migration, and traditional backgrounds and attitudes, which
together led to misunderstandings between Mexicans and Anglos in Texas. Lowrie
concludes that differences in culture were at the heart of the break between Texas
colonists and Mexicans. Some cultural exchanges did occur; Anglo-Americans adopted
the Spanish land system and some of the Spanish/Mexican legal traditions and
language; the Mexicans adopted some English words and democratic concepts.

327 **Mexican-Americans of south Texas.**
William Madison. New York: Holt, Rinehart, and Winston, 1964.
112p. map. bibliog. (Case Studies in Cultural Anthropology).

An anthropological study of Mexican-American culture in Hidalgo County, Texas. The author has defined three levels of acculturation among Mexican-Americans. The first group has retained most of its traditional folk culture, although it is strongly influenced by American economic and technological factors. The second level of acculturation embraces those Mexican-Americans who are caught between two cultures; they frequently compartmentalize their lives by observing folk culture in some instances, especially during celebrations and social occasions, and the customs of American society at other times. The third level constitutes those middle- and upper-class Mexican-Americans who are fully assimilated into American culture. Among the topics discussed in terms of assimilation are family, marital patterns, religion, the emerging middle- and upper-classes, political participation, superstition and folk medicine, and the internal conflicts caused by acculturation in the Mexican-American community.

328 **Poorest of Americans: the Mexican Americans of the lower Rio Grande valley of Texas.**
Robert Lee Maril. Notre Dame, Indiana: University of Notre Dame Press, 1989. 228p. map. bibliog.

A survey, based primarily on secondary sources, of the more than 300,000 people living at or below the poverty line in the Rio Grande Valley and of the issues that affect them: racism, economic 'colonization', education, and health care. After indicting most of the policies of the local, state, and federal governments, Maril recommends that the economy of the Valley region should be re-evaluated. Finishing industries – as opposed to the production of raw materials and produce – should be expanded and the cattle industry limited; there should be more agricultural processing in the Valley; local banks should invest more of their assets locally; there should be better land and resource management; the church must take the lead in advocating changes; Mexican-Americans must improve their political participation and grass roots organizing; and both the federal and the state governments must become more active in creating an economy in the Rio Grande Valley that is less dependent on factors beyond the control of its residents.

329 **Older Mexican Americans: a study in an urban *barrio*.**
Kyriakos S. Markides, Harry W. Martin. Austin, Texas: Center for Mexican-American Studies, 1983. 139p.

An overview of the circumstances and conditions faced by elderly *Tejanos*, compared to the experiences of elderly Anglo-Americans. Individual chapters examine socio-economic standing, family structure and relations, psychological well-being, health and health care, religion, and retirement. The authors conclude that elderly Mexican-Americans are disadvantaged (although many owned homes), are not as dependent on their families and children as had been suspected, suffer from psychological distress, and are in somewhat worse health and more devoted to the church than their white counterparts. Markides and Martin do not suggest major policy shifts; rather, their useful statistics are meant to set the stage for further research into the experiences of elderly Mexican-Americans and what should be done to help them. Over 500 interviewees – seventy per cent Mexican-American and thirty per cent Anglo-American – provided the data for the study; the twenty-four page survey is appended.

330 **Power and politics in a Chicano barrio: a study of mobilization efforts and community power in El Paso.**
Benjamin Marquez. Lanham, Maryland: University Press of America, 1985. 264p. map. bibliog.

Marquez uses the issue of public housing as a case study in tracing the development of Chicano political activity in South El Paso's Second Ward from 1960 to 1980. Public housing encountered opposition from the Anglo-dominated city government; burdened by poverty and inexperience, Chicanos were unable to mount a sustained protest movement or political activity. The community failed to shape municipal policy or to change conditions for the better; the author warns that the south side may lose its identity and fade from El Paso's collective memory as it merges with the rest of the city's growing slums.

331 **North from Mexico: the Spanish-speaking people of the United States.**
Carey McWilliams, Matt S. Meier. New York: Greenwood Press, 1990. 2nd ed. 372p. bibliog. (Contributions in American History).

A very readable, fast-moving, and often dramatic account of movement into the Southwest of Spanish-speaking peoples from Mexico and of their often violent contacts with Anglos. There is some analysis of Mexican-American culture, but the book is at its best in providing a narrative of Anglo-Mexican relations over the course of a century and a half. First published by McWilliams in 1949, Meier's additions in the second edition consist of three chapters on Chicano politics and education and on recent immigrants (legal and illegal). Texas obviously plays an important part in the larger story told in this very useful survey of race relations in the entire region.

332 **Reflections of the Mexican experience in Texas.**
Edited by Margarita B. Melville, Hilda Castillo Phariss. Houston, Texas: Mexican-American Studies Center, University of Houston, 1979. 374p. maps.

A collection of papers presented at a 1979 symposium on aspects of Mexican-Texan history, culture, and socio-economic conditions. The essays examine Mexican-American demography, Mexican labourers from 1848-1900, the origins and importance of the term 'Chicano', oral histories of survivors of the turbulent events along the Texas-Mexico border between 1910-20, contemporary Mexican poets, problems in Hispanic education in Texas, and the failure of Mexican-Americans to influence the political system through the two traditional parties or through the *Raza Unida Party* in the 1960s and 1970s. Two maps provide demographic information about *Tejanos* by county, and 16 tables provide statistics on the income, occupation, and education of Hispanics.

333 **'Let all of them take heed': Mexican-Americans and the campaign for educational equality in Texas, 1910-1981.**
Guadalupe San Miguel, Jr. Austin, Texas: University of Texas Press, 1987. 256p. bibliog. (Mexican-American Monograph Series).

A scholarly analysis of the development of the state-wide effort by Mexican-Americans to achieve educational equality. The influx of agricultural workers and refugees from the Mexican revolution created extraordinarily unequal school conditions for *Tejanos* in the first third of the 20th century. San Miguel explores the legal challenges to the status quo, the attempts to create an intellectual tradition within the Hispanic community, and curriculum reform, which culminated in the drive for bi-lingual education. The results of these campaigns were hardly a total victory for the reformers. Mexican-American children still attend segregated, inferior schools and the curriculum is still mainly directed toward assimilation. The author believes that failure stemmed partly from targeting administrative practices rather than finances and structure and from the reformers' inability to remove local school policy makers. For the most part, however, they failed because they remained politically impotent, which left their legal successes unenforceable. This is both a history of the efforts to bring quality education to Texas Hispanics and an attempt to influence policy and future campaigns to eradicate inequality.

334 **Anglos and Mexicans in the making of Texas, 1836-1986.**
David Montejano. Austin, Texas: University of Texas Press, 1987.
383p. maps. bibliog.

Focusing on a 200-mile wide area of the Texas-Mexico border from Brownsville to El Paso, Montejano provides an analysis of race relations and economic development. Part one (1836-1900) discusses the annexation and incorporation of different races into the Republic and the state of Texas. Despite discrimination against Mexicans, a peace structure was sought by authorities in order to provide stability and economic growth. Part two (1900-20) examines the period when the closing of the frontier and improving technology 'reconstructed' Anglo-Mexican ranch society; this process, along with the repression of Mexican protests by Texas Rangers, created an agricultural Anglo elite. Part three (1920-40) details the in-migration of farmers and farm labourers, which broke down traditional Anglo paternalism, increased agricultural wage labour, and promoted segregation of the races. During the period covered in part four (1940-86), industry and urban merchants took the power base away from agricultural elites and Mexican-Americans began to gain political power, breaking down Jim Crow discrimination and generally improving their conditions. The emphasis throughout this solid, respected work, is on the influence of Mexican-Americans on the Texas economy, politics, society, and culture.

335 *Tejano* **origins in eighteenth-century San Antonio.**
Edited by Gerald E. Poyo, Gilberto M. Hinojosa. Austin, Texas:
University of Texas Press, 1991. 198p. map. bibliog.

This is a collection of essays on a variety of topics related to the *Tejanos*. It includes a piece on the historiography of the borderlands region, and another on the emergence of a *Tejano* community in Spanish San Antonio in the contexts of economic, social, political, and cultural developments. They include pieces on Spanish immigrants to San Antonio from the Canary Islands, the founders of the military outposts at San Antonio, Indian-clerical relations, Indian culture and community (including those Native Americans affiliated with missions and those unaffiliated), and other immigrant groups to the area. A number of pen-and-ink drawings of Indians, missionaries, army officers, and San Antonio sites by José Cisneros complement the essays nicely.

336 **Stolen heritage: a Mexican Americans' rediscovery of his family's lost land grant.**
Abel G. Rubio, edited by Thomas H. Kreneck. Austin, Texas: Eakin Press, 1986. 224p. maps. bibliog.

A first-person account of a retired Marine's discovery of the facts regarding an 8,900 acre land grant his ancestors had held in South Texas in the early 19th century. Based on his family's oral tradition as well as public documents, maps, and other county records, this is partly an autobiography, but also the history of a tough frontier family, of race relations along the violent South Texas frontier, and of Anglo graft and legal manipulations. Kreneck provides a brief history of the region's settlement and of the widespread fraud used by Anglos to relieve Mexicans of their old Spanish land grants. This unique book is colourful, depressing, painstaking, and often moving.

337 **Across the tracks: Mexican-Americans in a Texas city.**
Arthur Rubel. Austin, Texas: University of Texas Press, 1966. 266p. map. bibliog.

An anthropologist's examination of a Mexican-American working class community in Hidalgo County, Texas. Rubel did field work in the town for two years, during which he explored race relations, problems associated with health care, illiteracy, economic forces, tradition versus modernity, and political participation. The findings are considered in the light of social science models and precedents. Several tables quantify the occupations and income of Hidalgo County residents, while sixteen black-and-white photographs document the lives of migrant workers in the county.

338 *La Raza*: **the Mexican-Americans.**
Stan Steiner. New York: Harper & Row, 1970. 418p. bibliog.

Written in a popular style, this is a chronicle of the 1960s Mexican-American movement to gain civil rights and to unionize migrant workers, especially in Texas, New Mexico, and California. Based largely on first-hand accounts of participants. Steiner emphasizes the oppression of Mexican-Americans and their political, legal, and economic responses, such as Cesar Chavez's movement to organize migrant farm workers in California and Reies Lopez Tijerina's efforts to regain lost lands in New Mexico. Related in a dramatic style, this is a fast-paced introduction to 1960s activism among southwestern Hispanics.

339 **Vaqueros in blue and gray.**
Jerry Thompson. Austin, Texas: Presidial Press, 1976. 148p. bibliog.

About 9,900 Mexican-Americans from New Mexico and Texas fought for both sides in the American Civil War. They served primarily on the Texas-Mexico border and gained a reputation as poor soldiers; some units had desertion rates as high as 100 per cent. Thompson argues that the severe prejudice and discrimination directed against them by whites caused their disastrous military record. Many Mexican-American units went without food, uniforms, and pay for extended periods of time and were assigned out-dated and unworkable weapons. Many did not even understand the conflict between the North and the South and joined the army only because they were encouraged to do so by community leaders, while others signed up to escape New Mexico's peonage system. Another source of dissatisfaction stemmed from the fact that Mexican-Americans were frequently passed over for promotions. An extreme example of the mistreatment accorded them by Anglo-American commanders and men on both sides is reflected in the experiences of Adrian J. Vidal, who as a Confederate captain deserted with his entire company and joined the Federal army near Brownsville in late 1863. The Yankees continued the racist remarks and poor treatment, and Vidal soon deserted from the Union forces. This is a useful, albeit brief, look at a usually forgotten aspect of the Civil War.

340 **The history of Mexican Americans in Lubbock County.**
Andrés A. Tijerina. Lubbock, Texas: Texas Tech University Press, 1977. 73p. bibliog.

This is a very brief account of Mexican-Americans in a northwest Texas city from the Spanish conquest to the present. Tijerina stresses the mixture of cultures between Anglos and *Tejanos* and the diversity within the Mexican-American community. Some feel a strong affinity for their Aztec heritage, while others claim their Spanish roots; some consider themselves Chicano, while still others are simply 'Americans'. The author also provides examples of how Hispanic customs and language have survived and influenced southwestern United States culture (especially in music, art, Americanized Spanish terms, and food).

341 **The Mexican-American family: tradition and change.**
Norma Williams. Dix Hills, New York: General Hall, 1990. 170p. bibliog. (Reynolds Series in Sociology).

A sociological analysis of Mexican-American life cycles and rituals (including religion, birth, marriage, death, generational differences), role-making, and decision-making (among both working class and professional Mexican-Americans). Williams conducted her field work in Austin, Corpus Christi, and the Kingsville region of Texas. She is especially interested in determining how generational change and class development have contributed to changes in rituals and attitudes about family; she concludes that urbanization, assimilation, and the decline of religion have made traditional rituals less important, the extended family less central, and male dominance a little less apparent among Mexican-Americans.

African Americans

342   **Black leaders: Texans for their times.**
Edited by Alwyn Barr, Robert A. Calvert.   Austin, Texas: Texas
State Historical Association, 1981. 237p.

A very useful work on African-Americans in Texas whose lives have been significant but who are now little-known. The essays span Texas history from the slave period through the 1970s, and offer brief analyses of educators, business people, civil rights activists, and artists. Specifically, the essays examine a slave named Dave whose refusal to work on a plantation led to his imprisonment; William Goyens, who was a free black landowner before the Civil War; the Reconstruction politician Matt Gaines, who served in the Texas State Senate in the 1870s; William MacDonald, who was a Texas Republican Party leader from 1886 to 1896; Mary Branch, who was the first black woman to administer a college when she became president of Tillotson College in 1930; W. R, Banks, president of Prairie View A & M College; Herman Marion Sweatt, the plaintiff in one of the civil rights cases that desegregated the University of Texas; and John Biggers, who was a prominent figure in Afro-American art in the 1970s.

343   **Black Texans: a history of Negroes in Texas, 1528-1971.**
Alwyn Barr.   Austin, Texas: Jenkins; Pemberton Press, 1973. 259p.
bibliog. (Negro Heritage Series).

A sympathetic narrative written for a general audience. Barr chronicles the experiences of black Texans, slave and free, from the beginnings of Texas through the civil rights era. He highlights race relations (including racism and violence toward blacks) as well as the achievements of notable black Texans, African-American political movements, and the work of organizations like the National Association for the Advancement of Colored People. The author also provides useful sections on social life, employment, and education. This is a clearly written, balanced survey.

344   **Negro legislators of Texas and their descendants.**
John Mason Brewer.   Dallas, Texas: Mathis, 1935; Austin, Texas:
Jenkins, 1970. 154p. bibliog.

A collection of facts lifted directly from primary sources, this compilation of the names, records, and genealogies of the 19th-century black members of the Texas State Legislature – in the 20th century, no African-American won election to the legislature until the 1960s – remains an important contribution to African-American historiography in the Lone Star State. Brewer establishes who served in the legislature and when, emphasizes their dignity and independence, records white reactions (they were often disappointed at the blacks' credible performances), and traces the careers of some of the legislators' descendants. He also describes the various constitutional conventions in which blacks took part, voting patterns among blacks, and the disfranchisement of African-Americans in the 1890s. For many years, this was the only serious work on black politicians in Texas.

345 **Barbara Charline Jordan: from the ghetto to the capitol.**
Ira Babington Bryant. Houston, Texas: D. Armstrong, 1977. 105p.

A very laudatory biography of Barbara Jordan (1932–) from her birth to 1976, when she was about to begin her third term in the United States House of Representatives. Although she attended the segregated public schools of Houston, she managed to infiltrate the 'white man's' government, first as a Texas State Senator (elected in 1966, she was the first black in the Senate since 1883) and then as a Congresswoman. Bryant describes how Jordan used her debating experience, tact, and bargaining skills to gain white male support in the legislature and in Congress for bills that dealt with issues such as the elderly, small businesses, immigrants and women, education and health care, and poverty. Although this is not a particularly balanced view of Jordan, it is a useful biography that must suffice until a more objective one appears.

346 **Invisible Houston.**
Robert D. Bullard. College Station, Texas: Texas A & M University Press, 1987. 160p. maps.

A history of the black community in Houston, the largest concentration of urban blacks in the South. Not surprisingly, Bullard finds that African-Americans have been excluded from decent housing, employment, police protection, resource allocation, and even local histories. Bullard considers black contributions to politics (through the NAACP), the economy, culture and society, and sports. Individual chapters are devoted to the most important issues facing blacks: poverty, housing, racism, neighbourhood quality of life, business, law enforcement, and civil rights. Four maps and 23 tables provide quantitative data on black population, home ownership, public housing, discrimination complaints, landfills, the labour market, median income by race, poverty levels in southern urban areas, educational attainment by race, black businesses, crime, and political organizations.

347 **An empire for slavery: the peculiar institution in Texas, 1821-1865.**
Randolph B. Campbell. Baton Rouge, Louisiana: Louisiana State University Press, 1989. 306p. maps. bibliog.

The winner of several awards from the Texas State Historical Association and written by one of the most thorough and best-known historians of Texas. This analysis of slavery in Texas relies heavily on quantitative evidence drawn from census returns and county records and on a vast amount of qualitative evidence. Campbell finds that slavery in Texas did not differ much from slavery elsewhere in the South, although he does argue that slavery was vital to the economic growth of Texas before the Civil War. He methodically examines the institution in its economic and human dimensions; he describes the black experience, white attitudes, and black – white relationships within slavery. This is not a complicated book, but a well-researched and clearly presented look at an important topic.

348 **The Freedmen's Bureau and black Texans.**
Barry A. Crouch. Austin, Texas: University of Texas Press, 1992. 216p. bibliog.

A revisionist analysis of the Bureau of Freedmen, Refugees, and Abandoned Lands, organized by the United States government in 1865 to help the South and southern blacks make the transition from war to peace and from slavery to freedom. Most accounts of the Bureau have emphasized its shortcomings, but Crouch argues that it was more effective than previously thought and actually acted as the first social welfare agency in American history through its education, labour, and other programmes.

349 **Biracial politics: conflict and coalition in the metropolitan south.**
Chandler Davidson.   Baton Rouge, Louisiana: Louisiana State University Press, 1972. 301p.

A political scientist's examination of ethnic politics in Houston, the largest city in Texas and the southern city with the largest black population. This work challenges the optimistic assessments of black political participation and power since the 1965 Voting Rights Act. In Houston, Chandler argues, blacks have been politically active, yet they have had little overall impact on policy making and have not been assimilated into mainstream political parties. The author's quantitative evidence (he includes forty-nine tables of statistics) concentrates on voter registration, white and black differences in voter turnout and occupations, and racial matters as political issues. Chandler concludes that African-American voters cannot achieve their political goals alone; they must form bi-racial coalitions in order to have a real impact on the political process.

350 **Overcoming: a history of black integration at the University of Texas at Austin.**
Almetris M. Duren, Louise Iscoe.   Austin, Texas: University of Texas Press, 1979. 45p.

An illustrated chronicle of the black struggle for equality of life and education at the main campus of the University of Texas at Austin, as told by Mrs Almetris Duren – called 'Mama Duren' by black students attending 'UT'. Mrs Duren provided housing, food, help, and encouragement to African-American students from the 1950s through the 1970s. This memoir is organized chronologically, with individual chapters providing information on the burgeoning civil rights movement at UT, campus protests, ethnic studies programmes, the increasing percentage of black students at the university, and their changing image. Many of the sources were Mrs Duren's own collection of clippings, letters, publications, and her personal recollections. The nearly eighty photographs and sketches depict black leaders, students, and alumni, as well as student life and living conditions.

351 **The negro cowboys.**
Philip H. Durham, Everett L. Jones.   New York: Dodd, Mead, 1965. 287p. maps. bibliog.

As in any book dealing with facets of the Old West and the cattle industry, Texas is featured prominently in this scholarly treatment of African-American cowboys. The authors organize their material more or less chronologically, beginning with slave cowboys and moving through the post-Civil War era of the long cattle drives. Durham and Jones survey all of the West, from Texas to Deadwood, Dakota Territory, and from Tombstone, Arizona, to Lincoln County, Wyoming, with separate chapters on black outlaws and black members of Wild West Shows.

352 **The black infantry in the west, 1869-1891.**
Arlen L. Fowler. Westport, Connecticut: Greenwood Publishing, 1971. 167p. bibliog. (Contributions in Afro-American and African Studies).

The United States Army formed four black infantry regiments in 1866-67: the 38th, 39th, 40th, and 41st United States Infantry; they were later combined into the 24th and 25th Infantry. The author became interested in their histories in the 1950s, when he served in the 25th Armored Infantry Battalion, the descendant of the 25th Infantry. The regiments were stationed in frontier posts all over the West, from the Rio Grande to the Canadian border. Fowler provides a full chapter on the regiments' Texas experiences within the chronological framework of the book. The men in these units – which were officered by whites – endured frontier conditions and racist treatment and fought Indians and Mexican bandits. The author also details educational programmes for the men in the army and racism they experienced from white soldiers.

353 **Norris Wright Cuney: a tribune of the black people.**
Maud Cuney Hare. Austin, Texas: Steck-Vaughn, 1913, 1968. 230p.

This adulatory biography by one of Cuney's daughters lacks objectivity as well as scholarly apparatus. Yet it is still the only book-length biography of this late 19th-century African-Texan leader. Born in Hempstead, Texas, Cuney (1846-97) was educated in Pittsburgh, Pennsylvania, and later became a Galveston attorney. From 1872 to the 1890s, he was one of the leaders of the state's Republican Party; he was delegate to every Republican national convention between 1872 and 1896 and was inspector and collector of customs for Galveston – a plum office awarded to Republican stalwarts by the federal government, which was usually controlled by Republican presidents – for most of that period. Toward the end of his life, Cuney led the unsuccessful fight against white Republicans in Texas, who wanted to make the Party leadership 'Lily White'. The author presents her father's life chronologically, emphasizing his successes and his compassion for disadvantaged people of all kinds – the poor, convicts, and juvenile delinquents, as well as blacks. In a telling demonstration of the dated nature of this book, Hare frequently resorts to quoting influential whites about her father's positive attributes.

354 **A night of violence: the Houston riot of 1917.**
Robert V. Haynes. Baton Rouge, Louisiana: Louisiana State University Press, 1976. 338p. maps. bibliog.

A case study of the state of race relations in the United States during the era of the First World War. The August 1917 'mutiny' of members of the all-black 24th United States Infantry Regiment resulted in the deaths of fourteen white residents of Houston. It led to the largest court martial (involving sixty-three men) in United States military history and to the execution of thirteen black soldiers and the sentencing to life terms of forty-one others. Hayne provides a balanced account of this incident, rightly placing it in the context of the racial conflict during this 'Nadir' period in American race relations. He details the events leading up to the riot (tensions between white Houstonians, especially white policemen, and the black soldiers stationed there had been building for weeks), the investigation, and the courts martial, which were shrouded in secrecy.

355 **Private black colleges in Texas, 1865-1954.**
Michael R. Heintze. College Station, Texas: Texas A & M University Press, 1985. 211p. bibliog.

This is a revisionist work that defends black-only institutions of higher education. Despite their grave deficiencies, the author argues that for the ninety years following the Civil War they were the only institutions training doctors, lawyers, teachers, and other professionals for black communities. He concentrates on the founding of private, mostly church-orientated African-American colleges from 1865-1954, and on controversies and problems that confronted those colleges, such as developing clear-cut goals, attracting good administrators and faculty, improving curricula, bolstering finances, and enhancing student life. He also compares these institutions to one another and to other black schools in the United States. The author provides over forty black-and-white illustrations of educators and students and of the campuses of the colleges, as well as eleven tables showing statistics on enrollment, types of classes offered, and post-graduate occupations of students.

356 **Wake up dead man: Afro-American worksongs from Texas prisons.**
Collected and edited by Bruce Jackson. Cambridge, Massachusetts: Harvard University Press, 1972. 326p. bibliog.

A collection of songs sung by black prisoners while working in a variety of prison activities. Jackson divides the book into songs sung as solos and as groups in the cotton and cane fields, songs sung while logging, and songs sung while 'flatweeding' (other field work). One chapter is devoted entirely to J. B. Smith, a noted prison work-song artist. The editor stresses that these are only worksongs; he does not deal with blues or gospel music. He places the work songs and prison music as a whole in their historical contexts, building on the work of the pioneering folklorists John A. and Alan Lomax. The bulk of the book consists of the words and music to the songs he taped, with brief explanations of the lyrics and of the conditions under which they were recorded. Other scholarly aids include a glossary, notes on nicknames, the response patterns in the songs, and an alphabetical list of the songs.

357 **Violence in the city.**
Blair Justice. Fort Worth, Texas: Texas Christian University Press, 1969. 289p. maps.

An attempt to determine the attitudes toward and the contours of violence in Houston's black community in the late 1960s. Based on interviews with residents, government records, and a wide variety of statistical information (forty graphs and tables detail employment, government expenditures in black neighbourhoods, and patterns of violence, among other things), the book examines the causes of discontent; black revolutionaries and student protestors; relationships between African-Americans, the police, and the government; and methods of breaking the cycle of violence and unrest and entering the mainstream through community activism, jobs, and better relationships with law enforcement organizations.

358 **The buffalo soldiers: a narrative of the negro cavalry in the west.**
William H. Leckie.   Norman, Oklahoma: University of Oklahoma
Press, 1967. 290p. maps. bibliog.

A scholarly narrative of the experiences and operations of the 9th and 10th United
States Cavalry regiments, which were made up of black troopers commanded by white
officers. Both units served primarily on the Southern Plains between 1867 and 1891.
Leckie not only recounts the battles fought against Indians, but also the soldiers' battle
against discrimination; he argues that the 9th and 10th were much more effective than
they were given credit for and had fewer discipline problems than white regiments.
Three chapters deal specifically with their campaigns in Texas during the Red River
War and in West Texas; other chapters describe their operations against Apaches,
Utes, and Mexican bandits. Twenty black-and-white photographs of officers, men, and
posts, and four maps of campaigns provide useful graphic information.

359 **Life styles in the black ghetto.**
William McCord, (et al.).   New York: W. W. Norton, 1969. 334p.
bibliog.

A sociological study of African-American life compiled from questionnaires distributed
just after the most violent period in black urban history, the 'Red Summers' of 1966-
68. As the title indicates, the authors seek to describe the lives of black ghetto
dwellers; they also look at the opinions of urban blacks about their situation. Seventy-
four tables provide statistics on demography, occupation, income, family structure, and
other economic and social data. Three ghettos – in Houston, Los Angeles, and
Oakland, California – are highlighted; the 1967 riot at Texas Southern University, then
an all-black school, is also examined.

360 **History of the Teachers State Association of Texas.**
Vernon McDaniel.   Washington, DC: National Education
Association, 1977. 165p. bibliog.

This is less a history than a compilation of statistical information, by-laws,
chronological charts, biographies of important personnel, and association initiatives
from 1884-1966. The Teachers State Association of Texas was the primary union and
professional organization for African-American teachers in Texas during that period.

361 **Through many dangers, toils and snares: the black leadership of Texas,
1868-1900.**
Merline Pitre.   Austin, Texas: Eakin Press, 1985. 260p. maps. bibliog.

A chronicle of the activities of black Texas politicians during Reconstruction in Texas,
including their performance in constitutional conventions, the state legislature, and in
Republican Party conventions. Blacks provided an overriding majority of Republican
votes in post-war Texas and at conventions, yet they were rarely able to control the
Party. Pitre also describes the unethical and often violent means used by Texas whites
to control or to eliminate black voters and politicians. The most useful parts of the
book are the mini-biographies, which are actually character analyses of several of the
most prominent black political leaders in Texas between the Civil War and 1900.
Richard Allen comes across as selfishly ambitious, while Robert L. Smith was well-
meaning but spineless. Norris Cuney was helpful to blacks, but his political ambition
led him to ignore discrimination and racism and to promote accomodationist attitudes.
Matt Gaines was the most militant of the black leaders, while George Ruby is

presented as a Republican Party operative. Appendixes provide rosters of black legislators and their committee assignments, and the names of black delegates to Republican National Conventions.

362 The negro in Texas, 1874-1900.
Lawrence D. Rice. Baton Rouge, Louisiana: Louisiana State University Press, 1971. 309p. bibliog.

This effective work is the only available overview of African-Americans in Texas during the period from the end of Reconstruction to the beginning of the 20th century. Rice emphasizes politics: blacks' efforts to influence the policies of the Republican Party, their uneasy relationship with the Populist Party and brief-lived attempts at fusion with other white-dominated interest groups, their involvement with federal patronage, and their eventual disfranchisement in the 1890s. Rice also devotes chapters to economic issues, social life, and the legal system. This is a sobering story of declining rights and opportunities for black Texans after Reconstruction, as they found few sources of income outside of agriculture. Rice concludes that blacks' lives were not stable during this period; despite their technical freedom they were buffeted by racism and discrimination that limited their ability to explore opportunities or to improve their quality of life. This is a scholarly, clearly written, and often-cited 'sequel' (although it was written nearly twenty years earlier) to Campbell's book on Texas slavery.

363 The bell rings at four: a black teacher's chronicle of change.
Dorothy Redus Robinson. Austin, Texas: Madrona, 1978. 142p.

Dorothy Redus Robinson (1909-), was born in Sublime, Texas, and began her career teaching in a one-room school for African-American children at the age of nineteen. In addition to the elementary grades, she later taught homemaking and special education and served as a school principle retiring in 1974. Mrs. Robinson recounts the trials, successes, and memorable children she encountered during her career, and also provides valuable insights into the economic and social problems that plagued the education of blacks, and continue to influence them, especially in the South.

364 The accommodation: the politics of race in an American city.
Jim Schutze. Secaucus, New Jersey: Citadel, 1986. 199p.

A lively journalistic account of race relations in Dallas throughout the period of the civil rights movement. Schutze examines how the main interest groups – white businessmen and community leaders seeking order, working class whites wanting to protect their status, the growing black community needing room to expand (more jobs, additional housing) – grappled in the legal, political, and social arenas throughout the 1950s and 1960s. They managed to accomodate one another through constant pressure and grudging acceptance. Blacks, of course, fought for equal rights, while whites merely wanted to preserve peace without necessarily achieving justice. The author's emphasis is on institutions – the fair housing movement, urban renewal, Civil Rights; he argues that the 'accomodation' was successful in that change occurred without major outbreaks of violence.

365 **Across the Rio Grande to freedom: United States negroes in Mexico.**
Rosalie Schwartz. El Paso, Texas: Texas Western Press, 1975. 64p.
bibliog.

White Texans believed that Mexicans often aided their slaves to escape to freedom in
Mexico; this brief volume looks at the diplomatic ramifications of the movement in the
late 1840s and the 1850s of slaves into Mexico – a country which had abolished slavery
in 1824. Extradition of escaped slaves was not allowed, and as tension between North
and South mounted in the late antebellum period, United States-Mexican relations
became more strained. Although it only begins to examine this topic and is based
primarily on secondary sources, it is the only attempt to analyse this aspect of slavery
in Texas.

366 **Time of hope, time of despair: black Texans during reconstruction.**
James M. Smallwood. Port Washington, New York: Kennikat Press,
1981. 202p. map. bibliog.

This is a survey of African-Americans in Texas during the decade after the Civil War
that accepts the main outlines of revisionist histories of Reconstruction. Rejecting
earlier historians' arguments that blacks in Texas did not suffer as much as blacks in
other southern states, Smallwood tends to concentrate on white terrorism and
discrimination and black efforts to build a stable community despite overwhelming
obstacles. The author examines the impact of Texas's white leaders and of the Federal
government (especially through the ill-fated Freedmen's Bureau) on the lives of blacks.
He devotes separate chapters to a brief overview of slavery, the freedmen's first
reactions to freedom, their attempts to deal with economic peonage and to create
educational and religious institutions, and their participation in politics despite the
violent opposition of whites.

367 **The Brownsville raid.**
John D. Weaver. New York: Norton, 1970. 320p. map. bibliog.

An analysis of the 1906 incident in Brownsville, Texas, in which black soldiers of the
25th United States Infantry stationed at Fort Brown were blamed for violence in which
several white Brownsville residents were killed. Although the regiment had recently
arrived in Brownsville, racial tensions and rumours of the rape of a white woman by a
black soldier helped convince the Army and President Theodore Roosevelt to deal
with the soldiers harshly; 167 were dishonourably discharged from the military.
Weaver places the incident in its larger racial and political contexts and provides a
coherent narrative of the 'raid' and the hearings that followed it.

368 **No quittin' sense.**
C. C. White, Ada Morehead Holland. Austin, Texas: University of
Texas Press, 1969. 216p.

A useful memoir of a black preacher's 20th century Texas odyssey. The grandson of a
slave, Reverend C(harley) C. White was born into poverty in the piney woods country
of East Texas and raised by his mother. He claims that he began preaching at the age
of three; this informal autobiography describes his experiences as an evangelical
minister encountering white racism, hostile blacks, and Indians (his mother was half
Native American). Among the topics about which he reminisces are rural poverty,
black superstitions and folklore, home medicine, and his own brand of charity for the
needy of all races.

369　Black community control: a study of transition in a Texas ghetto.
Joyce E. Williams.　New York: Praeger, 1973. 277p. map. bibliog.

An extremely well-focused study of one black community's struggle for control of its own destiny through political and social activism, community centres, children's organizations, and other activities. The community is in the Lake Como area of Fort Worth, a black working class district; this is, in effect, a progress report on the effectiveness of community initiative. Thirteen tables provide data on demography, occupations, income, family structure, and social activities in the neighbourhood. The emphasis is on the growing politicization of blacks in Lake Como and their realization that constructing a playground and other tentative steps are not enough to break down the 'walls' built by whites around the community.

370　I am Annie Mae, an extraordinary woman in her own words: the personal history of a black Texas woman.
Edited by Ruthe Winegarten, Frieda Werden.　Austin, Texas:
Rosegarden Press, 1983. 151p.

Born in 1909, the granddaughter of former slaves, Annie Mae McDade Prosper Hunt tells the story of black females in Texas from her grandmother to herself – lives that have spanned 120 years. Annie Mae worked as a domestic, like her mother and grandmother (and most black women) and picked cotton in near-slavery conditions. She later became a self-employed seamstress and cosmetics saleswoman serving the black community. Married three times, she spent most of her life as a single mother with six children, although she suffered three miscarriages and three of her children died as infants. Her autobiography provides fascinating material on slavery – her grandmother could clearly remember the day her mother was sold; the family and friendship networks developed by black women; the depression of the 1930s; single motherhood; black political participation after the 1950s (she attended President Jimmy Carter's inauguration in 1977); black churches; and the civil rights movement. Annie Mae is remarkable mainly because she recorded her experiences; her narrative, while a bit disjointed and often plagued by frustrating brevity, is a useful first-hand account of over a century of African-American life in Texas.

371　Prairie View: a study in public conscience, 1878-1946.
George Ruble Woolfolk.　New York: Pageant, 1962. 404p. bibliog.

Founded as a land grant college and normal school for African-Americans in 1879, Prairie View A & M typified the philosophy of 'industrial education' for blacks in the post-Reconstruction South. Woolfolk discusses northern philanthropy and the farmers' movement of the late 19th century as influences in the founding of the school. The narrative emphasizes administrators and political fights over public funding, black student life, the up-grading to a four-year institution after the turn of the century, and the transformation of ideology from purely agricultural and mechanical pursuits to a broader curriculum after the Great Depression. Six tables provide statistics on state funding, salary scales, and enrollment.

Europeans

372 **The first Polish-Americans: Silesian settlements in Texas.**
T. Lindsay Baker. College Station, Texas: Texas A & M University Press, 1979. 268p. maps. bibliog.

A chronological look at the Silesians who emigrated to Texas in the 1850s, precursors to the millions of Poles who began arriving in the United States in the last part of the 19th century. Baker carries their story into the 20th century and shows that their experiences represent a microcosm of the immigrant process in the United States. He provides a broad look at their motivations, problems, progress, accomplishments, and relationships with other Texans, and emphasizes their long-lasting distinctiveness and Polish consciousness as well as their eventual assimilation into Texas and American culture. Three dozen illustrations, including many photographs, complement this sympathetic, extensively researched, and clearly written book.

373 **The Germans in Texas: a study in immigration.**
Gilbert G. Benjamin. Philadelphia: The author, 1909; San Francisco: R and E Research Associates, 1970. 157p. maps. bibliog. (Americana Germanica).

Benjamin's book is a very old but still useful examination of German settlement in Texas before the Civil War, with effective summaries of their economic and political contributions, their attitudes on slavery, their cultural institutions (singing and fraternal societies, gymnasiums, newspapers), the process of settlement, and the Germans' first impressions of their new home. The appendixes include the constitution and laws of the German settlements (in German).

374 **The history of German settlement in Texas, 1831-1861.**
Rudolph L. Biesele. Austin, Texas: Boeckmann Jones, 1930. 259p. maps. bibliog.

The classic scholarly account of Germans in pre-Civil War Texas, this book is still a reliable and often-cited work. Biesele describes German immigration to Texas in general; the histories of most of the German communities founded on the Lower Brazos, Guadalupe, and Colorado Rivers; the work done by the Society for the Protection of German Immigrants in Texas to help Germans settle in Texas; the Germans' relations with the Indians; and their participation in politics (for instance, they earned a reputation for their opposition to slavery and devotion to the United States government at a time when neither attitude was popular in the South). The book also covers the economic and social life of German communities and the institutions which the immigrants transferred from Germany to Texas.

375 **The English-Texans.**
Thomas W. Cutrer. San Antonio, Texas: Institute of Texan Cultures, 1985. 187p. maps. bibliog. (Texians and Texans).

Beginning with Stephen F. Austin in the 1820s, Cutrer chronicles the rise of prominent Anglo-Texans such as Edward Manell House and his descendants, James Pinckney Henderson, and others. He then goes on to describe the experiences of less well-known 'common' English-Texans as farmers, ranchers, and small businessmen. He has methodically found English-born Texans who were doctors and lawyers, politicians and military men, as well as a few prominent women. Two short chapters describe life for post-frontier Anglo-Texans and Welsh immigration to the state. One highlight of this informal book is provided by the eighty-two black-and-white photographs, sketches and documents relating to the English in Texas.

376 **The Irish-Texans.**
John Brendan Flannery.   San Antonio, Texas: Institute of Texan Cultures, 1980. 170p. maps. bibliog. (Texians and Texans).

Irish immigrants were among the first settlers of Texas. In fact, drawing on their shared religion, some openly sided with Mexico during the Texas Revolution. In two dozen short chapters, Flannery describes Irish colonies in Texas and Irish communities in cities like Galveston, Houston, Victoria and San Antonio, from their beginnings to about 1900. He attempts to show that Irish-Texan history paralleled Texas history as a whole. The author examines Irish customs brought to Texas, especially the importance of the Catholic church to the Irish community; the prosperity and political influence of Irish who settled in coastal cities; Irish activities during the Texas Revolution and the Civil War; and Irish railroaders and outlaws. Six maps of Ireland and of Texas and ninety illustrations of prominent Irish Texans, artifacts, places, events, and documents are included.

377 **El Paso merchant and civic leader from the 1880s through the Mexican Revolution.**
Samuel J. Freudenthal.   El Paso, Texas: Texas Western Press,1965. 44p. bibliog.

The autobiography of Samuel J. Freudenthal (1863-1939), an El Paso businessman and politician (he served on the school board and on the city council) who for many years was one of the most prominent Jews in El Paso. Floyd S. Fierman has contributed additional research and notes to Freudenthal's memoirs, which focus on his business and civic activities; marriage and family life; the Jewish community and a fraternal organization – the Nobles of the Mystic Shrine – which he helped to organize; baseball; visits to El Paso by United States Presidents; and Freudenthal's experiences in Mexico.

378 **Texians and Texans.**
Institute of Texan Cultures.   Austin, Texas: University of Texas Press for the Institute of Texan cultures, 1972-87.

Between 1972-86, the University of Texas's Institute of Texan Cultures, located in San Antonio, issued a series of pamphlets providing brief histories of a number of ethnic groups in Texas, with special attention paid to their customs, religions, and everyday lives. The groups included in the series, along with the date of publication and length of the pamphlet, are: *Afro-American Texans* (1987. 2nd ed.), 31p; *Anglo-American Texans* (1985), 24p; *Chinese Texans* (1978), 21p; *Czech Texans* (1972), 32p; *French Texans* (1973), 32p; *German Texans* (1987), 240p; *Greek Texans* (1974), 32p; *Italian Texans* (1986), 32p; *Jewish Texans* (1974), 32p; *Mexican Texans* (1986), 23p; *Norwegian Texans* (1985), 32p; *Polish Texans* (1972), 32p; *Swiss Texans* (1977), 23p; *Syrian and Lebanese Texans* (1974), 32p; and *Wendish Texans* (1982), 120p.

379   John O. Meusebach: German colonizer in Texas.
       Irene M. King.   Austin, Texas: University of Texas Press, 1967. 192p.
       map. bibliog.
A scholarly, but unobjective biography by a descendant of Meusebach (1812-97), a
prominent promotor of German immigration to Texas. Meusebach was an extremely
well-educated politican and bureaucrat in Germany who administered German
colonization to Texas and later served as a state senator. After migrating to Texas in
1845, he was commissioner general of the German Immigration Company and a leader
in the German-Texas community. This is a simple biography divided into three parts:
his life in Germany from 1812-45; his role in the colonization of Texas from 1845-47
(including German experiences with their Indian and Anglo neighbours and other
frontier hardships), and the last fifty years of his life, during which time he served in
the state government, raised a family, and built a reputation as an amateur naturalist.
A fold-out map locates all of the German settlements in Texas.

380   Czech voices: stories from Texas in the *Amerikán Národni Kalendár*.
       Translated and edited by Clinton Machann, James W. Mendl Jr.
       College Station, Texas: Texas A & M University Press, 1991. 192p.
       bibliog. (Centennial Series of the Association of Former Students,
       Texas A & M University).
First published in the Czech journal *Amerikán Národni Kalendár*, these are the
personal narratives of Czechs on the Texas frontier. An interpretative introduction and
extensive notes place the stories in their historical context. They emphasize Czech
customs as practiced in Texas, religious conflicts, the Civil War, the challenges of
assimilation, relationships with the Anglo-American majority, and economic contributions. The speakers comprise an articulate and (obviously) literate, cross-section of the
early Czech community ranging from adventurers to leaders to common farmers.

381   Texas politics, 1906-1944: with special reference to the German counties.
       Seth Shepard McKay.   Lubbock, Texas: Texas Tech University Press,
       1952. 486p. bibliog.
An extremely thorough and methodical examination of every major and minor election
in Texas during the first four decades of the century (each chapter covers a different
campaign) and of the voting patterns and attitudes of Texas Germans. McKay
describes the Germans' reactions to strong nativist and anti-black sentiment in Texas,
the political activities of the Ku Klux Klan, the economic effects of the Depression and
of the Second World War, and the dominance of the Democratic Party. He finds that,
even as late as the mid-20th century, Germans tended to stray from the mainstream in
Texas politics. At least half remained committed to the Republican Party that
Germans had joined in large numbers during Reconstruction, despite its clear minority
status in the state as a whole. Although many German-Texans had assimilated into the
larger culture, many had retained their ethnic identity, at least politically.

382   *Krasna Amerika*: a study of Texas Czechs, 1851-1939.
       James W. Mendl.   Austin, Texas: Eakin Press, 1983. 280p. maps.
       bibliog.
A methodical, clear study of the impact of the broader American and Texas cultures
on Czechs which is thoroughly researched in both American and Czech sources. This is
not a dramatic tale of immigrants' hardships and struggles on the frontier; their story is

taken well into the 20th century, and this is one of the strengths of this book. Mendl devotes chapters to the original Czech immigrants to Texas and the early histories of their settlements, the diaspora of those communities, the Czech-Texans' social structure, religion, and folk culture, newspapers and literature, and the ways in which Czechs assimilated yet retained at least symbolic fragments of their culture. A number of appendixes provide further information on Czech folklore and newspapers, a chronology of the settlement of Czechs in Texas, Texas counties with their Czech populations, and a guide to Czech pronunciation.

383 **In search of a home: nineteenth century Wendish immigration.**
George R. Nielsen.   College Station, Texas: Texas A & M University Press, 1989. 213p. maps.

This is a revision of the 1977 edition published by the University of Birmingham, England. Nielsen describes (with little analysis) this tiny and little-known Slavic-German ethnic group's journey from Germany to Australia and (for the most part) Texas. The Wendish shared with German immigrants their political and economic reasons for migrating, and settled near the Germans, associating with German Lutheran sects (especially the Missouri Synod Lutherans). The author examines religious organization and leaders and describes the everyday lives of ordinary people. A useful source for genealogists is the long appendix, which lists all of the Wendish immigrants to Australia who went on to settle in Texas.

384 **Texas pioneers from Poland: a study in ethnic history.**
Jacek Przygoda.   Waco, Texas: Texian Press, 1971. 171p. bibliog.

Although Polish Texans did not come to Texas in the mid-19th century to build a 'New Poland', they did retain characteristics of their native land, such as a strong religious faith, a moral code of individual, family, and social conduct, a love of freedom, and the hope for economic improvement. The author asserts that material progress came for the Poles as a group and that even in the 20th century Texas Poles retain the concept of a pluralistic, rather than an individualistic, society. As a result, he focuses on three Polish-Texan communities: two parishes in San Antonio – St Hedwig's and St Michael's – and on Panna Maria settlement and parish in South Texas. Przygoda adds a chapter on Poles elsewhere in the state and another on Polish miners, businessmen, and professionals. Three tables and nearly a dozen appendixes provide quantitative evidence on the Polish population in Texas, their economic progress, and their employment, and lists the pastors of Panna Maria Parish between 1854-70.

385 **We're Czechs.**
R. L. Skrabanek.   College Station, Texas: Texas A & M University Press, 1988. 240p. bibliog. (Centennial Series of the Association of Former Students, Texas A & M University).

An autobiographical account of the Czech community of Snook, Texas, a rural farming community in the south-central portion of the state. Much of it is based on the author's personal reminiscences, and on interviews with other residents about growing up in Snook in the 1920s and 1930s. The author discusses every day life in Snook during this era. Residents had no electricity, heated their houses with wood-burning stoves, drove on un-surfaced roads, and used mules for field work. The tight-knit Czech community spoke their native language in school, in church, and in conversation, and extended family groups were quite common. In addition to farm work, family ties, and the town's one-room school, the author discusses the Czech benevolent and mutual aid societies and the Moravian Church to which many of Snook's Czechs belonged. The author finishes with a wistful account about how things have changed for the Czech community in the half-century since he grew up.

386   **Coming to terms: the German hill country of Texas.**
      Wendy Watriss, Fred Baldwin, Lawrence Goodwyn.   College Station,
      Texas: Texas A & M University Press, 1991. 160p. (The Charles and
      Elizabeth Prothro Texas Photography Series).

An artistic, historical, almost anthropological examination of the modernization of a traditionally isolated corner of Texas. The rugged Hill Country, north of San Antonio and west of Austin, was settled in the 1850s by German immigrants, and even today is characterized by tidy towns and small farms. Its unique architecture (including rock houses) and lifestyle (the prevalence of the German language and the Germans' political distinctiveness) have survived but are fading in the 20th century. With an essay by noted Texas historian Lawrence Goodwyn that places the Hill Country in its historical context, *Coming to Terms* offers nearly thirty historical and over eighty contemporary duotone photographs of sites and scenes from this geographically and ethnically intriguing region of Texas.

387   **Castro's colony: empresario development in Texas, 1842-1856.**
      Bobby D. Weaver.   College Station, Texas: Texas A & M University
      Press, 1985. 158p. maps. bibliog.

The Republic of Texas administered an 'empresario' programme similar to Mexico's, whose purpose was to grant huge tracts of land to individuals or organizations who agreed to sponsor immigration to this sparsely settled region. The author uses the empresario grant and colony of Henri Castro (1786-1865) to illustrate how the system developed, how it operated, and its impact on Texas. Texas hit hard times in 1837 and it tried to sell some of its public lands to ease its financial crisis. Castro was the French consul to Texas when he became involved in the land speculation business; he settled his colony southwest of San Antonio in Medina County. Many of the settlers were German Catholics who emigrated to Texas in the mid-1840s. Weaver describes the nuts and bolts of organizing and settling the grant, the management of water resources, the hardships endured by the settlers, the creation of Castroville (the primary town within the land grant), the rise of the livestock industry in the 1850s, and the Civil War in Castro's colony (many residents sympathized with the Confederate cause, but most of the men joined frontier regiments to avoid service in the Confederate Army).

Asians

388   **The Chinese in El Paso.**
      Nancy Farrar.   El Paso, Texas: Texas Western Press, 1972. 44p.
      bibliog.

A succinct account of the Chinese in late 19th-century El Paso, from their arrival in the 1880s as railroad workers through their expansion into other occupations such as launderers, restauranteurs, servants, and gardeners. Farrar briefly surveys Chinese customs as practiced in the overcrowded 'Chinatown' and describes the career of Sam

Hing, a successful businessman, but she concentrates on the more colourful opium dens, smugglers (especially of illegal aliens), and Tong organizations (societies that developed into gambling rings and criminal gangs).

Women

389 The labor of women in the production of cotton.
Ruth Allen. Austin, Texas: University of Texas, 1931; New York: Arno Press, 1975. 285p. bibliog.

This reprint of a 1930 University of Texas Research Bulletin is out-dated but useful from a historical standpoint, providing a quantitative study of women who lived on Texas farms where cotton was the main crop. Allen shows that poor women and single women who were the daughters of farmers were, logically, more likely to work in the fields than middle-class women. Race was also a factor; a higher percentage of black and *Tejano* than white women worked in the fields. The author demonstrates that wages and working conditions for most women field workers were below subsistence levels. Although her study focuses on women, it also provides evidence of the chronic economic depression caused by an over-dependence on cotton. Allen places women's labour in the cotton-growing industry in the context of the migration of Mexican agricultural workers to Texas. She concludes by predicting that many of these women will eventually join the unskilled factory labour force as the Texas industrial base expands. Allen includes eighteen black-and-white photographs of Texas women cotton workers, their homes, and their families. More interesting are the eighty-two tables provided by the author that furnish information on such topics as race, parentage, marital status, magazine subscriptions, social contacts, housework methods, children, canned and preserved goods, soap-making, gardens, income, hours of field work per day, and luxury items owned.

390 Women of the depression: caste and culture in San Antonio, 1919-1939.
Julia Kirk Blackwelder. College Station, Texas: Texas A & M University Press, 1984. 279p. bibliog.

An analysis of social structure and discrimination in terms of social and occupational mobility, and the relationships between white, black, and Hispanic female workers in 1930s San Antonio. Blackwelder bases her arguments on quantitative research in United States Census Bureau records; she analyses income, crime, motherhood, unemployment, occupations, family size and status, race, school attendance, housing, and more general demographic information. She concludes that the Depression touched San Antonio women differently, depending on their race and social class. For instance, black women tended to work in domestic service, Mexican-Americans in industrial jobs, and whites in sales and clerical positions. The latter left the Depression in better shape than their black and Hispanic counterparts, who, due to the double handicap of their gender and race, were kept from entering better, higher-paying occupations. In addition to numerous statistical appendixes, Blackwelder summarizes her use of economic and social theory in an appendix.

391 Women in early Texas.
Edited by Evelyn M. Carrington.   Austin, Texas: Jenkins, 1975. 308p.

An informally written series of profiles of more than fifty notable women from various ethnic groups (including a handful of blacks, Hispanics, and Indians, and a number of women from European immigrant stock, especially Germans) in 19th century Texas. There is little analysis in these short biographies, but plenty of specifics about each woman's family, experiences, attitudes, and contributions to society and to the economy. The emphasis is on their toughness, adaptability, strength, and grace under pressure.

392 Women in Texas: their lives, their experiences, their accomplishments.
Ann Fears Crawford, Crystal Sasse Ragsdale.   Burnet, Texas: Eakin Press, 1982. 394p. bibliog.

Another collection of mini-biographies of a wide variety of black, white, and Mexican-American women from the 19th and 20th centuries. The purpose is to contrast the various roles played by women: as farmers, cattlewomen, members of élites, politicans, writers, artists, and in other fields. The authors emphasize the women's accomplishments and argue that Texas frontier conditions and the ethos of rugged individualism encouraged women, as well as men, to be strong and ambitious. This is a useful source for its basic information, its bibliography of secondary sources, and the photographs it provides of the women in question.

393 Women in the Texas workforce: yesterday and today.
Edited by Richard Croxdale, Melissa Hield.   Austin, Texas: People's History in Texas, 1979. 54p.

Although this is a very short and not widely distributed booklet, the four essays in it fill a neglected niche in the history of Texas women. The focus is on women workers in the garment and pecan-shelling industries in Texas between the 1930s and the 1950s, especially their activities in organized labour. Black women are considered in a variety of work situations during the same period as well as more recent times and the author gives attention to the entrance of women into white collar jobs. The authors point out the problems faced by women who want or need to work outside the home, such as low wages, the paucity of child care, and job discrimination. They also describe methods, including (but not restricted to) labour union activity, which women have used in attempting to overcome such problems.

394 **Ella Elgar Bird Dumont: an autobiography of a west Texas pioneer.**
Ella Elgar Bird Dumont, edited by Tommy J. Boley. Austin, Texas:
University of Texas Press, 1988. 227p. bibliog. (Barker Texas History
Center Series).

Dumont lived between 1861 and 1943, and this is a first-hand account of daily life on
the developing West Texas frontier from the 1870s to the early 20th century. In
addition to the events and details it provides of this ordinary woman's life, the book is
also valuable for the editors' substantial notes and bibliography, and for Emily Cutrer's
foreword which places the memoir in the context of recent historiography of frontier
women.

395 **Texas women in politics.**
Edited by Elizabeth E. Fernea, (et al.). Austin, Texas: Foundation of
Women's Resources, 1977. 287p.

This combines history, collective biography, and bibliography on Texas women in
local, state, and federal political offices, and on political organizations for Texas
women. The first section of the book provides an historical narrative of Texas women
in politics, while the second furnishes personal narratives of women who have served
as political campaigners and administrators, and in every office from school boards to
county courts, the state legislature to Congress, and from United States District Courts
to the US President's cabinet. The third section focuses on statistics from the Texas
Women's Voter Education Project and includes tables on women in Texan political
offices and women's views on political issues and political participation. The last
section provides lists of current legislators and women's political organizations,
and bibliographies of women's issues and women's suffrage.

396 **Claiming their land: women homesteaders in Texas.**
Florence C. Gould, Patricia N. Pando. El Paso, Texas: Texas
Western Press, 1991. 94p. map.

Between 1845-98, 1,481 female heads-of-household claimed homesteads in Texas. The
authors look at the differences between homesteaders on state and federal lands,
examine the changing legal and political contexts that allowed women to become
homesteaders, and describe the lives of women homesteaders in Texas. A great deal of
information is presented on size of homesteads (especially comparing male and female
homesteaders), differences in the percentages of women homesteaders in the various
land districts around the state, and Texas land law. An appendix provides a list of all
female claimants in Texas during those years.

397 **Revolt against chivalry: Jesse Daniel Ames and the women's campaign
against lynching.**
Jacquelyn Dowd Hall. New York: Columbia University Press, 1979.
373p. bibliog.

Hall examines the ways that middle-class southern women confronted the issues of sex,
race, power, and feminism in the early 20th century through the work of Jessie Daniel
Ames (1883-1972), a Texas suffragist and leader at the state, regional, and national
levels of the Commission on Inter-racial Cooperation. In many ways, Ames
represented all well-off, late-Victorian American women; yet she was also deeply
involved in political and social reform. In addition to providing a biography of Ames,
the author describes the work of the Association of Southern Women for the

Prevention of Lynching, which fought the murders and extra-judicial executions of African-Americans. Hall adeptly links feminism with racial justice; she uses her professional but affecting biography of Ames to illustrate the backgrounds, decisions, life-styles, personalities, and goals of women in her place, time, and class.

398 **Concealed under petticoats: married women's property and the law of Texas, 1840-1913.**
Kathleen Elizabeth Lazarou. New York: Garland, 1986. 236p. bibliog. (Garland Series of Outstanding Dissertations).

Lazarou argues in her unrevised PhD dissertation that women's property rights – governed by the several Married Women's Property Acts passed by the state legislature between 1840-1913 – reflected national trends and were not merely local phenomena. These acts were rooted in English common law, which was supposed to protect married women's property from irresponsible husbands. Although on the surface these acts looked much fairer to women than English common law, the author's research into diaries, newspapers, and letters shows otherwise. In fact, the acts recognized a woman's rights to own property (a right carried over from Spanish customs) but English common law prevented her from controlling it. Although the legislature did loosen the laws during the decades following the Civil War, it was not until 1913 that Texas legislators liberalized the law and allowed married women control over their own property.

399 **Women on the Texas frontier: a cross-cultural perspective.**
Ann Patton Malone. El Paso, Texas: Texas Western Press, 1983. 78p. bibliog.

Malone offers a comparison of the Texas frontier experiences of Anglo-American, Indian, and black women. Native American women were adapted to frontier life, but were threatened by the increased presence of non-Indians. Anglo-American women had households to build and to run, and dangers and illnesses to fight. Black women were often slaves or heads of households, or both, which made their experiences especially grueling. Although the conclusions are unsurprising, this is the only, albeit brief, attempt to deal with women from all three major ethnic groups in Texas.

400 **The search for Emma's story: a model for humanities detective work.**
Marian L. Martinello. Fort Worth, Texas: Texas Christian University Press, 1987. 223p. maps.

This shows the reconstruction, through the use of artifacts such as photographs and personal belongings, public records, oral histories, and newspapers, of the life of Emma Beckmann, a young wife and mother in Stonewall, Texas, who happened to be a neighbour of Lyndon B. Johnson in the period 1910–20. The life of this hitherto unknown Texas woman is interesting in its own right, but the book is also valuable, as the title suggests, as a model for researching and writing life stories of ordinary people. The author explains possible sources and methodologies in her final chapter. This is a helpful guide for those interested in women's, family, or public history, and is also a good account of late 19th and early 20th century life in the Texas Hill Country.

401 **Westering women and the frontier experience, 1800-1915.**
Sandra L. Myres. Albuquerque, New Mexico: University of New
Mexico Press, 1982. 365p. maps. bibliog. (Histories of the American
Frontier).

A study of women's contributions to the development of the frontier, based on
women's writings, many of them from Texan archives. Myres includes not only white
women, but also the French, Spanish, Native American, black, and Mexican-American
women who shared the frontier experience. The author shows how women's
expectations of the frontier differed from those of men and how those preconceptions
changed when confronted with reality. Myres' chapters explore historical stereotypes
of frontier women, women's views of the wilderness and of the Indians, women on
wagon trains and in the home, women as voters and entrepreneurs, and family values
and community on the frontier.

402 **The cowgirls.**
Joyce Gibson Roach. Denton, Texas: University of North Texas
Press, 1990. 2nd ed. 259p. bibliog.

Roach considers women ranchers as struggling pioneers whose hard work allowed
them to function at a level of social equality with their husbands. She also examines the
second generation of ranch women who popularized the cowgirl in Wild West shows.
Three elements were significant to the growth of the myth and legend of the cowgirl:
their clothes, their horses, and their guns. The author reveals that, for all the
hardships, rancher women had certain freedoms that other women did not, such as
dressing the way they pleased. In addition, in taking on men's work and
responsibilities, they also had to ride horses and carry guns like men. As a result,
cowgirls found ranch life to be something of an equalizer. The author also examines
modern day cowgirls and rodeo stars, stereotypes of cowgirls, the roles of cowgirls in
movies and in western humour, and the relationships between ranch men and ranch
women.

403 **Citizens at last: the women's suffrage movement in Texas.**
A. Elizabeth Taylor. Austin, Texas: Ellen C. Temple, 1987. 242p.
map. bibliog.

A three-part narrative and source book on the movement by Texas women to gain the
vote. Part one provides a brief history of the movement in Texas, the first southern
state to extend the vote to women, and includes the women's ideology, the hardships
they endured, and their campaign strategies. Part two provides a chronological
presentation of documents relating to the movement, such as speeches, letters, and
essays by Texan suffragettes. Part three consists of a bibliography of the suffrage
movement and a bibliography on women in Texas politics and public affairs. Forty-five
photographs, broadsides, and cartoons pertaining to suffrage in Texas accompany the
text.

404 **Texas quilts, Texas women.**
Suzanne Yabsley. College Station, Texas: Texas A & M University
Press, 1984. 99p. bibliog.

An examination of 19th and 20th century quilts and the Texas women who produced
them. Quilting was a social phenomenon that provided interaction as well as artistic
expression. Yabsley provides an account of quilt making throughout the history of

Texas. She also profiles many Texas women quilters by using the diaries and letters of 19th century women and interviews with more recent quilters. The book examines quilting as an art form, as a means of self-expression, and as a way of developing female networks. Significantly, the author includes quilting in slave and African-American communities. Finally, she also details modern quilting clubs and Texas museums that display quilts. Twelve black-and-white and eleven colour photographs demonstrated the styles and messages of a century and a half of Texas quilting.

Religion

405 Nothing better than this: the biography of James Huckins, first Baptist missionary to Texas.
Eugene W. Baker.   Waco, Texas: Baylor University Press, 1985. 175p. bibliog. (Baylor University Founders).

Heavily rooted in church sources, along with a few other primary and secondary works, this is the biography of the New Englander, James Huckins (1807-63), who arrived in Texas in 1839. Despite his northern origins, Huckins was a pro-slavery minister, which had helped force him out of his New England parish before his journey to Texas as a missionary. This simple narrative describes his role in the creation of Baptist churches in Houston – where the First Baptist church grew into a congregation of 18,000 – and Galveston, Baylor University, the Baptist State Convention, and the Union Baptist Association. Huckins left Texas to become a pastor in Charleston, South Carolina, in 1859; he died as a Confederate chaplain during the Civil War.

406 The Southern Baptist Convention and its people, 1607-1972.
Robert Baker.   Nashville, Tennessee: Broadman Press, 1974. 477p. bibliog.

A social history of the Southern Baptists in the United States, aimed at ministers and at students attending Baptist seminaries. Baker examines the demography of local and regional Baptist congregations (shown in thirty tables) as well as the formation of individual congregations, the effects of national events (the American Revolution, the slavery controversy, the Civil and World Wars), and the rise of foreign mission work as an important element of church activities. The Southern Baptist Convention was actually formed in 1845, when the debate over the morality of slavery split the northern and southern wings of the Baptist church. Several appendixes list the presidents and meeting places of the Southern Baptist Convention, the number of churches in each state convention, and seminaries and academies.

407 The Southern Baptists holy war: the self-destructive struggle for power
within the largest protestant denomination in America.
Joe Edward Barnhart.   Austin, Texas: Texas Monthly Press, 1986.
273p.

An analysis of the internecine warfare between 'Moderates' and 'Fundamentalists' or
'Inerrantist' Southern Baptists over Biblical interpretation, the role of women in the
church, the relationship between church and state, academic freedom, birth control,
and creedalism (whether or not every Baptist must subscribe to the same creed). The
'war' is basically a Fundamentalist uprising, and they have been gradually winning
control of the denomination. Despite his unwieldy title, Barnhart presents a useful
description of the controversies and argues that the two groups have different world
views that cannot be reconciled without serious compromise by one or both sides. Such
a compromise seems to be less likely as time goes on.

408 Lone-star vanguard: the Catholic re-occupation of Texas.
Ralph Francis Bayard.   St Louis, Missouri: The Vincentian Press,
1945. 453p. bibliog.

This is a heavily biographical narrative of the work of twelve missionaries from the
Catholic Order of Saint Vincent De Paul, who arrived in Texas in 1838. Partly inspired
to journey from the United States because of Irish Texans' desire for an organized
church, they were led by Father John Timon. In addition to detailed information on
the missionaries themselves, there is a great deal on papal and church politics; this is
more an administrative history than anything else. The book culminates in 1848, with
the dedication of St Mary's Cathedral in Galveston.

409 Religion on the Texas frontier.
Carter E. Boren.   San Antonio, Texas: Naylor, 1968. 375p. bibliog.

A fact-filled narrative of the Disciples of Christ in Texas, from 1824 to 1906, when
there were roughly 100,000 members of the sect. Boren, a deacon of the church,
concentrates on missionary work, higher education, internal divisions (such as the
debate over slavery), and church structure. Although he calls his work a 'ringing
affirmation' of the movement and of its democratic form of Christianity, he is critical of
the 19th century Disciples' lack of concern for social issues, their racial prejudice, their
indifference to historical and contemporary events and thought, their isolation from
the religious mainstream, and their informal organization.

410 Social justice and church authority: the public life of Archbishop Robert
E. Lucey.
Saul E. Bronder.   Philadelphia, Pennsylvania: Temple University
Press, 1982. 215p. bibliog.

Lucey (1891-1977) was a native of Los Angeles, California, who eventually became the
first Bishop of the Diocese of Amarillo, Texas, in the 1920s and later, in 1941, the
Archbishop of San Antonio. This scholarly biography stresses his social activism
throughout his career; he often took unpopular stances in favour of organized labour in
the 1920s and 1930s, the rights of Mexican migrant workers in the 1940s and 1950s, and
racial integration in the 1960s.

411 **Our Catholic heritage in Texas, 1519-1936.**
Carlos Eduardo Castañeda. Austin, Texas: Von Boeckmann-Jones,
1936-58. 7 vols. maps. bibliog.

Although subsequent historians have found factual errors, this encyclopaedic account is still the most important and frequently cited work on Catholicism in Texas from 1519-1950. Casteneda finished the last volume on his deathbed. The author is concerned more with facts than with analysis, and follows a chronological approach until the final volume. Volume one describes exploration in Texas, Catholic martyrs, and the beginnings of mission work among the Indians, while volume two deals primarily with the founding of missions and exploration in the Big Bend area. Volume three details the functioning of the missions, the exploration of the Gulf Coast, and the interests of France and Great Britain in Texas. Volumes four and five explore the decline of the missions and their eventual secularization, the San Saba massacre, and the founding of the last mission at Nuestra Senoro del Refugio. Volume six incorporates political history with religious history in recounting both the Mexican and Texas Revolutions. Finally, volume seven, published as a supplement, takes a topical approach to over a century of post-Texas Revolution Catholic history.

412 **Four decades of Catholicism in Texas, 1820-1860.**
Sister Mary Angela Fitzmorris. Washington, DC: The Catholic
University of America, 1926. 109p. bibliog.

A minimally revised doctoral dissertation on the Catholic Church in Texas after the secularization of the missions at the turn of the 19th century. Although the author is unabashedly sympathetic to the work of the church, this is an honest narrative, firmly rooted in Texas history, of church development and politics and the growth of Catholicism on the frontier. The most prominent figure in the book is Bishop John Odin, who worked in Texas from 1842-61.

413 **Iglesia Presbiteriana: a history of Presbyterians and Mexican-Americans of the southwest.**
Francisco O. García-Treto, R. Douglas Brackenridge. San Antonio,
Texas: Trinity University Press, 1974. 2nd ed. 278p. map. bibliog.
(Presbyterian Historical Society Publications).

A well-researched and objective narrative by professors in the Department of Religion at Trinity University in San Antonio. They divide the history of the contact between Presbyterians and Mexican-Americans into three sections. Part one, 1830-1910, stresses missionary work and schools. Part two, 1910-60, describes the Presbyterians' adoption of a social services mission at the national and local levels; by the end of this period, there was an all-time high of 10,000 Mexican-American communicants. Part three, 1960 through the early 1970s, shows how the Chicano movement disrupted normal mission work and altered attitudes. Events in Texas are especially important in chapters one and four.

414 **Diamond jubilee album: Archdiocese of San Antonio, 1874-1949.**
Edited and compiled by Rev. M. J. Gilbert. San Antonio, Texas:
Schreider Printing, 1949. 304p. map.

This is a typical celebratory volume commemorating the 75th anniversary of the
founding of the Archdiocese of San Antonio. One hundred and fifty contributors wrote
200 entries concentrating on biographies of important churchmen and brief histories of
the parishes in the South Central Texas Archdiocese.

415 **Dominican women in Texas: from Ohio to Galveston and beyond.**
Sheila Hackett. Houston, Texas: Sacred Heart Convent of Texas,
1986. 782p. bibliog.

This is a history of the work of the Dominican Sisters in Houston's Congregation of the
Sacred Heart. The original group of nuns arrived in Texas from Ohio in 1882; during
the next century, they established dozens of elementary schools, high schools, and
colleges in Texas, California, and Guatemala. Hackett provides a thoroughly
researched chronicle that includes information on church politics, problems, and
successes; separate histories of the more than fifty schools founded and administered
by the sisters, and thirty-nine appendixes that provide lists ranging from school
uniforms and awards at Pius X High School in 1985, to the names of the sisters serving
in Guatemala in 1966, to the first student roll at Our Lady of Perpetual Help School in
Beaumont, Texas, in 1895.

416 **God's last and only hope: the fragmentation of the Southern Baptist
Convention.**
Bill J. Leonard. Grand Rapids, Michigan: W. B. Erdmans, 1990.
187p.

A case study of the Southern Baptist Convention as a reflection of tensions between
church and culture in the United States. The author examines in a scholarly manner
the factions within the denomination – fundamentalists versus non-fundamentalists,
liberals versus conservatives, blacks versus whites – throughout the history of the
Convention from the 1880s to the present. Each element of the Convention is
discussed, not as static systems of ideas, but as developing interest groups and policies
(concerning internal politics, race relations, and the relationships between the South
and the rest of the United States and between the Baptists and other religious
denominations). Southern Baptist theology and political activities are also discussed, as
is the future of the organization, which will continue to fragment, argues the author, if
a new consensus fails to develop.

417 **Frontiersmen of the faith: a history of Baptist pioneer work in Texas,
1865-1885.**
Zane Allen Mason. San Antonio, Texas: The Naylor Company, 1970.
219p. bibliog.

This is not a general study of Baptists in Texas, but only of the problems they
encountered and the lives they built on the Texas frontier. The author focuses on
challenges such as hostile Indians, vast distances, and meagre resources, and on the
ways in which these pioneering Baptists dealt with those problems. Other areas studied
include missionary work, the importance of frontier revivals, the growth of the Baptist
church, and its role in the 'civilizing' process. Three appendixes list Baptist associations
and the names of the missionaries who operated in the state.

Religion

418 **Blessed assurance: at home with the bomb in Amarillo, Texas.**
A. G. Mojtabai. Boston, Massachusetts: Houghton Mifflin, 1986.
255p.

The author attempts to explain why and how Amarillo, Texas, has become so well-adapted to the presence of Pantex (the final assembly plant for all nuclear weapons in the United States), especially in the face of constant anti-nuclear demonstrations outside the plant. Mojtabai interviewed Amarillo residents, Pantex workers, and city leaders, and conducted research into newspapers and government records in tracing the city's history and its relationship with the United States nuclear industry. He concludes that faith and reality have intersected to make Amarillans resigned to the existence of the plant. They respond in two ways: the apocalyptic (a belief that the end of the world and the second coming of Christ are near) and the technocratic (a belief that the bomb denotes technological progress).

419 **The calvary of Christ on the Rio Grande, 1849-1883.**
Bernard Poyon. Milwaukee, Wisconsin: Bruce Press, 1956. 252p.
maps. bibliog.

A narrative of the missionary work of the Oblates of Mary Immaculate, a Roman Catholic religious order headquartered in France, along the Mexican border, from 1849, when they first arrived in Brownsville, to 1883, when the order underwent a continent-wide reorganization. A total of about forty priests and brothers served in Texas during these years; an appendix includes all of their names. Poyon begins the book with a brief introduction on the mission era in Texas from 1690-1821, then presents a straightforward, chronological account that stresses hardships, the sometimes bitter debates within the order, and the difficulties of reconciling the needs of the Spanish-speaking majority with the wishes of the more dominant Anglo-American minority.

420 **Cold anger: a story of faith and power politics.**
Mary Beth Rogers. Denton, Texas: University of North Texas Press,
1990. 222p.

Written by a political scientist, *Cold Anger* chronicles the work of Ernesto Cortes, Jr, and other members of the Industrial Areas Foundation Network. Cortes and IAF have worked in cities and communities throughout Texas to get poor, minority, and working class people into the political mainstream and involved in programmes to improve their communities. Through a mixture of progressive politics and Christian values, much of the organizing occurs through local churches and parishes. Although this grass roots movement to regain control of their communities by the residents of slums and working class neighbourhoods began in San Antonio, it has spread to other Texas cities.

421 **The Southern Baptists: a subculture in transition.**
Ellen Rosenberg. Knoxville, Tennessee: University of Tennessee
Press, 1989. 240p. bibliog.

Rosenberg has produced an anthropological work on the culture of Southern Baptists from the time of the American Revolution to the late 1980s. It looks at the denomination's power structure, the massive changes that have occurred in the last thirty years due to the destruction of the southern caste system and the Southern Baptist response to those changes, the sect's role in fostering 'Bible Belt' sexual conservatism, and its connection to the New Religious Right movement, which mixes fundamentalist Christianity with conservative politics. Texas looms very large in this analysis; since it has a larger number of Baptists than any other state and serves as headquarters for the fundamentalist branch of the Southern Baptists, it sets the pace for the rest of the Southern Baptist Convention. The main sections of the book deal with Southern Baptists as southerners and as Americans; the social history of the church; its role in American politics; congregational, pastoral, and family interaction; and Southern Baptist ideology.

422 The Society of Mary in Texas.

Joseph W. Schmitz. San Antonio, Texas: Naylor, 1951. 261p. bibliog.

The Society of Mary, or Marianists, is a religious order founded in France in 1817. Members of the order came to San Antonio in 1852 at the request of Bishop John Odin. There, they established St Mary's Institute, which in 1926 merged with St Louis College to become St Mary's University. Schmitz also discusses the parish associated with St Mary's and the order's founding of the Central Catholic High School in San Antonio.

423 Texas Baptist leadership and social Christianity, 1900-1980.

John Storey. College Station, Texas: Texas A & M University Press, 1986. 236p. bibliog.

A scholarly, revisionist book that challenges the traditional interpretations of the Social Gospel movement – concerned with the application of scripture to social justice – which reached its peak prior to the First World War. Historians have tended to believe that this urban credo did not really affect the rural, agrarian South. The author attempts to refute this point of view, at least as it applies to Texas. Texans, he argues, were far more progressive than the rest of the South due to the state's steady urban growth, the progressive orientation of the Baptist General Convention of Texas and the educational level of its leaders, and their prominence in the Christian Life Commission (which set out to study the application of Christianity to real life issues in the latter half of the 20th century). Among the topics examined are prohibition, race relations, the impact of the Great Depression and the Second World War, and examples of both continuity and change in the perceptions and operations of Texas Baptists.

Social Conditions

424 **Migration into east Texas, 1835-1860: a study from the United States census.**
Barnes F. Lathrop.   Austin, Texas: Texas State Historical
Association, 1949. 114p. maps. bibliog.

This is an old, but still cited, exploration of the origins of antebellum migrants into seventeen East Texas counties (between the Red and Trinity Rivers) drawn entirely from United States manuscript census returns. Lathrop presents a dry basic analysis of the data, with year by year and county by county tabulations of the states of origin of the migrants. Twenty-seven maps, figures, and tables furnish statistics on white and black population figures, the birthplaces of parents and children who moved to Texas, the rate of migration, annual migration patterns, and real estate ownership.

425 **Death without dignity: the story of the first nursing home corporation indicted for murder.**
Steven Long.   Austin, Texas: Texas Monthly Press, 1987. 280p.

Long provides a fast-paced and outraged account of the 1986 case in which Autumn Hills Convalescent Centers, Inc. was charged with the willful killing of an eighty-seven-year-old woman and with the abuse and neglect of sixty other residents, some of whom also died. In addition to describing much of the testimony in court, Long also examines such chronic nursing home problems as space shortages and high personnel turnover. Although Autumn Hills was not convicted after the six-month trial (one of the state's longest murder trials ever), this is a useful look at the growing problem of care of the elderly in Texas and the United States.

426 **Christmas in Texas.**
Elizabeth Silverthorne. College Station, Texas: Texas A & M
University Press, 1990. 210p. bibliog. (Clayton Wheat Williams Texas
Life Series).

Silverthorne commemorates the varied and colourful ways that Texans have celebrated
Christmas since the introduction of Christianity. She describes the food, music,
decorations, and celebrations of the various ethnic groups – mainly Europeans – who
came to Texas, and suggests ways in which those customs were adapted to new
conditions or remained the same. The book is illustrated with nearly twenty colour and
thirty black-and-white photographs.

427 **Plantation life in Texas.**
Elizabeth Silverthorne. College Station, Texas: Texas A & M
University Press, 1986. 234p. maps. bibliog. (Clayton Wheat Williams
Texas Life Series).

Although presented in a large format and containing five dozen illustrations, this is not
a typical 'coffee-table' book. True to the name of the series to which it belongs,
Plantation Life describes the daily lives of blacks and whites on antebellum Texas
plantations, with chapters devoted to such topics as 'Necessities and Luxuries', 'The
Seasons', 'Body and Soul', and 'Mind and Spirit'. Although she does not ignore
entirely the ugly realities of slavery, Silverthorne focuses on anecdotal examples of
work, society, family, and black-white relationships, and places them competently in
their historical contexts.

428 **The family secret: domestic violence in America.**
William A. Stacey, Anson Shupe. Boston, Massachusetts: Beacon
Press, 1983. 237p. bibliog.

An overview of domestic violence in the United States, drawn largely from interviews
with residents of battered women shelters in Dallas and Arlington, Texas. The authors
outline the scope, types, and history of family violence. They look at the effects of
family violence on women and children, portray the victims' situations when they
arrive at the shelters, and detail the backgrounds of battering men. They trace
women's experiences at shelters, examine the victims' options upon leaving the shelter,
and explore the legal and rather limited law enforcement aspects of domestic violence.
The authors conclude that family violence occurs in all social classes, that the level of
violence is greater than previously thought, that woman and child battering are often
related, and that the scale of violence will continue to escalate if drastic actions are not
taken.

Urban Affairs and History

429　**Politics of San Antonio: community, progress, and power.**
Edited by John A. Booth, David R. Johnson, Richard Harris.
Lincoln, Nebraska: University of Nebraska Press, 1983. 248p. maps.

In this collection of essays, the authors show that from 1925-52, San Antonio politicians entrenched themselves in city government through patronage, voter manipulation, and election fraud. The 1952 transition to a metropolitan government, composed of a city manager and a city council, corrected those abuses, but opened the way for business interests to take over. By 1970, however, no group had enough power or resources to monopolize the government, so citizens gained new access and participation, although business still played a large part. The authors conclude optimistically that San Antonio will continue this democratic trend into the future. Individual essays examine San Antonio's political history in the one hundred and fifty years since 1836, in terms of San Antonio's spatial economic structure from 1955-80, Mexican-American occupational patterns, the transition of leadership in modern San Antonio, mayoral politics from 1955-79, the political context of unequal educational opportunity, the Edwards Aquifer controversy, and the rise of citizen and community influence on public policy. A collection of tables provide statistics on private sector employment, election results, income, ethnicity, voting patterns, and educational differences.

430　**San Antonio during the Texas Republic: a city in transition.**
Ray F. Broussard.　El Paso, Texas: Texas Western Press, 1967. 40p. bibliog.

Broussard's pamphlet provides a very short but useful narrative of the transitions through which San Antonio de Bexar passed during its first 150 years. The pamphlet follows the city from its days as the civil and military outpost attached to the missions established in the area, to its incorporation into the Texas Republic and its demographic transition from being dominated by Spanish speakers to its control by Anglo-Americans and European immigrants (especially Germans). One of the constants in the pre-1850 history of the city was the fear of attack by Indians and, both during and after the Texas Revolution, by Mexican troops.

431 **Texas cities and the great depression.**
    Edited by Robert Cotner. Austin, Texas: Texas Memorial Museum,
    1973. 215p.

A collection of graduate student papers on the ways the Great Depression of the 1930s affected eleven Texas cities: separate essays examine Temple, Taylor, San Marcos, San Antonio, Midland, Kilgore, Dallas, Galveston, Houston, San Angelo, and Austin. The depression impacted on different parts of the economy differently. The agricultural sectors of the state suffered high unemployment and much hardship, while the booming oil industry continued to boom and, actually, expanded. The cities hardest hit by bank failures were San Antonio and Taylor. Numerous tables present information on unemployment rates, relief services, New Deal programmes, and banking statistics. The book includes many extended quotations from first-hand accounts of Texans' depression experiences.

432 **Let there be towns: Spanish municipal origins in the American southwest, 1610–1810.**
    Gilbert R. Cruz. College Station, Texas: Texas A & M University
    Press, 1988. 236p. maps. bibliog.

Historians have often stressed the role of Spanish missions and *presidios*, but Cruz presents the first scholarly study of urban development on the Spanish southwestern frontier. Cruz emphasizes the importance of towns and their *cabildos*, or town governments, in organizing labour among natives, creating water systems, building and maintaining roads, and regulating local economies. He also studies how town administrators maintained law and order, promoted economic development, and fashioned partial democracies. The book is basically a legal and institutional history of Santa Fe, New Mexico; El Paso, San Antonio, and Laredo, Texas; and San Jose and Los Angeles, California, with little direct information about what it was like to live in these towns. The inclusion of eight maps, six population charts, and illustrations, add to the value of this original approach to southwestern history.

433 **San Antonio legacy.**
    Donald E. Everett. San Antonio, Texas: Trinity University Press,
    1979. 121p.

An entertaining series of reports, descriptions, and tall tales drawn from the pages of the *San Antonio Express* between 1865–1929, with line drawings by José Cisneros. Categories of stories include 'Frontier Town' about daily life and Old West colour; 'The Ladies', including Hispanics; and 'Legendary Stories' about the Alamo and local ghost stories.

434 **Essays on sunbelt cities and recent urban America.**
    Edited by Robert B. Fairbanks, Kathleen Underwood. College
    Station, Texas: Texas A & M University Press, 1990. 176p.

A collection of essays originally delivered for the 1988 Walter Prescott Webb Memorial Lectures at the University of Texas at Arlington. Raymond Mohl explores demographic, spatial, economic, and political developments in recent urban America; Robert Fisher uses a comparative approach to examine various economic, demographic, and political factors in Houston's growth as a 'sunbelt' city; Carl Abbott examines unique characteristics of southwestern cities such as appearance, form, and function; Robert W. Lotchin uses San Diego to illustrate the special relationship that many sunbelt cities have with the military (especially after the Second World War) and the military's impact on urban growth; Robert B. Fairbanks studies the dominance of business leadership in the politics of sunbelt cities, concentrating on Dallas, from 1930-60; and Zane L. Miller uses the writings of Webb and the Chicago school of sociology to examine how sunbelt cities have handled regional, ethnic, and racial diversity.

435 **Free enterprise city: Houston in political-economic perspective.**
Joe R. Feagin.   New Brunswick, New Jersey: Rutgers University
Press, 1988. 322p. maps.

An examination of the conflict between creating a good business climate and achieving a good quality of life for all the residents of a city. Feagin uses a number of theories on urban development to demonstrate Houston's growth and decline as a business centre and as a place to live. He argues that in the late 1970s Houston provided a positive model of a 'free enterprise, laissez-faire approach to urban development'. Yet the lack of planning or regulation and remarkably low taxes had their costs, too. The author explores Houston's economy, politics, and spatial development in the contexts of the capitalistic world market, the business community's involvement in local, state, and national politics, and the heavy social cost of free enterprise development, such as flooding, pollution, declining street maintenance and public works, and the increasing plight and burden of Houston's poor. This is a disturbing analysis, as well as a useful source of information. The author includes more than a dozen statistical tables regarding employment, population, occupations, manufacturing, club membership, and office building construction and occupancy.

436 **The Galveston era: the Texas crescent on the eve of secession.**
Earl Wesley Fornell.   Austin, Texas: University of Texas Press, 1961.
355p. map. bibliog.

Fornell explores the development of the Texas Gulf Coast during the booming 1850s. He focuses on the expansion of the cotton industry and the natural transportation advantages of Galveston, as well as the political ramifications of the economic ties that Texas enjoyed with the rest of the plantation South, which resulted in attempts to re-open the African slave trade, and in the state's eventual secession from the Union in 1861.

437 **Goals for Dallas.**
Goals for Dallas Conference.   Dallas, Texas: Graduate Research
Center of the Southwest, 1966. 310p. map.

A very optimistic, not to say utopian, effort to explain ways to improve the quality of life in Dallas. In many ways, this is a photograph in words of the people and institutions of Dallas – their status, their problems, their goals – at a moment in the mid-1960s. The product of a conference of nearly ninety residents and leaders of Dallas and nearby communities, the thirteen essays tackle issues ranging from government to health and welfare, from public safety to education, from culture to recreation. The book is fact-filled, with plenty of statistics. It proposes a series of general and specific goals (land use, economic development, transportation needs, expanding literacy, inter-agency cooperation, expanded taxi service) for each of the thirteen issues covered in the essays.

438   A borderlands town in transition: Laredo, Texas, 1755-1870.
      Gilberto M. Hinojosa.   College Station, Texas: Texas A & M
      University Press, 1983. 148p. bibliog.
This work places 115 years of Laredo's history in its Spanish, Mexican, and American
contexts. The author argues that Laredoans did not act according to the whims of their
national or even state governments, but acted mostly out of self-interest. Laredo was
an economic crossroads important to both settlers and travellers and to residents on
both banks of the Rio Grande. Hinojosa shows Laredo as a unified community with a
definite sense of its own interests and purposes. Supporting his assertions are nearly
twenty statistical tables on population, ethnicity, marital status, sex ratios, wealth,
employment, income, and housing. Finally, a glossary of Spanish terms which have
entered the vocabularies of Anglo-Texans is included.

439   **Minorities in the sunbelt.**
      Franklin J. James.   New Brunswick, New Jersey: Center for Urban
      Policy Research, 1984. 256p. maps. bibliog.
A study of Denver, Colorado, Phoenix, Arizona, and Houston, Texas, that focuses on
economic opportunity and status for minorities (black and Hispanic) and on housing
issues: segregation, discrimination, the housing market, and the implementation and
effectiveness of federal and state policies. The author suggests a number of ways to
make housing truly public and truly fair: expanding the areas covered under fair
housing laws, toughening federal power, and making the complaint and enforcement
process more effective. This is a very authoritative and factual analysis; along with
twelve maps, James provides four apendixes on methodology, statistics, and
comparison of state fair housing laws, and seventy-two statistical tables on population,
housing, economic indicators, and segregation.

440   **Houston: the unknown city, 1836-1946.**
      Marguerite Johnston.   College Station, Texas: Texas A & M
      University Press, 1991. 448p. bibliog.
A chatty look at over a century of Houston's elite, with dozens of black-and-white
photographs of leading families and their activities. The author portrays these wealthy
and powerful Houstonians as pioneers, entrepreneurs, adventurers, cosmopolites, and
philanthropists, and focuses on the colourful and noteworthy events, murders and
machinations, public service and public display.

441   **Fort Worth: outpost on the Trinity.**
      Oliver Knight, Cissy Steward Lale.   Fort Worth, Texas: Texas
      Christian University Press, 1990. 2nd ed. 256p. maps. bibliog.
      (Chisholm Trail Series).
Written as a supplement to the *Fort Worth Star-Telegram* in 1947 and first published in
book form in 1953, Knight's work is reissued here as a paperback. This is a popular
history of Fort Worth by a journalist-historian emphasizing the 'wild west' aspects of
the city's past. Knight focuses on crime and corruption, boosterism and cattle drives,
vices and railroaders, the taming of the city after the turn of the century, and the rise
of the oil, aircraft, and meatpacking industries in the early 20th century. An essay
written for the new edition by Lale brings Fort Worth's story up to the present.

442 **Baker & Botts in the development of modern Houston.**
Kenneth J. Lipartito, Joseph A. Pratt. Austin, Texas: University of
Texas Press, 1991. 253p.

A history of one of Texas's oldest and most powerful law firms. Established in 1840 by
William and Peter Gray, the firm helped codify the laws of Texas when it entered the
United States. W. B. Botts and James A. Baker joined the business shortly after the
Civil War and gave the firm their names in 1875. The authors' main thesis is that the
development of Baker & Botts paralleled the development of Houston. The firm has
been involved with many of the city's major corporations and its partners have often
been civic leaders. In the 1980s, the firm employed nearly 400 lawyers and enjoyed a
national practice and reputation. An appendix lists Baker & Botts partner admissions
from 1840 to 1990, while ten tables offer information on profits, starting salaries, and
birthplaces of partners, and other items of interest.

443 **The city moves west: economic and industrial growth in west Texas.**
Robert L. Martin. Austin, Texas: University of Texas Press, 1969.
190p. map. bibliog.

An analysis of the ecomomic forces that contributed to the growth of towns and cities
in west-central Texas between the end of the Civil War and the early 1960s. Martin
follows a chronological format, beginning with the cattle industry, then moving to the
development of West Texas agriculture through 1930. Two chapters examine the oil
industry before and after 1930, while another looks at the rise of industry and business
in the region. Three useful appendixes provide statistics on political affiliations and
attitudes, agricultural practices and production, and on 1963 gas and oil production in
the Permian Basin.

444 **Border boom town: Ciudad Juárez since 1848.**
Oscar J. Martínez. Austin, Texas: University of Texas Press, 1978.
231p. bibliog.

This book is written by a migrant from central Chihuahua who came to Ciudad Juarez
in the 1940s and is now a history professor at the University of Texas at El Paso. He
focuses on the development of the city from a frontier town to a major North Mexican
city, especially in terms of its economic growth and the resultant influx of population.
Martínez places the history of Juárez, which lies across the Rio Grande from El Paso,
in the context of the development of the entire Rio Grande Valley region. He
examines transportation improvements, political situations on both sides of the River,
the ecomomy of vice, revolutions, industrialization since the 1960s, the relationship
between Juárez and El Paso, the increasing importance of decisions at the capital in
Mexico City (free trade, industrialization programmes), and the extraordinarily tough
(and worsening) living conditions in the city.

445 **Houston: a history.**
David G. McComb. Austin, Texas: University of Texas Press, 1981.
2nd ed. 288p. bibliog.

A straightforward, chronological 'urban biography' of Houston that details the city's
rapid economic growth in the 19th century due to banking, railroads, shipping, the oil
industry, and, much later, the space programme. McComb also provides a useful
survey of other aspects of Houston's growth: technology, natural resources, culture,
and urban renewal. Nine tables provide statistics on bank deposits, shipping out of the

Port of Houston, and demographic information on blacks and whites. The first edition of the book was published as *Houston: The Bayou City* (Austin, Texas: University of Texas Press, 1969).

446 **Ethnic groups of Houston.**
Edited by Fred von der Mehden. Houston, Texas: Rice University, 1984. 240p.

Ten essays that each provide a historical narrative of one of Houston's primary ethnic groups are included in this volume. Each author describes one group's early history; religious and cultural aspects; fraternal, youth, and other organizations; business and political activities; and modern ethnic festivals. The ethnic groups included are: African-Americans, Mexican-Americans, Indochinese, Japanese, Chinese, Greeks, Jews, Scandinavians, Germans, and the French.

447 **Urban Texas: politics and development.**
Edited by Char Miller, Heywood T. Sanders. College Station, Texas: Texas A & M University Press, 1990. 208p. (Texas A & M Southwestern Series).

A collection of nine essays that focus on elite, white leadership and interests in Texas cities and on the roles of women and blacks. An introductory historical overview of urban Texas looks primarily at San Antonio, Dallas, and Houston; the remaining articles deal with wide-ranging events and periods, such as women reformers in Galveston between 1880-1920; the growth of one black neighbourhood and of civic clubs in Houston; 1940s economic development in Dallas; Gilded Age politics; post-Second World War bond issues; the rise of an exclusive suburb in San Antonio; and boss politics and Progressivism in the early 20th century. Although this is hardly a survey of the urban history of Texas, these factual accounts are generally successful in placing the state's urban conditions into their national and southern contexts.

448 **Searching for the sunbelt: historical perspectives on a region.**
Edited by Raymond A. Mohl. Knoxville, Tennessee: University of Tennessee Press, 1990. 250p.

A collective effort, by a number of urban historians, to define and describe the 'sunbelt'. The authors reach no concise conclusions, but they do offer a number of interesting essays on various aspects of 'Sunbelt' economics, politics, and culture (including immigration, air conditioning, ethnic groups, industrialization, and defence spending). Although most of the essays deal with urban areas in Texas in the larger context of sunbelt issues, none addresses a particular Texas city (or, for that matter, any other southern or southwestern city).

449 **Oil booms: social change in five towns.**
Roger Olien, Diana Olien. Lincoln, Nebraska: University of Nebraska Press, 1982. 220p. map. bibliog.

In this work, the authors offer an examination of the effects of the oil industry on the towns of Midland, Odessa, McCamey, Wink, and Snyder, Texas. All five oil towns faced the same problems, such as the boom and bust nature of the oil business, transient populations, and frequent housing shortages. However, each town had its unique problems, especially in terms of how long its oil field produced oil. Today, for instance, Midland is still booming (at least when this book was written), while nearby

Odessa is in decline. Another variation stemmed from each city's ability to set up permanent institutions and to attract businesses other than oil. Individual chapters cover population, housing, public services and education, women and the family, African- and Mexican-Americans, crime and vice, spare time and legal amusements, and life after the boom. The author provides tables on population by age, sex, and ethnicity, divorce rates, and housing construction.

450 **Power, money, & the people: the making of modern Austin.**
Anthony M. Orum. Austin, Texas: Texas Monthly Press, 1987. 404p. bibliog.

This is a detailed look at the last thirty years of the state capital of Texas from a socio-political point of view. Designed as a text for graduate students in urban affairs and political science, *Power, Money, & the People* traces the tensions and opportunities created by the quadrupling of the Austin metropolitan population between 1960 and 1990. Topics include the conflict between pro- and anti-growth forces, the role of the state and of individual leaders in fostering city development, land policy, ethnic tensions, neighbourhood interests and activists, environmental concerns versus economic development, and Austin's struggle with the South Texas Nuclear Project. This is a wide-ranging, useful case study of the sunbelt phenomenon.

451 **City building in the new south: the growth of public services in Houston, Texas, 1830-1915.**
Harold L. Platt. Philadelphia, Pennsylvania: Temple University Press, 1983. 252p. maps.

Platt argues that urbanization was the result of interaction between people and their environment. *City Building in the New South* applies this paradigm to the origins and growth of public services and the construction of Houston as a commercial metropolis, especially during the late 19th and early 20th centuries. The author analyses the tensions created by the clash between the public's desire for essential services and the entrenched political elite, as well as the role of Texas Progressives in passing legislation aimed at creating a more comfortable urban environment as well as a friendly business climate. Nearly twenty tables and charts provide data on city government and finances, population growth and make-up, and the economies of both Houston and Galveston.

452 **The forgotten frontier: urban planning in the American west before 1890.**
John W. Reps. Columbia, Missouri: University of Missouri Press, 1981. 169p. maps. bibliog.

A useful introduction to urban planning in the developing west, including Spanish towns in the Southwest, mining and lumbering towns in the mountain and Pacific West, and Mormon towns in Utah. Chapter three focuses on urban planning – before 'urban planning' was a field of endeavour – by Mexicans and Anglos in Texas as it applied to Austin, Gonzales, Matagorda, Houston, Galveston, Dallas, Forth Worth, Fredericksburg, New Braunfels, and Indianola. Reps dicusses the role of speculators, the impact of location and geography on trade, the factors that contributed to the selection of a town site, and efforts to lay out towns in an orderly fashion. Chapter two, on Hispanic cities and towns, includes a discussion of San Antonio. The author provides over forty black-and-white lithographs of western cities, sixty-three maps, and an appendix with population data (for 1850–90 and for 1970) for the seventy largest western cities.

453 **Progressive cities: the commission government movement in America, 1901-1920.**

Bradley Robert Rice. Austin, Texas: University of Texas Press, 1977. 160p. bibliog.

A study of the origins, dissemination, and decline of the commission idea for municipal government. Commission government originated in Galveston in 1900 and spread across the country; the author examines its administration in Galveston, Houston, and Des Moines, Iowa. He describes the ways in which the commission system was geared to the needs of individual communities and explores the adoption of many municipal reforms, such as the 'short' election ballots, at-large representation and non-partisanship in city government elections, the establishment of municipal civil service systems, and direct legislation. But Rice also shows that commission government offered little in the way of social reform. He also explains its relationship with other progressive reform movements and the social and practical perspectives of its decline. An appendix provides a list of American cities that adopted the system, their populations, and the dates of operation of the system in those cities.

454 **Houston: a twentieth century urban frontier.**

Edited by Francisco A. Rosales, Barry J. Kaplan. Port Washington, New York: Associated Faculty Press, 1983. 208p.

A collection of nine essays on different aspects of Houston's urban history from the mid-19th century through the mid-20th century. Topics include the commercial rivalry between Houston and Galveston, the role of civic elites in urban planning, labour relations, Mexican immigrant experiences, law enforcement, the development of 'high culture', African-American attempts to participate in the 'whites-only' political system, anti-communism in the early 1950s, and environmental issues. The last essay on the environment includes six statistical tables on land use, population, automobiles, and air quality.

455 **Hell's half-acre: life and legend in a red-light district.**

Richard F. Selcer. Fort Worth, Texas: Texas Christian University Press, 1991. 364p. maps. bibliog. (The Chisholm Trail Series).

An historian's look at a colourful episode in Texas history: the heyday of the Fort Worth vice district during the city's cattle-boom decades in the 1870s and 1880s. Based on published sources and newspapers, the book highlights the personalities and outrageous events that earned the area its notoriety, but also examines its impact on the local economy, the social pressures that caused early 20th century reformers to wage a successful campaign to clean up the district, and even the nearby social clubs patronized by the city's businessmen and 'better class of people'.

456 **Houston: growth and decline in a sunbelt boomtown.**

Beth Anne Shelton, (et al.). Philadelphia, Pennsylvania: Temple University Press, 1989. 155p. maps.

Four sociologists and a political scientist provide a largely descriptive volume that argues for the multiplicity of Houston's communities. Individual chapters trace the economic growth and decline of Houston's economy from 1836-1986. The emphasis is on the oil and gas industries (rather than the city's involvement in commerce and shipping); the city and suburbs' relationship with the federal government; neighbourhood groups; and blacks and Hispanics. There is also a summary of future issues:

diversity, the oil crisis, sewerage, traffic congestion, housing for minorities, fiscal crisis, and politics. This is a broad oveview that, despite its lack of detailed analysis, is a useful introduction to urban issues in Houston.

457 Pass of the north: four centuries on the Rio Grande.

C. L. Sonnichsen.   El Paso, Texas: Texas Western Press, 1968. 467p. maps. bibliog.

Written in a highly entertaining fashion by a long-time resident of El Paso, this book examines the interplay of Hispanic and Anglo influences on El Paso from the 16th century explorations of conquistadors through Indian fights and little-known Civil War battles, to Old West days and turn of the century reformers who finally 'cleaned up' the town. Numerous photographs are included, together with generous segments on Ciudad Juarez, the Mexican city which lies across the Rio Grande from El Paso.

458 El Paso: a borderlands history.

W. H. Timmons.   El Paso, Texas: Texas Western Press, 1990. 387p. maps. bibliog.

As the title of this scholarly, yet readable volume indicates, Timmons places the story of Texas's most western city in the much broader context of the history of the borderlands; that sometimes vague region where Hispanic, Native American, and United States interests and cultures have met and clashed. Timmons provides plenty of colourful incidents of frontier and political history, but also sketches the lives of the Mexican-Americans, Jews, Chinese, and Syrians who settled in El Paso. Some of his larger themes include the importance of water laws and usage to the fortunes of El Paso, the economic and cultural links to Ciudad Juárez, the meshing of the Anglo and Mexican communities, and the importance of federal government spending – from the military to the social welfare system – to the local economy. The text is divided into three roughly equal segments for the Spanish period, the 19th century, and after 1917, and is accompanied by nearly three dozen photographs and twenty drawings by José Cisneros.

459 Water out of the desert.

Christopher M. Wallace.   El Paso, Texas: Texas Western Press, 1969. 48p. bibliog.

A somewhat technical, albeit brief, analysis of the means by which the growing industrial and commercial city of El Paso acquired water. Basing his work on personal interviews and records from the Texas Water Commission and the Public Health Services, Wallace provides a case study of one of the least understood but most important elements of Texas urban life – the problem of providing water for people and industry.

460 To wear a city's crown: the beginnings of urban growth in Texas, 1836-1865.

Kenneth W. Wheeler.   Cambridge, Massachusetts: Harvard University Press, 1968. 222p. map. bibliog.

A comparative study of Houston, Galveston, Austin, and San Antonio during the thirty years after the Texas Revolution. The author examines why these four cities, which shared a common cultural heritage and geographical advantages, developed such diverse characteristics. He also examines economic growth among the four cities.

Galveston's early leaders were not far-sighted enough, Houston's wisely invested in economic improvements. San Antonio had the most diverse population and worked hard from the beginning to help all its citizens to become productive, while Austin was content to not have a railroad or be involved in interstate commerce until after the Civil War. Although Wheeler's primary emphasis is on commerce, he does not ignore the cultural factors in the development of these cities.

Education

461 Centennial history of Texas A & M University.
Henry C. Dethloff. College Station, Texas: Texas A & M University Press, 1975. 2 vols. maps.

A chronological history of Texas A & M University (originally called the Agricultural and Mechanical College of Texas) spanning its first century. Chartered in the 1860s, enrollment at the school grew from 106 in 1876 to over 8,000 in 1946, when veterans of the Second World War swelled the student body. After twenty years of stable figures, a rapid expansion raised enrollment to 25,247 in 1976. Dethloff focuses on these trends, as well as organizational and administrative changes; the addition of programmes like the veterinary school and the forestry and agricultural extension programmes; the role of the 'cadre' (the military training programme to which all students belonged until the 1950s) in the life of the university and in America's wars; and on the controversies over the admittance of women for the first time in the early 1960s. Appendixes list presidents, chancellors, and members of the Board of Directors; A & M alumni who died while serving the United States in the military; football and basketball records; honorary degrees and distinguished alumni awards conferred by the school; and emeriti faculty members. Statistical tables present enrollment from 1876–1976, university income, and construction figures.

462 Pictorial history of Texas A & M University.
Henry C. Dethloff. College Station, Texas: Texas A & M University Press, 1975. 232p. (Centennial Series of the Association of Former Students of Texas A & M University).

A nostalgic and evocative history of A & M, with scores of black-and-white and dozens of colour photographs of the campus, the students, and celebrated personalities associated with the school. The text and illustrations highlight A & M traditions, including sports, the Corps of Cadets (and their exploits in the United States Army), and agricultural research. This is not an objective rendering of A & M history, nor a particularly close look at the University as an educational institution, but it is useful as an explanation for A & M myths and legends and the 'Aggie' mystique.

463 **Saint Edward's University: a centennial history.**

William Dunn, C.S.C. Austin, Texas: Nortex Press, 1986. 444p. bibliog.

Saint 'Ed's', as local residents call it, was founded in Austin by the Congregation of the Holy Cross in 1876. Dunn emphasizes the national economic and political events that affected the school, changes in the make-up and size of the student body and policies of the administration, and the dwindling yet still important role of religion and of members of the order on campus. This comprehensive history is valuable for the wealth of facts it presents and for the religious and regional contexts into which Dunn places them.

464 **The development of education in Texas.**

Frederick Eby. New York: Macmillan, 1925. 354p. bibliog.

A history of education in Texas from the Spanish regime through to 1920. Following a number of chapters that chronicle the achievements and changes in individual decades, Eby provides separate sections on the growth of high schools, black education, college education and teacher training, and 'present' problems facing educators. Although this work is, of course, very out-dated, it remains useful as a source of statistics and information on early Texas education.

465 **Land, oil, and education.**

Berte R. Haigh. El Paso, Texas: Texas Western Press, 1986. 351p. maps. bibliog.

In 1838, Texas President Mirabeau Lamar set aside 211,000 acres of public lands for higher education in Texas. Additional land grants in 1875 and 1883 totalling two million acres were crucial to the establishment of Texas A & M University and the University of Texas, respectively. The West Texas land managed by the Universities – the Permanent University Fund was later created by the revenue from the land – was found in 1923 to be rich in oil as well as sulphur and potash. Haigh's dry but thorough book examines the management, sale, and leasing of the university lands in a strictly chronological fashion, from the beginning through to the mid-20th century. Four maps show the sites of the major oil wells sunk on University land and eight tables provide statistics on leases, sales, and other revenues.

466 **History of Texas Christian University: a college of the cattle frontier.**

Colby Dixon Hall. Fort Worth, Texas: Texas Christian University Press, 1947. 380p. bibliog.

The TCU was founded in the late 1860s as a private school in Fort Worth (its original name was Add-Ran College) and endured several moves and a couple of name changes before it received its present title in 1902 and its present location in Fort Worth in 1910. Affiliated with the Christian Church, it opened a medical school in 1912, and Brite College of the Bible in 1914. Hall focuses on environmental and personnel changes, the religious mission of the school, its administrators and trustees, the effects of the World Wars and of the Great Depression, and the relationship between TCU and Fort Worth.

467 **Down the corridor of years: a centennial history of the University of North Texas in photographs, 1890-1990.**
Richard S. La Forte, Richard L. Himmel. Denton, Texas: University of North Texas Press, 1989. 292p.

The book is not strictly a history of this North Texas institution of higher learning, but a valuable collection of photographs with detailed captions. The photos are divided into seven roughly chronological sections, each introduced by a short historical essay that establishes the themes and tone of the chapter. The subjects of the illustrations are, of course, mainly people and structures, but also included are facsimiles of important documents and letters.

468 **Hill country teacher: oral histories from the one-room school and beyond.**
Edited by Dianne Manning. Boston, Massachusetts: Twayne Publishers, 1990. 191p. bibliog.

A collection of the oral reminiscences of eight women whose educational careers began in one-room rural schools in the Texas Hill Country before the Second World War. Although the editor provides summaries of the oral histories and 'then-and-now' photographs of the interviewees, the bulk of the book consists of their reminiscences about students, facilities, parents, relationships with local school boards, and their personal motivations for choosing a career in education. Inevitably, the book leans at times toward nostalgia, yet the women's earthy and sometimes angry memories of expectations and hardships lend their testimony a solid dose of realism.

469 **A history of Rice University.**
Fredericka Meiners. Houston, Texas: Rice University Studies, 1982. 249p. bibliog.

A chronological (each chapter examines a different decade) look at Houston's Rice University. When it began as Rice Institute in 1912, it was a school for mechanical engineers and military officers; eventually it offered a full range of courses in the liberal arts and sciences and a wide range of graduate programmes. Meiners focuses on the growth and transformation of the faculty and student body (especially in the 1920s and the 1950s), the increasing importance of the revenue from the school's investments in the oil industry, and on the key presidents and administrators who contributed to the institution's progress. Over 150 photographs chronicle campus life, important people associated with the school, sports teams, and other events.

470 **School desegregation in Texas: the implementation of United States vs State of Texas.**
School Desegregation in Texas Policy Research Project. Austin, Texas: University of Texas Press, 1982. 64p.

Filled with statistics and information on scores of Texas school districts, this report examines the process of enforcing the lawsuits that led to the legal desegregation of Texas public schools. It provides brief histories of the lawsuits, exploring the role of the Texas Education Agency, and its methods of enforcing the decisions. The report concludes that the TEA has been passive, at best, in implementing public school desegregation.

471 **Southern Methodist University: founding and early years.**
   Mary Martha Hosford Thomas.   Dallas, Texas: Southern Methodist
   University Press, 1974. 224p. map. bibliog.

Chartered in 1911, SMU opened in 1915 in response to the educational needs of
Methodists in Texas. It grew from 700 to 4,000 students within twenty-five years, and
was transformed from a regional liberal arts college to a national university with
schools of law, engineering, and business. This book chronicles the first twenty-five
years of the school's history as well as the University's relationship with the Methodist
Church and with the state of Texas. It considers individuals who were instrumental in
the school's founding and development. Fifty photographs portray early 20th century
faculty, administrators, students, and campus events; an appendix lists founders,
administrators, and faculty members.

Economy and Business

Banking and Finance

472 **But also good business: Texas Commerce Banks and the financing of Houston and Texas, 1886-1986.**
Walter L. Buenger, Joseph A. Pratt. College Station, Texas: Texas A & M University Press, 1986. 450p. maps. bibliog.

The history of one of Texas's largest banks from its founding late in the 19th century through to the 1980s. Texas Commerce Banks took on its present configuration in the 1930s, when a number of hard-pressed institutions merged. Since then, with the continuing acquisition of other banks in Texas, it has financed much of the expansion in the Texas oil, construction, and agriculture industries. Buenger and Pratt focus on bankers and bank policies, the rise of Houston as a financial centre, and the growing national and international prominence of Texas businessmen and financiers. Nearly fifty graphs and tables provide wide-ranging statistics on population, oil prices and production, office space, sources of bank income, loans, and acquisitions.

473 **I'm an endangered species: the autobiography of a free enterpriser.**
David Harold Byrd. Houston, Texas: Pacesetter Press, 1978. 108p.

An entertaining but self-congratulatory autobiography of the author's transformation from a Texas oil field roughneck and carnival bear wrestler to a millionaire by the age of thirty. Although Byrd made his reputation as an oil man (he was president of the Independent Oil Producers Association) many of the fifty-two businesses he has managed were not involved with the oil industry. The author preaches in favour of self-reliance and 'American values', but against government intervention in business. Although there is little information of value about the oil industry in Texas in this little book, it is an interesting expression of Texan attitudes in its unabashed glorification of free enterprise and of Texas individualism.

474   **History of savings and loan in Texas.**
      Jack W. Cashin.   Austin, Texas: Bureau of Business Research,
      University of Texas, 1956. 171p. map.

A rather prescient, if dry, report on savings and loan associations. Although the author furnishes a history of the venerable institutions since the late 19th century, with sixty-six tables of statistics on the financial condition of the savings and loans, and on state and federal regulations, he also provides a warning. Nearly three decades before the 'S & L' crisis that struck the United States in the 1980s, Cashin wrote that savings and loans must accurately evaluate the properties in which they invest. He also asserts – in vain, it turns out – that rigid standards for organizing new S & L's must be maintained as they become more like commercial banks in their loan and investment practices.

475   **Transition in the Texas commercial banking industry, 1956-1965.**
      Lawrence L. Crum.   Austin, Texas: Bureau of Business Research,
      University of Texas at Austin, 1970. 170p. (Studies in Banking and
      Finance).

This is a heavily statistical examination (there are forty tables and seventy-three figures) of an important decade in the history of commercial banking. Crum places the changes in the organizational and financial structures of Texas banks in the context of similar changes in the United States and the Southwest. Among the changes are: innovations in customer service; the growth of assets of state banks (in comparison to national banks); the decline in cash assets and rise of non-federal securities (such as municipal bonds) as assets; the large growth of loans (especially commercial and industrial) as a percentage of assets; the growth of time deposits; and increasing automation.

476   **Banks and bankers in early Texas, 1835-1875.**
      Joe E. Ericson.   New Orleans, Louisiana: Polyanthos, 1976. 170p.
      map. bibliog.

This is largely a reference work, with listings and data about early Texas banks and bankers. The information includes biographical sketches, financial holdings, and business dealings. Texas banking was privately controlled until 1834, when Samuel May Williams and Thomas Freeman McKinney formed the First State Bank at Galveston. As Texas expanded, so did its public banking system, which was largely formed as the result of the needs of the railroads, agricultural interests, and industry. After the incorporation of banks became legal in Texas in 1869, other state banks were chartered and national banks began forming. At the same time, private banks became larger and more numerous.

477   **Saving the savings and loan: the United States thrift industry in the
      Texas experience, 1950-1988.**
      M. Manfred Fabritius.   New York: Praeger, 1989. 161p. map.

Fabritius provides an historical look at Texas S & Ls that concentrates on the years since the Second World War and on the crises of 1979-82 and 1983-88, especially as they affected Texas institutions. As thrifts were freed to make commercial and consumer loans and property investments (aided in part by the appointment of Texas's first S & L comissioners in 1961) their business became riskier; unsecured loans and inflated property assessments caused the multi-billion dollar collapse of most of Texas's S & Ls in the 1980s. The author complements his text with fourteen statistical tables showing S & L income, assets, investment yields, liabilities, and interest rates. He predicts that Texas S & L's will survive their current crisis, but that these complex institutions will require more complex regulations. For an overview of the history of American S & Ls, and of the conditions that led to the debacle of the 1980s, see Paul Zane Pilzer and Robert Deitz, *Other People's Money: the Inside Story of the S & L Mess* (New York: Simon & Schuster, 1989).

478   **The development of state-chartered banking in Texas: from predecessor systems until 1970.**
Joseph M. Grant.   Austin, Texas: Bureau of Business Research, University of Texas at Austin, 1978. 281p.

A useful survey of the development of state banks after the 1905 State Bank Law. Although three chapters provide a brief history of pre-1905 banking, and later chapters cover more recent decades, the emphasis is on the period 1910 to 1930. Grant offers detailed information on the evolution of laws regarding banks, on the economic and political contexts for bank development, and on the growth of deposit insurance programmes and government agencies regulating state banks. Nearly two dozen tables furnish quantitative evidence on resources, bank failures, deposits in state and national banks, and income from the cotton and the oil industries; an appendix contains lists and photographs of the banking commissioners of Texas.

479   **Oleander odyssey: the Kempners of Galveston, Texas, 1854-1980s.**
Harold M. Hyman.   College Station, Texas: Texas A & M University Press, 512p. bibliog. (Kenneth E. Montague Series in Oil and Business History).

This is an exhaustive family biography of one of the oldest moneyed families in Texas. The Kempner family of Galveston rose from the hard work and ambition of Harris Kempner, a Russian Jew who arrived as a teenager on Ellis Island in 1854 and died as a Texas millionaire four decades later. After working as a peddler in East Texas, he and his descendants eventually became cotton agents and wholesalers and branched out into banking, insurance, and the sugar industry (they eventually owned the Imperial Sugar Company). The Kempners, almost single-handedly, helped Galveston survive the disastrous hurricane of 1900. Ike Kempner, Harris's son, directed relief efforts and instigated several preventative measures including the construction of a protective sea wall and a causeway to the mainland, and the elevation of the city's grade. Hyman places this family's history in the contexts of the acculturation of southern Jews, the tradition of Progressive urban reformers, and the politics and economy of South Texas.

480   **The State National since 1881.**
C. L. Sonnichsen, M. G. McKinney.   El Paso, Texas: Texas Western Press, 1971. 171p. maps. bibliog.

A colourful corporate history of nearly a century of El Paso's State National Bank, from its founding in 1881 by Charles R. Morehead to 1971. Sonnichsen and McKinney describe the turbulent politics and economy of 1880s El Paso, and the founder's unsuccessful political campaigns. The authors pay close attention to the crisis of the Great Depression and the recovery that followed, and detail the bank's numerous managerial changes and the transformation of the physical plant that culminated in the building of a twenty-two story skyscraper in 1971. Thirty black-and-white photographs show famous personalities and important events in the history of the bank.

481   The Murchisons: the rise and fall of a Texas dynasty.
      Jane Wolfe.   New York: St Martin's Press, 1989. 505p. bibliog.
An entertaining chronicle of Texas wealth that traces the creation and the destruction
of a single family's fortunes. Early in the 20th century, Clint Murchison Sr. began
creating that fortune in the east central Texas cattle trade. The ever-optimistic
Murchison later made millions in the oil business, but built his fortune with a risk-
taking, money-borrowing style that led him to own, at one time, over one hundred
companies and have a personal worth of $350 million. His style succeeded in a growth
economy, but when the oil industry hit hard times in the 1980s and when his sons could
not find time for the business (as in John's case) or took unrealistic risks (in the case of
Clint, Jr.), the fortune evaporated and the family ended up in bankruptcy court. This is
a journalistic narrative with plenty of details on 20th century Texan society and high-
life, as well as business.

Agriculture and Ranching

482   The Texas land and development company: a Panhandle promotion,
      1912-1956.
      Billy R. Brunson.   Austin, Texas: University of Texas Press, 1970.
      248p. maps. bibliog.
Operating from 1912-56, the Texas Land and Development Company did not produce
a profit for its original investors and did not successfully develop all of its lands. Yet it
benefited hundreds of tenants, purchasers, and employees and it undertook
innovations in crop management, irrigation, and fertilization. Brunson describes both
the business side (including the 1919 reorganization of the company and the final
retirement of its debt) and the personal aspect (the daily lives of employees and
Depression-era hardships). In addition to the chronologically organized text, the
author provides maps of the Texas Panhandle and of a model farm, as well as home
plans used by new settlers. Also provided are thirteen tables showing crop values,
expenditures, production levels, the acreage cultivated for individual crops, property
values, salaries, investment funds, and prices.

483   Texas woolybacks: the range sheep and goat industry.
      Paul H. Carlson.   College Station, Texas: Texas A & M University
      Press, 1982. 236p. maps. bibliog.
Although Texas is far better known for its cattle industry, Carlson shows in this
detailed account that the Texas sheep and goat industry has flourished since the
Spanish first settled Texas. He argues that the Anglo-Americans' disdain for sheep
caused them to leave sheep ranching to English, Basque, Mexican, and German
immigrants. When it proved to be more profitable than cattle, Anglos began entering
the business. Carlson focuses on personalities such as George Wilkins Kendall and
William Leslie Black, and on popular sheep grazing areas like the Rio Grande plain,
the Panhandle, and the Edwards Plateau. Most of the book deals with the 19th
century, although the final two chapters survey the decades after 1900. A number of
photographs show owners and workers (mainly blacks and Hispanics) on the job and at
warehouses, sales, and meetings. Tables provide information on sheep, goat, and cattle

143

populations from 1867-90, mohair production, tariffs and wool duties, and sheep and wool production cycles from 1870-1943.

484   **A special kind of doctor: a history of veterinary medicine in Texas.**
Henry C. Dethloff, Donald H. Dyal.   College Station, Texas: Texas A & M University Press, 1991. 240p. bibliog.

A narrative of the veterinary profession in Texas since veterinary training began at Texas A & M University in 1888, and of the Texas Veterinary Medical Association, which was formed in 1903. The authors concentrate on the technological, scientific, and organizational evolution of the profession. Although the bulk of the book details the work of typical agricultural veterinary practitioners, Dethloff and Dyal also describe the challenges of treating zoo animals and chimpanzees flying into outer space as a part of the United States space programme.

485   **The longhorns.**
J. Frank Dobie.   Boston, Massachusetts: Little, Brown, 1941. 388p.

This is a profusely illustrated history of Texas's most famous breed of cattle, the longhorn. Dobie traces their arrival in Texas to the Spanish explorer Coronado's journey through the territory in 1540, and provides descriptions of the beasts by travellers and settlers in the centuries that followed. By the time of the Civil War, the cattle industry had grown in the state, with the sturdy, range-experienced longhorns as the major product of Texas ranches. These were the cattle driven north over the Chisholm trail from the 1860s until 1895; about ten million were taken to market during that time. Dobie does not focus on the cattle industry as an economic force, but looks at the longhorn as a cultural symbol and at the lore surrounding the animal and its keepers.

486   **Gail Borden: dairyman to a nation.**
Joe B. Frantz.   Norman, Oklahoma: University of Oklahoma Press, 1951. 310p. maps. bibliog.

The rags to riches story of a newspaper publisher and inventor (he also happened to be a Texas revolutionary) who developed a sanitary means of canning and shipping milk. Frantz provides a chronological, comprehensive, and entertaining narrative that examines much of the technical aspect of the research that Borden (1801-74) conducted into the preparation of sanitary foods and dairy products, as well as his other business and political interests.

487   **The Chisholm trail.**
Wayne Gard.   Norman, Oklahoma: University of Oklahoma Press, 1954. 296p. maps. bibliog.

The story of the famous route over which South Texas cattle were driven to railheads in Kansas and Missouri during the 1860s and 1870s. The Chisholm Trail was actually several different trails, as the railroads that took the beef to market inched closer to Texas. Gard provides an anecdotal but serious account that includes information on feeder routes, the economic forces acting on the industry (and which altered the routes over which the trail led), the growth and decline of the 'cow-towns' at the end of the journey, and the hazards of life on the trail. The author concludes that the millions of cattle driven up the Chisholm Trail helped Texas escape post-Civil War poverty, provided meat to eastern cities and even European markets, helped stock new ranches on the northern plains, and contributed to the development of the meat-packing industry and of refrigerated railroad cars.

488 **The old world background of the irrigation system of San Antonio, Texas.**
Thomas F. Glick.   El Paso, Texas: Texas Western Press, 1972. 67p. maps. bibliog.

An extensive look at the transferral of Canary Island irrigation technology, dating from the 16th and 17th centuries, to San Antonio. Although the focus is on the origins of the technology far from San Antonio, this little volume provides a useful background to one means in which Texans have dealt with their water resources.

489 **Land of the underground rain: irrigation on the Texas high plains, 1910-1970.**
Donald Green.   Austin, Texas: University of Texas Press, 1973. 295p. maps. bibliog.

Green begins with the migration of cattlemen to the high plains in the 1870s and 1880s when the lack of water was a barrier to settlement. The irrigation movement began in the 1890s and was led by land speculators like Artemus Baker and Frederick S. Pearson. The author examines their efforts, as well as the transformation in technology from early windmills to vertical centrifugal pumps, the development of which was aided by the drought of the 1930s and New Deal economic programmes. The increased demand for agricultural products during the Second World War also increased the demand for irrigation; by the 1940s natural gas-powered pumps provided a technological breakthrough that allowed the greater development of the high plains.

490 **Charles Goodnight, cowman and plainsman.**
J. Evetts Haley.   Norman, Oklahoma: University of Oklahoma Press, 1949. 485p. bibliog.

An epic biography of a larger-than-life Texan. Goodnight (1836-1929) rode from Illinois to Texas at the age of nine, hunted with Indians, fought as a Texas Ranger, launched his own business at the age of twenty, and blazed cattle trails to Kansas, Colorado, Wyoming, and New Mexico before the age of thirty. He established a cattle ranch in the Texas Panhandle, hundreds of miles beyond the frontier and built it into the 20,000,000 acre J A Ranch, where he became a scientific breeder of cattle and an expert on the range economy. Evetts paints a vivid picture of the colourful Goodnight, but does not ignore his business practices or political activities. The author followed Goodnight's trails and spoke to his contemporaries en route to creating an earthy, extraordinarily sympathetic, and very readable biography of a legendary character.

491 **The XIT ranch of Texas and the early days of the Llano Estacado.**
J. Evetts Haley.   Norman, Oklahoma: University of Oklahoma Press, 1953. 2nd ed. 258p. maps. bibliog.

Although the author is fond of the dusty legends of cowboys and cattleman (he dedicated the book to his cowhorses) this is a very scholarly look at the reality of the ranching business. He traces the history of the growth of the XIT ranch and of the 'staked plains' of the Texas Panhandle from the Spanish period until the early 20th century, when it consisted of parts of ten huge counties in the far northwestern corner of the Panhandle. The XIT itself grew out of over 3,000,000 acres of public land given to John V. Farwell and others in exchange for building the Texas state capitol, which was completed in 1888. Haley includes the trials and tribulations of ranch life and cowboying, but also details the political and economic history of the ranch. At the turn of the century the ranch began to be broken up, the cattle were sold off, and the land was developed by others in much smaller units.

492 **Cowboys and cattleland: memories of a frontier.**
     H. H. Halsell.   Nashville, Tennessee: Parthenon Press, 1937; Fort
     Worth, Texas: Texas Christian University Press, 1983. 276p. maps.
     (Chisholm Trail Series).

The story of frontier Texas life as told by Harry H. Halsell (1860-1957), who was born on the Texas frontier and carved out large ranch holdings in Indian Territory (present-day Oklahoma). He worked as a cowboy in New Mexico, eventually becoming a wealthy rancher. When his first wife received the bulk of his property in a divorce settlement, he started over again at age forty-eight. His colourful narrative stresses cowboy hardships, roundups, fights with Indians and rustlers, and other facets of the life of an archetypal cowboy.

493 **Lambshead before Interwoven: a Texas range chronicle, 1848-1878.**
     Francis M. Holden.   College Station, Texas: Texas A & M University
     Press, 1982. 230p. maps. bibliog.

The author draws on the 1936 personal narrative written by Sallie Reynolds Matthews for her children, about the coming of the Reynolds and the Matthews families to northwest Texas in the late 1850s. She highlights the building of the 50,000 acre Lambshead Ranch, family and frontier personalities, and relationships with the Indians of the region – especially wars and the 'civilizing process'. The narrative provides a memorable look at a large Texas ranch and the family that built it. There are brief chapters on the geology of Lambshead Ranch by Glen L. Evans and on the flora and fauna found on the ranch by A. S. Jackson. Both present the scientific and colloquial names and descriptions of the elements of the ranch's ecosystem.

494 **The Espuela Land and Cattle Company: a study of a foreign-owned
     ranch in Texas.**
     William C. Holden.   Austin, Texas: Texas State Historical
     Association, 1970. 268p. map. bibliog.

Focusing on the Spur Ranch holdings of the company, the author describes the land and wildlife of the ranch, and each group of white occupants (from hunters and traders to soldiers), and the evolution of ranch management and activities in the late 19th century. Individual chapters highlight ranch life, duties, and personnel; business practices; relations with Native Americans, neighbours, and predators; and the challenges and hardships associated with administering a ranch.

495 Los mestenos: Spanish ranching in Texas, 1721-1821.
Jack Jackson.   College Station, Texas: Texas A & M University Press,
1986. 704p. maps. bibliog.

A narrative of Spanish ranching operations in the region that became Texas during the century before the Mexican Revolution in 1821. Jackson describes ranching during the mission periods and during the period of secularization, as well as the problems faced by ranchers throughout Texas history: water shortages, Indian raiders, and cattle thieves. He also analyses business practices, the effects of the revolution on the ranching industry, and the influence of Spanish ranching practices on Anglo ranchers. Profusely illustrated, with nine maps, nine tables (establishing the numbers of cattle on Spanish ranches and export figures), and fourteen appendixes detailing such items as exports, the major Spanish ranchers, and their brands, this is a very useful source concerning an all but ignored period in Texas ranching history.

496 Trails to Texas: southern roots of western cattle ranching.
Terry G. Jordan.   Lincoln, Nebraska: University of Nebraska Press,
1981. 220p. maps. bibliog.

A cultural geographer's perspective on an old and myth-obscured topic, Jordan approaches the rise of the Texas cattle industry as an example of cultural diffusion. He briefly analyses the various theories accounting for the creation of this 'cultural type' and argues that Texas cattle ranching methods and culture evolved from colonial South Carolina Anglo- and African-American traditions and blended with Hispanic methods to create a 'hybrid' system that spread through much of the Great Plains. He describes the two major routes taken by this cultural diffusion, the major areas in which it developed, and the favourable market and environmental conditions that led to this 'creolization' of a number of ethnic traditions. The book includes numerous illustrations depicting ranch and cowboy life, brands and ear marks, as well as a wide variety of maps, charts on vegetation, cattle and population distribution, 'herding traits' and other ethnic and geographical characteristics, and ranching vocabularies.

497 Renderbrook: a century under the spade brand.
Steve Kelton.   Fort Worth, Texas: Texas Christian University Press,
1989. 221p. maps.

Renderbrook was founded late in the 19th century by Isaac Ellwood, a barbed-wire merchant, and continues to be operated nearly one hundred years later. Kelton's often anecdotal narrative presents Renderbrook's history as a microcosm of the history of ranching in Texas. He emphasizes the personalities of the men involved as well as the business practices of the managers, relying on traditional archival sources as well as interviews with family members and long-term employees. A number of black-and-white photographs portray livestock, staff members, buildings, and documents important to the ranch's history.

498 The golden hoof: the story of the sheep of the southwest.
Winifred Kupper.   New York: Alfred A. Knopf, 1945. 302p.

A history of shepherding in West Texas and New Mexico, including Spanish, Indian, and (in the 19th century) Anglo sheepmen. Kupper discusses the range wars that occurred between cattle and sheepmen in the 1870s, 1880s, and early 1900s, as well as the sheepmen's fight against predators, blizzards, and other natural enemies. Despite

147

its rather romantic portrayal of the lives of Texas and New Mexico sheep raisers in the 19th century, this is a useful introduction to the southwestern sheep industry.

499 Texas cowboys: memories of the early days.

Jim Lanning, Judy Lanning. College Station, Texas: Texas A & M University Press, 1984. 233p. bibliog.

Thirty-two personal narratives (including four women, two African-Americans, and one Mexican-American) selected from over 400 interviews compiled during the 1930s from persons associated with the King, Kennedy, Slaughter, Sevenson, Waggoner, and Burnett ranches. The selections were chosen as representative in detailing ranch and cowboy life, as well as the unique experiences they recount (such as encounters with Billy the Kid, Jesse James, and Will Rogers). Two short sections provide narratives from minority and female points of view.

500 The King ranch.

Tom Lea. Boston, Massachusetts: Little, Brown, 1957. 2 vols. maps.

An account of the first century of one of the most famous ranches in Texas. Richard King was born in New York City in 1824, served in Texas during the Mexican War, and purchased the Santa Gertrudis, or King Ranch, forty-five miles southwest of Corpus Christi in 1853. The narrative includes the obligatory battles with Indians and cattle rustlers, but focuses on the growth and prosperity of the huge operation, which in the 1920s passed to the Kleberg family. The Ranch continued to flourish, and in the 1930s the Klebergs began to raise race horses. This is a very positive account of the achievements of this important South Texas institution.

501 A market analysis of the cattle industry of Texas.

George M. Lewis. Austin, Texas: Bureau of Business Research, University of Texas, 1928. 171p. maps.

A detailed but narrow examination of the Texas cattle industry over several years during the 1920s. Fifty-seven tables, sixteen graphs, two maps, and a dry text provide statistical information on the state's seven livestock districts, including the numbers of cattle raised and shipped to points outside the state and to markets in the state, methods and costs of marketing cattle, agricultural conditions and stock raising practices, transportation costs, and the distribution and effects of 'Texas fever' among other complex and highly technical economic issues.

502 Rich grass and sweet water: ranch life with the Koch Matador Cattle Company.

John Lincoln. College Station, Texas: Texas A & M University Press, 1989. 148p. maps.

Lincoln, a friend and employee of the Kansas industrialist Fred Koch, has written a personal, nostalgic memoir about post-Second World War ranching in Wyoming, Montana, and in Texas where Koch owned the Matador Ranch in the Panhandle and the Yellow House Ranch on the South Texas plains. Lincoln describes life on each ranch in detail, including the differences in how the ranches were operated. His narrative is very matter-of-fact; he presents the pre-Koch history of the ranches, problems, descriptions of the employees on each ranch, and work routines and management plans. This is an anecdotal and uncritical account, yet it is full of important, practical details about ranching in the modern West.

503　**Planters and plain folk: agriculture in antebellum Texas.**

Richard G. Lowe, Randolph B. Campbell.　Dallas, Texas: Southern
Methodist University Press, 1987. 216p. maps. bibliog.

A highly quantified, comparative analysis of farming in Texas before the Civil War.
The authors show that farm size and ownership in Texas resembled that in the North,
that the percentage of slaveowners in Texas was about the same as in the Deep South,
and that Texas plantations were larger and worth more than elsewhere in the South.
Lowe and Campbell provide over sixty statistical tables on: property ownership,
population, land values, slavery; and production of cotton, corn, peas, beans, wheat,
and other crops. One of the authors' discoveries is that Texas produced more cotton
per slave than any other slave state. They also present useful descriptions of 'typical'
farmers: a non-slaveholder on the northern and eastern Texas prairies and a
slaveholder in far eastern Texas and the coastal plains.

504　**Marvin Jones: the public life of an agrarian advocate.**

Irvin M. May Jr.　College Station, Texas: Texas A & M University
Press, 1980. 296p. maps. bibliog. (Centennial Series of the Association
of Former Students, Texas A & M University).

This is an authorized biography by a close friend of this prominent jurist,
Congressman, and agrarian reformer. Although May examines most aspects of his
subject's public life, he focuses primarily on Jones (1882-1976) as a spokesman for
agricultural interests in Congress from 1917-41 and during the Second World War as a
food programme administrator. Jones was one of the prime instigators of farm credit
reform during the New Deal in the 1930s, and was a supporter and promoter of the
Agricultural Adjustment Administration, the government's first attempt to regulate
agriculture through price supports and production limits.

505　**The cattlemen.**

W. R. McAfee.　Alvin, Texas: Davis Mountain Press, 1989. 326p.

A biography of Roy (1886-1977) and Wade (1888-1974) Reid, and a history of their
Bar Eleven Ranch. Born in Wise County, they were raised on their father's Texas
Panhandle ranch. In 1909 they left home to work as cowboys; they eventually bought
their own ranch northeast of Fort Davis in West Texas's Barrilla Mountains. This was
never a large or a famous ranch and they did most of their own work; that work and
the privations they endured provide the basis for most of the narrative. The Reids were
20th century examples of 19th century style individualists and frontiersmen. McAfee
bases this useful book on interviews with both men, family members, and friends,
along with other local sources. The Bar Eleven was an excellent example of the small
operations that were far more typical of Texas ranching than the better-known, giant
spreads like the King Ranch.

506　**McNeills' SR Ranch: 100 years in Blanco Canyon.**

J. C. McNeill III.　College Station, Texas: Texas A & M University
Press, 1988. 205p.

An account of another small, family-owned ranch from 1883 to the present, written by
the grandson of the ranch's founder. McNeill obviously has very fond memories of his
life on the ranch and of his grandfather; he devotes half of the book to the first three
decades of its history and only forty pages to the last fifty years. His primary topics are
the hardships faced by his ranching family and their business practices, but he also

offers information on family affairs and the impact of world events and environmental changes on cattle markets in general, and on this ranch in particular.

507   **Great roundup: the story of Texas and southwestern cowmen.**
    Lewis Nordyke.   New York: Morrow, 1955. 288p. maps.

An informal history of the Southwestern Cattle Raisers Association, founded in Graham, Texas, in 1877 to stop cattle thieves. The author focuses in a rather dramatic fashion on the presidents who led the Association and the issues they promoted. The early years were spent cracking down on crime and in coercing the Texas legislature to ban the practice of setting fire to prairies to starve out competitors, and to pass more stringent trespassing laws. The members often acted together at regional cattle conventions to fight cattlemen from other states over issues such as new cattle trails from Texas to railroad terminals. In the 20th century, issues included the leasing of Comanche and Kiowa reservation lands, the quarantine of cattle carrying ticks that spread 'Texas fever', and efforts to catch increasingly sophisticated cattle thieves. This is a useful institutional history of what was a powerful force in Texas ranching and politics for a number of decades.

508   **Cattlemen vs. sheepmen: five decades of violence in the West, 1880-1920.**
    Bill O'Neal.   Austin, Texas: Eakin Press, 1989. 212p. maps. bibliog.

The story of the struggle for Texas land, first between ranchers and Indians, then, as the country began getting crowded, between different kinds of ranchers. After setting his story of violence in its broad economic context in the first chapter, O'Neal focuses on different geographical regions. He devotes one chapter to the violence between sheep and cattle raisers in Texas and northeastern New Mexico; other chapters examine Colorado, Arizona, and Wyoming (which gets three chapters). Although the author gives some consideration to economic issues, this is primarily a narrative of colourful (if deadly) Old West range wars.

509   **Gilbert Onderdonk: the nurseryman of Mission Valley, pioneer horticulturalist.**
    Evelyn Oppenheimer.   Denton, Texas: University of North Texas Press, 1991. 200p. bibliog.

Onderdonk (1829-1920) came to Texas from New York in 1851 as an invalid; he died nearly seventy years later, after a crowded lifetime as a Confederate soldier, pioneer botanist and horticulturalist, rancher, researcher in Mexico for the United States Department of Agriculture, essayist, and travel writer. He began his nursery business in the 1870s and founded the first industry in South Texas; he eventually became an internationally known horticulturalist. Oppenheimer bases this straightforward biography on Onderdonk's personal letters and travelogues. As the title suggests, she emphasizes the subject's agricultural and scientific careers.

510   **Livestock legacy: the Fort Worth stockyards, 1887-1987.**
    J'Nell L. Pate.   College Station, Texas: Texas A & M University Press, 1988. 332p. bibliog.

As the railroad came to Fort Worth in the 1880s, major cattle drives to terminals in Kansas and other towns farther North declined, and Fort Worth's meat-packing industry began its ascendancy. The author follows a strictly chronological approach that emphasizes the business side of this history, beginning with the origins of the city's stockyard industry in the 1870s and 1880s, when city fathers succeeded in linking Fort Worth by rail to eastern markets. In 1893 the Fort Worth Stockyards Company was formed, while Armour and Swift entered the stockyards business in 1902. Other chapters are devoted to life at the yards, the introduction of hogs into the Fort Worth operation, the Depression, early attempts at government regulation, the Second World War, promotional efforts in the 1950s, the decline of the industry in the 1960s, and the movement to preserve the stockyards as a historic district in the 1970s.

511 **The Matador Land and Cattle Company.**

William W. Pearce. Norman, Oklahoma: University of Oklahoma Press, 1964. 244p. maps. bibliog.

The Matador Cattle Company was formed by Hank Campbell in 1879 in the northwest Texas county of Motley. It was sold to a group of Scottish investors based in Dundee in 1882 and reorganized as the Matador Land and Cattle Company. Murdo MacKenzie became the company's American manager in 1890, and he moved the corporate headquarters from Austin to Trinidad, Colorado. MacKenzie managed the company for thirty-five years, while Alexander Mackay ran the Scottish end of the business. The former led the modernization of the company's management techniques and the transition from open range to enclosed ranching. Although the company survived the Depression and prospered during the Second World War, it fell on hard times in the late 1940s and in 1951 was broken up into fifteen smaller corporations. Several maps show the evolution of the company's landholdings, while appendixes list ranch personnel and provide statistics on production and prices for Matador Cattle from 1891-1950.

512 **The Southwestern International Livestock Show and Rodeo.**

Nora Ramirez. El Paso, Texas: Texas Western Press, 1972. 40p. bibliog.

This is a useful pamphlet on the history of one of the state's oldest livestock shows and rodeos, which began in El Paso in 1902 and turned into a regular event in 1931. The author gives a financial history of the show, relating how supporters hoped to demonstrate the value of a balanced system of agriculture, encourage the feeding of Texas stock on Texas farms, and to promote the development of packing houses in Texas. The rodeo was added to the show as a revenue-earning event that could support the livestock show.

513 **Cowboy life on the Texas plains: the photographs of Ray Rector.**

Ray Rector. College Station, Texas: Texas A & M University Press, 1982. 119p.

After an introductory chapter describing Texas cowboy life, Rector presents eighty-nine of his mostly full-page black-and-white photographs of Texas cowboys. His subjects include roping, bronco busting, branding, herding, ranch chores, cooking on the range, rope tricks, recreation, courtship, the Spur Ranch, the coming of the railroads and automobiles, rodeos, and horse-racing. Most of the photographs date from the early 20th century and show the transition of the occupation of cowboy from one of utility to one of nostalgic showmanship.

514 **Cattle raising on the plains, 1900-1961.**
John T. Schlebecker. Lincoln, Nebraska: University of Nebraska
Press, 1963. 323p. bibliog.

A general, chronological history of the cattle industry on the Great Plains in the 20th
century. It discusses the numerous changes the industry faced in the first sixty years of
the century, especially the application of science and technology, which allowed
cattlemen to raise more cattle on less land with less work. The author also discusses the
growing market for beef in the early 20th century; the numerous natural disasters that
often imperiled the industry, such as droughts and epidemics; and the impact of the
Depression, the World Wars, and the effects of the New Deal on the cattle industry.
Finally, the book summarizes the important role of 1950s biochemistry and food
processing on the cattle industry.

515 **The Francklyn land and cattle company: a Panhandle enterprise, 1882-
1957.**
Lester F. Sheffy. Austin, Texas: University of Texas Press, 1963.
402p. maps. bibliog. (M. K. Brown Range Life Series).

The Francklyn Land and Cattle Company was established in 1882 when Kentuckian
B. B. Groom bought 529,000 acres of the Texas Panhandle and made Charles B.
Francklyn president of the company. He attracted numerous British investors and
Groom, who ran the ranching side of the company, brought Hereford and Polled
Angus breeds from Britain. The company was dissolved in 1886, when a new company
was organized from the old called White Deer Lands, which was run by George Tyng.
Tyng brought modern beef and agricultural methods to the business, which was
liquidated in 1957. The book explores early Indian troubles, the modernization of the
cattle industry in northwest Texas, the economic and social development of the region,
and the business history of ranching in the late 19th and first half of the 20th century.

516 **The cattle-trailing industry: between supply and demand, 1866-1890.**
Jimmy M. Skaggs. Lawrence, Kansas: University Press of Kansas,
1973. 173p. map. bibliog.

An analysis of the companies which contracted with cattle ranchers from Texas and
other Great Plains states to drive their stock to railheads in Kansas, Missouri,
Nebraska, and New Mexico. It was more economical for a rancher to hire someone to
take his cattle to market than it was to ship his cattle on expensive rail lines; the
rancher could also avoid shutting down his operations while he was on the trail. The
author focuses on the major operators such as John T. Lytle, Eugene B. Millett, and
Charles Schreiner, analysing their methods and business practices and describing the
economies of the frontier towns that lay at the end of the trail. The cattle trailing
business collapsed in 1889, when South Texas cattle were quarantined in their
respective counties due to the highly contagious Texas fever.

Industry

517 **Texas resources and industries.**
Stanley Arbingast. Austin, Texas: Bureau of Business Research,
University of Texas, 1971. 233p. maps.

A useful source for information on business and industrial conditions in Texas in the
early 1970s. The author discusses the climate and geography of Texas; the use and
production of various natural resources such as lumber, minerals, oil, and natural gas;
income distribution among Texas workers; and the demographic composition of the
Texas work force. He provides analyses of the Texas transportation, recreation,
aviation, paper, rubber, and housing industries, as well as agricultural products,
especially cotton. Finally Arbingast briefly explores the process of urbanization and
examines in detail business and industry in the Rio Grande Valley and on the Texas
coast. Much of the wealth of quantitative information found in the book is shown on
the twenty-seven maps of Texas (which show, among other things, the distribution of
natural resources and industries, and demographic, geographic, and climatic data) and
well over 100 tables and graphs.

518 **The history of apparel manufacturing in Texas, 1897-1981.**
Dorothy DeMoss. New York: Garland, 1989. 270p. bibliog. (Garland
Studies in Entrepreneurship).

In this reprinted 1981 dissertation, DeMoss examines twenty-one apparel companies in
Dallas, Fort Worth, San Antonio, and El Paso which originated in Texas and whose
home offices remain there. Her approach is basically chronological, with chapters also
devoted specifically to management and labour relations, and to eight post-Second
World War companies and their creative approaches to manufacturing, marketing, and
fashion. By the 1940s, Texas ranked third in the United States in manufacturing
clothing. The author points out that a number of factors contributed to the growth of
the Texas apparel industry: the presence of railroads, the two World Wars, a cheap
labour supply, the rise of mass production techniques, the diversification of
production, and the 'Sun Belt' boom of the 1970s.

519 **A short history of the sugar industry in Texas.**
William R. Johnson. Houston, Texas: Texas Gulf Coast Historical
Association, 1961. 83p. bibliog.

Johnson provides a straightforward examination of an often over-looked niche of the
Texas economy. After several unsuccessful attempts to grow cane in Louisiana,
Etienne Bore succeeded in growing and refining quality cane sugar in 1795. Despite the
expense, others rushed to follow his example and the industry soon spread to the Texas
gulf coast in the 1820s and 1830s. The sugar communities of Brazoria, Matagorda, Fort
Bend, Wharton, Liberty, Victoria, and Rusk were soon thriving. Johnson examines the
economic and political factors that encouraged the transformation of the Texas sugar
industry from the production of cane to the refining of sugar. By 1920, the Imperial
Sugar Company was the primary producer in Texas, limiting its business mostly to
refining cane imported from Louisiana and the Caribbean. Useful statistics are
provided in ten tables on sugar production, the use of convict labour, and refinery
production.

520   The realtor in Texas: the story of the Texas Association of Realtors,
      1920-1970.
      Cora Biesele Matlock.   Austin, Texas: Texas Association of Realtors,
      1970. 138p.

An official history of the Texas Association of Realtors (TAR). In 1920, the TAR was
formed to regulate companies within the Texas realty market so that development
would take place more ethically, efficiently, and profitably. They implemented such
programmes as the 'TAR Institute schedule', the 'Make America Better Program', and
appraisal, counselling, and brokerage services. The organization promoted the 1939
passage of the Texas Real Estate License Act and the creation of the Texas Real
Estate Commission of 1949. This is a very positive and straightforward narrative of one
of the most important forces in the Texas real estate industry.

521   Sawdust empire: the Texas lumber industry, 1830-1940.
      Robert S. Maxwell, Robert D. Baker.   College Station, Texas: Texas
      A & M University Press, 1983. 228p. maps. bibliog.

Before 1901, lumbering was Texas's largest manufacturing industry, taking second
place to oil until 1930. Although logging of Texas lumber began when white settlers
first arrived, commercial lumbering was instigated in 1880. The authors chronicle the
competition between several lumber companies throughout the boom period of the late
19th century, as well as the decline and near collapse of the industry during the Great
Depression and the move toward conservation prior to the Second World War.
Maxwell and Baker discuss individual logging company owners, the railroads and
shipping companies, lumber and paper millers, and labourers.

522   The brimstone game: monopoly in action.
      R. H. Montgomery.   New York: Vanguard, 1940. 94p.

A technical but accessible explanation of how monopolies in the United States work,
with an eventual focus on the sulphur industry. The author blames the poverty,
shortages, and unemployment of the Depression on monopolistic practices which were
actually encouraged by the United States government's over-regulatory practices. In
the first three chapters, Montgomery gives brief descriptions of how railroads, oil
companies, steel companies, and others have expanded both vertically and horizontally
to control their respective industries, as well as related industries. The remainder of
the book traces the origins of the monopoly in the 'brimstone', or sulphur industry,
including the Texas Gulf Sulphur Company in the 1930s.

523   Perpetual jeopardy: the Texas Gulf Sulphur affair; a chronicle of
      achievement and misadventure.
      Kenneth Gilbert Patrick.   New York: Macmillan, 1972. 363p. (Studies
      of the Modern Corporation).

This is partly a description of the growth and prosperity of the Texas Gulf Sulphur
Company, which was founded just after the First World War. Although initially the
company's major sources of sulphur were in Texas and Louisiana, it eventually struck a
large deposit in Canada. Patrick's other goal is to analyse a 1965 Securities Exchange
Commission suit against a number of stockholders for 'insider trading' – the unfair use
of special knowledge to profit from fluctuations in their company's stock prices. After a
tumultuous set of court decisions and appeals, the Texas Gulf Sulphur Case – which

the defendants won – became important not because it settled anything, but because it blurred the distinctions between legal and illegal stock market activities.

524 **Economic and business issues of the 1980s.**
Edited by Joseph E. Pluta.   Austin, Texas: Bureau of Business Reseach, University of Texas at Austin, 1980. 235p.

This is not a unified monograph but a collection of specialized, if brief, explorations into important factors in the Texas business climate in the 1980s. All of these articles – complemented by ten maps and scores of statistical charts and grafts – are reprinted from the *Texas Business Review*. Section one examines general economic and market conditions like migration, local planning, inflation, interest rates, and manufacturing. Section two describes factors that contribute to the strengths and weaknesses of industrial location, such as taxes, physical plants, regional planning, relocation problems, and rural industrialization. Section three focuses on labour and employment issues, including costs, minorities in the work force, public employees, and unionization. Section four provides case studies of the insurance, housing, air travel, apparel, and agricultural industries, while section five shows small business success stories. Section six examines the banking industry, especially holding companies and federal reserve membership, and section seven takes a look at taxing and regulatory trends.

525 **Indians, cattle, ships, and oil: the story of W. D. Lee.**
Donald F. Schofield.   Austin, Texas: University of Texas Press, 1985. 205p. maps. bibliog.

A biography of William McDole Lee, a Wisconsite who came to Texas before the Civil War. After service in the Union Army, Lee returned to Texas and influenced the late-19th century's most important economic trends. He participated in the buffalo hide trade in Indian Territory, cattle ranching in the Texas Panhandle, the construction of the Brazos River channel which allowed Houston to grow as a shipping centre, and the exploration for oil in Brazoria County. This is a brief, but useful look at frontier entrepreneurship and one man's role in the economic history of developing Texas.

526 **The road to Spindletop: economic change in Texas, 1875-1901.**
John S. Spratt.   Dallas, Texas: Southern Methodist University Press, 1955; Austin, Texas: University of Texas Press, 1970. 337p. bibliog.

This is an analysis of Texas during the last quarter of the 19th century. In 1875, 95 per cent of the population of the state lived or worked on farms and three-fifths of the state's territory was still wilderness. Much of this changed over the course of the next generation, as urbanization, industrialization, the commercialization of agriculture, and the construction of railroads altered Texas's economy forever. Agriculture expanded into West Texas, ranching was changed by fencing, and railroads created a transportation network within Texas and connected the state to outside markets. Spratt also provides information on farmer protest organizations, the regulation of railroads in the 1890s, and on the origins of migrant workers in Texas. He concludes that, by January 1901, when the first major oil well was discovered at Spindletop, the economic shifts that the oil industry would accelerate had already been under way for a generation.

527 **Basic industries in Texas and northern Mexico.**
University of Texas Institute of Latin American Studies.   Austin,
Texas: University of Texas Press, 1950. 193p. maps. (Institute of Latin
American Studies Series).

A somewhat dated examination of the most important industries in Texas and northern
Mexico, especially steel, oil, and chemicals; of the available resources, such as land,
minerals, and especially water; of infrastructure development in terms of dams, hydroelectric power, and immigration; and of the trade between northern Mexico and Texas.
This old report is probably most useful for the statistics on industrial products and
resources, which are presented in seventy-six tables and nine maps.

Energy

528 **The last boom.**
James A. Clark, Michael Halbouty.   New York: Random House,
1972. 305p. maps. bibliog.

The authors describe the oil boom in the northeast Texas counties of Gregg and Rusk
during the late 1920s and early 1930s. Columbus Joiner and A. D. Lloyd began
pumping oil out of the 'Daisy Bradford 3' well in 1929; the operation was later financed
by the future Texas billionnaire H. L. Hunt. Over the next few years, other wells
began producing on this hitherto untapped northeastern Texas oil field. The authors
focus on the work of geological discovery, the economic effects of the boom, the
government regulation of the oil industry that resulted from the boom, life in the wild
boom towns near the oil fields, disputes among the oil men (and the eventual
declaration of martial law in 1931), and the construction of pipe lines to carry the oil
from Texas to New Jersey.

529 **Spindletop.**
James A. Clark, Michael T. Halbouty.   New York: Random House,
1952. 306p. map. bibliog.

Spindletop is perhaps the most famous oil field in Texas history. When it yielded a
'gusher' on 10 January 1901, it catapulted Texas into a brand new economy and
changed its political and social systems forever. The authors cover the first fifty years of
Spindletop: they examine in narrative fashion Pattillo Higgins's prediction of a major
oil source in East Texas and the daily routine of oil prospecting and drilling. The
sudden growth of Beaumont and life in the boom towns near the oil fields are
discussed, along with the legal challenges to mineral rights claims, Standard Oil's
appearance in East Texas, and the Young-Lee Oil Company, the most successful of the
companies drilling at Spindletop.

530   **Texas energy: a twenty-five year history.**
Ginny Cummings.   Austin, Texas: Governor's Energy Advisory
Council, Forecasting and Policy Analysis Division, 1977. 156p.
A basic source of information consisting of nearly 120 charts and tables, and a very
brief text on the development, production, pricing, and consumption of energy resources
in Texas between 1952 and 1977. Individual chapters provide statistics on exploration and
drilling for oil and gas; energy imports and exports; energy processing, conversion, and
distribution; the electric and gas utility industry; energy prices and consumption; tax
collections; population and employment; personal income; and price indexes.

531   **The politics of oil.**
Robert Engler.   New York: Macmillan, 1961. 565p. bibliog.
Texas frequently appears in this book about the larger issue of the oil industry's
political influence in the 1950s. Engler treats this as a case study of the relationship
between the American industrial system and the American political system. The author
addresses such issues as the use of public resources by private oil companies, the role
of industry in a democracy, national security, public opinion, and lobbying. His main
concern is to outline all the ways that the oil industry determines and pursues its
interests. This is, perhaps not surprisingly, a negative portrayal of how the oil industry,
which operates as a sort of private government, subverts American political and
democratic principles.

532   **Flush production: the epic of oil in the Gulf-southwest.**
Gerald D. Forbes.   Norman, Oklahoma: University of Oklahoma
Press, 1942. 253p. maps. bibliog.
A survey of the oil industry in the Southwest, from early exploration for oil in the
region during the antebellum period through to the 1901 Spindletop 'gusher' and the
proliferation of the industry over the next forty years. Forbes explores technological
changes in the industry, and the political, social, and economic problems which the
industry brought to the region. He examines regulatory attempts at the state and
federal levels, the rise of the natural gas business, the construction of pipelines, and
the legal aspects of drilling for oil. An appendix lists the major oil fields of the
Southwest, the locations of which are shown on a map.

533   **And work was made less: Texas Electric Service Company.**
Vance Gillmore.   Fort Worth, Texas: Branch-Smith, 1976. 219p.
maps.
A congratulatory institutional history of the first power companies in Fort Worth.
Gillmore focuses on growth, organizational changes, and especially the gradual
centralization of services from a number of small electric companies during the first
twenty or thirty years of the 20th century to the creation, through a series of mergers,
of the Texas Electric Service Company.

534   **Wildcatters: a story of Texas, oil, and money.**
Sally Helgesen.   New York: Doubleday, 1981. 198p.
This book chronicles, in dramatic narrative style, the story of the Moncrief family of
Amarillo and Fort Worth, and of Moncrief International's rise to prominence in the oil
industry. The author begins with the story of Monty Moncrief and ends with Dick

Moncrief, who was head of the company in 1980. Helgesen relates their beginnings in the mid-1800s and expansion throughout Texas and into the Gulf of Mexico and the Middle East by the mid-20th century. She shows how, as they grew, the Moncriefs had to learn to deal with industry, economics, and politics on an international scale, and reveals them here as tough, daring, risk-taking entrepreneurs who fit the popular image of Texan oil men.

535 **Pattillo Higgins and the search for Texas oil.**
Robert W. McDaniel, Henry C. Dethloff. College Station, Texas: Texas A & M University Press, 1989. 174p. bibliog.

Higgins (1863-1955) was a self-taught geologist who identified over seventy oil fields in East Texas and along the gulf coast, including the famous Spindletop oil field. The authors concentrate on Higgins's efforts to diversify the oil business and to prevent out-of-state investment, as well as the technical obstacles that he faced. McDaniel (Higgins's great-grand-nephew) and Dethloff cannot explain how Higgins found oil, and his methods were very controversial among professional geologists. The book is strong on the colourful Higgins's family background and early life; he was a womanizing eccentric who later became religious.

536 **Easy money: oil promoters and investors in the jazz age.**
Roger M. Olien, Diana Davids Olien. Chapel Hill, North Carolina: University of North Carolina Press, 1990. 216p.

The authors offer a discussion of the boom in the oil industry following the First World War (the 'Jazz Age'), and of the wild financial speculation and corruption that accompanied it. The authors stress that the oil industry was a favourite high-risk investment during this period because of the potential for huge profits in the volatile boom-bust cycles which characterized it. During this period, the saying was that 'anyone could get rich' in oil, and there were many Americans from all walks of life and income brackets investing in oil. The Oliens also examine oil promoters who risked, and often stole, other people's money. One such man was Seymour E. J. Cox, a slippery Houston promoter who skimmed away half of the money people gave him to invest in oil. Another untrustworthy promoter was Dr Frederick A. Cook, who, like Cox, went to trial in 1923 with ninety-two other promoters for their shady activities. However, this crackdown did not end oil promotion: promoters simply turned to new and more legitimate strategies. This is something of a corrective to the dramatic accounts of heroic oil men favoured by Texas authors.

537 **A saga of wealth: the rise of the Texas oilmen.**
James Presley. New York: G. P. Putnam's Sons, 1978. 464p. map. bibliog.

Presley claims that the discovery of oil opened a new era in Texas and United States history and transformed the frontier experience, which he defines as a new and rowdy way of life that survived long into the 20th century. Oil pulled Texas into the industrial era, bringing the state urbanization, wealth, and political influence. The narrative explores the history of the oil industry, describes the oil frontiersmen, traces what happened to the great wealth spawned by oil, and examines how the money affected these new oil barons; his most general theme is that oil broke down the state's isolation from the rest of the world.

538 **Petroleum politics and the Texas Railroad Commission.**
David Prindle. Austin, Texas: University of Texas Press, 1981. 230p.
maps.

The Texas Railroad Commission was established in 1891 to regulate railroads within the state, but in 1930 the oil industry was also put under its control. Prindle examines the interaction of policy-making and politics on such topics as 'well-spacing', 'slant' wells, conservation of natural gas, oil exploration, prices, and the energy crisis of 1973. Railroad commissioners are elected in Texas, and the author also examines the process of choosing regulators. This is a scholarly and at times critical study of an important facet of the Texas economy and of Texas politics.

539 **Early Texas oil: a photographic history, 1866-1936.**
Walter Rundell, Jr. College Station, Texas: Texas A & M University
Press, 1977. 260p. map. bibliog.

Rundell has put hundreds of black-and-white archival photographs into chapters organized geographically by oil field, town, or region; the pictures are arranged chronologically within those chapers. The illustrations portray oil field workers, technology, towns, working and living conditions, prominent oil men and financiers, and 'gushers' from 1866-1936 (especially the 1890s). Accompanying the excellent selection of photographs is a brief text which places the illustrations in their appropriate contexts and is full of statistics and facts.

540 **Economics of natural gas in Texas.**
John R. Stockton, Richard C. Henshaw, Richard W. Graves. Austin,
Texas: Bureau of Business Research, University of Texas, 1952. 316p.
maps. bibliog.

A basic economic study of natural gas production, distribution, utilization, technological innovation, regulation (including taxes and public control of the industry) and conservation in Texas. The most valuable information can be found in 125 tables and charts showing production, price, tax, and distribution statistics; five diagrams describing the obtaining and processing of natural gas; and fourteen maps locating major production and consumption centres, processing plants, and pipe lines in Texas and the United States.

541 **Oil field child.**
Esther Briscoe Stowe. Fort Worth, Texas: Texas Christian University
Press, 1989. 181p.

This is Esther Briscoe Stowe's autobiographical account of her nomadic childhood in West Texas and Oklahoma oil fields in the 1920s. She relates the communities established by the transient population, the joys and sorrow of transitory friendships, her happy family life, and her mother's struggle with tuberculosis (she was sent to a sanitorium while Esther stayed with her father). Stowe also describes the various occupations on the oil rigs such as the driller, pipeliner, and derrick builder, and although she does not dwell on it, she briefly examines the dangers of working in the oil fields. Stowe's father worked on the original Santa Rita Well No. 1, which began the great Permian Basin oil boom in 1923. Accompanying the text are thirty-five black-and-white photographs of oil fields in which her father worked and boom towns in which her family lived.

Trade, Transport and Technology

542 **Then came the railroads: the century from steam to diesel in the southwest.**
Ira G. Clark. Norman, Oklahoma: University of Oklahoma Press, 1958. 336p. maps. bibliog.

In this comprehensive, scholarly survey of railroad building in the Southwest from 1850-1950, Clark discusses how the Southwest was neglected at first, since transcontinental systems were a priority, even though the 1870s were a boom decade for southwestern railroads. He also discusses the lives and work of famous entrepreneurs, especially railroad barons like Jay Gould, A. A. Robinson, and William B. Strong, as well as the numerous railroad lines that operated during this century in the Southwest, such as Gould's Texas and Pacific, the Missouri Pacific, and the Central Branch Railway Corporation. The author explains the social and economic changes the railroads brought to the Southwest, such as the settlement of towns, farms, and ranches; the creation of commercial agriculture and industrialization; and the displacement of Native Americans. Six maps show the evolving railroad networks of the gulf region and the Southwest from 1860 to 1950.

543 **Trails south: the wagon-road economy in the Dodge City-Panhandle region.**
C. Robert Haywood. Norman, Oklahoma: University of Oklahoma Press, 1986. 312p. maps. bibliog.

Haywood, a professional historian, draws attention to the freighting trails of the Old West rather than the much better-known cattle trails. His focus is on the economic and military contexts of the overland trails leading from Dodge City, Kansas, through Oklahoma to the Texas Panhandle during the period 1860-90. He describes the transition of this network of trails from military supply routes to commercial highways, with Dodge City as the primary supplier for a large part of the southern Great Plains. The buffalo hide trade, the cattle drives, and homesteaders were all part of Dodge City's market; the nation-wide 1890s depression and the coming of railroads ended the trails' usefulness and profitability. Separate chapters are included on the freighters themselves, on stage drivers, way stations, and P. G. Reynolds (the region's leading entrepreneur and mail contractor during this period).

544 **The Quanah route: a history of the Quanah, Acme, & Pacific Railway.**
Don L. Hofsommer. College Station, Texas: Texas A & M University Press, 1991. 226p. bibliog.

The Q A & P operated in four counties in northwest Texas from the early 20th century through to the 1980s. Hofsommer, who had full access to the Q A & P archives, deals with the political, economic, and regulatory contexts of this short-line railroad, and describes its impact on the development of the region. He argues that the line's decline was brought about by the trucking industry, the improvement of Texas's system of roads, and Texans' passion for automobiles. Well over one hundred black-and-white photographs accompany the text.

545   **The Southern Pacific, 1901-1985.**
Don L. Hofsommer.   College Station, Texas: Texas A & M University
Press, 1986. 373p. maps. bibliog.

Although it is not entirely approving of Southern Pacific practices, this is an official
history of the line's 20th century expansion and management which works particularly
well as a business history. Hofsommer places the So Pac's history in a number of
contexts: regional and national railroad development; technological change, the growth
of organized labour; and the rise of government regulations. He also provides
anecdotes on the more colourful, personal sides of railroading. Two hundred black-
and-white and nine colour photographs together with twenty-seven maps provide
graphic portrayals of the railroad's operations. The So Pac, which runs through the
entire Southwest and all along the Pacific Coast, extends from East Texas to West
Texas – from Beaumont to El Paso – with a branch running into Dallas.

546   **River of lost dreams: navigation on the Rio Grande.**
Pat Kelley.   Lincoln, Nebraska: University of Nebraska Press, 1986.
149p. maps. bibliog.

A brief and thinly researched history of the mostly futile efforts to launch commercially
viable shipping companies in the often-difficult waters of the Rio Grande River. Kelley
provides a basic history of the various firms involved in Rio Grande commerce, but
also blames the railroads and irrigation companies for draining trade and water from
the river.

547   **100 years of science and technology in Texas.**
Leo Klosterman, Lloyd S. Swenson, Jr. Sylvia Rose.   Houston, Texas:
Rice University Press, 1986. 391p. maps. bibliog.

A methodical study of a century of scientific and technological research in Texas, with
great emphasis on the period after the Second World War. Individual chapters are
devoted to separate fields, with nearly two dozen tables, several maps, and over eighty
photographs. Although technological development is an important element of the
narrative, the authors also focus on the founding and activities of professional
organizations and research institutions. Among the fields covered are geology,
oceanography, meteorology, astronomy, mathematics, space sciences, physics,
chemistry, petroleum and petrochemicals, civil and mechanical engineering, com-
puters, biology, health sciences, archaeology, anthropology, psychology, and psychiatry.

548   **The promotion of exports from Texas.**
Lyndon B. Johnson School of Public Affairs.   Austin, Texas:
University of Texas Press, 1981. 199p. bibliog. (Lyndon B. Johnson
School of Public Affairs Research Project Report).

An analysis of the growth of almost every facet of Texas agricultural and industrial
production from the late 1950s to the early 1980s. Through a highly detailed text and
116 tables, graphs, and charts, the book offers basic information on the Texas economy
(the gross state product, income, the labour force, population, and export figures);
Texas manufacturing; agricultural production and exports; export opportunities in
Mexico; and the promotion by the state of its exportable products. This is not only a
summary of past activity, but a projection of production and exports into the 1980s.

549   **The Katy Railroad and the last frontier.**
V. V. Masterson.   Norman, Oklahoma: University of Oklahoma
Press, 1952. 312p. maps. bibliog.

A strictly chronological history of the Missouri, Kansas, and Texas Railroad from its formation in 1861 to 1952. Beginning in Emporia, Kansas, in 1869, the 'Katy' line was the first to enter Indian Territory (present-day Oklahoma). In 1872 it crossed the Red River to Denison, Texas, and later it continued on to Fort Worth and to Houston. The road's significance lay in its linking of the central Great Plains region with the Gulf of Mexico. In addition to his coverage of the obstacles to construction – hostile Indians and geographic difficulties – Masterson also discusses the administration of M K & T land grants and the many communities that sprang up along the line. Fourteen maps and over thirty illustrations accompany the text.

550   **The rebirth of the Missouri Pacific.**
H. Craig Miner.   College Station, Texas: Texas A & M University
Press, 1983. 236p. maps.

A modern history of the Missouri and Pacific, from its 1956 reorganization to 1983. During the 1950s, 1960s, and 1970s, the M & P worked to modernize itself through better technology (new locomotives, computerization) and a modern system of management. Miner emphasizes corporate history and the leadership of several presidents of the line; he also analyses the 1983 merger of the M & P with the Western Pacific and Union Pacific Railroads. This history of the 'Mo Pac' line is relevant to Texas because the M & P operates extensively in the state and because it merged with the Texas and Pacific Railroad in 1976.

551   **Gulf to the Rockies: the heritage of the Fort Worth and Denver-
Colorado and Southern Railways, 1861-1898.**
Richard C. Overton.   Austin, Texas: University of Texas Press, 1953.
410p. maps. bibliog.

A history of the construction of railroads between Texas and Colorado during the latter part of the 19th century, which culminated in the creation of the Colorado and Southern Railroad in 1896. Overton focuses on railroad entrepreneurs such as Grenville M. Dodge, John Evans, Morgan Jones, and Charles L. Frost, and on the numerous other lines that preceded the Colorado and Southern and played a fundamental part in building the region's rail system (including the Union Pacific and the Fort Worth and Denver City Railroad). The author provides a narrative of the construction of these lines, a history of the corporations that financed them, and an analysis of the economic development of the region serviced by these railroads.

552   **A history of the Texas railroads.**
St Clair Griffin Reed.   Houston, Texas: St Clair Publications, 1941.
822p.

Although it lacks citations and a bibliography, this is a massive and useful source on railroads in Texas. Reed offers a history of every railroad in Texas, no matter how small, and discusses proposed railroads that were never built. He covers regulatory and tax issues, land grants to Texas railroads, consolidations and the development of regional systems, terminal and electric rail companies, 'ghost' railroads that were abandoned, important legal cases concerning railroads, revenues and principal commodities shipped on Texas lines, and issues of stocks and bonds by railroads. The last three chapters examine Texas ports and steamship lines, the Texas Intercoastal Canal, and Texas railroads on the eve of the Second World War. Twenty-two tables provide information on track mileage, freight rates, chartered railroads in Texas, and land grant acreage.

553 **Intercity bus lines of the Southwest: a photographic history.**
Jack Rhodes. College Station, Texas: Texas A & M University Press, 1988. 158p. bibliog.

Although this is a pictorial work, it contains a useful amount of business history on Texas, Oklahoma, and New Mexico bus lines from 1907 to 1955. About eighty per cent of the book is devoted to Texas; there were 108 bus companies in the state in the 1930s. Rhodes presents their history in an entreprenuerial context: men opportunistically taking advantage of population shifts, highway programmes, and the decline of rail service to create, in effect, a brand new industry. Although the author does provide information on technological change, he offers less detail on state regulations and the consolidation of various bus lines. The text makes this more interesting than most photographic histories.

554 **The port of Houston.**
Marilyn McAdams Sibley. Austin, Texas: University of Texas Press, 1968. 246p. maps. bibliog.

Sibley begins with the earliest Spanish description of Galveston Bay and Buffalo Bayou in 1766, and moves on to discuss the use of Buffalo Bayou as an outlet to the Gulf of Mexico from the 1830s to the 1850s. After the Civil War, steamship operations were controlled by Commodore Charles Morgan, who also conducted most of the shipping along the Texas gulf coast. Morgan led the effort to expand the Bayou from Galveston Bay to Houston during the last quarter of the 19th century; the waterway was completed in 1914, when deep draft, ocean-going vessels could finally reach Houston. Oil and gas pipelines soon connected production areas to the port. Sibley discusses the profound impact the port had on the prosperity and population of Houston in the 20th century. Over seventy black-and-white illustrations portray important people and places connected with the port.

555 **San Antonio stage lines, 1847-1881.**
Robert Thonhoff. El Paso, Texas: Texas Westen Press, 1971. 38p.

A very brief look at stagecoach services to and from San Antonio in the second half of the 19th century. Thonhoff focuses on passenger and mail routes, competition between rival lines (especially through their advertisements), routes to El Paso and Mexico, and the negative effects of the construction of railroads on the stage industry.

556 **Texas railroads: a record of construction and abandonment.**
Charles Zlatkovich. Austin, Texas: Bureau of Business Research, University of Texas at Austin; Texas State Historical Association, 1981. 139p. maps.

Aided by twenty state and regional maps, Zlatkovich provides a list of the construction and abandonment of virtually all of the railroad lines in Texas, large and small, including the years in which specific sections of the lines were built and abandoned. In another section, he offers a chronological table of construction and abandonment organized by year and by company. Two more brief parts of the book provide histories of the state's relationship with the railroad industry and of the companies that built roads in the state. This is a matter-of-fact presentation of statistical material that is more a primary than a secondary resource.

Labour and Trade Unions

557 Chapters in the history of organized labor in Texas.
Ruth Allen. Austin, Texas: Bureau of Research in the Social Sciences, University of Texas, 1941. 258p.

Allen's book is a useful introduction to labour relations in Texas between 1880 and 1936. Each chapter covers a different topic: the relationship between railroad workers, owners and the 'Knights of Labor' in the 1880s; cowboy strikes in the 1880s; strikes by the International Granite Cutters Union against the builders of the state capitol in the 1880s; the role of the United Mine Workers Union in miners' strikes in the 1880s; the history of the Texas State Federation of Labor in the 1890s; the part played by African-Americans in the Texas State Federation of Labor; and the history of the oil workers' union from 1903-36.

558 East Texas lumber workers: an economic and social picture, 1870-1950.
Ruth A. Allen. Austin, Texas: University of Texas Press, 1961. 239p. maps. bibliog.

A social and economic history of the workers in the East Texas lumber industry during the heyday of lumbering in Texas. Allen explores the growth of the industry and the companies involved in it; labour problems and issues; company towns, pay scales, and the workers' standard of living; and the nature of work in the lumber industry. Seventeen tables summarize economic and social data about the workers, while two maps of Texas show per-capita income and employment rates for each county.

559 Texas shrimpers: community, capitalism, and the sea.
Robert Maril. College Station, Texas: Texas A & M University Press, 1983. 222p. maps. bibliog.

Maril's book is divided into three sections: part one emphasizes how the sea shapes the work and life of the shrimper, whilst part two is a social history of the community of shrimpers, including their lives and behaviour on land (surprisingly, the author claims that community anxieties are highest when the shrimpers are home from a long haul). Part three puts the shrimpers of Texas into the larger context of the United States fishing industry and includes sections on labour unions and government regulation. The shrimping industry is the largest and most lucrative fishing enterprise in the area and has a significant impact on other industries, particularly the food processing and restaurant businesses. Maril notes the hard times the shrimpers experienced in the early 1980s and predicts that consolidation within the industry will be necessary. He also looks briefly at the problems caused by the influx of Mexican-Americans into the industry.

560 **The history of the Oil Workers International Union – CIO.**
Harvey O'Connor.   Denver, Colorado: Oil Workers Labor Union –
CIO, 1950. 442p.

An official history of the OWIU from 1913-50. The author examines the conflict
between Texas oil workers and Standard Oil in 1917 and the birth of the OWIU a year
later. He goes on to discuss factionalism within the union, its growth in the 1920s and
1930s, the New Deal, and how the Union helped increase productivity during the
Second World War. The second part of the book provides a history of labour
organizing activity among oil workers in general, beginning with the first union
(formed in 1872 in Pennsylvania), the formation of the International Brotherhood of
Oil and Gas Well Workers in 1899, the International Workers of the World in the oil
industry, and so-called company unions. Part three is by far the longest section of the
book; it offers histories of local chapters and district councils of the OWIU, many of
which are in Texas, as well as the names of officers and OWIU convention delegates.

561 **A way of work and a way of life: coal mining in Thurber, Texas, 1888-
1926.**
Marilyn D. Rhinehart.   College Station, Texas: Texas A & M
University Press, 1992. 256p. bibliog.

Thurber, in north central Texas, was the site of a coal mine operated by the Texas and
Pacific Coal Company from the late 19th century to 1926. Most of the population
consisted of Italian and Polish immigrants. Rhinehart examines ethnic customs and
tensions, community spirit and labour protests, and the efforts of labour organizers and
the United Mine Workers. The UMW helped organize a massive strike in 1902; after
which the presence of the union and the welfare capitalism practiced by the company
encouraged generally calm employee-employer relations. This is an excellent study of a
single company town and of the economic and ethnic relationships between its
residents.

Folklore and
Linguistics

562 **The bounty of Texas.**
Edited by Francis E. Abernethy.   Denton, Texas: University of North
Texas Press, 1990. 220p. bibliog.

An eclectic collection of essays on ethnic and other styles of folk tales, folk music, and folk art in Texas, ranging from prison tales to Oliver North, hometowns to railroads, and ethnic food to J. Frank Dobie.

563 **The folklore of Texas cultures.**
Edited by Francis E. Abernethy.   Austīn, Texas: Encino Press, 1974.
366p.

These forty essays cover the history and folklore of two dozen ethnic and national groups in Texas. Some provide analyses of religious and secular customs, legends, or folk survivals in modern Texas; others offer the histories of specific ethnic groups; still others retell important folk tales. Native Americans, Mexican-Americans, and African-Americans receive the greatest coverage, but at least one entry deals with groups like the Spanish, French, Anglo-Saxons, and Germans, as well as seldom-discussed nationalities like the Dutch, the Danes, the Greeks, and the Lebanese – the major Asian groups and even Gypsies appear in at least one essay. This is not a survey of the folk culture of each of these groups, but a sampling of folk tales and customs.

564 **Tales from the Big Thicket.**
Edited by Francis E. Abernethy.   Austin, Texas: University of Texas
Press, 1966. 244p. maps.

A collection of essays on the folklore, history, and life of the Big Thicket of East Texas. Although one essay describes tales of the Alabama-Coushatta tribe, the book is concerned overwhelmingly with white folklore on such topics as bear hunts, local songs and ballads, early settlers, the oil boom at the turn of the century, family legends, and tales about a number of lakes, creeks, and marshes. Three maps and nearly ninety photographs from the early 20th century complement the essays.

565 **Texas toys and games.**
Edited by Francis E. Abernethy. Dallas, Texas: Southern Methodist
University Press, 1989. 253p. bibliog.

With detailed descriptions and scores of black-and-white photographs, diagrams, and
drawings, this book places toys and games in the contexts of the frontier experience
and socialization, the recreational outlets and lessons toys and games provided, the
skills they enhanced, the dangers they created, and the pleasures they gave. The
authors of these collected essays offer the histories of toys and games from kites to
knives, tree houses to party games, and dolls to gambling, but also describe present-
day practices and adaptations.

566 **The regional vocabulary of Texas.**
Elmer Atwood. Austin, Texas: University of Texas Press, 1962. 273p.
maps.

The author studies the constantly changing vocabulary of Texas in terms of Texans'
conversations about the weather, housing, landscape, personal property, food, flora
and fauna, and objects and mannerisms from family and daily life. He traces the
origins of specific phrases and usages from other parts of the country and their
transformation and, in some cases, eventual obsolescence in Texas. This is a highly
technical work; Atwood provides a methodological appendix and over six score maps
indicating the geographical distributions of selected words or groups of words.

567 **And horns on the toads.**
Edited by Mody C. Boatright, Wilson M. Hudson, Allen Maxwell.
Dallas, Texas: Southern Methodist University Press, 1959. 237p.

A wide-ranging compilation of Texas folklore that takes its name from the first tale,
which explains how the devil put horned toads in Texas. Subsequent selections detail
the histories of, or tales about, Mexican folk cures, famous story tellers and tricksters,
left-handed people, animal stories, vigilantism, buried treasure, folk music, rain,
African-American folk heroes and tales about whites, and ghost stories of military life
in the Southwest.

568 **Folk laughter on the American frontier.**
Mody C. Boatright. New York: Macmillan, 1949. 182p. bibliog.

Boatright focuses on various aspects of frontier humour, from the 18th and 19th
centuries. He analyses bragging and tall tales, notions of feminine beauty and ugliness,
frontier manners and etiquette, jokes played on 'greenhorns' new to the frontier,
stump speeches and frontier politicians, the law, religion, and the formation of a
distinctive frontier vocabulary. The author describes the reactions of Europeans and
easterners to the frontier sense of humour. Chapter seven concentrates on Texans'
enthusiasm for their own region.

569 **Folklore of the oil industry.**
Mody C. Boatright. Dallas, Texas: Southern Methodist University
Press, 1963. 220p. bibliog.

An examination of oil-related folklore in Texas from 1859 to 1940, and of the ways in
which the tales from older oil-producing states like Pennsylvania, West Virginia, Ohio,
Kansas, and Oklahoma influenced Texas oil folklore. Part one deals with finding oil

167

(such as early notions that oil could only be found near creeks), the early work of geologists, tales of men who used 'X-ray eyes', the occult, and 'doodlebugmen', who used divining rods and other unscientific methods to locate oil. Part two covers specific myths and stereotypes of certain oil men, such as the geologist, the 'slick', the manipulative oil promoter, the 'shooters', who set charges of nitroglycerin to break up rock formations, and the driller, who was considered the aristocrat of oil field labourers. Part three examines the songs, tales and anecdotes of oil folklore in Texas and other states.

570 **Dog ghosts and other Negro folk tales.**
John Mason Brewer. Austin, Texas: University of Texas Press, 1958. 124p.

This is a compilation of sixty-three African-American tales collected mostly in the 1950s. Brewer has retained the dialect and structure of these folk tales as he heard them and has presented them in a direct fashion, unencumbered by scholarship. They deal with slavery, leisure activities, animals, ranch life, religion, and ghosts.

571 **The word on the Brazos: Negro preacher tales from the Brazos bottom of Texas.**
John Mason Brewer. Austin, Texas: University of Texas Press, 1953.

A simple collection of fifty-six stories dating back to the last thirty years of the 19th century. The categories of tales include 'Bad Religion', 'Baptisms, Conversions, and Church Meetings', 'Good Religion', 'Heaven and Hell', and 'Preachers and Little Boys'. The stories are generally humourous and are presented as told (or as creatively retold), complete with 'Negro' dialect.

572 **J. Mason Brewer: Negro folklorist.**
James W. Byrd. Austin, Texas: Steck-Vaughn, 1967. 44p. bibliog. (Southwest Writers Series).

Brewer (1896-1975) was a prominent folklorist, author, essayist, historian, poet, and editor. A member of a well-educated Texas family, he served as an interpreter in the United States Army during the First World War and was associated after the war with J. Frank Dobie. He finally received his doctorate in 1951. For many years, Byrd taught at small black schools, including Hutson-Tillotson and Texas Southern in Texas and Livingston College in North Carolina. His many books and articles contributed much to the early historiography on Texas blacks and to the folklore of slavery. This booklet stresses his accomplishments in the field of folklore rather than his historical research.

573 **The tongue of the Tirilones: a linguistic study of a criminal argot.**
Lurline H. Coltharp. University, Alabama: University of Alabama Press, 1965. 313p. map. bibliog. (Alabama Linguistic and Philological Series).

Coltharp argues that the language spoken in the crime-ridden and economically depressed South El Paso of the early 1960s comprised a 'third' language (after English and Spanish). The author portrays the residents of slums and members of under-privileged ethnic groups as sub-cultures that develop their own languages. This is a highly technical, very scholarly work; the bulk of it (190 pages) is devoted to a vocabulary of words she discovered in South El Paso, a combination of Spanish, English, and slang useful to this sub-culture's everyday lives.

574 **Black cats, hoot owls, and water witches: beliefs, superstitions, and sayings from Texas.**
Edited by Kenneth W. Davis, Everett Gillis.   Denton, Texas: University of North Texas Press, 1989. 101p.

A collection of hundreds of brief sayings, anecdotes, epigrams, and metaphors from Texas. Accompanied by a dozen attractive black-and-white drawings by Teal Sale, the entries are presented in a straightforward manner and are organized into three major sections: Field and Farm (including the weather, planting, finding water, insects, and reptiles), Home and Hearth (health problems, the family, deaths, and clothing), and superstitions.

575 **Legends of Texas.**
Edited by J. Frank Dobie.   Hatboro, Pennsylvania: Folklore Associates, 1964. 279p.

These legends, collected by Texas's most famous folklorist, are paraphrased by the contributors and generally presented without jargon or analysis. The categories of legends include buried treasure and lost mines, the supernatural, lovers and pirates, origins of Texas flowers and place names, and miscellaneous legends. Many of the legends have Mexican or Native American origins, and date back to the 19th century or earlier.

576 **Man, bird, and beast.**
J. Frank Dobie.   Dallas, Texas: Southern Methodist University Press, 1965. 185p.

A collection of scholarly but accessible articles on Anglo, Indian, and Hispanic folktales and legends. Among the topics are ranch remedies (for people and animals) and folk cures in northwestern Oklahoma; stories and songs (complete with music and lyrics in Spanish and English) of Mexican-Texans; Anglo-American outlaws, Texas Rangers and other lawmen; and cowboys. The two final articles examine the sources of folklore (especially oral history and family documents) and recent scholarship on balladry and folk songs.

577 **Children's riddling.**
John Holmes McDowell.   Bloomington, Indiana: Indiana University Press, 1979. 272p. bibliog.

In this examination of the ways children use riddles, McDowell explores the differences between riddles he heard from working class Chicano children and middle-class white children in Austin, Texas. This is a very technical book, whose key concept in defining the meaning and functions of riddles is interrogative ludic routine, which adapts the verb sequence of interrogative language to the purposes of play. Within this theoretical structure, the author seeks to elucidate differences among Chicano and white children in the form and content of their riddles. The social processes of riddling, the acquisition of riddling competence, social and cognitive functions of children's riddling, and the reflexivity of riddling are among the topics included in this analysis.

578 **I heard the old fisherman say: folklore of the Texas Gulf coast.**
Patrick B. Mullen.   Austin, Texas: University of Texas Press, 1978.
183p. bibliog.

An analysis of the folklore and folk beliefs of professional fishermen and shrimpers on
the Texas gulf coast. The author distinguishes between the folklore of deep sea
fisherman and those who work close to shore; he also places the folklore of these
Texans in the context of the folk beliefs of other coastal regions. Many of the folk
beliefs and superstitions revolve around the hazards of the profession, such as omens
that foretell bad weather or small catches. Since fishing is usually a family endeavour,
folk beliefs are passed from one generation to another, and the author discusses the
process of folklore transmission. Other topics include tall tales, buried treasure, and
colourful personalities found in local tradition. Part one discusses folklore associated
with the profession at large and differences between such ethnic groups as Italians,
blacks, Anglos, and Yugoslavians. Part two discusses differences in the folklore among
various parts of the Texas coastal region.

579 **Witchcraft in the southwest: Spanish and Indian supernaturalism on the
Rio Grande.**
Marc Simmons.   Lincoln, Nebraska: University of Nebraska Press,
1980. 2nd ed. 184p. map. bibliog.

An historical survey and contemporary account of the nature of witchcraft belief in the
southwestern United States. Simmons illuminates the belief in witchcraft and the
supernatural that still pervades southwesten Hispanic and Indian societies, although
practitioners often conceal it from the whites who ridicule their beliefs. The book
provides many tales and folklore from several tribes, and much detail on supernatural
beliefs and rituals both past and present. The author devotes separate chapters to types
of witchcraft (executions and herbalism, for instance), and to individual tribes such as
the Pueblo, Zuni, Navja, and Apache. A number of intriguing historic and
contemporary photographs show witches performing rituals and sites of witchcraft
ceremonies.

Media

580 **The Texas country editor: H. M. Baggarly takes a grass-roots look at national politics.**
Herbert M. Baggarly, edited by Eugene W. Jones.   Cleveland, Ohio: World Publishing, 1966. 341p. map.

Baggarly (1915–), a columnist and later editor of the weekly *Tulia* (Swisher County, Texas) *Herald* in the 1950s and 1960s, provides the authentic voice of a southern liberal. The *Herald*, where Baggarly began working in 1946 (he bought a controlling interest in 1955) reached 4,500 subscribers in the Texas Panhandle. As an editorialist, Baggarly won many state, regional, and two national awards; his columns promoted liberal causes such as racial integration, farm programmes, an active federal government, and the policies of John F. Kennedy. Most of the editorials included in this volume deal with presidential politics. The editor has included a chart showing at least circumstantial statistical evidence of Baggarly's persuasive influence in the formation of public opinion in his readership area.

581 **Drawing power: Knott, Ficklen, and McClanahan, editorial cartoonists of the *Dallas Morning News*.**
Robert F. Darden.   Waco, Texas: Markham Press Fund, 1983. 105p. bibliog.

A collection of editorial cartoons by a trio of *Dallas Morning News* cartoonists whose work appeared in the paper from the 1910s through the mid-1970s. John Francis Knott (1878-1963) was the finest artist of the three; he was patriotic, civic-minded, and concerned with rural issues. Jack Ficklen (1911-80) focused largely on Dallas politics and personalities, while William McClanahan (1907-81) drew cartoons on sports as well as Texan politics. These cartoonists were generally conservative Democrats and boosters for both Dallas and Texas; however, their work seems quite mild compared with contemporary editorial cartoonists.

Media

582 **The press and the law in Texas.**

Norris G. Davis.   Austin, Texas: University of Texas Press, 1956.
244p.

A dated but nonetheless useful description of Texan (not federal) laws pertaining to
the press, and an analysis of their application to actual news-reporting situations. After
a brief introduction on the history of freedom of the press in Texas, Davis examines
the issues of civil and criminal libel, invasion of privacy, contempt of court, trial by
publicity, public records access, disloyalty, obscenity, and advertising. In every case he
provides a historical context of the development of laws regulating and protecting the
press. Despite its age, this well organized, detailed, precise, and practical book
remains an important introduction to its subject.

583 **Amon: the life of Amon Carter, Sr., of Texas.**

Jerry Flemmans.   Austin, Texas: Jenkins Publishing, 1978. 520p.

Amon Carter Sr, (1879–1955) published the *Fort Worth Star Telegram*, a leading Texas
newspaper that boisterously promoted Fort Worth, West Texas, and Texan interests
(in that order). He was not a journalist, but a businessman, promoter, and, often
problematically, one of the area's biggest news makers. Carter was 'a professional
Texan' with all of the positive and negative characteristics of the stereotype. Through
his wide-ranging business interests and impressive wealth, he was very influential in
Fort Worth and in much of West Texas. This is a colourful retelling of a colourful
man's life, newspaper, and city. Flemmans highlights anecdotes (positive and negative)
about Carter that detail his influence and philanthropy, and press room legends.

584 **John Henry Brown: Texian journalist, 1820-1895.**

Laurence E. Honig.   El Paso, Texas: Texas Western Press, 1973. 55p.

Brown (1820-95) was a pioneering editor who came to Texas in 1840. He worked as a
reporter or editor for newspapers in Austin, Victoria, Indianola, Galveston, and
Belton during the twenty years prior to the Civil War. Although Brown also served as
a legislator, Confederate officer, and mayor of Dallas, Honig focuses on Brown's
journalistic career and his attitudes concerning Indians, slavery, and the Civil War.
Brown was also one of Texas's earliest historians; his *History of Texas* (St Louis,
Missouri: L. E. Daniell, 1892) and *Indian wars and pioneers of Texas* (Austin, Texas:
L. E. Daniell, 1892) are still cited by historians.

585 **Lone stars and state gazettes.**

Marilyn McAdams Sibley.   College Station, Texas: Texas A & M
University Press, 1983. 403p. bibliog.

Sponsored by the Texas Daily Newspaper Association, this is an exhaustive look at
Texas newspapers during the decades before the Civil War. Sibley offers her usual
thorough research and clear writing: this is not merely a celebration of sturdy pioneer
editors, but an analysis of their backgrounds, practices, and experiences. She devotes
separate chapters to the Texas Revolution, political patronage and government
contracts for public printing, and secession. The author also includes Spanish-language
newspapers in her survey. The focus is on the political side of newspaper publishing.
Also included is a checklist of 347 Texas newspapers published in the state from
annexation to the Civil War.

Performing Arts

586 The theatre in early El Paso, 1881-1905.
Donald V. Brady. El Paso, Texas: Texas Western Press, 1966. 39p.

This is a brisk and erratically organized history of the theatre in El Paso from the cultural awakening in the city after the Civil War to the turn of the century. Brady describes the construction of the Coliseum and of the Myar Opera House, and provides a short look at the management of these two primary theatres of El Paso.

587 The BFI companion to the western.
Edited by Edward Buscombe. New York: Atheneum, 1988. 432p. map. bibliog.

A profusely illustrated and useful reference work on movies about the American West. After a brief history by Buscombe of western films, forty contributors offer over 400 thoughtful essays which provide biographical information and analyses of movies dealing in various ways with a plethora of western topics, from Billy the Kid and 'bankers' to Populism, prostitution, and the Second World War. The book also includes an annotated list of 300 western films with brief reviews and credits, and a listing of every western television series and movie with synopses, running dates, and credits.

588 Houston by stages: a history of theatre in Houston.
Sue Dauphin. Burnet, Texas: Eakin Press, 1981. 498p. bibliog.

Dauphin offers an exhaustive look at theatre in Texas's largest city. More encyclopaedic than analytical, and rigidly chronological, it concentrates on producers and productions. After a brief chapter on the late 19th century and vaudeville, she offers sections on the 'Little Theatre' movement and the regional theatres of the 1930s and 1940s, community theatres, musical theatres, college drama departments, dinner theatres, and ethnic theatres in Houston. The text is followed by an index of theatres, producers, and plays.

589 **Footlights on the border: the Galveston and Houston stage before 1900.**
Joseph Galleghy.   The Hague, Netherlands: Mouton, 1962. 262p.
bibliog.

This text examines the history of the theatre in Houston and Galveston from the days
of the Texas Republic up to 1900. Galleghy provides an account of and commentary on
every dramatic season held during this period. He also gives the histories of many of
the theatres in the cities and the men who founded them. Most of the narrative consists
of descriptions of each play, opera, and musical performance – as well as their on- and
off-stage personnel – that took place in the two cities. The author also reprints reviews
of these performances from local newspapers. Forty-one black-and-white photographs
of actors, theatres, and playbills are included.

590 **The midnight special: the legend of Ledbelly.**
Richard M. Garvin, Edmund G. Addeo.   New York: Bernard Geis,
1971. 312p.

This is an unusual biography of this legendary blues and folk artist in that it is written
as a novel based closely on historical events. A native of Louisiana, Huddie 'Ledbelly'
Ledbetter (1887-1949) served many years in Louisiana, Texas, and New York prisons;
the authors chronicle this aspect of his life but also, of course, emphasize his music. He
learned the twelve-string guitar at an early age, organized bands in Louisiana oil fields,
on Dallas's East Side, and in prison, and was 'discovered' by the folklorist John
Lomax, who recorded his prison work songs in 1934 and took Ledbelly to New York to
perform. An idiosyncratic but interesting look at a ground-breaking musician.

591 **The early years of rhythm & blues: focus on Houston.**
Alan Govenar.   Houston, Texas: Rice University Press, 1990. 96p.
bibliog.

Although it contains a very brief introductory essay on the history of the blues and of
blues artists in Houston, this is primarily a photographic history of the city's rhythm
and blues scene in the 1950s and 1960s. The author includes seventy-four black-and-
white photographs by Benny Joseph, a well-known community and promotional
photographer for Peacock Records. His subjects include entertainers, producers, night
club owners, and events and sites from the black community in Houston.

592 **No name on the bullet: a biography of Audie Murphy.**
Don Graham.   New York: Viking Press, 1989. 396p.

Murphy (1924-71), who was America's most decorated war hero for his exploits during
the Second World War, became a movie star in the 1940s and 1950s. Graham provides
a balanced portrayal of a man who demonstrated a great number of contradictions.
Murphy was a shy sharecropper's son with a craving for excitement; he was generous
to friends but often displayed a violent temper and penchant for cruel practical jokes;
he was a hero in his films but a chronically unfaithful husband and compulsive gambler.
The author carefully traces the rise of the soldier and hero, as well as the fall of the
unwise businessman and big-time gambler. This is a good story, and Graham provides
plenty of context for Murphy's life, including the rural Texas poverty in which he grew
up, combat during the Second World War, and the political and social tawdriness of
Hollywood and the movie industry.

593 **Scott Joplin.**
James Haskin, Kathleen Benson. Garden City, New York:
Doubleday, 1978. 248p.

A simple, yet thoroughly researched biography of Scott Joplin (1868-1917), the son of
a former Texan slave who became one of the greatest American composers of popular
music, and creator of the opera *Treemonisha*. Although not close, his family were
musically inclined and Joplin formed his first musical group at the age of sixteen, when
he joined the ranks of the itinerant musicians who moved across the South and West
developing 'ragtime' music. Joplin ended up in Chicago in 1893, where he quickly
became a success with such compositions as the 'Maple-Leaf Rag', and 'The
Entertainer'. With the onset of the 'Jazz Age' in the 1920s, he lost popularity, although
his music was rediscovered in the 1970s. The authors place ragtime in the context of
African-American music and explain how it entered the musical mainstream in the
20th century.

594 **'The whorehouse bells were ringing': and other songs cowboys sing.**
Collected and edited by Guy Logsdon. Urbana, Illinois: University of
Illinois Press, 1989. 388p. bibliog. (Music in American Life Series).

This sometimes quite bawdy volume contains sixty-one cowboy songs not published
elsewhere (at least in the versions presented here). Many originated outside the West
and were first sung by workers in other occupations. The extensive annotation for each
song includes other titles by which it was known, its origins, its music and lyrics, and
recordings made of the song. In a separate section, six cowboys who acted as
informants detail their lives and how they learned the songs and passed them along.
Finally, Logsdon provides a sixty-page essay on the history and collection of cowboy
songs.

595 **Willie: an autobiography.**
Willie Nelson, Bud Shrake. New York: Simon & Schuster, 1988.
334p.

In this book Willie Nelson, perhaps Texas's most long-lasting and popular native
musician, reminisces about his life, from his poverty-stricken childhood in central
Texas to his often-tumultuous rise to country music stardom. Nelson's descriptions of
incidents or periods of his life are printed along with statements or memories from
friends, family members, and colleagues. Although this is obviously a very commercial
book, it is fairly honest; it includes Nelson's struggles with alcohol, and his several
wives, as well as inside information about the music business and life on tour. In
addition, Nelson also presents his philosophy of life, which draws on astrology,
reincarnation, and a vaguely populist admiration of the common man.

596 **The Texas-Mexican *conjunto*: a history of working-class music.**
Manuel Peña. Austin, Texas: University of Texas Press, 1985. 218p.

A scholarly community study of Mexican-Americans from 1860 to the present, with a
focus on this highly popular type of accordion music which has a strong symbolic
importance to the Mexican-American working class. The author examines its stylistic
evolution from a single accordion to several instruments plus a contra-bass and a drum.
The major shift in style occurred immediately after the Second World War, as *Tejano*
society changed in response to rising educational attainment, employment mobility,

and assimilation. This caused tension within the community and the *conjunto* was itself split between traditional and more modern approaches and interpretations.

597 The Houston Symphony Orchestra, 1913-1971.

Herbert Roussel.   Austin, Texas: University of Texas Press, 1972. 247p. bibliog.

A chronological, but eccentrically organized history of a major Texas musical establishment. Roussel recounts the story of how the musically gifted Ima Hogg (daughter of Texas governor James Hogg), funded every facet of the early years of the orchestra, and describes its quantitative and artistic growth during its first fifty-eight years. The author chronicles the effects of two world wars, the Great Depression, and the civil rights movement on the orchestra in terms of attendance, financial support, and the demography of the orchestra. The appendixes list musical and administrative personnel, while thirty-three black-and-white photographs show musicians, patrons, and venues.

598 Music in El Paso, 1919-1939.

Robert M. Stevenson.   El Paso, Texas: Texas Western Press, 1970. 40p.

This is a useful look at two decades of music in El Paso. Stevenson offers short biographies of a number of musicians, composers, and music instructors who lived or worked in the city in the 1920s and 1930s, as well as descriptions of certain types of music (including jazz, classical, and Mexican-American music), and a short history of the El Paso orchestra.

599 San Antonio Rose: the life and music of Bob Wills.

Charles Townsend.   Urbana, Illinois: University of Illinois Press, 1976. 395p. bibliog.

Written by an historian, this is a biography of Bob Wills (1905-75), the legendary Texas bandleader and singer who originated 'Texas swing' music. Based on 200 interviews, including extensive talks with Wills, this is a complete biography set in the contexts of Texas, popular music, and the entertainment industry. Townsend describes Wills' life (including his drinking binges and several failed marriages); the diverse origins of Wills' unique style; and his business dealings. Although Townsend obviously admires Wills and his music, this is an objective examination of the entertainment business and of a giant in Texas popular music history. The author also provides a discography of the 500-plus recordings made by Wills and his Texas Playboys.

600 The yellow rose of Texas: the story of a song.

Martha Anne Turner.   El Paso, Texas: Texas Western Press, 1971. 19p.

A short piece, this is a popular history of Texas's most famous song. Turner traces changes in the lyrics and music from before the Civil War through the early 20th century.

Fine Arts

Literature

601 **Elmer Kelton and west Texas: a literary relationship.**
Judy Alter. Denton, Texas: University of North Texas Press, 1989.
161p. bibliog. (Texas Writers Series).

By 1987, Elmer Kelton (1926-) had published twenty-seven novels, over fifty short stories, and two collections of short stories. His novels fall into two categories: popular westerns and serious literary works. Alter argues that Kelton uses the 'western' novel as a vehicle for studying man; his strengths, weaknesses, actions, and reactions. Her book chronicles how Kelton developed his art from the 'powderburner' western to regional novels of the highest quality, and reveals him as an example of a writer who writes from his own experiences or through serious research. Some of Kelton's better-known novels (all published in Garden City, New York, by Doubleday) are *The day the cowboys quit* (1971), *The time it never rained* (1973), *Stand proud* (1984), and *The man who rode Midnight* (1987).

602 **Talking with Texas writers: twelve interviews.**
Patrick Bennett. College Station, Texas: Texas A & M University Press, 1980. 307p. bibliog.

Transcriptions of interviews with a dozen leading Texas essayists, fiction writers, playwrights, journalists, biographers, and historians are collected together in this volume. Most of the authors write about subjects dear to Texans' hearts (cowboys, Texas, the West), while a few are better known for writing about the Southwest or the South, other authors, or contemporary America. These men are not necessarily Texas natives, but have been long-time residents of the state. Among the topics they discuss are their writing processes, how they perceive themselves and other Texas writers, their life and work (and how the two intersect), and the themes found in their books. The twelve writers are: Larry McMurtry, A. C. Greene, John Graves, Max Apple, Shelby Hearon, Leon Hale, Preston Jones, Elmer Kelton, Francis Mossiker, William Goyen, Larry L. King, and Tom Lea. A bibliography lists their major publications.

603 **Benjamin Capps and the south plains.**
Laurence Clayton. Denton, Texas: University of North Texas Press, 1990. 205p. bibliog. (Texas Writers Series).

Capps (1922-) has written a dozen novels and popular histories on the West, Texas, and Native Americans. The grandson and son of cowboys, he is a serious novelist rather than a formula writer; he writes about both the Old West and the contemporary West. Clayton applauds Capps' character development and realism in this useful summary of the writer's main themes and career. His novels include *White man's road* (New York: Harper & Row, 1969) and *Trail to Ogallala* (New York: Duell, Sloan and Pierce, 1964); his non-fiction work includes the very accessible *The great chiefs* (New York: Time-Life Books, 1975) and *The Indians* (New York: Time-Life Books, 1973).

604 **In the deep heart's core: reflections on life, letters, and Texas.**
Craig Edward Clifford. College Station, Texas: Texas A & M University Press, 1985. 145p.

A collection of Clifford's essays that blend personal narratives and anecdotes with literary criticism and interpretation. He examines and offers criticism on Texas men of letters, such as Walter Prescott Webb, Larry McMurtry, J. Frank Dobie,and Roy Bedicheck. He analyses the work of other Texas writers (historians, essayists, political commentators, and creative writers) in the contexts Texas, and the Texan experience: cowboys, South and West Texas, Houston, ethnic groups (including Germans, Irish, Czechs, Anglos, blacks, and Mexican-Americans), music, and many other topics that Texas writers have explored in the last twenty to thirty years are covered. This is an idiosyncratic but valuable introduction to a wide-ranging coterie of recent Texas authors.

605 **Range wars: heated debates, sober reflections, and other assessments of Texas writing.**
Edited by Craig Clifford and Tom Pilkington. Dallas, Texas: Southern Methodist University Press, 1989. 188p. bibliog.

This is a compilation of spirited essays about Texas writers written by prominent Texas writers and critics. The essays provide a sense of the history of Texas writing as well as the history of the criticism of Texas writing. Among the essays is a list of the fifty best Texas books by A. C. Greene; Craig Clifford's examination of 'The Reality of Myth in Texas Letters' and his reflections on the characteristics of Texas writers; Texas women writers (Celia Morris), literature dealing with Indian-white relations (Don Graham); and James Wardlee's analysis of 'Arbiters of Texas Literary Taste'. There are also pieces by Larry McMurtry, Marshall Terry, and Tom Pilkington.

606 **John C. Duval: first Texas man of letters – his life and some of his unpublished writings.**
J. Frank Dobie. Dallas, Texas: Southern Methodist University Press, 1965. 105p.

A hero of the Texas Revolution, Duval (1816-97) was a frontier surveyor and prospector, Texas Ranger, Confederate soldier, and author of stories and books on Texas topics. His most important writings were *Early times in Texas* (published serially in 1867 in *Burke's Weekly*; a facsimile edition was published in Austin, Texas: by Steck-Vaughn in 1967) which detailed his adventures during and after the Texas Revolution, and *The adventures of Big Foot Wallace, the Texas ranger and hunter*

(Philadelphia, Pennsylvania: Claxton, Remsen, and Haffelfinger, 1871), about a famed Texas frontiersman with whom Duval had served in the Texas Rangers. Dobie's short book is divided into three parts: biographical, critical, and bibliographical.

607 Three men in Texas: Bedichek, Webb, and Dobie.
Edited by Ronnie Dugger. Austin, Texas: University of Texas Press, 1967. 285p.

An eclectic series of essays about Roy Bedichek (the famed naturalist); Walter Prescott Webb (Texas's best-known historian); and the folklorist J. Frank Dobie. All three men were well-known professors at the University of Texas. The essays originally appeared in the *Texas Observor*, which Dugger edited. The articles vary widely in topics and quality: some are reviews of their books, while others analyse their personal philosophies. Several are simply biographical sketches, while a number of them are memoirs by friends and former students of these important Texas writers.

608 Poets laureate of Texas, 1932-1966.
Margret R. Edwards. San Antonio, Texas: Naylor, 1966. 140p.

In 1932, Texas newspaper editors convinced the state legislature to establish the position of poet laureate of Texas. Poets were initially appointed for a period of two years (it later became every one year) by a committee comprised of the governor and six legislators. Edwards devotes five to six pages to each of the first two dozen poets laureate, providing biographical sketches, a photograph, and notable examples of their poetry.

609 Texas, a literary portrait.
Don Graham. San Antonio, Texas: Corona, 1985. 243p. bibliog.

Drawing on a wide-ranging assortment of writers, essayists, playwrights, and historians spanning a century of Texas literature, Graham examines the main sub-regions of Texas (including urban Texas). He attempts to reach the realities behind the myths surrounding Texas history and literature and to explain how the myths developed. Graham explores the defensiveness and aggressiveness of Texans and Texas writers, the reactions of Texans to outsiders and vice versa, and Texans' responses to ethnicity and to national issues. He concludes that there is room for a regional literature, but not at the exclusion of more comprehensive or inclusive themes and visions.

610 The Texas literary tradition: fiction, folklore, history.
Edited by Don Graham, James W. Lee, William T. Pilkington. Austin, Texas: College of Liberal Arts, University of Texas at Austin, Texas State Historical Association, 1983. 238p. bibliog.

The product of a 1983 conference at the University of Texas at Austin, which explored the current literary scene in Texas and the ways that contemporary Texan writers view their state's literary past. The nineteen essays examine such diverse topics as J. Frank Dobie, Walter Prescott Webb, and Roy Bedichek; the southern roots of Texas literature and historical writing; the frontier; Texas-Mexican perspectives; the myths of Texas; and recent writing on the urban experience and on women's issues.

611 A part of space: ten Texas writers.

Edited by John Howard Griffin. Fort Worth, Texas: Texas Christian University Press, 1969. 179p.

This compilation offers a sampling of prose, fiction, and poetry from ten writers who are identified with the Dallas-Fort Worth area. The authors are John Howard Griffin, Edwin Shrake, William Burford, William D. Barney, John Graves, James Newcomers, Ilse Skipana Rothrock, Larry McMurtry, Tom Pendleton, and Ramona Maher Weeks. Although these writers are associated with Texas, their work is not necessarily concerned with the Texas legacy or attitudes (although some, of course, are); these selections simply represent the writing of prominent contemporary Texas writers.

612 Fred Gipson at work.

Glen E. Lich. College Station, Texas: Texas A & M University Press, 1990. 125p. bibliog.

The author does not intend this to be a comprehensive biography of Fred Gipson (1908-73); instead, he highlights those aspects and events of Gipson's life that had the greatest influences on his literary work. Special emphasis is placed on Gipson's relationship with the Texas Hill Country, including both its negative and positive influences and the notoriety his writings gave to this sub-region of Texas. The book traces changes in Gipson's conception of the region and how this was manifested in his writings as both memories and aspirations. Gipson wrote pulp westerns and stories for *Reader's Digest* and the *Southwest Review*, but also books like *Fabulous empire* (Boston, Massachusetts: Houghton Mifflin, 1946), *Big Bend: a homesteader's story* (Austin, Texas: University of Texas Press, 1973), and his most famous book, *Old Yeller* (New York: Harper, 1956).

613 Katharine Anne Porter and Texas: an uneasy relationship.

Clinton Machann, William Bedford Clark. College Station, Texas: Texas A & M University Press, 1990. 208p. bibliog.

Several of the essays in this collection describe Porter's background and experiences in Texas, the remainder providing literary criticism and an annotated bibliography. The authors attempt to place this Texas-born author in her appropriate Texas context as well as in the southern context in which she is generally considered. Among Porter's books are *Ship of Fools* (Boston, Massachusetts: Little, Brown, 1962), *Noon-Wine* (Detroit, Michigan: Schuman's 1937), *Never-Ending Wrong* (Boston, Massachusetts: Little, Brown, 1977), and a number of short story collections.

614 The children of the sun: Mexican-Americans in the literature of the United States.

Marcienne Pocard, translated by Edward G. Brown, Jr. Tucson, Arizona: University of Arizona Press, 1989. 393p. bibliog.

The author examines the transition of the Mexican-American image in American literature, both from the Hispanic and from the Anglo-American points of view. Pocard divides the study into three periods. Between 1848 and 1940 literary images of Mexican-Americans grew out of American ideas about 'Manifest Destiny' and their Mexican War experiences. The myth of Anglo superiority dominated this century. The author examines the origins of the derogatory term 'greasers' and other negative language and stereotypes, which declined with increasing Mexican and Anglo interaction in the 1940s. The period from 1940-65 witnessed a degree of Mexican-American assimilation into the larger American society and as Anglo authors became more sympathetic, more positive images appeared in the media. In addition, more Mexican-American authors began writing in English. Finally, the decade after 1965 saw a further decline in literary stereotypes of Mexican-Americans; many Anglos sympathized with Chicanos but were confused about their origins and goals, and tentative about Chicanos' radical political efforts. Mexican-American literature promoted nationalism and positive aspects of the *barrio*, but also the negative aspects. In general, argues Pocard, images of Mexican-Americans in literature over the last century and a half, written by Anglos as well as Hispanics, reflected a growing integration and sophistication, and a decreasing use of stereotypes.

615   **Taking stock: a Larry McMurtry casebook.**
Edited by Clay Reynolds.   Dallas, Texas: Southern Methodist
University Press, 1989. 450p. bibliog.

Larry McMurtry has written over fifteen novels (several of which have been made into movies) and more than 500 essays and critical studies dealing with the 19th and 20th century Texas experience. Reynolds provides over forty essays, reviews and articles describing McMurtry's work and ideas. The contributors deal with McMurtry's writings, and also his conflicts with the Texas literary establishment; his relationship with the film industry; and more traditional discussions of his growth as a writer. Among McMurtry's best-known books are *Lonesome dove* (New York: Simon & Schuster, 1985), which won a Pulitzer Prize, *The last Picture show* (New York: Dial, 1966), and *Terms of endearment* (New York: Simon & Schuster, 1975).

616   **The southwest in life and literature.**
Compiled and Edited by C. L. Sonnichsen.   New York: Devin-Adair,
1962. 554p.

Sonnichsen has included works spanning a century of writing in this book, which offers ten to twenty page extracts from book-length fiction, history, travellers' accounts, and memoirs that help to define and describe the American Southwest (Arizona, New Mexico, Oklahoma, and Texas). The editor has chosen forty different writers from a wide-range of backgrounds and periods and he provides useful mini-biographies along with selections of writing. Among the authors with Texas connections are: John C. Duval, a Texas Ranger, surveyor, and chronicler of the frontier; Frederick Law Olmsted, who wrote a famous account of his 1850s journey through Texas; the Native American novelist Frank Waters; the naturalist Roy Bedichek; Edna Ferber, the popular novelist and author of the epic novel about Texas oil men, *Giant*; and the folklorist J. Frank Dobie. This is a good introduction to the literature and historical writing about Texas and the Southwest, but has limitations; for instance, there are no works by African-Americans.

617   **An American original: the life of J. Frank Dobie.**
Lon Tinkle.   Boston, Massachusetts: Little, Brown, 1978. 264p.
bibliog.

Dobie (1888-1964) was the leading Texas literary critic, folklorist, and preserver of Texas heritage. After serving as an Army officer in the First World War, he taught in the University of Texas English Department and became a well-known author, columnist, and radio personality. Among his books on Texas legends, history, and folklore are *Coronado's children: tales of lost mines and buried treasure in the southwest*

(New York: Grosset and Dunlap, 1930), *The longhorns* (Boston, Massachusetts: Little, Brown, 1941), and *On the open range* (Dallas, Texas: Banks, Upshaw, 1940). This is an informative biography of the man called 'Mr Texas'.

618 C. L. Sonnichsen: grassroots historian.
Dale L. Walker. El Paso, Texas: Texas Western Press, 1972. 99p. bibliog.

A simple biography of one of Texas's best-known popular historians. After receiving a PhD from Harvard University in English, Sonnichsen (1901-92) taught at the University of Texas at El Paso for forty-one years, where thousands of students took his course on the 'Life and Literature of the Southwest'. However, Sonnichsen was actually better known as an historian; he was the author of *I'll die before I run: the Story of the great feuds of Texas* (New York: Devin-Adair,1962) and *Pass of the north: four centuries on the Rio Grande* (El Paso, Texas: Texas Western Press, 1968). Sonnichsen lived on for another twenty years after the publication of this biography, part of which he spent editing the *Journal of Arizona History*.

Art

619 Folk art in Texas.
Edited by Francis E. Abernethy. Dallas, Texas: Southern Methodist University Press, 1985. 203p.

The editor defines 'folk art' as objects that were designed for utilitarian purposes but which still possess artistic qualities, and this is an examination of such art (mostly modern) in Texas. Although the text provides some background and descriptions, the book is given over mostly to both black-and-white and colour photographs. The wide-ranging chapters cover ethnic groups, important folk artists, tattoos, cowboy hats, painted handkerchiefs made by Bexar County jail inmates, whittlers, grave stones, 19th century Indian pine needle art, saddle-making, and murals in El Paso.

620 Black history, black vision: the visionary image in Texas.
Lynne Adele. Austin, Texas: The Gallery, 1989. 93p. bibliog.

The catalogue of an exhibition that appeared in a number of Texas museums, this book includes many black-and-white and several colour prints of the art work. The artists are six self-taught African-Americans, born late in the 19th or early in the 20th centuries, who deal with dreams, visions, religious revelations, and other mystical themes in their art. The artists are: John W. Banks (felt marker and ballpoint depicting rural scenes and the second coming of Jesus Christ); Ezekial Gibbs (watercolours, pastel drawings creating impressionistic portrayals of every day life from his own experiences); Frank Jones (coloured pencil drawings of devils and 'haunts'); Naomi Polk (watercolours; primitive religious themes); Johnnie Swearingen (oil paintings of Biblical and contemporary religious scenes); and Willard Watson (watercolour and felt marker pictures of autobiographical incidents – he also executes African-inspired sculptures). This is an interesting look at the importance of African survivals and mystical religion even in the 20th century black community.

621 **Texas gulf coast: interpretations by nine artists.**
Al Barnes, (et al.), introduction by Leon Hale. College Station,
Texas: Texas A & M University Press, 1979. 112p.

After a brief introduction on the history, economy, and ecology of the gulf shore, the
nine artists present forty-six colour prints, with one-paragraph comments by the artists.
The paintings are generally realistic or representational in style; their subjects (most of
which are contemporary) include the flora and fauna of the shore, boats, residents, and
tourists. These are mostly popular artists, although several are art professors and the
works of others have been shown at major galleries around Texas and the Southwest. In
addition to Barnes, the artists whose work is included in this collection are Herb
Booth, John P. Cowan, Michael Frary, John Guerin, Harold Phenix, E. M. Schiwetz,
Everett Spruce, and Dan Wingren.

622 **Faces of the borderlands: twenty-one drawings by José Cisneros.**
José Cisneros. El Paso, Texas: Texas Western Press, 1977. 52p.
bibliog.

Twenty-one sketches of representative people of the borderland region by one of
Texas's most prominent contemporary illustrators. Most of the drawings are head or
bust portraits only, with appropriate headgear and accessories. The artist draws
'typical' representations of a number of border 'types' and provides a paragraph or two
about each, including information on his or her role in borderland society, attitudes,
and dress. Cisneros includes drawings of a Cuera dragoon, a conquistadore, a soldier,
an officer, a child, a viceroy, and a pioneer woman from the Spanish period, as well as
a merchant, an outlaw, a stagecoach driver, and a cowhand from the Anglo period.
Rounding out the collection are an Apache warrior, a Mexican soldier, and a Mexican
vaquero (cowboy).

623 **Riders of the border: a selection of thirty drawings by José Cisneros.**
José Cisneros. El Paso, Texas: Texas Western Press, 1971. 64p.
bibliog.

This volume contains thirty black-and-white sketches of different types of horsemen
and horsewomen of the United States and Mexican border region, with a descriptive
paragraph about the function, customs, and behaviour of each. Cisneros covers
Spanish soldiers, conquistadores, dragoons, lancers, borderland pioneers, Franciscan
missionaries, women, and most other groups of settlers in his work.

624 **The art of the woman: the life and work of Elisabet Ney.**
Emily Fourmy Cutrer. Lincoln, Nebraska: University of Nebraska
Press, 1988. 270p. bibliog.

The first female student at Munich's Art Academy, Ney (1833-1907) sculpted many of
the most prominent European men of her time, from Jacob Grimm to Guiseppi
Garibaldi and Otto von Bismarck. Idealistic and romantic, Ney and her husband came
to a German utopian settlement in Georgia in 1870 and in 1871 she moved to Texas.
She was rather eccentric for a woman of her time; she wore trousers and ran the family
farm. She began sculpting again in the 1880s and won a number of important
commissions. Her statues of Stephen F. Austin and Sam Houston are now displayed in
the state capitol and the United States capitol respectively, while other pieces of her
work are in the National Museum of American Art and the Elisabet Ney Museum in
Austin. Cutrer places Ney in the contexts of the lives of other 19th century female

artists and the development of Texas culture, which Ney promoted as enthusiastically as she promoted her own work.

625 **Impressions of the Texas Panhandle.**
Michael Frary.   College Station, Texas: Texas A & M University
Press, 1977. 112p. maps. (The Joe and Betty Moore Texas Art Series).

Frary offers seventy-seven paintings (most shown in colour) of contemporary scenes of the Texas Panhandle. Frary's short history of the region and description of its physical geography, its people, and its towns accompanies his paintings. The artist's subjects include cattle and ranchers; physical landmarks on the Panhandle such as Cap Rock, Ceta Canyon, and the open prairie; wildlife, such as bison and prairie dogs; and scenes from Panhandle towns like Lubbock, Clarendon, Farwell, and Bovina.

626 **Watercolors of the Rio Grande.**
Michael Frary.   College Station, Texas: Texas A & M University
Press, 1984. 131p. map.

Nearly fifty of Frary's watercolours showing the places and people of the Rio Grande River Valley, from the river's headwaters to its mouth, are collected in this book. Frary provides a brief descriptive and historical introduction to his realistic paintings of natural landmarks and sites (the bulk of the paintings), people at work, small towns, and scenes featuring Native Americans and Hispanics.

627 **The art of Tom Lea.**
Compiled by Kathleen G. Hjerter, introduction by William Weber
Johnson.   College Station, Texas: Texas A & M University Press,
1989. 256p.

Lea is an artist, illustrator, and writer from El Paso. Along with very useful biographical information on his life and times, the introduction provides an effective analysis of Lea's artistic and intellectual achievements. Nearly 300 photographs of his work are provided, including portraits, paintings, and murals, mostly of the Southwest. One section of the book features his work as a Second World War artist and correspondent for *Life* magazine.

628 **The Texas landscape, 1900-1986.**
Susie Kalil.   Houston, Texas: Museum of Fine Arts, 1986. 96p.

This is the catalogue of the Texas Sesquicentennial Exhibition at Houston's Museum of Fine Arts. The exhibition spotlighted seventy-six artists, from Frederick Remington to Robert Onderdonk who, in their paintings, sculptures, drawings, and photographs depicted or were influenced by the Texas landscape. These are not simply pretty pictures of scenic grandeur or representations of a space often occupied and changed by humans. Many of the selections do portray Texas directly, but other artists are included because their work was affected by their residence in Texas. The compiler includes brief biographies of many of the artists featured, as well as a fifty-page historical and critical essay on the various regions of Texas, genres of art, and periods covered in the exhibition. Some of the examples are reproduced in full colour.

629 **Gentilz: artist of the old southwest.**
Dorothy Steinbomer Kendall, Carmen Perry. Austin, Texas: University of Texas Press, 1974. 127p. (The Elma Dill Russell Spencer Foundation Series).

Theodore Gentilz (1819-1906), a Parisian, came to San Antonio in 1844 and taught at St Mary's College. The first part of this volume describes his travels and life in Texas. Part two furnishes reproductions (thirty in colour and thirty in black-and-white) of Gentilz's paintings which depict the everyday life of the Mexican-Texans, Anglos, and Native Americans of Texas; Texas landscapes and villages; and famous sites like the Alamo. Part three consists of the diary Gentilz kept and the thirty sketches he drew while touring Texas in the 1840s.

630 **Hermann Lungkwitz: romantic landscapist on the Texas frontier.**
James Patrick McGuire. Austin, Texas: University of Texas Press, 1983. 225p.

A native of Germany, Karl Friedrich Hermann Lungkwitz (1813-91), arrived in the Texas hill country west of Austin in 1851. He supported his family in a number of different jobs (including a stint in the State Land Office), moving to San Antonio during the Civil War and to Austin afterwards. McGuire has identified 341 paintings, drawings, lithographs, and other works by Lungkwitz of Texas cities and Hill Country landscapes; although he sold few of his works during his lifetime, he remains, according to the author, Texas's first important landscape artist.

631 **Gary Niblett: a new look at the old west.**
Mary Terrence McKay. Loveland, Colorado: Action Press, 1990. 95p.

McKay seeks to elevate the work of the well-known 'cowboy' artist Niblett to respectability. He documents Niblett's roots in Texas and New Mexico, examining the artistic merits of 'cowboy' art, and exploring the career of this western artist who also attempts to move beyond that genre by painting Polish peasants. The author compares Niblett to other western artists, but also to 17th century Dutch genre painters. She takes western art seriously, not romanticizing it, but considering it as valid art, and places Niblett in the larger context of 'artistic geography' rather than 'residential geography'. This is a scholarly look at the kind of artist rarely considered by experts; a number of colour plates of Niblett's paintings, showing scenes of the every day life of cowboys and Polish peasants, are included.

632 **The Wendy and Emery Reeves collection.**
Steven A. Nash, David F. Owsley, Robert V. Rozelle. Dallas, Texas: Dallas Museum of Art, 1985. 224p.

The Wendy and Emóry Reeves collection has been located since 1985 in a recreated 'Villa La Pausa' (the collectors' home in France) within the decorative arts wing of the Dallas Museum of Art. It offers a wide-ranging selection of decorative art, including collections of dishware, rugs, frames, and furnishings, as well as valuable paintings, sculptures, and drawings. This catalogue of the collection includes biographies of Wendy (a fashion model) and Emery (a writer) and analyses of the pieces featured in dozens of colour photographs from the holdings.

633 **Cowboy spurs and their makers.**
Jane Pattie. College Station, Texas: Texas A & M University Press, 1991. 180p. bibliog. (Centennial Series of the Association of Former Students, Texas A & M University).

Pattie, a journalist and photographer based in Texas, traces the process of making spurs and devotes individual chapters to the most prominent spur makers. Her book spans the 19th century to the present, while the geographical area covered ranges from Connecticut and New Jersey to the Southwest. She discusses spur-making as a business and as an art form, and argues that spur design depended on who was to wear them (cowboys as opposed to gentlemen riders) and the environment in which they would be worn. Nearly 100 photographs accompany the text and an appendix lists many past and present artisans, with their locations and the distinctive characteristics of their spurs.

634 **Painting in Texas: the nineteenth century.**
Pauline A. Pinckney. Austin, Texas: University of Texas Press, 1967. 232p. bibliog.

This is a very useful survey of 19th century painters of Texas, illustrated with almost 120 examples of their works. Pinckney makes connections between diverse groups of artists; her book is organized chronologically and thematically, with genres or backgrounds or circumstances providing the main chapter headings, and individual artists the subjects of chapter sub-divisions. Most of these artists had little formal training; the author approaches them as personalities and as artists. She categorizes them as provincials (from the earliest days of Anglo-Texas through the Texas Republic), travellers (Americans and Europeans), portrait and landscape painters, artists accompanying surveying expeditions, native-born Texans, and patrons of the arts.

635 **The Onderdonks: a family of Texas painters.**
Cecilia Steinfeldt. San Antonio, Texas: Trinity University Press, 1976. 238p. bibliog.

Three short biographies of three Texas artists are provided here: Robert Onderdonk, best known as an art teacher, and two of his children – Julian, a landscape artist, and Eleanor, a painter of portraits and natural subjects and a museum curator. Following each biographical section Steinfeldt gives a catalogue of that artist's paintings and sketches. The Onderdonks came to Texas in 1879, and their efforts, according to Steinfeldt, made Texas art less 'European' and more 'American'. A total of 275 illustrations accompany the text, some in colour.

636 **Lone star regionalism: the Dallas nine and their circle, 1928-1945.**
Rick Stewart. Austin, Texas: Texas Monthly Press, 1985. 199p.

This is the catalogue of an exhibition commemorating the Texas sesquicentennial mounted at the Dallas Museum of Art and other museums around the state. The show focused on nine Dallas artists who achieved national prominence based on their expression of regional character and traditions; they were instrumental in the formation and activities of the Dallas Arts League in the 1930s. They painted primarily rural scenes, the oil industry, landscapes, and Texans of all ages and races. Stewart provides an extensive analysis of this movement and considers the artists in their regional and national contexts. Well over 100 reproductions of the art work are included. The best-known artists from this group are Jerry Bywaters, Charles Bowling, Alexandre Hogue, William Lester, and Otis Dozier.

637   **Pecos to Rio Grande: interpretations of west Texas by 18 artists.**
Introduction by Ron Tyler.   College Station, Texas: Texas A & M University Press, 1983. 125p.

The bulk of this book consists of forty-nine full-colour Texas landscapes by Al Brouilette, Marbury Hill Brown, Jerry Bywaters, Finis F. Collins, Otis Dozier, Heather Edwards, Michael Frary, Frank Gerrasi, John Guerin, William Hoey, DeForrest Judd, William Lester, Clay McGaughy, Ancel F. Nunn, Stephen Rascoe, Everett Spruce, and E. Gordon West. Their artistic styles include realism, post-impressionism, and many others. Tyler's introduction provides a travelogue of the remote areas depicted.

638   **Views of Texas: watercolors by Sarah Ann Lillie Hardinge together with a journal of her departure from Texas.**
Introduction and captions by Ron Tyler.   Fort Worth, Texas: Amon Carter Museum, 1988. 80p.

Hardinge, a New Englander, spent four years in Texas in the 1850s. Her watercolours portray scenes from Seguin and San Antonio, old Spanish missions, river landscapes, ferries, stagecoaches, and plantation houses. Tyler's introduction and a portion of the artist's journal (kept while she travelled out of Texas in 1856), highlight her family and care for her children, women's roles in antebellum Texas, and her adventures and accidents during the journey out of the state.

639   **Black art in Houston: the Texas Southern University experience.**
John Edward Weems, John Biggers, Carroll Simms.   College Station, Texas: Texas A & M University Press, 1978. 106p.

An analysis of the work and careers of John Biggers, a muralist and painter, and Carroll Simms, a sculptor and ceramicist. In the 1950s, Biggers and Simms established the Negro Art Department at Texas Southern University, which has produced a number of notable African-American artists in the decades since. Weems discusses the men's lives, their inspirations, and their early efforts to train African-American artists at TSU. Included in the book are numerous examples of the work of Biggers and Simms and their students, especially their 1970s murals on some of the buildings at the college.

640   **The Texas cowboy.**
Don Worcester.   Fort Worth, Texas: Texas Christian University Press, 1986. 136p. map.

This book contains over 100 colour and black-and-white reproductions of paintings, photographs of sculptures, and illustrations featuring scenes of cowboy life from the early 18th century to the present. All of the contributors are contemporary artists; they include painters Mark Storm, Justin Wells, and Lee Herrington; sculptors Cynthia Rigden and Garland Weeks; and the illustrator Harold Holden. Their art, accompanied by a brief descriptive text, deals with typical western scenes such as roundups, mustangs on the open range, night cavalry patrols, cattle drives, the arrival in Texas of pioneers, branding cattle, stampedes, Indians, and Texas longhorn cattle.

Architecture

641 **Texas homes of the 19th century.**
Drury Blakeley Alexander, foreword by Harry H. Ransom. Austin, Texas: University of Texas Press, 1966. 276p. bibliog. (The Texas Architectural Survey).

This is a survey of more than 200 Texan homes, divided into three main sections – frontier settlement architecture, antebellum South architecture, and Victorian architecture. A photograph and specific information (location, date of construction, builder, and distinctive architectural features) are presented for each house. The styles range from log cabins and adobe structures from the first era to Greek Revivals in the second and Italianate, Queen Anne, and Second Empire styles in the third. Alexander includes the homes of some of Texas's most famous residents, such as Sam Houston, Beriah Graham, and Sam Bell Maxey. Fourteen diagrams show designs and architectural features common to Texas.

642 **Lighthouses of Texas.**
T. Lindsay Baker, foreword by F. Ross Holland, paintings by Harold Phenix. College Station, Texas: Texas A & M University Press, 1991. 168p. bibliog.

This is a survey of the different styles of lighthouse found in Texas. After an introductory chapter that provides a general account of lighthouses and the people who kept them, Baker gives ten chapters, each detailing the construction, history, and navigational service of a surviving Texas lighthouse. The author highlights the personalities and hardships endured by the engineers, keepers, and inspectors who operated the lighthouses until they were closed in the mid-20th century. Supplemented by thirty colour and black-and-white illustrations, this is a useful look at some of the Texas coast's most unique architectural landmarks at some of its best-known historical sites: Brazos Santiago, Aransas Pass, Galveston, and Sabine Pass.

643 **Houston's forgotten heritage: landscape, houses, interiors, 1824-1914.**
Sadie Blackburn, (et al.). Houston, Texas: Rice University Press, 1991. 350p.

A study of the society and architectural landscape of 19th century Houston with nearly 300 black-and-white photographs. Separate sections, by separate authors, examine landscaping and horticulture, the development of Houston architecture, home interiors, and the everyday lives of Houstonians. An introduction places those lives and developments in their larger historical contexts.

644 **Inside Texas: culture, identity, and houses, 1878-1920.**
Cynthia A. Brandimarte. Fort Worth, Texas: Texas Christian University Press, 1991. 416p. bibliog.

An examination of the tastes of Texans as displayed in their interior decorating. Brandimarte examines differences in home interiors based on the resident's occupation, ethnicity, socio-economic group, region in Texas, and degrees of culture and refinement. Chronologically, *Inside Texas* covers styles from late 19th century homes to the more open arts and crafts movement of the early 20th century. The author also explores another transition: the shift from individualized, personal decorating, to the use of professional decorators and widely available commercial products. Three hundred black-and-white photographs are used to support her text.

645 Dallas architecture, 1936-1986.
David Dillon, photographs by Doug Tomlinson. Austin, Texas: Texas Monthly Press, 1985. 213p.

The result of a 1976 exhibition at the Dallas Museum of Fine Arts, this is a chronological account of a half-century of Dallas architecture, with short profiles of leading architects and chapters examining the 1940s-1950s, 1960s-1970s, 1980s, historic preservation, and city planning. Dillon emphasizes the mercantile, entrepreneurial, and affluent nature of Dallas's history and architecture; the dominant styles have been relentlessly modern. He also focuses on 'downtown', on public buildings, and on the business side of architecture more than the art of it. Tomlinson provides dozens of black-and-white photographs of building exteriors as well as a few interiors.

646 Henry C. Trost: architect of the southwest.
Lloyd C. Englebrecht, June-Marie F. Englebrecht. El Paso, Texas: El Paso Library Association, 1981. 154p. bibliog.

Trost (1860-1933) designed many buildings in Arizona, New Mexico, and the Trans-Pecos region of Texas. A resident of El Paso for the last thirty years of his life, he dominated architecture in these three states from 1890-1920 and was influenced by the architects Louis Sullivan and Frank Lloyd Wright, by the mission revival movement, and by Pueblo motifs. He was one of the first architects to design buildings using steel reinforced concrete, yet he insisted that regional architectural styles were both desirable and necessary. He also argued that architects must design buildings for specific environments by taking into consideration factors such as climate and terrain. About half the text deals with his designs and innovations in El Paso. The author includes eighty black-and-white photographs of Trost's work.

647 Houston architectural guide.
Stephen Fox, edited by Nancy Hadley, foreword by Peter C. Papademetriou. Houston, Texas: The American Institute of Architects, Houston Chapter, 1990. 318p. maps.

A guide to 850 architecturally significant buildings and houses, as well as a few bridges, parks, and statues in Houston and its surrounding suburbs. Each entry provides a photograph (taken by Gerald Moorhead), address, date of construction, and a description of the site. The structures have been arranged into nineteen driving tours, complete with easy-to-read maps. The brief architectural analyses in the text are subjective and sometimes quite critical. Given the history of Houston – especially in the 20th century – it is not surprising that most of the structures included in this guide are modern and post-modern in orientation.

648 Abner Cook: master builder on the Texas frontier.
Kenneth Hafertepe. Austin, Texas: Texas State Historical Association, 1991. 240p.

An analysis of the life and times and work of Abner Cook, who, during his forty-five years in the city, designed Greek Revival houses for many of Austin's most prominent residents, including the governor's mansion. Hafertepe links Cook to eastern designers and builders, Cook having worked extensively in the northeastern United States and in

Virginia and Tennessee before moving to Texas. After the Civil War, he built a
number of commercial buildings in Austin, as well as the original main building at the
University of Texas. One of the author's primary contributions is his identification of
buildings actually designed and built by Cook.

649   Ashton Villa: a family and its house in Victorian Galveston, Texas.
Kenneth Hafertepe.   Austin, Texas: Texas State Historical
Association, 1991. 60p. (Popular History Series).

The story of an Italianate mansion on Galveston's legendary Broadway is related in
this book. Built of brick and cast iron, it was begun in 1859 by the merchant James M.
Brown. Hafertepe examines the evolution of the house's interior through various
architectural styles and periods. He explores archaeological findings, such as the kinds
of food eaten by the inhabitants of the house and other aspects of everyday life, and
uses the recently discovered diary of Brown's daughter for information on the
mundane details of Victorian family life and courtship. Ashton Villa survived
Galveston's hurricane in 1900 and has recently been restored. It now belongs to the
city and is administered by the Galveston Historical Foundation.

650   Log cabin village.
Terry G. Jordan.   Austin, Texas: Texas State Historical Association,
1980. 146p. maps. bibliog.

This guide to Log Cabin Village, an historical park in Fort Worth, is also a history of
the log cabin in the United States. Jordan discusses the origins of the log house in
colonial America, its adaptation to the frontier in the 19th century, and the several
designs and building methods demonstrated in the Fort Worth buildings. The second
half of the book contains detailed histories and over 100 photographs of the seven
homes in Log Cabin Village. Jordan has also provided seven maps of Texas and the
United States showing the distribution of various types of architectural styles, including
log cabins.

651   Texas log buildings: a folk architecture.
Terry G. Jordan.   Austin, Texas: University of Texas Press, 1978.
230p. maps. bibliog.

Jordan provides here a more detailed and wider-ranging study of log buildings in Texas
than in his book *Log cabin village*. The author emphasizes differences in the designs
and construction techniques of several ethnic groups (especially Anglo-Americans,
German-Americans, and African-Americans), as well as regional differences due to
the availability of certain building materials. The author provides great detail regarding
the building process, from laying the foundations of log buildings to attaching their
chimneys, and includes chapters on public buildings and outbuildings constructed of
logs. The book is illustrated with nearly 100 black-and-white photographs and two
dozen maps showing the distribution of various styles of log buildings throughout
Texas counties.

652 **Restoring Texas: Raiford Stripling's life and architecture.**
Michael McCullar. College Station, Texas: Texas A & M University
Press, 1985. 161p. map. bibliog.

Raiford Stripling (1910-), the son of a pharmacist, has restored many East Texas
buildings over the last forty years. This book is partly a biography, but over half of the
volume is devoted to his work and contributions to Texas history and culture through
his preservation and restoration work. His restoration projects include the old Saint
Augustine jail, numerous mission chapels, the Earle-Harrison and Milton Garrett
Houses, Ashton Villa, and Sabine City hospital.

653 **Historic Galveston.**
Richard Payne, Geoffrey Leavenworth. Houston, Texas: Herring
Press, 1985. 99p. bibliog.

A coffee-table book with a veneer of historical and architectural scholarship, a number
of full-colour photographs of buildings or building details, and a twenty-page
'Architectural Inventory' of fifty-three architecturally significant residential, commercial, and ecclesiastical buildings representing a number of architectural styles. Each
building is shown in a tiny black-and-white photograph and described with the history
of its builders and owners and a summary of its architectural details. Also included is a
very brief historical essay that highlights the economic growth that led to the
architectural flowering of Galveston, summarizes the ravages of the 1900 hurricane,
and describes the 'Galveston Style' – a mixture of Greek Revival, Italianate, and the
Victorian 'gingerbread' popular in Galveston during the 19th century.

654 **Gone from Texas: our lost architectural heritage.**
Willard B. Robinson. College Station, Texas: Texas A & M
University Press, 1981. 296p. bibliog.

Robinson provides a cross-section of the architectural history of Texas from the
Spanish colonial period to the early 20th century. He explains the development of each
type of architecture (residential, religious, industrial, and governmental), Texans'
attitudes toward architecture (its function and aesthetic appeal), and why buildings
were destroyed. He advocates the preservation and restoration of various now-
endangered structures. Over 250 black-and-white photographs show buildings that
have now been destroyed or greatly altered.

655 **The people's architecture: Texas courthouses, jails, and municipal
buildings.**
Willard B. Robinson. Austin, Texas: Texas State Historical
Association, 1983. 365p. bibliog.

Robinson surveys the factors that gave form and character to local government
buildings in Texas, and the material and human conditions (such as income and tax
base, population and cultural heritage, crime rates, climate and industry, attitudes
about wealth) that affected their design and construction. He argues that Texans had a
special pride in their public buildings: nevertheless, many fell victim to the anti-
Victorian wave of destruction in the 1920s. The author provides detailed descriptions
of the buildings as well as the craftmanship and technology used to construct them.
The book includes photographs, drawings, and diagrams of selected public structures.

656 **Texas public buildings of the 19th century.**
Willard B. Robinson, foreword by Drury Blakeley Alexander.
Austin, Texas: University of Texas Press, 1974. 290p. map. bibliog.

This is an attempt to preserve in photographs many endangered, but still standing, 19th century public buildings and to describe some that have already vanished. Robinson emphasizes those regions most fully developed by 1900. He suggests that Texans of the late 19th century took great pride in their government architecture as symbols of progress, culture, permanence and future growth. He includes chapters on Spanish and Mexican architecture in Texas, antebellum public buildings, and military and institutional architecture. Over 200 black-and-white photographs and 16 diagrams of floor plans and layouts of town squares provide graphic evidence for Robinson's text.

Medicine

657 Texas folk medicine: 1333 cures, remedies, preventives, and health practices.
John Q. Anderson. Austin, Texas: Encino, 1970. 91p.

Very brief descriptions of over 1300 folk cures for many different ailments, including recognized diseases and injuries, as well as fright, freckles, crossed eyes, and other less traditional 'diseases'. Many of the cures employ magic, including chants, charms, and amulets, and the use of plants; there are Hispanic origins for many of these natural cures.

658 Crazy water: the story of Mineral Wells and other Texas health resorts.
Gene Fowler. Fort Worth, Texas: Texas Christian University Press, 1991. 315p. map. bibliog.

An account of the mineral water resorts and bottlers that have thrived in Texas from 1877 to the present. Although places like Indian Hot Springs in Hudspeth and Hot Sulphur Wells Resort near San Antonio are mentioned, the author concentrates on Mineral Springs, Texas, where numerous resorts flourished and water was bottled for sale all over the United States. These resorts were popular in Texas, especially before the Second World War, and the mineral baths were said to cure just about any affliction. Fowler details the efforts of Mineral Springs and other towns to bottle their water and describes the quacks and charlatans who purported to cure ailments with 'magnetic baths', old Indian methods, and uranium waters. The last chapter discusses the battle in 1948 between Perrier, and the Artesia Water Company and other mineral water bottlers in Texas to gain control of the American mineral water market. Eighty black-and-white photographs of mineral springs, advertisements, and customers enliven this thorough and entertaining book.

659   **A history of the Texas Medical Association, 1853-1953.**
      Pat I. Nixon.   Austin, Texas: University of Texas Press, 1954. 476p.

Nixon begins with the unsuccessful formation of the first Texas Medical Association (TMA) in 1853. It was reorganized in 1869 and, despite another slow start, became established by the 1880s, publishing the *Texas State Journal of Medicine* from 1905 onwards. Nixon describes the TMA's contributions to the war efforts during both the First and Second World Wars, and the association's rapid growth after 1945. The author focuses on the TMA's work to instill professional ethics, efforts to disseminate new treatments and technologies, and its promotion of public health laws.

660   **The medical story of early Texas, 1528-1853.**
      Pat I. Nixon.   Lancaster, Pennsylvania: Lancaster Press, 1946. 507p.
      bibliog.

An exhaustive history of medicine in Texas from the Spanish period to the formation of the Texas Medical Association in 1853. Nixon includes discussions of the herbal medicines of Native Americans, which were often adopted by whites. He also covers Hispanic medical practices; French and Spanish doctors and medicines; the role of doctors in the military campaigns of the Texas Revolution; the beginning of medical education in Texas; and medical ethics and quackery. The author describes diseases and cures, as well as changing technology and early hospitals.

661   **The Methodist Hospital of Houston: serving the world.**
      Marilyn McAdams Sibley.   Austin, Texas: Texas State Historical
      Association, 1989. 244p. bibliog.

Now a 3,800 bed hospital with an annual gross revenue of $150 million, the Methodist Hospital has been affiliated with Baylor University Medical School since 1943. Sibley, who bases her narrative mainly on hospital sources and documents, portrays the hospital and its staff in a very positive light. Her theme is the rather bland proposition that the Methodist Hospital has always sought to provide quality service. The book is more about management than about medicine or patients highlighting the individuals and institutions that built and maintained the giant complex. Although clearly written, *The Methodist Hospital* is less analytical, perhaps, than some of Sibley's other works.

662   **Texas College of Osteopathic Medicine: the first twenty years.**
      Edited by C. Ray Stokes.   Denton, Texas: University of North Texas
      Press, 1991. 124p.

The College was begun in 1970 by three Fort Worth osteopaths seeking to promote 'wellness' and prevention as opposed to merely treating diseases, and is now affiliated with the University of North Texas. It is a nationally recognized institution with a fifteen-acre campus, 150 faculty members, and 450 students. This is basically a collection of extremely admiring oral accounts collected together by Stokes; they focus on the early struggles for acceptance, the growth of the college's facilities, and the success of 1,000 alumni. An appendix lists the primary benefactors of the school.

Sports

663 **Friday night lights: a town, a team, and a dream.**
H. G. Bissinger. Reading, Massachusetts: Addison-Wesley, 1990.
357p.

More than a description of one Texas city's obsession witih football, this is an analysis of the ways in which Odessa's Permian High School Panthers' 1988 football season reflected community priorities and civic pride, provided social activities in an isolated West Texas oil city, and, displayed much of what is wrong with Texas and American society. Through high school football, Bissinger explores racism, problems with the country's educational system, social beliefs, violence, and even political machinations. Football and football players are larger than life in Texas; this fast-paced and interesting work shows how and why that is the case.

664 **The Dallas Cowboys and the National Football League.**
Donald Chipman, Randolph Campbell, Robert Calvert. Norman,
Oklahoma: University of Oklahoma Press, 1970. 252p. bibliog.

In a 'behind the scenes' history of the Dallas Cowboys the authors examine the business side of the 'Cowboys' and of the National Football League (including agreements between the league and television networks); the social and cultural impact of professional football on Dallas and on the United States in general; the competition between the NFL and the American Football League (to which the Cowboys originally belonged) before the 1966 merger of the two leagues; and the eventually very successful struggle to build a winning team in the 1960s. The book contains ten tables of NFL standings in the 1960s, season statistics, attendance records, and Cowboy rosters.

665   **The twelfth man: a story of Texas A & M football.**
Wilber Evans, H. B. McElroy.   Huntsville, Alabama: Strode, 1974.
315p.
A fan's history of Texas A & M football, presented in an enthusiastic narrative that focuses on the coaches, stars, and school traditions. The authors provide year-by-year team records; school records; members of all-Southwest Conference and all-America teams from A & M; the outcomes of post-season bowl games; the rosters of the A & M teams that won conference championships; and the names of team captains. The name of the book originates from the legend of the 'twelfth man' – the enthusiasm of the A & M cheering section – encouraging the on-field eleven to victory.

666   **The Aggies and the 'Horns': 86 years of bad blood and good football.**
John D. Forsyth.   Austin, Texas: Texas Monthly Press, 1981. 159p.
bibliog.
The oldest and most fierce football rivalry in Texas college football exists between Texas A & M University's 'Aggies' and the University of Texas at Austin's 'Longhorns'. This is a breezy history of that rivalry, which concentrates, of course, on the big games between the two schools, but also offers information on the teams' coaches (especially at A & M, where coaches tended not to stay around long during the 1950s and 1960s, when UT dominated the rivalry) and on important matches with other Southwest Conference schools.

667   **American rodeo: from Buffalo Bill to big business.**
Kristine Fredriksson.   College Station, Texas: Texas A & M
University Press, 1985. 255p.
Although the author makes reference to the early history of rodeo, when it was merely a diversion for cowboys from their hard work, Fredriksson's discussion is mainly concerned with the 20th century rodeo. She focuses on the formation of institutions like the Cowboy Turtle Association (the rodeo cowboys' union), which fought for fair prize money; the early Rodeo Association of America (R A A), which sought to standardize rules; and the Professional Rodeo Cowboys Association, which was formed in the 1970s to help promote the sport. The author also discusses the popularization of the sport as well as some of its leading heroes and prize-winners. More than sixty black-and-white photographs of rodeo personalities and events are included.

668   **Hook 'em horns: a story of Texas football.**
Denne H. Freeman.   Huntsville, Alabama: Strode, 1974. 231p.
In the first few chapters, Freeman describes the first sixty years of University of Texas football from 1893 onward, and goes on to tell the story of the reign of legendary head coach Darrell Royal. From 1957-73, Royal won a number of Southwest Conference championships, the national championship in 1963, and numerous other big games and important post-season games. Throughout the book, the focus is on star players and dramatic moments, with an analysis of Royal's most important innovation, the 'Wishbone' offense. The author includes over sixty black-and-white photographs and numerous statistical tables.

669   **Texas sport: the illustrated history.**
Jon Holmes.   Austin, Texas: Texas Monthly Press, 1984. 126p.
bibliog.

Holmes focuses primarily on teams and individuals who rose to prominence in baseball (major and minor league teams and the 'Negro leagues' in Texas); football (major college and professional teams); basketball (college teams and players who became professional players); golfers and tennis players (college and professional); and boxing, track and field, rodeo, and horse racing. The brief entries are copiously illustrated with black-and-white photographs of leading participants in all of these sports.

670   **The Texas League: a century of baseball, 1888-1987.**
Bill O'Neal.   Austin, Texas: Eakin Press, 1987. 389p. bibliog.

The Texas League was one of the premier minor baseball leagues in the United States during the first half of the 20th century. O'Neal focuses on colourful players and owners. He describes each season and offers a summary of the history of each franchise that ever belonged to the league. Lists of champions, playoff results, league standings, and numerous other statistics are also included. The Texas League declined as major league baseball teams were established in Houston and Dallas, and as television brought major-league baseball to the small towns in which the minor league teams flourished. Although O'Neal packs his book full of information, he neglects interpretation; for instance, he barely discusses the league's relationship with the major leagues.

671   **Autumn's mightiest legions: history of Texas schoolboy football.**
Harold V. Ratliff.   Waco, Texas: Texian Press, 1963. 174p.

In this narrative history of high school football in Texas, Ratliff discusses briefly the first non-school sponsored teams in Dallas in the 1920s, the founding of the Interscholastic Football League in 1920, and the changes in Texas high school football during the early 1960s. The author describes championship games, legendary teams and coaches, the evolution of rules (regarding on-the-field play as well as eligibility requirements), and community support for high school football.

672   **Papa Jack: Jack Johnson and the era of white hopes.**
Randy Roberts.   New York: Free Press, 1983. 274p. bibliog.

A native of Galveston, Johnson (1878-1946) defeated Jim Jeffries in 1910 to become the first African-American world heavyweight boxing champion. Although this is a scholarly biography, it is written with the verve of a sportswriter. Roberts focuses on his subject's boxing matches, but also on his sometimes violent and often controversial lifestyle, and on his experience as a black man in a white society. He recounts Johnson's personal life: his prison experiences, his relationships with the press, with prostitutes, and his white wife; and his attempts (usually over-shadowed by racism and poor personal choices) to defy the restrictions imposed upon members of his race. While this is certainly not a whitewash of Johnson's life, it is clear that the author has a great admiration for the legendary boxer.

673 **Red Raiders: Texas Tech football.**
Ralph Sellmeyer, James E. Davidson.   Huntsville, Alabama: Strode,
1978. 418p.

Each season of Texas Tech University football from 1925-77 receives its own chapter, whilst specific games, coaches, players, and the team's 1976 Southwest Conference championship season are also discussed. Appendixes list the scores of every Texas Tech football game, the names of every football letter-winner of 1977, and team and individual records.

674 **Saturday's children.**
Giles Tippette.   New York: Macmillan, 1973. 270p.

This is an account of the Rice University football team during the 1971 season. Tippette describes games and practices, relationships among players and coaches, and the pressures of the win-at-all-costs atmosphere of college football in the Southwest Conference. Although much of the text deals with on-the-field action, Tippette uses this Rice University team as an example of the strengths (the teamwork and effort required to win) and weaknesses (the opportunities for corruption and for distorting the relationship between college sports and academics) of big-time college football in the United States.

675 **Football, Texas style: illustrated history of the Southwest Conference.**
Kern Tips.   Garden City, New Jersey: Doubleday, 1964. 275p.

The leading major college football conference in Texas is the Southwest Conference, founded in 1915 and comprising of most of the major universities in the state: the University of Texas, Texas A & M University, Rice University, the University of Houston, Texas Tech University, Texas Christian University, Southern Methodist University, and the University of Arkansas (until the 1990s). This is a profusely illustrated history of the conference which focuses on great coaches, players, and teams; on changes in rules and in strategies for playing football; and on the status of the Southwest Conference among other major college conferences around the United States.

Reference Works and Bibliographies

676 **Texas bibliography: a manual on history research materials.**
Compiled and edited by Gilberto Rafael Cruz, James Arthur Irby.
Austin, Texas: Eakin Press, 1982. 337p.

An unannotated listing of over 6,300 books, articles, PhD and MA theses, and some printed primary sources published over the last 100-plus years. Two-thirds of the entries are found in listings for the chronological periods of Texas history, and the editors have also focused primarily on history in the other categories of works: biographies, the frontier, Texas Rangers, folklore, diplomacy, travellers' accounts, ethnic groups, architecture, art, nature, and children's literature.

677 **Exploring the Johnson years.**
Edited by Robert A. Divine.   Austin, Texas: University of Texas Press, 1981. 280p. bibliog.

A collection of seven essays that combine historiographical and factual material as well as a discussion of the appropriate sources from the Lyndon B. Johnson Presidential Library in Austin. Following an introductory essay by the editor are essays on: the war in Vietnam, by George Herring; Latin American policy, by Walter LaFeber; civil rights, by Steven F. Lawson; the 'War on Poverty', by Mark I. Gelfand; federal educational policy, by Hugh Davis Graham; Johnson's relationship with the White House staff, by Larry Berman; and Johnson's relationship with the media, by David Culbert. Finishing the book is a sixteen-page appendix that lists the vast primary sources in the Johnson library, ranging from Johnson's Congressional, Senate, and Presidential papers to oral histories and the records of government agencies during Johnson's tenure in office (1963-69).

Reference Works and Bibliographies

678   **A bibliography of Texas government and politics.**
Arnold Fleischmann.   Austin, Texas: Policy Research Institute,
University of Texas at Austin, 1985. 106p.

The authors begin with a fourteen-page research guide to depositories and sources on Texas government and politics. This is followed by sections listing: bibliographies, works on political institutions (such as the state constitution, legal system, and the branches of government), political participation (including parties, ethnicity, and interest groups), public policy (regarding state finances, education, social services, natural resources, transportation, business and the economy, and agriculture), and local government and politics (including entries on thirteen individual cities). The listings include books, articles, and reports by scholars, journalists, government agencies, and interest groups. All were written after 1900 most dating from after 1945.

679   **Cracker barrel chronicles: a bibliography of Texas town and county histories.**
John H. Jenkins.   Austin, Texas: Pemberton Press, 1965. 509p.

A quite useful bibliography of 5,040 Texas country histories of every size and quality, and from virtually every historical period. Jenkins lists the author, title, place and date of publication, publisher, number of pages, and the value (from a book collector's standpoint) of each book or pamphlet. Although the entries are arranged by county, an appendix cross references towns and counties. Another appendix provides population figures for Texas towns and counties from 1850-1960.

680   **Manuscript sources in the Rosenberg Library: a selective guide.**
Edited by Jane A. Kenamore, Michael E. Wilson.   College Station,
Texas: Texas A & M University Press, 1983. 174p.

This is an annotated bibliography of the manuscript collections available in Galveston's Rosenberg Library. The holdings focus on Galveston history from the 1820s to the mid-20th century, and on the history of early Texas. Entries are organized by call number, in ascending order, and include a brief biography of the individuals involved with the documents, the number of items in the collection, and a description of those items. A very detailed index enhances the volume's usefulness.

681   **The University of Texas Archives: a guide to the historical manuscripts collections in the University of Texas library.**
Compiled by Chester V. Kielman.   Austin, Texas: University of Texas
Press, 1967. 594p.

A dated but still very useful resource. Now housed in the 'Eugene C. Barker Texas History Center', the University of Texas Archives were established in 1899 and are the major repository of primary source materials for Texan history. The guide includes entries on 2,430 separate manuscript collections, ranging in size from one or two letters to dozens of boxes of documents. A descriptive entry includes the names of the individuals and families connected to each collection, the time span covered by the collection, the types of documents, and the important people, places, and events mentioned in the documents. An extensive index consists primarily of names, places, and institutions.

682 **The Big Thicket of Texas: a comprehensive annotated bibliography.**
Compiled by Lois Williams Parker. Arlington, Texas: Sable, 1977.
225p.

This is a partially annotated bibliography on the flora and fauna of the Big Thicket of East Texas. It is divided into nine sections: books and chapters of books; journals and periodicals; interviews, speeches, manuscript sources; songs and verse; audio and visual recordings; government documents; newspaper articles (this is by far the largest category of entries); a list of newspapers published in the Big Thicket (from the 19th and 20th centuries); and theses and dissertations.

683 **Mexican Americans: a research bibliography.**
Compiled by Frank Piño. East Lansing, Michigan: Latin American Studies Center, Michigan State University, 1974. 2 vols.

A massive bibliography of books, monographs, MA and PhD theses, articles, and local, state, and federal government publications in both English and Spanish, dealing with Hispanics, Mexican-Americans, and Chicanos. Texas occupies forty-four pages of entries in volume two; other subjects are: (in volume one) art, theatre, bibliographies, economics, education, cinema, geography, Arizona, California, Colorado, Mexico, New Mexico, Spain in America, Southwestern history, and (in volume two) the United States, linguistics, English-Spanish languages, images, literature, law, medicine/health, music, journalism, political science, psychology, migration, sociology, and journals. An author index is also included.

684 **Lyndon B. Johnson: a bibliography.**
Compiled by the Staff of the Lyndon B. Johnson Library (vol. 1), Craig Roell (vol. 2). Austin, Texas: University of Texas Press, 1988. (2nd ed.). 2 vols.

With accessible formats and citations, this is a very useful uncritical bibliography of books and articles (scholarly, journalistic, popular) by and about the only Texan to serve as president of the United States. Topics are organized in a chronological fashion and are highly detailed; for instance, entries relating to Johnson's presidential administration are separated into nearly two dozen different categories. The editors consulted fifty indexes and bibliographies for this work. Volume two provides an update of material not included in volume one.

685 **Bibliography of Texas, 1795-1845.**
Thomas Winthrop Streeter. Cambridge, Massachusetts: Harvard University Press, 1955-60. 3 vols.

A guide to books, documents, and maps published in and about Texas within this period. Each entry includes a description of the work, the author, title, publisher, place of publication, year, pagination, and the archives and libraries in which the item can be located. Streeter has included travellers' and explorers' diaries; lists of government reports put out by the Mexican government, Texas Republic, and United States government; and books and documents by Europeans. Volume one contains United States and European imprints relating to Texas from 1795-1839, volume two contains Texas imprints from 1839-45, and volume three contains Mexican imprints relating to Texas from 1803-45. The entries are organized chronologically by year and alphabetically within each year, with author, subject, and title indexes.

686   **The Indians of Texas: an annotated research bibliography.**
Michael L. Tate.   Metuchen, New Jersey: Scarecrow Press, 1986.
514p. maps. (Native American Bibliography Series).

Includes both published and unpublished works on the Indian tribes who at one time
or another lived in Texas or the greater Southwest. Organized by tribe, geographic
area, and chronologically, the book provides references to both the cultural history of
Native Americans in Texas and their relationships with whites from historical,
archaeological, and sociological standpoints. Tate has included texts, monographs,
state and federal documents, articles, catalogues, bibliographies, pamphlets, theses,
dissertations, and published primary sources. Many of the entries are in Spanish. Tate
provides brief, descriptive annotations for most entries.

687   **A dictionary of the old west.**
Peter Watts.   New York: Knopf, 1977. 399p. bibliog.

A wide-ranging and profusely illustrated reference work on words and terms common
to the American West 1850-1900. There is an emphasis on cowboys and the cattle
industry (with a number of entries related to Texas), but the book covers all aspects of
the frontier experience in the Southwest, Far West, and Great Plains. It also includes
Mexican and Indian terms that were adopted by white settlers.

688   **The handbook of Texas.**
Edited by Walter Prescott Webb.   Austin, Texas: Texas State
Historical Association, 1952, 1976. 3 vols. bibliog.

First published in two volumes in 1952 (a supplement was added in 1976), this oft-cited
work is an encyclopaedia of Texas history, natural history, government, and the arts.
Entries range in length from a short paragraph on obscure ghost towns and creeks to
several pages on issues and institutions like slavery, universities, and Indian tribes.
Although most items are descriptive, some selections provide critical interpretations of
important political and social movements. Every county, settlement, and body of water
receives an entry; persons mentioned include governors, senators, Congressmen, state
legislators, editors, settlers, Indian fighters, and heroes of the Texas Revolution. Over
1,000 authors contributed about 16,000 entries, most of which provide (somewhat
dated) citations for several primary and secondary sources on their subjects.

689   **Texas women's history project bibliography.**
Edited by Ruthe Winegarten.   Austin, Texas: Texas Foundation of
Women's Resources, 1980. 349p.

An annotated bibliography of sources available for the study of women's contributions
to Texan culture, economy, and politics, in all periods of the state's history. Presenting
a fairly equal mix of books and articles (plus a few theses and dissertations), written for
both academic and popular audiences, this resource provides separate sections on:
community building, diaries, education, health, legal rights, life cycles, literature,
pioneer women, politics, religion, work, and black, Hispanic, and Native American
women. A separate section lists reference aids, such as bibliographies and group
biographies.

Journals and Periodicals

690 **Southwestern historical quarterly.**
Austin, Texas: Texas State Historical Association.
Published since 1897, this quarterly is one of the better state historical journals published in the United States. Each issue contains two or three scholarly articles by professional historians, edited primary documents, book reviews, and news from the Historical Association. This is the best single source for information on Texas history.

691 **Southwestern entomologist.**
College Station, Texas: Southwestern Entomology Society, Texas A & M University.
A scholarly journal, published since 1976, devoted to the scientific study of insects for agricultural pest control.

692 **Southwest review.**
Dallas, Texas: Southern Methodist University.
A long-running quarterly (established in 1915) devoted to serious fiction, poetry and literary criticism, including occasional interviews with authors. Most articles deal with southwestern literature or with southwesterners who are writers.

693 **Texas almanac and state industrial guide.**
Dallas, Texas: *Dallas Morning News*.
An eclectic and extremely useful semi-annual that dates back to the 1860s. A number of departments provide up-to-date information on science, history, the environment, crime, constitutional issues, sports, culture, business, industry, agriculture and education in the state. Heavily quantified, the most recent population and economic statistics are provided for each county and city in Texas. Other information includes a zip code directory and pronunciation guides to Texas towns and phrases.

694 **Texas business review.**

Austin, Texas: Bureau of Business Research, University of Texas at Austin.

A bi-monthly published since 1927 that focuses on the current condition of the Texas economy, this journal pays special attention to future trends in the state as a whole, and in the various sub-regions of Texas. The technical articles offer employment data and interpretations of the leading economic indicators in Texas.

695 **Texas facts.**

Dallas, Texas: Clements Research II.

A triennial founded in 1984, *Texas facts* presents information on the land, economy, people, government, history, community services, and attractions of each county of Texas.

696 **Texas folklore society publications.**

Denton, Texas: University of North Texas Press.

This journal has been produced annually since 1916 by the Texas Folklore Society. Each volume contains folk stories and songs from most ethnic groups, most regions, and every historical period of Texas. Some articles are merely retellings of folk tales, while others are more scholarly; articles on linguistics are also included occasionally.

697 **Texas gardener.**

Waco, Texas: Suntex Communications.

Published twice a month since 1981, this is a glossy magazine. It provides information and tips on ornamental and food-producing gardening in Texas, and includes articles on plant varieties, pests, products (wine, for instance), maintenance, and climate.

698 **Texas highways.**

Austin, Texas: Texas Department of Transportation.

The official travel magazine of Texas, this monthly has provided brief, beautifully illustrated articles on the wildlife, historic sites, recreation areas (lakes, zoos, museums), and cities and towns of Texas for nearly forty years. The glossy format, colour photography, and information on how to reach the places described make this an attractive and useful guide for planning trips in Texas.

699 **Texas horticulturalist.**

Bryan, Texas: Texas Pecan Growers Association.

This specialist monthly has been published since 1973, and has only a small circulation. It contains articles dealing with raising fruits, vegetables, and roses, in greenhouses and in the open.

700 **Texas journal of science.**

Lubbock, Texas: Texas Academy of Science.

A scholarly quarterly published since 1949 by Texas Tech University. The articles cover every scientific field, including biology, chemistry, mathematics, geology, nutrition, zoology, and ecology.

701 **Texas law review.**
Austin, Texas: University of Texas at Austin Law School.
Founded in 1922, the *Review* is published six times per year. Like law reviews at most American law schools, it examines current legal issues that do not necessarily focus on Texas.

702 **Texas lawyer.**
New York: American Lawyer Media.
A weekly publication that appeared in 1985, this is a magazine aimed at Texas attorneys featuring articles on legal cases, law firms, and politics in Texas. It also provides court summaries of notable cases in the state.

703 **Texas libraries.**
Austin, Texas: Texas State Library and Archives Commission.
A quarterly journal for professional librarians that began publication in 1906 and includes articles on Texas writers, depositories, and recently accessioned manuscript collections; book reviews; information for genealogists; and library news.

704 **Texas medicine.**
Austin, Texas: Texas Medical Association.
First published in 1905, this monthly offers wide-ranging professional articles on all aspects of medical care, from research to diagnosis and treatment.

705 **Texas monthly.**
Austin, Texas: Texas Monthly Press.
A lively, breezy, sometimes controversial monthly begun in 1973, which features articles on politics, entertainment, leisure activities, business, sports, dining, and gossip from around the state. Some of the articles are written as exposes of corruption or hypocrisy; one of the most popular annual articles ranks the 'best and worst' state legislators in Texas.

706 **Texas observor.**
Austin, Texas: Texas Observor Publishing Company.
A bi-weekly published since 1954, the *Observor* calls itself 'A Journal of Free Voices'. It is probably the most liberal periodical in Texas, although Democrats and liberal politicians are criticized nearly as often as conservatives. Its writers specialize in hard-hitting political articles that are always controversial if sometimes superficial.

707 **Texas parks and wildlife.**
Austin, Texas: Texas Parks and Wildlife Department.
A glossy monthly, first published in 1942, whose colourfully illustrated articles on nature and environmental issues are aimed at tourists and Texans interested in hunting, fishing, bird watching, and other outdoor activities.

708   **Texas studies in literature and language.**

Austin, Texas: University of Texas Press.

Published since 1959, this scholarly quarterly rarely deals with Texas subjects, but is the leading journal of its type produced in Texas. The articles deal with literary criticism and rhetorical studies.

Index

The index is a single alphabetical sequence of authors (personal and corporate), titles of publications and subjects. Index entries refer to both the main items and to other works mentioned in the note to each item. Title entries are in italics. Numbers refer to bibliographic entries.

1941: Texas goes to war 195
100 Years of science and technology in Texas 547

A

Abernethy, F. E. 562-565, 619
Abner Cook: master builder on the Texas frontier 648
Accomodation: the politics of race in an American city 364
Across the Rio Grande to freedom: United States negroes in Mexico 365
Across the tracks: Mexican-Americans in a Texas city 337
Adams, E. D. 130
Adams, J. A. 187
Addeo, E. G. 590
Adele, L. 620
Adventure in glory, 1836-1849 136
Adventures with a Texas naturalist 57
African-Americans 6, 71-72, 99, 171, 173, 181, 188, 224, 249, 325, 342-371, 446, 449, 456, 499
    bibliography 689
    civil rights 249, 255, 350, 364, 369, 410, 467

culture 342, 346, 350, 356, 416, 590-591, 593, 620, 630
    discrimination against 346, 354, 358, 362, 367, 397
    folk culture 356, 563, 567, 570-572, 578
    political activities 342, 344, 346, 349, 361, 364, 366, 454
    slavery 28, 153-154, 160, 167-168, 347, 365, 427
    society 357, 359, 366, 369
    women 389-383, 399, 401, 404
After San Jacinto: the Texas-Mexican frontier, 1836-1841 155
Aggies and the 'Horns: 86 years of bad blood and good football 666
Alamo 103, 149, 151, 162, 216, 433
Alamo chain of missions: a history of San Antonio's five old missions 122
Alamo images: changing perceptions of a Texas experience 103
Albert Sidney Johnston: soldier of three republics 230
Alexander, C. C. 188
Alexander, D. B. 641
Allan Shivers: the pied piper of Texas politics 205

Allen, Richard 361
Allen, R. 389, 557-558
Almaraz, Jr., F. D. 110-111
Along Texas old forts trail 228
Alter, J. 601
Amarillo, Texas 410, 418
Amazing armadillo 51
Ambition and the power 248
American original: the life of J. Frank Dobie 617
American rodeo: from Buffalo Bill to big business 667
Ames, Jesse Daniel 397
Amon: the life of Amon Carter, Sr., of Texas 583
And horns on the toads 567
And work was made less: Texas Electric Service Company 533
Anders, E. 189
Anderson, A. 101
Anderson, J. Q. 657
Anglo-Americans 6, 59, 100, 112, 123, 375, 378
Anglos and Mexicans in the making of Texas, 1836-1986 334
Annexation of Texas 160
Annexation, Texas to United States 154, 156, 158, 160, 163
Anson Jones: the last president of Texas 140
Apple, Max 602
Arbingast, S. A. 13, 517

Architecture 641-656
  interior design 644
Arciniega, T. A. 319
Arnold, R. E. 33
Art 73, 103, 342, 619-620,
  624, 627, 629-631,
  633-635, 638-640
  collections of artists'
  works 621-623,
  625-627, 635, 637
  exhibition catalogues
  628, 632, 636
*Art of the woman: the life
  and work of Elisabet
  Ney* 624
Art of Tom Lea 627
*Ashbel Smith of Texas:
  pioneer, patriot,
  statesman, 1805-1886*
  159
*Ashton Villa: a family and
  its house in Victorian
  Galveston, Texas* 649
Asian-Americans 378, 388,
  446, 458
Askins, C. 78
Aston, B. W. 228
Aten, L. 272
Atherton, L. E. 176
*At home in Texas: early
  views of the land* 8
Atlas of Texas 13
Atwood, E. 566
Audubon, John J. 60
Austin, Moses 121
Austin, Stephen F. 113,
  114
  See also History: Spanish
  and Mexican Periods;
  Texas Revolution and
  Republic
Austin, Texas 341, 431,
  450, 452, 460, 577, 584
*Autumn's mightiest legions:
  history of Texas
  schoolboy football* 671

B

*Bad medicine and good:
  tales of the Kiowas* 295
Baggarly, H. M. 580

Bailey, A. J. 210
Bailey, Jr. A. R. 72
Bainbridge, J. 1
*Baker & Botts in the
  development of
  modern Houston* 442
Baker, E. W. 405
Baker, R. 406
Baker, R. B. 521
Baker, T. L. 79, 372, 642
Baldwin, F. 386
*Banks and bankers in early
  Texas, 1835-1875* 476
Banks, J. 247
Bannon, J. F. 112
Bar 11 ranch 505
*Barbara Charline Jordan:
  from the ghetto to the
  capitol* 345
Barker, E. C. 113
Barker, Eugene C. 75
Barnes, Al 621
Barnes, D. A. 177
Barney, William D. 611
Barnhart, J. E. 407
Barr, A. 178, 211, 342-343
Barrera, M. 301
Barry, J. M. 248
*Bartlett's West: drawing the
  Mexican boundary* 21
Baseball, 669, 670
*Basic industries in Texas
  and northern Mexico*
  527
Bats of Texas 47
Battles of Texas 216
Bayard, R. F. 408
Baylor University 405, 661
Beals, C. 114
Bean, J. L. 9
Bean, Roy 269
Beaumont, Texas 529
Beckmann, Emma 400
Bedichek, R. 57-58
Bedichek, Roy 604, 607,
  610, 616
Belfrage, Gustaf Wilhem
  60
*Bell rings at four: a black
  teacher's chronicle of
  change* 363
Benjamin, G. G. 373
*Benjamin Capps and the
  south plains* 603

Benner, J. A. 179
Bennett, P. 602
Benson, K. 593
Berlandier, J. L. 60, 273
Bermal, J. 267
*Between sun and sod: an
  informal history of the
  Texas panhandle* 94
*Between the enemy and
  Texas: Parsons's Texas
  Cavalry in the Civil
  War* 210
*Beyond the cross timbers:
  the travels of
  Randolph B. Marcy,
  1812-1887* 23
*BFI companion to the
  western* 587
Bibliographies 9, 29,
  71-72, 403, 602,
  676-683, 685-686, 689
*Bibliography of Texas
  government and
  politics* 678
*Bibliography of Texas,
  1795-1845* 685
Biesele, R. L. 374
Big Bend 12, 54, 55, 88,
  105, 227
*Big bend: a history of the
  last Texas frontier* 105
*Big Thicket: a challenge for
  conservation* 62
*Big Thicket of Texas: a
  comprehensive
  annotated bibliography*
  682
Big Thicket *see* East Texas
Biggers, J. 639
Biggers, John 342, 639
Binkley, W. C. 131-132
*Biracial politics: conflict
  and coalition in the
  metropolitan south* 349
Bird life of Texas 40
Birds 37, 40, 43, 45, 52, 55,
  57-58
  birdwatching 39, 42, 44,
  46, 54
Birds of Big Bend National
  Park and vicinity 54
Birds of Houston 46
*Birds of north central
  Texas* 44

Birds of Texas and adjacent states 42
Birds of the Texas coastal bend: abundance and distribution 45
Bissinger, H. G. 663
Black art in Houston: the Texas Southern University experience 639
Black cats, hoot owls, and water witches: beliefs, superstitions, and sayings from Texas 574
Black community control: a study of transition in a Texas ghetto 369
Black history, black vision: the visionary image in Texas 620
Black infantry in the west, 1869-1891 352
Black leaders: Texans for their times 342
Black Texans: a history of Negroes in Texas, 1528-1971 343
Black victory: the rise and fall of the white primary in Texas 255
Blackburn, S. 643
Blacklock, G. W. 45
Blackwelder, J. K. 390
Bland, R. W. 259
Blessed assurance: at home with the bomb in Amarillo, Texas 418
Boatright, M. C. 567-569
Bolivar Peninsula 108
Boll, Jacob 60
Bollaert, W. 18
Bolton, H. E. 115-116, 274
Bonnie, M. E. 13
Booth, J. A. 429
Booth, John 621
Borden, Gail 486
Border boom town: Ciudad Juarez since 1848 444
Borderland in retreat: from Spanish Louisiana to the far southwest 125
*Borderlands town in

transition: Laredo, Texas, 1755-1870* 438
Boren, C. E. 409
Boss rule in south Texas: the progressive era 189
Bounty of Texas 562
Bowles, Chief 277
Bowling, Charles 636
Boyd, M. 275
Brackenridge, George W. 186
Brackenridge, R. D. 413
Brady, D. V. 586
Branch, Mary 342
Brandimarte, C. A. 644
Brewer, J. M. 344, 570-571
Brewer, J. Mason 572
Brimstone game: monopoly in action 522
British interests and activities in Texas, 1838-1846 130
Bronder, S. E. 410
Brouilette, Al 637
Broussard, R. F. 430
Brown, John Henry 584
Brown, Marbury Hill 637
Brown, N. 190
Brownsville raid 367
Brownsville, Texas 367, 419
Brunson, B. R. 482
Bryant, I. B. 345
Bryson, C. 249
Buenger, W. L. 71, 166, 472
Buffalo Bayou 554
Buffalo hunting 180, 184
Buffalo soldiers: a narrative of the negro cavalry in the west 358
Buffalo war 218
Bullard, R. D. 346
Burford, William 611
Burnet, David G. 134
Buscombe, E. 587
But also good business: Texas Commerce Banks and the financing of Houston and Texas, 1886-1986 472
Byrd, D. H. 473

Byrd, J. W. 572
Bywaters, Jerry 636-637

C

C. L. Sonnichsen: grassroots historian 618
Cacti of the Southwest: Texas, New Mexico, Oklahoma, Arkansas, and Louisiana 56
Calendar history of the Kiowa Indians 291
California 432
Texans in 93
Calvary of Christ on the Rio Grande, 1849-1883 419
Calvert, R. A. 71, 80, 342, 664
Campbell, R. B. 167-168, 347, 503, 664
Cannatella, M. M. 33
Cannibals and condos: Texans and Texas along the Gulf Coast 63
Canonge, E. 276
Capps, Benjamin 603
Caprock canyonlands 34
Carleton, D. 200
Carlson, P. H. 483
Caro, R. 201
Carrington, E. M. 391
Carroll, H. B. 133
Carter, Sr., Amon 583
Carter, K. 2
Cartwright, G. 81
Casdorph, P. 250
Casey, R. J. 82
Cashin, J. W. 474
Castaneda, C. E. 411
Castle Gap and the Pecos frontier 83
Castro's colony: empresario development in Texas, 1842-1856 387
Castro, Henri 387
Cattle kings 176
Cattlemen 505

Cattlemen vs. sheepmen: five decades of violence in the West, 1880-1920 508

Cattle raising on the plains, 1900-1961 514

Cattle-trailing industry: between supply and demand, 1866-1890 516

Céliz, F. 19

Centennial history of Texas A & M University 461

Champagne, A. 202, 251

Chance, J. E. 212

Chapters in the history of organized labor in Texas 557

Charles Goodnight, cowman and plainsman 490

Chavira, J. A. 302

Chicano workers and the politics of fairness: the FEPC in the southwest, 1941-1945 304

Chicanos and Native Americans: the territorial minorities 319

Chief Bowles and the Texas Cherokees 277

Chief executive in Texas: a study in gubernatorial leadership 241

Children 3, 565, 577, 676

Children of the sun: Mexican-Americans in the literature of the United States 614

Children's riddling 577

Chinese in El Paso 388

Chipman, D. 664

Chisholm trail 487

Christian, D. 263

Christmas in Texas 426

Cisneros, J. 433 and 458, 622-623

Citizens at last: the women's suffrage movement in Texas 403

City building in the new south: the growth of public services in Houston, Texas, 1830-1915 451

City moves west: economic and industrial growth in West Texas 443

Ciudad Juarez *see* El Paso

Claiming their land: women homesteaders in Texas 396

Clarendon, Texas 94

Clark, I. G. 542

Clark, J. 528-529

Clark, W. B. 613

Clarke, M. W. 134-135, 277

Clayton, L. 603

Clifford, C. E. 604-605

Climate of Texas and the adjacent Gulf waters 65

Climates of Texas counties 64

Clinchy, E. R. 303

Clio's cowboys: studies in the historiography of the cattle trade 77

Coastal Texas water, land, and wildlife 52

Coerver, D. M. 191

Cold anger: a story of faith and power politics 420

Colley, C. C. 17

Collins, Finis F. 637

Colorado River 187

Colossal Hamilton of Texas: a biography of Andrew Jackson Hamilton, militant unionist and reconstruction governor 175

Coltharp, L. H. 573

Columbian consequences: archeological and historical perspectives on the Spanish borderlands west 299

Comanche texts 276

Comanches: lords of the south plains 284

Comanches: the destruction of a people 281

Coming to terms: the German hill country of Texas 386

Commodore Moore and the Texas navy 237

Common Texas grasses 35

Communism 200, 454

Concealed under petticoats: married women's property and the law of Texas, 1840-1913 398

Confederate cavalry west of the river 226

Conger, R. N. 213

Congressman Sam Rayburn 202

Connally, John 209, 247

Connie Hagar: the life history of a Texas birdwatcher 39

Connor, S. V. 136

Cook, Abner 648

Corder, J. W. 3

Coronado's quest: the discovery of the southwestern states 20

Coronado, knight of pueblos and plains 115

Coronado, Francisco Vazquez de 20, 115

Corpus Christi, Texas 341

Cotner, R. C. 192, 431

Cowboy hero: his image in American history and culture 102

Cowboy life on the Texas plains: the photographs of Ray Rector 513

Cowboy spurs and their makers 633

Cowboys *see* Ranching

Cowboys and cattleland: memories of a frontier 492

Cowgirls 402

Cracker barrel chronicles: a bibliography of Texas town and county histories 679

Crawford, A. F. 392

Crazy water: the story of Mineral Wells and

other Texas health resorts 658

Creel, G. 137

Crime 78, 173, 206, 263, 265-266, 268, 270, 425, 428, 455, 523, 573

Crimson desert: Indian wars of the American southwest 215

Crouch, B. A. 348

Croxdale, R. 393

Crum, L. L. 475

Crusade for conformity: the Ku Klux Klan in Texas, 1920-1930 188

Cruz, G. R. 432, 676

Cuanderismo: Mexican-American folk healing 302

Culture complexes and chronology in northern Texas: with extension of Puebloan datings to the Mississippi Valley 287

Culture conflict in Texas, 1821-1835 326

Cummings, G. 530

Cummins, L. T. 72

Cuney, Norris Wright 353, 361

Cutrer, E. F. 624

Cutrer, T. W. 375

Czech-Americans 378, 380, 382, 385

Czech voices: stories from Texas in the Amerikan Narodni Kalendar 380

D

Daddysman, J. W. 169

Dairy industry 486

Dallas architecture, 1936-1986 645

Dallas Cowboys and the National Football League 664

Dallas Morning News 581

Dallas Museum of Art 632, 636, 645

Dallas, Texas 197, 364, 428, 434, 437, 447, 452, 518, 584, 636, 645, 664

Damning the Colorado: the rise of the Lower Colorado River Authority, 1933-1939 187

Daniel, C. 304

Darden, R. F. 581

Dauphin, S. 588

David G. Burnet 134

Davidson, C. 252, 349

Davidson, J. E. 673

Davis, K. W. 574

Davis, N. G. 582

Dawson, J. M. 138

Day, A. G. 20

Day, J. M. 14, 117

De Witt colony of Texas 152

Deaf Smith, incredible Texas spy 146

Dearen, P. 83

Death of a president, November 20-November 25, 1963 206

Death row 263

Death without dignity: the story of the first nursing home corporation indicted for murder 425

Degener, Carl 174

Del Pueblo: a pictorial history of Houston's Hispanic community 324

Democratic promise: the Populist movement in America 181

Democratic Party 171-172, 178, 190, 193, 198, 202, 206, 209, 247, 249, 252-255, 260, 381

DeMoss, D. 518

Depression in Texas: the Hoover years 199

Depression, Great (1930s) 199, 389, 390, 431

Desert immigrants: the Mexicans of El Paso, 1880-1920 316

Dethloff, H. C. 461-462, 484, 535

Development of education in Texas 464

Development of state-chartered banking in Texas: from predecessor systems until 1970 478

Diamond jubilee album: Archdiocese of San Antonio, 1874-1949 414

Diary of the Alarcon expedition into Texas, 1718-1719 19

Dictionary of the old west 687

Dillon, D. 645

Divine, R. A. 677

Dobie, J. F. 485, 575-576, 606

Dobie, J. Frank 77, 572, 604, 607, 610, 616, 617

Dobkins, B. E. 262

Dodge City, Kansas 543

Dog ghosts and other Negro folk tales 570

Dominican women in Texas: from Ohio to Galveston and beyond 415

Dorsey, G. A. 278-279

Doughty, R. W. 8, 51, 59

Down the corridor of years: a centennial history of the University of North Texas in photographs, 1890-1990 467

Dozier, Otis, 636-637

Dr. Lawrence A. Nixon and the white primary 249

Drawing power: Knott, Ficklen, and McClanahan, editorial cartoonists of the Dallas Morning News 581

Dream of empire: a human history of the Republic of Texas, 1836-1846 163

Drummond, Thomas 60
*Duel of eagles: the Mexican
    and United States fight
    for the Alamo* 149
Dugger, R. 607
Dumont, E. E. B. 394
Dunlay, T. W. 214
Dunn, W. 463
Dunn, W. E. 118
Duren, A. M. 350
Durham, P. H. 351
Duval, John C. 606, 616
Dyal, D. H. 484

E

*Early economic policies of
    the government of
    Texas* 246
*Early Texas oil: a
    photographic history,
    1866-1936* 539
*Early years of rhythm &
    blues: focus on
    Houston* 591
*East Texas lumber
    workers: an economic
    and social picture,
    1870-1950* 558
East Texas 2, 5, 48, 53, 67,
    424, 529, 535, 558
    Big Thicket 43, 50, 62,
    564, 682
*Easy money: oil promoters
    and investors in the
    jazz age* 536
Eby, F. 464
*Economic and business
    issues of the 1980s* 524
*Economics of natural gas
    in Texas* 540
Economy 178, 208, 323,
    334, 435, 438, 448,
    450, 460
    agricultural 11, 13, 24,
    67, 167-168, 181, 389,
    443, 482, 484, 486,
    503, 526, 548
    banking and finance 143,
    186, 472-481, 524, 536
    industry 13, 62, 67, 251,
    517-527, 548

periodicals 694
Rio Grande Valley 23,
    311-312, 328, 517
see also Electric
    industry, natural gas
    industry, oil industry,
    ranching, trade
Edwards, Heather 637
Education 7, 13, 251, 333,
    342, 350, 355, 360,
    363, 371, 415, 422,
    429, 461- 471
Edwards, M. R. 608
Ekland-Olson, S. 266
*El Paso: a borderlands
    history* 458
*El Paso merchant and civic
    leader from the 1880s
    through the Mexican
    Revolution* 377
El Paso, Texas 12, 161,
    208, 316, 330, 377,
    388, 444, 457-459,
    480, 512, 518, 555,
    573, 586, 598, 646
Elections 249, 255,
    260-261
Electric industry 530, 533
Elizondo, V. P. 310
*Ella Elgar Bird Dumont:
    an autobiography of a
    west Texas pioneer* 394
*Elmer Kelton and west
    Texas: a literary
    relationship* 601
*Empire for slavery: the
    peculiar institution in
    Texas, 1821-1865* 347
Energy *see* Electric,
    Natural Gas, and Oil
    industries
Englebrecht, L. C. 646
Englebrecht, M. F. 646
Engler, R. 531
English-Texans 375
Environment 57-59, 61-63,
    66-67, 73, 88, 105,
    454, 707
*Equality of opportunity for
    Latin-Americans in
    Texas* 303
Ervendberg, Louis 60
*Espuela Land and Cattle
    Company: a study of a*

*foreign-owned ranch
    in Texas* 494
*Essays on sunbelt cities and
    recent urban America*
    434
*Essays on Walter Prescott
    Webb* 74
*Establishment in Texas
    politics* 254
Ethnic groups of Houston
    446
*Ethnicity in the sunbelt: a
    history of Mexican
    Americans in Houston*
    305
Ethnicity 9, 13, 92, 171,
    178, 251, 260,
    272-388, 425, 439,
    446, 496, 561, 578,
    604, 676 *see also*
    specific ethnic groups
Etulain, R. W. 73
*Eugene C. Barker:
    historian* 75
Evans, R. 203
Evans. W. 665
Everett, D. 280
Everett, D. E. 433
*Expansionist movement in
    Texas, 1836-1850* 131
Exploration 20, 100, 105,
    115, 118, 120
*Exploring the Johnson
    years* 677

F

Fabritius, M. M. 477
*Faces of the borderlands:
    twenty-one drawings
    by José Cisneros* 622
Fairbanks, R. B. 434
*Family secret: domestic
    violence in America*
    428
Farmers Alliance *see*
    Populists
*Farmers in rebellion: the
    rise and fall of the
    Southern Farmers
    Alliance and People's
    Party in Texas* 177

Farrar, N. 388
Faulk, O. B. 97, 119, 120, 215
Fauna 34, 36, 41, 43, 47, 48-49, 51, 52, 55, 57, 273, 493
Feagin, J. R. 435
Fehrenbach, T. R. 84-85, 281
Ferber, Edna 616
Ferguson, James 190
Ferguson, Miriam 190
Fernandez, R. A. 311-312
Fernea, E. E. 395
Ficklen, Jack 581
Films 587, 592
First Polish-Americans: Silesian settlements in Texas 372
Fischer, J. 86
Fish 36, 52, 55, 59, 578
Fishes of the Gulf of Mexico: Texas, Louisiana, and adjacent waters 36
Fishing industry 559, 578
Fitzmorris, M. A. 412
Flanagan, S. 4
Flannery, J. B. 376
Fleischmann, A. 678
Flemmans, J. 583
Flora 33-35, 38, 41, 43, 45, 52-53, 55-57, 60, 273, 493
Flores, D. 34
Flush production: the epic of oil in the Gulf-southwest 532
Foley, D. E. 313
Folk art in Texas 619
Folk culture 562-571, 574-575, 578, 617, 619, 633, 650-651, 657
  bibliography 676
  periodicals 696
  see also specific ethnic groups
Folk laughter on the American frontier 568
Folklore of Texas cultures 563
Folklore of the oil industry 569
Football, Texas style:

illustrated history of the Southwest Conference 675
Football 663-666, 668-669, 671, 673-675
Footlights on the border: the Galveston and Houston stage before 1900 589
Forbes, G. D. 532
Ford, John 145
Forgotten frontier: urban planning in the American west before1890 452
Fornell, E. W. 436
Forsyth, J. D. 666
Fort Belknap frontier saga: Indians, Negroes, and Anglo-Americans on the Texas frontier 224
Fort Griffin on the Texas frontier 229
Fort Worth: outpost on the Trinity 441
Fort Worth Star Telegram 441, 583
Fort Worth, Texas 197, 369, 441, 452, 455, 466, 470, 533, 549, 583, 650, 662
Four decades of Catholicism in Texas, 1820-1860 412
Fowler, A. L. 352
Fowler, G. 658
Fox, S. 647
France 116, 118, 123, 125
Francklyn Land and Cattle Company: a panhandle enterprise, 1882-1957 515
Frantz, J. B. 87, 216, 486
Frary, M. 621, 625-626, 637
Fred Gipson at work 612
Fredericksburg 452
Fredriksson, K. 667
Free enterprise city: Houston in political-economic perspective 435
Freedmen's Bureau and black Texans 348

Freedmen's Bureau 348, 366
Freeman, D. H. 668
French-Americans 378, 446
Freudenthal, S. J. 377
Friday night lights: a town, a team, and a dream 663
Friend, L. 139
From peones to politicos: class and ethnicity in a south Texas town, 1900- 1987 313
From the high plains 86
From token to triumph: the Texas Republicans since 1920 258
From Uncertain to Blue 2
Frontier forts of Texas 213
Frontier *see* Exploration, Settlement, The West
Frontiersmen of the faith: a history of Baptist pioneer work in Texas, 1865- 1885 417
Future is mestizo: *life where cultures meet* 310

G

Gail Borden: dairyman to a nation 486
Gaines, Matt 342, 361
Gallaway, B. P. 217
Galleghy, J. 589
Galveston era: the Texas crescent on the eve of secession 436
Galveston, Ellis Island of the west 196
Galveston: a history of the island 81
Galveston, Texas 70, 81, 108, 196, 376, 405, 408, 431, 436, 447, 452-453, 460, 479, 554, 584, 589, 649, 653
Gambrell, H. 140-141
Gantt, F. 241
Garcia, F. C. 314

Garcia, I. 315
Garcia, M. J. 316-317
Garcia, R. A. 318
Garcia-Treto, F. O. 413
Gard, W. 180, 487
Gardening 697, 699
Garment industry 393, 518, 524, 548
Garvin, R. M. 590
Gary Niblett: a new look at the old west 631
Garza, R. O. de la 319
Geaser, T. W. 103
Geiser, S. W. 60
Gentilz: artist of the old southwest 629
Gentilz, Theodore 629
Geography 8-11, 34, 92
George W. Brackenridge: maverick philanthropist 186
German-Americans 28, 171, 373-374, 378-379, 381, 386-387, 446
Germans in Texas: a study in immigration 373
Gerrasi, Frank 637
Ghost towns of Texas 79
Gibson, A. M. 282
Gilbert Onderdonk: the nurseryman of Mission Valley, pioneer horticulturalist 509
Gilbert, M. J. 414
Gillis, E. 574
Gillmore, V. 533
Gipson, Fred 612
Glick, T. F. 488
Goals for Dallas 437
God's last and only hope: the fragmentation of the Southern Baptist Convention 416
Golden hoof: the story of the sheep of the southwest 498
Goliad, massacre at 216
Gómez, A. R. 88
Gone from Texas: our lost architectural heritage 654
Gonzales, Texas 452
Goodnight, Charles 490

Goodwyn, L. C. 181, 386
Gould, F. C. 396
Gould, F. W. 35
Gould, L. L. 61, 193
Govenar, A. 591
Government, Texas 241-242, 244, 246, 257, 259, 450-451, 453, 531, 655- 656, 678
Governors of Texas 134, 137, 139, 141, 147, 164-165, 175, 179, 192, 205, 209, 240-241
Goyens, William 342, 602
Gracy, D. B. II 121, 194
Graham, D. 592, 609-610
Grant, J. M. 478
Grantham, D. W. 253
Graves, J. 5
Graves, John 602, 611
Graves, R. W. 540
Graveyards 92
Great Britain 130, 160
Great buffalo hunt 180
Great plains 11, 76
Great Plains 11, 549
Great river: the Rio Grande in North American history 91
Great roundup: the story of Texas and southwestern cowmen 507
Green, D. 489
Green, G. N. 254
Greene, A. C. 602
Gregg County, Texas 528
Gregory, J. 142
Griffin, John Howard 611
Guerin, John 621, 637
Guide to the history of Texas 72
Gulf of Mexico 36, 65
coast 5, 33, 45, 52, 58, 63, 272, 296, 549, 578, 621, 642
Gulf to the Rockies: the heritage of the Fort Worth and Denver-Colorado and Southern Railways, 1861-1898 551

Gunpowder justice: a reassessment of the Texas Rangers 267
Gunter, P. A. Y. 62
Gutiérrez, A. 321

H

Habig, M. H. 122
Hackett, S. 415
Haddox, J. 320
Hafertepe, K. 648-649
Hagan, W. T. 283
Haigh, B. R. 465
Halbouty, M. 528-529
Hale, Leon 602
Haley, J. E. 490-491
Haley, J. L. 89, 218
Hall, C. D. 466
Hall, J. D. 397
Hall, L. B. 191
Hall, T. D. 90
Halsell, H. H. 492
Hamilton, Andrew Jackson 174, 175
Hamilton, A. L. 219
Handbook of Texas 688
Hardinge, Sarah Ann 638
Hare, M. C. 353
Harris, R. 429
Harrison County, Texas 167
Hasinai: a traditional history of the Caddo confederacy 294
Hasinais: southern Caddoans as seen by the earliest Europeans 274
Haskin, J. 593
Hawkins, Charles 220
Haynes, R. V. 354
Haywood, C. R. 543
Hearon, Shelby 602
Heintze, M. R. 355
Helgesen, S. 534
Hell's half-acre: life and legend in a red-light district 455
Henderson, James Pickney 164

Henderson, R. 204
Henry C. Trost: architect of the southwest 646
Henshaw, R. C. 540
Henson, M. S. 143
Herman Lungkwitz: romantic landscapist on the Texas frontier 630
Hidalgo County, Texas 314, 327, 337
Hield, M. 393
Hill Country 373-374, 381, 386, 400, 468, 630
Hill country teacher: oral histories from the one-room school and beyond 468
Hill, J. D. 220
Himmel, R. L. 467
Hine, D. C. 255
Hine, R. V. 21
Hing, Sam 388
Hinkle, S. 221
Hinojosa, G. M. 335, 438
Hirsch, H. 321
Hispanics *see* Mexican-Americans
Historic Galveston 653
History 9, 10, 32, 67, 80, 84, 87, 89, 90, 96-99, 101, 106-107, 109, 441, 445, 457, 690
  historiography 71-77, 103, 240, 243, 277, 280
  Spanish and Mexican periods 110-129, 326, 335, 411-412
  Texas Revolution and Republic 4, 103, 126, 130-165, 211, 216, 220, 233, 237, 379, 387, 411, 430
  Civil War and Reconstruction 104, 145, 166-175, 179, 183, 186, 210, 212, 216-217, 226, 230, 232-233, 249, 256, 339, 347-348, 361, 365-366, 380
  Gilded Age 176-186, 353, 361-362
  Progressive Era, New

Deal, and Second World War 187-199, 354, 381, 431, 453
  Post-Second World War 200-209, 303
History of apparel manufacturing in Texas, 1897-1981 518
History of German settlement in Texas, 1831-1861 374
History of Hispanic theatre in the United States: origins to 1940 322
History of Mexican Americans in Lubbock County 340
History of Rice University 469
History of savings and loan in Texas 474
History of Texas (Calvert/De Leon) 80
History of Texas (Wortham) 109
History of Texas Christian University: a college of the cattle frontier 466
History of the Oil Workers International Union-CIO 560
History of the Republican Party in Texas, 1865-1965 250
History of the Teachers State Association of Texas 360
History of the Texas Medical Association, 1853-1953 659
History of the Texas railroads 552
Hjerter, K. G. 627
Hodge, F. W. 22
Hoebel, E. A. 284
Hoese, H. D. 36
Hoey, William 637
Hofsommer, D. L. 544-545
Hogan, W. R. 144
Hogg, James Stephen 192, 198
Hogue, Alexandre 636
Hoijer, H. 285

Holden, F. M. 493
Holden, W. C. 494
Holland, A. M. 368
Hollon, W. E. 23
Holloway, H. 260
Holmes, J. 669
Holmes, W. M. 9
Honig, L. E. 584
Hood's Texas brigade: Lee's grenadier guard 232
Hood, bonnet, and little brown jug: Texas politics, 1921-1928 190
Hook 'em horns: a story of Texas football 668
Hoover, Herbert 199
Horgan, P. 91
House, Edward M. 198
Houston: a history 445
Houston architectural guide 647
Houston: a twentieth century urban frontier 454
Houston by stages: a history of theatre in Houston 588
Houston: growth and decline in a sunbelt boomtown 456
Houston police: 1878-1948 265
Houston's forgotten heritage: landscape, houses, interiors, 1824-1914 643
Houston Symphony Orchestra, 1913-1971 597
Houston: the unknown city, 1836-1946 440
Houston, Margaret Lea 157
Houston, Sam 4, 134, 141, 157
  biographies 137, 139, 142, 147, 165
Houston, Temple 185
Houston, Texas 265, 445, 451-452, 460, 643, 647, 661
  economy 431, 434-435, 442, 454, 456, 472, 554

Houston, Texas *cont.*
  politics 200, 314, 345,
    349, 434-435, 447,
    453-454
  society 305, 324, 346,
    349, 354, 357, 359,
    439-440, 446, 454
Huckins, James 405
Hudson, W. M. 567
Huggins, Pattillo 535
Hughes, W. J. 145
Humour 568
Hurricanes 70
Huston, C. 146
Hutton, P. A. 103
Hyde, G. E. 222
Hyman, H. M. 479

I

I am Annie Mae, an
  extraordinary woman
  in her own words: the
  personal history of a
  black Texas woman
  370
If these walls could speak:
  historic forts of Texas
  234
If you don't like the
  weather . . . : stories
  of Texas weather 68
Iglesia Presbiteriana: a
  history of
  Presbyterians and
  Mexican-Americans of
  the southwest 413
I heard the old fisherman
  say: folklore of the
  Texas Gulf coast 578
I'll die before I'll run: the
  story of the great feuds
  of Texas 104
I'm an endangered species:
  the autobiography of a
  free enterpriser 473
Imperial Sugar Company
  518
Imperial Texas: an
  interpretative essay in
  cultural geography 10
Impressions of the Texas
  Panhandle 625

Indian frontier of the
  American west,
  1846-1890 235
Indian life in Texas 297
Indian tribes of Texas 300
Indianola, Texas 452, 584
Indians, cattle, ships, and
  oil: the story of W. D.
  Lee 525
Indians of Texas in 1830
  273
Indians of Texas: an
  annotated research
  bibliography 686
Indians of Texas: from
  prehistoric to modern
  times 292
Indians of the Rio Grande
  delta: their role in the
  history of southern
  Texas and northeastern
  Mexico 296
Indians of the upper Texas
  coast 272
Indians *see* Native
  Americans
In Search of a home:
  nineteenth century
  Wendish immigration
  383
Inside Texas: culture,
  identity, and houses,
  1878-1920 644
Intercity bus lines of the
  southwest: a
  photographic history
  553
In the deep heart's core:
  reflections on life,
  letters, and Texas 604
Invisible Houston 346
Irby, J. A. 676
Irish-Americans 376
Irish-Texans 376
Irrigation 488-489
Iscoe, L. 350
Italian-Americans 378,
  561, 578

J

J. Mason Brewer: Negro
  folklorist 572

Jackson, B. 263, 356
Jackson, J. 15, 495
James Pickney Henderson:
  Texas' first governor
  164
James Stephen Hogg: a
  biography 192
James, F. J. 439
James, M. 147
Jaques, M. J. 24
Jenkins, J. H. 679
Jews 196, 377, 378, 446,
  458
John C. Duval: first Texas
  man of letters-his life
  and some of his
  unpublished writings
  606
John Henry Brown: Texian
  journalist, 1820-1895
  584
John O. Meusebach:
  German colonizer in
  Texas 379
John, E. A. H. 123
Johnson, Claudia 'Lady
  Bird' 61
Johnson, D. R. 429
Johnson, Jack 672
Johnson, Lyndon B. 201,
  203, 205, 209, 247,
  677, 684
Johnson, W. R. 519
Johnston, Albert Sidney
  230
Johnston, M. 440
Jones, Anson 140
Jones, E. L. 351
Jones, Marvin 504
Jones, Preston 602
Jones, W. 286
Joplin, Scott 593
Jordan, Barbara 345
Jordan, T. G. 9, 92, 496,
  650-651
Jose Antonio Navarro:
  co-creator of Texas
  138
Journey through Texas; or
  a saddle trip on the
  southwestern frontier
  28
Judd, DeForrest 637
Justice, B. 357

K

Kanellos, N. 322
Kaplan, B. J. 454
Karankaway country 58
Katharine Anne Porter and Texas: an uneasy relationship 613
Katy Railroad and the last frontier 549
Keasby, Lindley M. 76
Kelley, P. 546
Kelton, Elmer 601-602
Kelton, S. 497
Kempner, Harris and family 479
Kenamore, J. A. 680
Kendall, D. S. 629
Kennamer, L. G. 13
Kennedy, John F. 206
Kerby, R. L. 170
Key, V. O. 252
Kibbe, P. R. 323
Kickapoos: lords of the middle border 282
Kickapoo tales 286
Kielman, C. V. 681
Kilgore, Texas 431
Kinch, S. 205
King ranch 500
King, I. M. 379
King, Larry L. 602
King, Richard 500
Kingsville, Texas 341
Kiowa voices 275
Kiowa years: a study in culture impact 289
Kiowas 290
Kipartito, K. J. 442
Kirby Smith's Confederacy: the trans-Mississippi south, 1863-1865 170
Klosterman, L. 547
Knight, O. 441
Knott, John Francis 581
Knox, J. A. 30
Koch, Fred 502
Koch Matador Cattle Company 502
Kofalk, H. 37
Krasna Amerika: a study of Texas Czechs, 1851-1939 382
Kreneck, T. H. 324

Krenek, H. 264
Krieger, A. D. 287
Kruszewski, Z. A. 319
Ku Klux Klan 173, 188, 190
Kupper, W. 498

L

La Forte, R. S. 467
La frontera: the United States' border with Mexico 12
La Raza: the Mexican-Americans 338
La Raza Unida Party 315, 320-321, 332, 338
Labor of women in the production of cotton 389
Labour and labourers 200, 254, 264, 313, 325, 338, 410, 454, 517, 524, 557
  fishing industry 559
  lumber industry 558
  mining industry 561
  oil industry 560
  women 389-390, 393
Lack, P. D. 148
Lady Bird Johnson and the environment 61
Lale, C. S. 441
Lamar, H. R. 93
Lamar, Mirabeau Bonaparte 141
Lamb County, Texas 194
Lambshead before Interwoven: a Texas range chronicle, 1848-1878 493
Lambshead Ranch 493
Lampasas County, Texas 182
Land of the bears and honey: a natural history of east Texas 67
Land of the underground rain: irrigation on the Texas high plains, 1910- 1970 489

Land, oil, and education 465
Landolt, R. G. 325
Lands, public 152, 243, 387, 396, 465
Landscapes of Texas: photographs from Texas Highways Magazine 5
Landscapes
  descriptions 8
  drawings and paintings 21, 621, 625-630, 635, 637
  photography 5, 41
Langtry, Texas 269
Lanning, Jim 499
Lanning, Judy 499
Laredo, Texas 12, 233, 322, 432, 438
Last boom 528
Last years of Spanish Texas, 1778-1821 119
Lathrop, B. F. 424
Latin Americans in Texas 323
Latinos *and the political system* 314
Latorre, D. L. 288
Latorre, F. A. 288
Law 74, 582
  journals 701-702
  practice of law 185, 398, 442
  water law 66, 262
Law enforcement 78, 251, 263, 265, 268-269, 357, 425, 454, 576
  prisons 263, 266, 270, 356
Lay, D. W. 67
Lazarou, K. E. 394
Lea, T. 500
Lea, Tom 602, 627
Learning to be militant 321
Leavenworth, G. 653
Leckie, W. H. 223, 358
Ledbetter, B. A. N. 224
Ledbetter, Huddie 'Ledbelly' 590
Lee, J. W. 195, 610
Lee, W. D. 525
Legends of Texas 575
León, A. de 80, 305-309

Leonard, B. J. 416
Lester, William 636-637
*Let all of them take heed:
Mexican-Americans
and the campaign for
educational equality in
Texas, 1910-1981* 333
*Let there be towns: Spanish
municipal origins in
the American
southwest, 1610-1810*
432
Lewis, G. M. 501
Lewis, T. H. 22
Lewis, W. N. 94
Libraries 72, 677, 680-681,
703
Lich, G. E. 612
*Life and death of the solid
south: a political
history* 253
*Life of Stephen F. Austin,
founder of Texas,
1793-1836: a chapter
in the westward
movement of the
Anglo-American
people* 113
*Life styles in the black
ghetto* 359
Lifestyles 1, 7, 144, 163,
426, 440
Lighthouses of Texas 642
Lincecum, Gideon 60
Lincoln, J. 502
Lindheimer, Ferdinand 60
Linguistics 566, 573, 577
Literature 73, 77, 102-103,
332, 601-616, 689,
692, 708
Littlefield, George W. 194
*Littlefield land:
colonization on the
Texas plains,
1912-1920* 194
Lively, F. 41
*Livestock legacy: the Fort
Worth stockyards,
1887-1987* 510
Llano Estacado 34, 491
Log cabin village 650
Logsdon, G. 594
*Lone star: a history of
Texas and the Texans*
84

*Lone star: life of John
Connally* 209
*Lone star regionalism: the
Dallas nine and their
circle, 1928-1945* 636
*Lone stars and state
gazettes* 585
*Lone-star vanguard: the
Catholic re-occupation
of Texas* 408
Longhorns 485
Long, J. 149
Long, Stuart 205
Long, Steven 425
Loomis, N. M. 150
Lord, W. 151
*Los Chicanos: an
awakening people* 320
*Los mesteños: Spanish
ranching in Texas,
1721-1821* 495
Lost in west Texas 3
Loughmiller, C. 38
Loughmiller, L. 38
Lowe, R. G. 168, 503
Lowrie, S. H. 326
Lubbock County, Texas
340
Lucey, Archbishop Robert
E. 410
Lukes, E. A. 152
Lumber industry 62, 67,
521
Lungkwitz, Hermann 60
*Lyndon B. Johnson: a
bibliography* 684
Lyndon B. Johnson
Presidential Library
680
*Lyndon B. Johnson: the
exercise of power* 203

M

MacCorkle, S. 242
MacDonald, William 342
Machann, C. 380, 613
MacKenzie, Ranald S. 236
Madison, W. 327
*Making of a history: Walter
Prescott Webb and the
Great Plains* 76

Malone, A. P. 399
*Mammals of trans-Pecos
Texas* 48
Man, bird, and beast 576
Manchester, W. R. 206
Manning, D. 468
*Manuscript sources in the
Rosenberg Library: a
selective guide* 680
*Mapping of the American
Southwest* 17
*Mapping Texas and the
Gulf coast: the
contributions of
Saint-Denis, Olivian,
and Le Maire* 15
*Maps of Texas and the
Southwest, 1513-1900*
16
*Maps of Texas, 1527-1900:
the map collection of
the Texas State
Archives* 14
Maps 10, 13, 16, 21
analysis 15, 17
catalogues 14
Marchiafava, L. 265
Maril, R. L. 63, 328, 559
Marinbach, B. 196
Marinello, M. L. 400
*Market analysis of the cattle
industry of Texas* 501
Markides, K. S. 329
Marks, P. M. 153
Marquez, B. 330
Marriott, A. 289
Marten, J. 171
Martin, H. W. 329
Martin, J. C. 16
Martin, R. L. 443
Martin, R. S. 16
Martin, S. J. 266
Martinez, O. J. 444
*Marvin Jones: the public
life of an agrarian
advocate* 504
Mason, Z. A. 417
Masterson, V. V. 549
*Matador Land and Cattle
Company* 511
*Matamoros trade:
Confederate
commerce, diplomacy,
and intrigue* 169

Matamoros, Mexico 169
Material world of the Texas big thicket 43
Matthews, Sallie Reynolds 493
Matlock, C. B. 520
Maury Maverick 204
Maverick, Mary 153
Maverick, Maury 204
Maverick, Samuel 153
Maxwell, A. 567
Maxwell, R. S. 521
May, Jr., I. M. 504
Mayhall, M. P. 290
McAfee, W. R. 505
McAlister, S. B. 244
McCaleb, W. F. 124
McCamey, Texas 449
McClanahan, William 581
McCleskey, C. 260
McComb, D. G. 95, 445
McCord, W. 359
McCracken, K. H. 39
McCullar, M. 652
McDaniel, R. W. 535
McDaniel, V. 360
McDonald, A. P. 96, 99
McDowell, J. H. 577
McElroy, H. B. 665
McGaughy, Clark 637
McGuire, J. P. 630
McIlvaine, M. H. 25-27
McKay, M. T. 631
McKay, S. S. 97, 207, 381
McKinney, M. G. 480
McMath, Jr., R. C. 182
McMurtry, Larry 602, 604, 611, 615
McNeill, J. C. III 506
McNeills' SR Ranch: 100 years in Blanco Canyon 506
McWilliams, C. 331
Media 580-585
Medical story of early Texas, 1528-1853 660
Medicine 302, 657-662, 704
Menden, F. von der 446
Meier, M. S. 331
Meiners, F. 469
Meinig, D. W. 10
Melville, M. B. 332
Mendl, Jr., J. W. 380, 382

Merk, F. 154
Methodist Hospital of Houston: serving the world 661
Meusebach, John O. 379
Mexican-Americans 6, 12, 59, 71-73, 86, 99, 138, 153, 171, 189, 267, 301- 341, 378, 429, 444, 446, 449, 454, 456-458, 499, 610
  assimilation 306, 310, 317-318, 327, 338, 341
  bibliographies 683, 689
  civil rights 303, 315, 319, 333, 410
  discrimination against 301, 304, 307, 309-313, 316, 320, 323, 325-326, 328-330, 336
  folk culture 302, 308, 340, 563, 567, 575, 579, 596
  immigration 305, 307, 313, 316, 331, 334, 335
  political activity 304-306, 308, 313-315, 317-318, 321, 330, 332, 334, 338-339
  religion 308, 328, 413, 420
  women 389-393, 401, 689
Mexican-American border region: issues and trends 311
Mexican-American family: tradition and change 341
Mexican Americans: a research bibliography 683
Mexican Americans: leadership, idology, and identity, 1920-1960 317
Mexican-Americans of south Texas 327
Mexican-American workers of San Antonio 325
Mexican frontier,

1821-1846: the American southwest under Mexico 127
Mexican Kickapoo Indians 288
Mexico 66, 90, 126-127, 131, 150, 155-156, 160, 169, 191, 221, 288, 311-312, 365, 377, 509, 527
Midland, Texas 431, 449
Midnight special: the legend of Ledbelly 590
Migration into east Texas, 1835-1860: a study from the United States census 424
Military affairs 88, 210-239, 339, 352, 354, 358, 367
  military installations 213, 219, 224, 228-229, 234, 238-239
Military conquest of the southern plains 223
Miller, C. 447
Miller, T. L. 243
Mineral Springs, Texas 658
Miner, H. C. 550
Mining industry 561
Minorities in the sunbelt 439
Mirabeau Bonaparte Lamar: troubador and crusader 141
Missions 21, 110, 117, 120, 122, 124, 128-129, 334, 411, 638
Mohl, R. A. 448
Mojtabai, A. G. 418
Moncrief International Oil Company 534
Money, marbles, and chalk 247
Moneyhon, C. H. 256
Montejano, D. 334
Montgomery, R. H. 522
Mooney, J. 291
Moore, Edwin Ward 237
Moore, R. H. 36
Moses Austin: his life 121
Mossiker, Francis 602
Most singular country: a history of occupation in Big Bend 88

Mr. House of Texas 198
Mullen, P. B. 578
Murchison, Sr., Clint, and
    family 481
Murchisons: the rise and
    fall of a Texas dynasty
    481
Murphy, Audie 592
Museums 31, 632, 636, 645
Music 590-591, 593-600
Music in El Paso,
    1919-1939 598
Myres, S. L. 401
Mythology of the Wichita
    278
Mythology 10, 85, 103, 610
    African-American 6
    Anglo-American 6, 102
    Mexican-American 6
    Native American 6,
      278-279, 285-286

N

Nackman, M. E. 98
Nance, J. 155
Nasatir, A. P. 125
Nash, G. D. 73
Nash, S. A. 632
National Guard, Texas 264
Nation within a nation: the
    rise of Texas
    nationalism 98
Native Americans 11, 21,
    30, 34, 59, 66, 86, 100,
    112, 119-120, 125,
    153, 184, 273, 299,
    399, 401, 494, 605,
    616, 629
    bibliographies 72-73,
      686, 689
    society and beliefs 6,
      272, 292-293, 297,
      335, 563, 575-576,
      579, 660
    warfare 214-216, 218,
      222-225, 230, 233,
      235-236, 238, 358
    Alabama-Coushatta 300
    Caddo 123, 274, 279,
      287, 294, 298, 300
    Cherokee 277, 280

    Comanche 123, 276, 281,
      283-284, 300
    Karankawa 58, 63, 108,
      300
    Kickapoo 282, 286, 288
    Lipan Apache 300
    Tonkawa 63, 123, 285,
      300
    Wichita 278, 300
Natural gas industry 530,
    532, 538, 540
Naturalists 37, 39, 57,
    59-60
Naturalist's Big Bend: an
    introduction to the
    trees and shrubs,
    wildflowers, cacti,
    mammals, birds,
    reptiles and
    amphibians, fish and
    insects 55
Naturalists on the frontier
    60
Nature of Texas: a feast of
    native beauty from
    Texas Highways
    Magazine 41
Navarro, José Antonio 138
Navy, Texas 220, 237
Negro cowboys 351
Negro in Texas, 1874-1900
    362
Negro legislators of Texas
    and their descendants
    344
Nelson, Willie 595
Newcomb, Jr., W. W.
    292-293
Newcomers, Larry 611
New Deal, The 187, 201,
    504
    see also Depression,
      Great
Newkumet, V. B. 294
New Mexico 131, 133, 150,
    338, 432
Ney, Elisabet 624
Niblett, Gary 631
Nielsen, G. R. 383
Night of violence: the
    Houston riot of 1917
    354
Nimmo, D. 257

Nixon, Lawrence A. 249,
    255
Nixon, P. I. 659-660
No name on the bullet: a
    biography of Audie
    Murphy 592
No quittin' sense 368
No woman tenderfoot:
    Florence Merriam
    Bailey, pioneer
    naturalist 37
Nordyke, L. 507
Norris Wright Cuney: a
    tribune of the black
    people 353
North from Mexico: the
    Spanish-speaking
    people of the United
    States 331
Norwegian-Americans
    378, 446
Not without honor: the life
    of John H. Reagan 183
Nothing better than this: the
    biography of James
    Huckins, first Baptist
    missionary to Texas
    405
Novack, R. 203
Nuclear weapons industry
    418
Nunn, Ancel F. 637
Nye, W. S. 225, 295

O

Oates, S. B. 226
Oberholser, H. C. 40
O'Connor, H. 560
O'Connor, R. R. 6
Oden, W. 257
Odessa, Texas 449, 663
Odin, Bishop John 412
Oil booms: social change in
    five towns 449
Oil field child 541
Oil industry 99, 108, 443,
    449, 456, 465, 481,
    525-526, 531, 536-538
    exploration 528-529,
      532, 534-535
    folklore 569

photographs 539
Oil Workers International Union 560
Older Mexican Americans: a study in an urban barrio 329
Old world background of the irrigation of San Antonio, Texas 488
Oleander odyssey: the Kempners of Galveston, Texas, 1854-1980s 479
Olien, D. 449, 536
Olien, R. M. 258, 449, 536
Olmsted, F. L. 28
Olmsted, Frederick Law 616
On a Mexican mustang through Texas, from the gulf to the Rio Grande 30
Onderdonks: a family of Texas painters 635
Onderdonk, Eleanor 635
Onderdonk, Gilbert 509
Onderdonk, Julian 635
Onderdonk, Robert 635
O'Neal, B. 508, 670
Oppenheimer, E. 509
Oral histories 7, 275, 332, 469, 499
Orton, R. B. 65
Orum, A. M. 450
Our Catholic heritage in Texas, 1519-1936 411
Overcoming: a history of black integration at the University of Texas at Austin 350
Overton, R. C. 551
Owsley, D. F. 632

P

Painting in Texas: the nineteenth century 634
Pando, P. N. 396
Panna Maria Settlement 384
Papa Jack: Jack Johnson and the era of white hopes 672

Parker, L. W. 682
Parsons, William H. 210, 217
Part of space: ten Texas writers 611
Party and factional division in Texas 260
Pass of the north: four centuries on the Rio Grande 457
Pate, J. L. 510
Patrick, K. G. 523
Patterson, C. P. 244
Pattie, J. 633
Pattillo Higgins and the search for Texas oil 535
Payne, R. 653
Pearce, W. W. 511
Pecos to Rio Grande: interpretations of west Texas by 18 artists 637
Peña, A. 267
Peña, M. 596
Penalogy for profit: a history of the Texas prison system, 1867-1912 270
Pendleton, Tom 611
People's architecture: Texas courthouses, jails, and municipal buildings 655
People's Party *see* Populists
Permian Basin 541
Perpetual jeopardy: the Texas Gulf Sulphur affair; a chronicle of achievement and misadventure 523
Perry, C. 629
Peterson, R. T. 42
Petroleum politics and the Texas Railroad Commission 538
Pettus, B. 259
Phariss, H. C. 332
Phenix, Harold 621
Philip, K. 74
Photographs 1, 4-5, 12, 41, 52, 79, 195, 225, 231, 297, 324, 386, 462, 467, 513, 539,

544-545, 553, 564, 591, 641, 643-644, 647, 653-656, 669, 698
Pictorial history of Texas A & M University 462
Pilkington, T. 605, 610
Pinckney, P. A. 634
Piño, F. 683
Pitre, M. 361
Pittman, B. 43
Plains Indian raiders 225
Plantation life in Texas 427
Planters and plain folk: agriculture in antebellum Texas 503
Plants of the Texas shore 33
Platt, H. L. 451
Pluta, J. E. 524
Pocard, M. 614
Poets laureate of Texas, 1932-1966 608
Polish-Americans 372, 378, 384, 561
Political history of the Texas Republic, 1836-1845 158
Politics 73, 135, 140, 148, 159, 163, 170, 173-174, 176, 181, 183, 188-189, 201, 240-261, 395, 403, 420, 429, 435-436, 448, 450, 538
bibliographies 678
African-Americans 342, 344-345, 349
European-Americans 374, 376
Mexican-Americans 314-315, 320-321, 332, 334, 338
see also Democratic Party; Elections; Government, Texas; Governors; Republican Party; United States Government
Politics of oil 531
Politics of San Antonio: community, progress, and power 429
Pool, W. C. 75

Poorest of Americans: the Mexican Americans of the lower Rio Grande valley of Texas 328

Populists 177-178, 181-182, 270, 526

Populist vanguard: a history of the Southern Farmers' Alliance 182

Porter, Katharine Ann 613

Port of Houston 554

Postwar readjustment in El Paso, 1945-1950 208

Power and politics in a chicano barrio: a study of mobilization efforts and community power in El Paso 330

Power vested: the use of martial law and the National Guard in Texas domestic crises, 1919-1932 264

Power, money, & the people: the making of modern Austin 450

Poyo, G. E. 335

Poyon, B. 419

Prairie View: a study in public conscience, 1878-1946 371

Prairie View A & M University 342, 371

Pratt, J. A. 442, 472

Presley, J. 537

Press and the law in Texas 582

Prindle, D. 538

Private black colleges in Texas, 1865-1954 355

Proctor, B. 99, 183

Progressive cities: the commission government movement in America, 1901-1920 453

Progressives and prohibitionists: Texas Democrats in the Wilson era 193

Progressivism 190, 192-193, 270, 453

Prohibition 189-190, 193

Promotion of exports from Texas 548

Przygoda, J. 384

Public lands of Texas, 1519-1970 243

Pulich, W. M. 44

Q

Quanah route: a history of the Quanah, Acme, & Pacific Railway 544

Quilting 404

R

Race and class in Texas politics 252

Race and class in the southwest: a theory of racial inequality 301

Ragged rebel: a common soldier in W. H. Parsons's Texas cavalry, 1861-1865 217

Ragsdale, C. S. 392

Ragsdale, K. B. 197, 227

Railroads 178, 184, 510, 526, 542, 551-552

    Central Branch Railway 542

    Missouri, Kansas, and Texas 549

    Missouri Pacific 542, 550

    Quanah, Acme, and Pacific 544

    Texas Pacific 542

    Union Pacific 550-551

Ramirez, N. 512

Ramsdell, C. W. 172

Ranald S. Mackenzie on the Texas frontier 236

Ranching 62, 77, 86, 88, 176, 184, 387, 443, 485, 487, 490, 492-497, 499-502, 505-509, 511, 516, 525

    cowboys 7, 102, 351, 492, 496, 557, 594

    cowgirls 402, 513

    popular images of cowboys 602-603, 612, 631, 640, 667

sheepraising 483, 498, 508

Range wars: heated debates, sober reflections, and other assessments of Texas writing 605

Rangers and regulars 222

Rappole, J. 45

Rascoe, Stephen 637

Rathjen, F. W. 100

Ratliff, H. V. 671

Raven: a biography of Sam Houston 147

Rayburn, Sam 202

Reagan, John 183

Realtor in Texas: the story of the Texas Association of Realtors, 1920-1970 520

Rebellious ranger: Rip Ford and the old southwest 145

Rebirth of the Missouri Pacific 550

Reconstruction in Texas 172

Reconstruction to reform: Texas politics, 1876-1906 178

Rector, R. 513

Red Raiders: Texas Tech football 673

Red river in southwestern history 106

Red scare! right-wing hysteria, fifties fanaticism, and their legacy 200

Reed, S. G. 552

Reeves, Wendy 632

Reeves, Emery 632

Reflections of the Mexican experience in Texas 332

Regional vocabulary of Texas 566

Reichstein, A. 156

Reid, Roy 505

Reid, Wade 505

Reinhartz, D. 17

Religion 86, 92, 94, 119, 308, 310, 368, 380, 383-385, 405-423, 466, 689

Catholics 408, 410-412, 414, 419, 422, 463
Disciples of Christ 409
Presbyterians 413
Southern Baptists 405-407, 416-417, 421, 423
Religion on the Texas frontier 409
Renderbrook: a century under the spade brand 497
Renderbrook Ranch 497
Reps, J. W. 452
Republicanism in reconstruction Texas 256
Republican Party 171-172, 175, 178, 186, 209, 247, 249-250, 252-254, 256, 258, 260, 353, 361-362
Rescheuthaler, P. 208
Reston, J. 209
Restoring Texas: Raiford Stripling's life and architecture 652
Reverchon, Julien 60
Revolt against chivalry: Jesse Daniel Ames and the women's campaign against lynching 397
Revolutionary decades, 1810-1836 126
Reynolds, C. 615
Rhinehart, M. D. 561
Rhodes, J. 553
Rice, B. R. 453
Rice, L. D. 362
Rice University 469, 674
Rich grass and sweet water: ranch life with the Koch Matador Cattle Company 502
Richardson, R. N. 101, 228
Riders of the border: a selection of thirty drawings by José Cisneros 623
Rio Grande River Valley 91, 546, 626
Rise of the lone star: the making of Texas 156

Rise of the Mexican American middle class: San Antonio, 1929-1941 318
Rister, C. C. 184, 229
River of lost dreams: navigation on the Rio Grande 546
Roach, J. G. 402
Road to Spindletop: economic change in Texas, 1875-1901 526
Roberts, R. 672
Robinson, D. R. 363
Robinson, W. B. 654-656
Robison, B. C. 46
Rock art of Texas Indians 293
Rodeo 402, 512-513, 667, 669
Roell, C. 684
Roemer, Ferdinand 60
Rogers, M. B. 420
Roland, C. P. 230
Roosevelt, Theodore 367
Rosales, F. A. 454
Rose, S. 547
Rosenberg, E. 421
Rosenberg Library 680
Ross, Lawrence Sullivan 179
Rothrock, Ilse Skipana 611
Roussel, H. 597
Royal, Darrell 668
Roy Bean: law west of the Pecos 269
Rozelle, R. V. 632
Rubel, A. 337
Rubio, A. G. 336
Ruby, George 361
Rundell, Jr. W. 539
Rural life
descriptions 3, 9, 24, 386
photography 5, 386
see also Ranching
Rusk County, Texas 528
Rusk, Thomas J. 135

S

Sabers on the Rio Grande 233

Saga of wealth: the rise of the Texas oilmen 537
Saint Edward's University: a centennial history 463
Salcedo, Manuel 111
Salinas, M. 296
Sam Houston: American giant 165
Sam Houston: colossus in buckskin 137
Sam Houston's Texas 4
Sam Houston's wife: a biography of Margaret Lea Houston 157
Sam Houston: the great designer 139
Sam Houston with the Cherokees, 1829-1833 142
Samora, J. 267
Samponaro, F. N. 231
Samuel May Williams, early Texas entrepreneur 143
San Angeleños: *Mexican-Americans in San Angelo, Texas* 306
San Angelo, Texas 306, 431
San Antonio, Texas 211, 410, 414, 429, 433, 460
economy 390, 431, 518, 555
politics 314, 429, 447
society 310, 318, 322, 325, 390
Spanish-Mexican Periods 110, 122, 335, 432
San Antonio during the Texas Republic: a city in transition 430
San Antonio Express 433
San Antonio legacy 433
San Antonio missions and their system of land tenure 110
San Antonio Rose: the life and music of Bob Wills 599
San Antonio stage lines, 1847-1881 555
San Jacinto, Battle of 216, 220

San Juan Bautista: a
gateway to Spanish
Texas 128
San Marcus, Texas 431
San Miguel, Jr., G. 333
San Saba Mission: Spanish
pivot in Texas 129
Sanders, H. T. 447
Santa Rita oil well 541
Saturday's children 674
Savage, Jr., W. W. 102
Saving the savings and
loan: the United States
thrift industry in the
Texas experience,
1950-1988 477
Savings and loans 474, 477
Sawdust empire: the Texas
lumber industry,
1830-1940 521
Schiwetz, E. M. 621
Schlebecker, J. T. 514
Schmidly, D. J. 47-49
Schmitz, J. W. 422
Schoelwer, S. P. 103
Schofield, D. F. 525
School desegregation in
Texas: the
implementation of
United States vs State
of Texas 470
Schutze, J. 364
Schwartz, R. 365
Science 484, 547, 662, 700
Scott Joplin 593
Seale, W. 157
Search for Emma's story: a
model for humanities
detective work 400
Searching for the sunbelt:
historical perspectives
on a region 448
Secession and the Union in
Texas 166
Second Texas infantry:
from Shiloh to
Vicksburg 212
Second World War 195,
304, 381, 504, 518, 592
Selcer, R. F. 455
Sellmeyer, R. 673
Senate, Texas State 245
Sentinel of the southern
plains: Fort

Richardson and the
northwest Texas
frontier, 1866-1878
219
Serials 690-708
Settlement of Texas 59,
62-63, 90, 94,
112-114, 116, 120,
123, 152, 161, 194,
374-375, 378-380,
382-383, 387, 394,
401, 409, 417, 432
Seven keys to Texas 85
Shaw, C. 297
Shaw, P. M. 245
Sheffy, L. F. 515
Shelton, B. A. 456
Shields, J. T. de 240
Shirley, G. 185
Shivers, Allan 206
Short history of the sugar
industry in Texas 519
Shrake, B. 595
Shrake, Edwin 611
Shupe, A. 428
Sibley, M. M. 29, 186, 554,
585, 661
Siegel, S. 158
Silverthorne, E. 159,
426-427
Simmons, Carroll 639
Simmons, M. 579
Simms, C. 639
Simpson, H. B. 232
Sitton, T. 268
Six missions of Texas 117
Six who came to El Paso:
pioneers of the 1840's
161
Sjilusgi, G. 50
Skaggs, J. M. 516
Skrabanek, R. L. 385
Slavery see
African-Americans
Slavery and the annexation
of Texas 154
Smallwood, J. M. 366
Smith, A. D. H. 198
Smith, Ashbel 159, 212
Smith, D. 242
Smith, E. Kirby 170
Smith, Erasmus, "Deaf"
146
Smith, J. H. 160

Smith, L. L. 51
Smith, Robert L. 361
Smith, Z. A. 66
Snook, Texas 385
Snyder, Texas 449
Social change in the
Southwest, 1350-1880
90
Social justice and church
authority: the public
life of Archbishop
Robert E. Lucey 410
Society of Mary in Texas
422
Soldiers, sutlers, and
settlers: garrison life
on the Texas frontier
239
Sonnichsen, C. L. 104,
269, 457, 480, 616,
618
Soukup, J. R. 260
Source material on the
history and ethnology
of the Caddo Indians
298
South, The 74, 182, 253,
496, 610
Southern Baptist
Convention see
religion
Southern Baptist
Convention and its
people, 1607-1972 406
Southern Baptists: a
subculture in transition
421
Southern Baptists holy war:
the self-destructive
struggle for power
within the largest
protestant
denomination in
America 407
Southern community in
crisis: Harrison
County, Texas,
1850-1880 167
Southern Methodist
University: founding
and early years 471
Southern Pacific,
1901-1985 545
Southwest, The 90, 112,

116, 123, 125, 127, 184, 215, 299, 301, 413, 432, 454, 498, 507, 532, 542, 579, 616, 646, 691-692
Southwest Conference 665-666, 673-675
Southwest in life and literature 616
Southwest review 692
Southwestern Cattle Raisers Association 507
Southwestern entomologist 691
Southwestern frontier, 1865-1881 184
Southwestern historical quarterly 690
Southwestern International Livestock Show and Rodeo 512
Spain 11, 59, 90, 111-112, 115-116, 118-120, 123, 125, 262, 432, 495, 622
Spanish and French rivalry in the Gulf region of the United States, 1678-1702 118
Spanish borderlands frontier, 1813-1821 112
Spanish element in Texas water law 262
Spanish explorers in the southern United States, 1528-1543 22
Spanish missions of Texas 124
Special kind of doctor: a history of veterinary medicine in Texas 484
Spindletop 529
Spindletop oil well 89, 97, 529
Sports 99, 663-675
Spratt, J. S. 526
Spruce, Everett 621, 637
Spur Ranch 494
Spurs 633
SR Ranch 506
Stacey, W. A. 428
Standard Oil Company 529

State and local government in Texas 244
State National since 1881 480
Statistics 9, 13, 32, 73, 168, 251, 259, 301, 307, 359, 395, 424, 517, 527, 540, 548
Steiner, S. 338
Steinfeldt, C. 635
Stephen F. Austin, father of Texas 114
Stevenson, R. M. 598
Stewart, K. L. 307
Stewart, R. 636
Stockton, J. R. 540
Stockyards, Fort Worth 510
Stokes, C. R. 662
Stolen heritage: a Mexican Americans' rediscovery of his family's lost land grant 336
Storey, J. 423
Storms brewed in other men's worlds: the confrontation of Indians, Spanish, and French in the Southwest, 1540-1795 123
Stowe, E. B. 541
Streeter, T. W. 685
Strickland, Reunard 142
Strickland, Ron 7
Strickland, R. W. 161
Stripling, Raiford 652
Successful failure 120
Sugar refining 519
Sul Ross: soldier, statesman, educator 179
Sul Ross State University 179
Sulphur industry 522-523
Sunbelt 208, 434, 439, 448, 456, 518
Super Americans: a picture of life in the United States, as brought into focus, bigger than life, in the land of the millionaires-Texas 1

Swanton, J. R. 298
Sweatt, Herman Marion 342
Sweet, A. E. 30
Swenson Jr., L. S. 547
Swiss-Americans 378
Syrian and Lebanese-Americans 378, 458

T

Taking stock: a Larry McMurtry casebook 615
Tales from the Big Thicket 564
Talking with Texas writers: twelve interviews 602
Tate, M. L. 686
Taylor, A. E. 403
Taylor, I. D. 228
Taylor, Texas 431
Tejano *community, 1836-1900* 308
Tejano *origins in eighteenth-century San Antonio* 335
Tejanos *and the numbers game: a socio-historical interpretation from the federal censuses, 1850-1900* 307
Temple Houston: lawyer with a gun 185
Temple, Texas 431
Texans, guns, and history 78
Texans in revolt: the battle for San Antonio, 1835 211
Texans: oral histories from the lone star state 7
Texas A & M University 179, 461-462, 465, 484, 665-666
Texas after Spindletop 97
Texas: a geography 9
Texas: a guide to the lone star state 32
Texas: a history 87

Texas, a literary portrait 609

Texas: all hail the mighty state 96

Texas almanac and state industrial guide 693

Texas: a modern history 95

Texas and the Fair Deal, 1945-1952 207

Texas and the Mexican revolution: a study in state and national border policy, 1910-1920 191

Texas: an informal biography 107

Texas Association of Realtors 520

Texas at the crossroads: people, politics, and policy 251

Texas auto trails: the northeast 25

Texas auto trails: the south and the Rio Grande valley 26

Texas auto trails: the southeast 27

Texas Baptist leadership and social Christianity, 1900-1980 423

Texas bibliography: a manual on history research materials 676

Texas border and some borderliners: a chronicle and guide 82

Texas business review 524, 694

Texas Centennial (1936) 197

Texas Cherokees: a people between two fires, 1819-1840 280

Texas Christian University 466

Texas cities and the great depression 431

Texas College of Osteopathic Medicine: the first twenty years 662

Texas Commerce Banks 472

Texas country editor: H. M. Baggarly takes a grass-roots look at national politics 580

Texas cowboy 640

Texas cowboys: memories of the early days 499

Texas crossings: the lone star state and the American far west, 1836-1986 93

Texas divided: loyalty & dissent in the lone star state, 1856-1874 171

Texas Education Agency 470

Texas Electric Service Company 533

Texas energy: a twenty-five year history 530

Texas facts 695

Texas folk medicine: 1333 cures, remedies, preventives, and health practices 657

Texas folklore society 696

Texas: from the frontier to Spindletop 89

Texas gardener 697

Texas government 242

Texas government today: structures, functions, political processes 259

Texas graveyards: a cultural legacy 92

Texas gulf coast: interpretations by nine artists 621

Texas Gulf Sulphur Company 522-523

Texas heritage 99

Texas high sheriffs 268

Texas highways magazine 5, 698

Texas homes of the 19th century 641

Texas horticulturalist 699

Texas in the 1960 presidential election 261

Texas in the middle eighteenth century: studies in Spanish colonial history and administration 116

Texas in turmoil, 1849-1875 174

Texas journal of science 700

Texas land and development company: a panhandle promotion, 1912-1956 482

Texas landscape, 1900-1986 628

Texas law review 701

Texas lawyer 702

Texas League: a century of baseball, 1888-1987 670

Texas libraries 703

Texas literary tradition: fiction, folklore, history 610

Texas log buildings: a folk architecture 651

Texas mammals east of the Balcones fault zone 49

Texas Medical Association 659, 704

Texas medicine 704

Texas-Mexican conjunto: a history of working-class music 596

Texas-Mexico border 12, 21, 78, 82, 155, 191, 221, 231, 312, 328, 332, 444, 622-623

Texas monthly 705

Texas museums: a guidebook 31

Texas myths 6

Texas navy: in forgotten battles and shirtsleeve diplomacy 220

Texas observor 706

Texas Panhandle 5, 34, 86, 94, 100, 482, 489, 515, 543, 580, 625

Texas panhandle frontier 100

Texas parks and wildlife 707

Texas pioneers from Poland: a study in ethnic history 384

Texas political system 257

Texas politics, 1906-1944: with special reference to the German counties 381

Texas prisons: the walls came tumbling down 266

Texas public buildings of the 19th century 656

Texas quilts, Texas women 404

Texas Railroad Commission 183, 538

Texas railroads: a record of construction and abandonment 556

Texas ranch life 24

Texas Rangers: a century of frontier defense 271

Texas Rangers 7, 78, 99, 145, 163, 179, 264, 267, 271, 334, 676

Texas Republic: a social and economic history 144

Texas resources and industries 517

Texas revolution 132

Texas revolutionary experience: a political and social history, 1835-1836 148

Texas-Santa Fe pioneers 150

Texas Santa Fe trail 133

Texas Senate: volume one: Republic to Civil War, 1836-1861 245

Texas shrimpers: community, capitalism, and the sea 559

Texas's last frontier: Fort Stockton and the trans-Pecos, 1861-1895 238

Texas Southern University 359, 639

Texas sport: the illustrated history 669

Texas State Federation of Labor 557

Texas State Historical Assocation 690

Texas studies in literature and language 708

Texas Tech University 673

Texas: the lone star state 101

Texas through time: evolving interpretations 71

Texas toys and games 565

Texas wildflowers: a field guide 38

Texas women in politics 395

Texas women's history project bibliography 689

Texas woolybacks: the range sheep and goat industry 483

Texians and Texans 378

Theatre 322, 586, 588-589

Theatre in early El Paso, 1881-1905 586

Then came the railroads: the century from steam to diesel in the southwest 542

They called them greasers: Anglo attitudes toward Mexican-Americans in Texas, 1821-1900 309

They made their own law: stories of Bolivar Peninsula 108

They sat in high place: the presidents and governors of Texas 240

Thomas J. Rusk: soldier, statesman, jurist 135

Thomas, D. H. 300

Thomas, M. M. H. 471

Thompson, J. 233, 339

Thonhoff, R. 555

Three men in Texas: Bedichek, Webb, and Dobie 607

Through many dangers, toils and snares: the black leadership of Texas, 1868-1900 361

Thurber, Texas 561

Tijerina, A. A. 340

Time of hope, time of despair: black Texans during reconstruction 366

Time to stand 151

Timmons, W. H. 458

Timon, John 408

Tinkle, L. 617

Tippette, G. 674

Tips, K. 675

To wear a city's crown: the beginnings of urban growth in Texas, 1836-1865 460

Tobin, G. M. 76

Tongue of the Tirilones: a linguistic study of a criminal argot 573

Tonkawa texts 285

Tornado 69

Townsend, C. 599

Toys 565

Trade 13, 93, 106, 133, 251, 451, 543, 546, 548, 553-555
see also Railroads

Traditions of the Caddo 279

Tragic cavalier: Governor Manuel Salcedo of Texas, 1808-1813 111

Trails south: the wagon-road economy in the Dodge City-panhandle region 543

Trails to Texas: southern roots of western cattle ranching 496

Transition in the Texas commercial banking industry, 1956-1965 475

Transportation see Trade

Travel accounts 18-19, 21-24, 28, 30, 676
analysis 29

Travelers in Texas, 1761-1860 29

Travel guides 25-27, 31-32, 55, 79, 82, 105, 228, 698

Travis County, Texas 314

Travis, William Barrett 162

Trees of east Texas 53

Trelease, A. W. 173

Trost, Henry C. 646
Trotter, R. T. II 302
Truett, J. C. 67
Truman, Harry S 207
Tulia (Texas) *Herald* 580
Turn your eyes toward Texas: pioneers Sam and Mary Maverick 153
Turner, M. A. 162, 600
Tveten, J. L. 52
Twelfth man: a story of Texas A & M football 665
Twentieth-century West: historical interpretations 73
Tyler, P. E. 31
Tyler, R. C. 31, 105, 637-638
Tyson, C. N. 106

U

Underwood, K. 434
United Mine Workers 557, 561
United States Army Air Corps 221, 227
United States-Comanche relations: the reservation years 283
United States Government 88, 149, 154, 156, 158, 160, 191, 199, 207
United States-Mexico border: a politico-economic profile 312
United we win: the rise and fall of La Raza Unida Party 315
University of North Texas 467, 662
University of Texas 75, 159, 186, 342, 350, 465, 666, 668, 681
University of Texas Archives: a guide to the historical manuscripts collections

in the University of Texas library 681
Urban life and urbanization 2, 9, 71, 73, 79, 188, 423, 429-460, 517, 610
see also individual cities
Urban Texas: politics and development 447
Utley, R. M. 234-235

V

Vanderwood, P. J. 231
Vaqueros in blue and gray 339
Veterinary medicine 484
Views of Texas: watercolors by Sarah Ann Lillie Hardinge together with a journal of her departure from Texas 638
Vigness, D. M. 126
Ville, W. de 15
Vines, R. A. 53
Violence 78, 104, 171, 173, 189, 354, 357, 367, 428, 508
Violence in the city 357
von der Mehden, F. 446

W

Waco, Texas 69
Wake up dead man: Afro-American worksongs from Texas prisons 356
Walker, D. D. 77
Walker, D. L. 618
Walker, D. R. 270
Wallace, C. M. 459
Wallace, E. 101, 174, 236, 284
Waller, J. L. 175
Waner, R. H. 54
War scare on the Rio Grande: Robert Runyon's photographs

of the border conflict, 1913-1916 231
Water 66, 73, 251, 262, 459, 488-489, 658
Water and the future of the Southwest 66
Water out of the desert 459
Watercolors of the Rio Grande 626
Waters, Frank 616
Watriss, W. 386
Watts, P. 687
Way of work and a way of life: coal mining in Thurber, Texas, 1888-1926 561
Weather 13, 64-65, 68-70, 517
We're Czechs 385
Wealth and power in antebellum Texas 168
Weaver, J. D. 367
Webb, W. P. 11, 271, 688
Webb, Walter Prescott 74, 76-77, 604, 607, 610
Weber, D. J. 127
Weddle, R. 15, 128-129
Weekend in September 70
Weeks, O. 261
Weeks, Ramona Maher 611
Weems, J. E. 68-70, 163, 639
Weisman, A. 12
Wells, T. H. 237
Wendish-Americans 378, 383
Wendy and Emery Reeves collection 632
Weniger, D. 56
Werden, F. 370
West, E. 74
West, E. Gordon 637
West, The 73, 93, 176, 214, 235, 351, 401, 452, 508, 514, 516, 568, 594, 687
Westering women and the frontier experience, 1800-1915 401
West Texas 3, 5, 48, 83, 238, 269, 394, 443, 541, 601, 637
Wheeler, K. M. 460

Whisenhunt, D. W. 199
White terror: the Ku Klux Klan conspiracy and southern reconstruction 173
White, C. C. 368
White, O. P. 107
Whorehouse bells were ringing: and other songs cowboys sing 594
Wiggins, M. 108
Wild flowers of the big thicket, east Texas, and western Louisiana 50
Wildcatters: a story of Texas, oil, and money 534
Wildlife and man in Texas: enviromental change and conservation 59
William Barrett Travis: his sword and his pen 162
William Bollaert's Texas 18
Williams, C. 238
Williams, J. E. 369
Williams, N. 341
Williams, Samuel May 143
Willie: an autobiography 595
Wills, Bob 599
Wilson, M. E. 680
Wilson, Woodrow 191, 193, 198
Winchester, R. G. 164, 689
Winegarten, R. 370, 689
Wingren, Dan 621
Wings over the border: the Army Air Service armed patrol of the

United States-Mexico border, 1919-1921 221
Wings over the Mexican border: pioneer military aviation in the Big Bend 227
Wink, Texas 449
Wisehart, M. K. 165
Witchcraft in the southwest: Spanish and Indian supernaturalism on the Rio Grande 579
Witt, Green de 152
Wolfe, J. 481
Wolves for the blue soldiers: Indian scouts and auxiliaries with the United States Army, 1860-90 214
Women 71-73, 99, 153, 157, 163, 190, 345, 369, 389-404, 415, 428, 447, 449, 499, 605, 610-611
bibliographies 689
Women in early Texas 391
Women in Texas: their lives, their experiences, their accomplishments 392
Women in the Texas workforce: yesterday and today 393
Women of the depression: caste and culture in San Antonio, 1919-1939 390
Women on the Texas frontier: a cross-cultural perspective 399

Women's Voter Education Project 395
Woolfolk, G. R. 371
Wooster, R. 239
Worcester, D. 640
Word on the Brazos: Negro preacher tales from the Brazos bottom of Texas 571
Wortham, L. J. 109
Wright, Charles 60
Wright, James 248

X

XIT ranch of Texas and the early days of the Llano Estacado 491

Y

Yabsley, S. 404
Year America discovered Texas: centennial '36 197
Years of Lyndon Johnson 201
Yellow rose of Texas: the story of a song 600
Young-Lee Oil Company 529
Yugoslavian-Americans 578

Z

Zant, L. V. 246
Zlatkovich, C. 556

Map of Texas

This map shows the more important towns and other features.

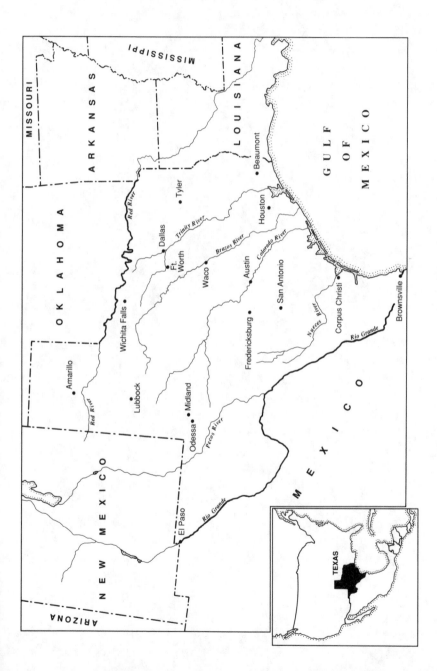